Towards a New Marxism

Proceedings of the First International
Telos Conference

October 8-11, 1970
Waterloo, Ontario

TOWARDS A NEW MARXISM

*Proceedings of the First International
Telos Conference*

*October 8-11, 1970
Waterloo, Ontario*

Edited by Bart Grahl and Paul Piccone

TELOS PRESS
ST. LOUIS, MO.

Library of Congress Catalog Card Number 73-87129

Contents

Introduction

Paul Piccone

The revival of radicalism in the sixties as a result of the Vietnam war and the shipwreck of both the New Frontier and the Great Society, took place in a theoretical vacuum. Almost two decades of the Cold War had decisively contributed to either the destruction or integration of any type of internal opposition to the general policies followed by the two ruling parties. At the theoretical level, the only critical remnants surviving the McCarthy era were a few Old Left sects with no popular base nor any relevant alternative. With the possible exception of Marcuse, Goodman, and a few other obscure intellectuals whose works had remained relatively unknown, there was no radical analysis available to either forecast the storm on the horizon or provide what was to become known as "the movement" with that minimal self-understanding necessary to conceptually prefigure viable alternatives and politically implement them.

At the beginning, this lack of historical identity, combined with a spontaneous resurgence of self-responsibility and social commitment in the face of meaningless death in a foreign land and racial and sexual injustices at home, presented itself as a breath of fresh air—a new optimism unshackled by the weight of the past. Only when this spontaneity had degenerated into chaos and the inability to turn "the movement" into a major political force did it become obvious that theory was unavoidable. Like Hegel's owl of Minerva, serious theoretical work began precisely at dusk: when the movement, through intensified governmental repression and the forestalled promise of ending the Indochina war, had already been defused and practically dissolved.

It is indicative that the conference where the following papers were originally presented took place roughly five months after the Cambodian invasion and the movement's last show of liveliness. Aware of the rapid internal disintegration of the movement, the staff of the journal Telos, *in collaboration with the student body of the University of Waterloo, organized a conference on "The New Marxism" in order to investigate the possibility of salvaging valuable theoretical indications from the forgotten Western Marxist tradition. Under attack from both official bourgeois ideology and Stalinism, this tradition had been completely obliterated, only to be gradually rediscovered in the late sixties by inquisitive New Leftists in search of historical self-understanding.*

Of all the papers delivered at the conference, two have been omitted and one has been substituted with another by the author. Robin Blackburn's paper on "Structuralist Marxism" was highjacked by Dick Howard and Karl Klare, and a subsequent version of it has already appeared in another anthology.[1] Silvia Federici's paper on "Gramsci's Theory of Education" was withdrawn by the author because of radical changes in her political perspective; and Lucio Colletti's original paper on "The Marxism of the

---

1. Cf. Robin Blackburn and Gareth Stedman Jones, "Louis Althusser and the Struggle for Marxism," in Dick Howard and Karl Klare, eds., *The Unknown Dimension: European Marxism since Lenin* (New York, 1972), pp. 365-387.

Second International," which has also been published elsewhere,[2] has been substituted, at the author's request, by a more appropriate one. Also excluded is James Hansen's paper "Marx's Concept of Praxis" which was never delivered at the conference[3] and, at any rate, did not pertain to the general theme of the conference. Many of the papers are extensively footnoted. This has been done not only in order to offer careful documentation, but also to provide a broad range of bibliographical references which, as a result, are not independently listed.

---

2. Cf. *Telos*, No. 8, Summer 1971, pp. 84-90. Earlier drafts of the following papers have also already appeared: Paul Breines, "Notes on 'The Old Culture and the New Culture'," in *Telos*, No. 5, Spring 1970, pp. 1-20; Georg Lukács, "The Old Culture and the New Culture," *ibid.*, pp. 21-30; Michael Kosok, "Dialectics of Nature," in *Telos*, No. 6, Fall 1970, pp. 47-103; Paul Piccone, "Phenomenological Marxism," in *Telos*, No. 9, Fall 1971, pp. 3-31; and Lucio Colletti, "The Theory of the Crash," in *Telos*, No. 13, Fall 1972, pp. 34-46. Raya Dunayevskaya's contribution is a chapter from her forthcoming book titled *Philosophy and Revolution*.

3. For a blow by blow account of the conference which includes a description of the disruption that prevented the presentation of Hansen's paper, see "The First *Telos* International Conference," in *Telos*, No. 6, Fall 1970, pp. 294-317.

Notes on Lukács' "The Old Culture and the New Culture"

Paul Breines

The essay first appeared in November, 1920 in *Kommunismus* (subtitled, "Journal of the Communist International for Countries of Southeastern Europe") which was published by the Communist party of Germany-Austria under the editorial direction of Gerhart Eisler. The journal itself, though short-lived—February, 1920 to September, 1921—was the most important central European forum of debate within the Third International in the latter's formative years. Its staff included and was decisively influenced by a number of Hungarian Communists—among them, Lukács, Josef Revai and Bela Fogarasi who, along with Karl Korsch, emerged as spokesmen for what came to be known as "Western Marxism" in distinction from the Moscow-centered brand—who had fled from Budapest to Vienna following the collapse of the Bela Kun-led "Hungarian Soviet Republic" (August, 1919) and the take-over by Horthy's fascist regime.[1] *Kommunismus* was founded in and its work was shaped by the general crisis of the communist movement in Europe. A capsule statement of the situation was

---

1. *Kommunismus*, Vol. I, No. 43 (Nov. 7, 1920), pp. 1538-49. Hereafter cited as *Komm.* The journal's politics were "ultra-Left": sympathetic to syndicalist currents in the proletarian movement; hostile to trade-union and electoral activity; largely insistent on the primacy of workers councils or soviets as the basic organizational form of the revolutionary movement; advocate of the "offensive tactic" and, as editorials throughout 1921 make clear, critical of the Comintern Executive's (successful) attempt to put brakes on militant action by stressing mass organizing, etc. Lukács appears to have been the guiding figure within the *Komm.* group. At the time, he, L. Rudas, Revai, and Fogarasi were already at odds with the Bela Kun leadership faction of the Hungarian CP. Kun, never independent in any case, had the advantage in this struggle of having fled to Moscow. For a statement of Lukács' position in this context see his "Noch Einmal Illusionspolitik" (1922) in *Georg Lukács Werke: Frühschriften II* (Neuwied and Berlin, 1968), pp. 155-60. His studies of "Rosa Luxemburg as Marxist," and of "Class Consciousness," both of which later appeared in *History and Class Consciousness*, were first published in *Komm.* His critique of parliamentarism is perhaps the main "Left-Wing Communist" statement on this question. See "Zur Frage des Parlamentarismus," *Komm.*, Vol. I, No. 6 (March 1, 1920), pp. 161-72. A summary of its theses can be found in James W. Hulse, *The Forming of the Communist International* (California, 1964), pp. 165-67. The journal also carried lengthy and exciting articles by the Dutch ultra-Leftists Anton Pannekoek and Henriette Roland-Holst. Among numerous other important articles, one of the most interesting in the context of the philosophical struggle within Marxism is a piece by a little-known figure, Erwin Ban. In his "Engels als Theoretiker," *Komm.*, Vol. I, No. 45 (Dec. 3, 1920), pp. 1595-1605, Ban presents a philosophical-biographical analysis of Engel's role in the gestation of Marxian theory and concludes that to the extent that Engels was not, like Marx, an "heir to classical German idealism," his role was nil, indeed, negative. Engels, Ban argues, had a positivist-naturalist conception of the dialectic—a dialectic of causation from lower to higher forms—and a mechanistic-instrumental conception of praxis. Further, his view of the "materialist conception of history" had an ontological and metaphysical character that was foreign to Marx's thought. Ban, in other words, tried to give documentation to the theses on Engels presented by Lukács in *History and Class Consciousness*. His little essay was doubtless one of numerous critical pieces in *Komm.* that must have blown the minds of those Marxists who sought to canonize theory into an air-tight *Weltanschauung*, especially Soviet Marxists for whom Engels' thought was already decisive. Ban concludes his essay by noting that Engels' real and revolutionary contribution was his critique of utopian socialism. The main part of his argument anticipates almost entirely the analysis of Engels recently offered by George Lichtheim, *Marxism: An Historical and Critical Study* (New York, 1961), pp. 234-43.

presented in the lead editorial of the journal's first issue in February, 1920: "[although with the Bolshevik Revolution the world proletariat entered a new epoch that heralded a global proletarian uprising, events had taken a different course. For] only the Finnish, Hungarian, and part of the German proletariat followed the Russian workers, but only to be beaten down in a blood-bath; beaten down not merely by the old reactionary forces but by traitors among the workers and the petit-bourgeois elements who had come to the workers' aid. The revolution was betrayed not only by the social-patriots, but also by the pre-war revolutionaries and social-pacifists...who fled in panic. But," the editorial continues, "the revolution marches forward nevertheless. We are in the midst of world revolution...victory will be ours."[2] To develop and sustain an active and aggressive revolutionary theory and strategy within the context of the apparent dissolution of revolutionary momentum was the task of *Kommunismus*.

Schematically, this was the situation in which Lukács' "The Old Culture and the New Culture" was published. Yet, among the several unusual aspects of the essay is the fact that although it appeared in print in late 1920 it actually originated in and reflects the brief moment of triumph and potential actualization of the communist revolution in Hungary during the preceding year. Specifically, the essay published in *Kommunismus* and translated here is a slightly revised version of two talks first given by Lukács in June, 1919, at the time of his work as Commissar of Public Education in the Soviet government.[3] But, insuring that there would be no forgetting the abyss that lay between the hopes and goals articulated by Lukács and the actual situation of the revolution in Central and Eastern Europe, the grim reality entered just one inch below the close of his essay. Immediately following his formulation of the concrete-utopian essence of communism—liberation of human relations from the hegemony of the economy and economic relations; collective self-actualization of man as an end in himself—there appears the following announcement: "HELP SAVE THOUSANDS OF COMRADES FROM DEATH BY FREEZING! Comrades: winter is at the door. Thousands of young and old comrades still languish in pain in Hungarian prisons and concentration camps. The mass arrests in recent weeks have even increased their number..."

As Lukács would write a few years later, "The Old Culture and the New Culture" is one of his works that "resonates with those overly optimistic hopes many of us then had regarding the pace and tempo of the revolution."[4] But, if the terror that liquidated those hopes (and many of the lives

---

2. "Zur Einführung," *Komm.*, Vol. I, Nos. 1 and 2 (Feb. 1, 1920), pp. 1-2.

3. David Kettler, *Marxismus und Kultur. Mannheim und Lukács in den ungarischen Revolutionen 1918/1919* (Neuwied and Berlin, 1967), pp. 45-54. Though restricted in time and scope, Kettler's little book is perceptive and extremely informative, detailing the terms in which the work of the "Spirit" group in Budapest, in which Lukács was the leading figure, decisively shaped his thought and the political work during the Kun regime. Kettler is the first analyst of Lukács' work to have called attention to the importance of "The Old Culture and the New Culture."

4. "Vorwort," *Geschichte und Klassenbewusstsein: Studien über marxistische Dialektik* (Berlin, 1923), p. 5. Lukács' remark is made in reference to another essay. "The Old Culture and the New Culture" is from 1919.

that bore them) has not vanished, neither have the hopes. In our view, the essay's importance—in the context of the genesis and development of Lukács' Marxism and in the context of its links to the present situation of radical theory and action—derives, in large part, precisely from its overdrawn, extremist and utopian character. To the extent that "The Old Culture and the New Culture" illuminates the *substratum* of the main and most problematic moment of Lukácsism—the moment of the "young Lukács"—so it may help illuminate the recent "return of the repressed." [5]

Within the intricate and often amazing "politics of Lukács republication"—a story consisting of recantations of his early works, feigned recantations, apparently feigned recantations, official (Comintern) bans, Lukács' own bans, underground circulation of his books, illegal reprints, etc.—the case of this essay is particularly perplexing; this provides additional grounds for presenting it here and now. [6] While it was among the material from which Lukács selected when putting together *History and Class Consciousness* in late 1922, there are evident reasons for its exclusion from that book. For one thing, the essentially cultural standpoint from which the essay is written was quickly *aufgehoben* in the trajectory of Lukács' work in the early 1920s, and thus several of its main themes were more fully developed in other writings: the functional change of historical materialism, the concept of ideology, the crisis of bourgeois ideology, the dialectics of proletarian class consciousness, etc. For another, the essay is not explicitly linked to the philosophical and strategic struggle against vulgar Marxism and Menshevism—as is *History and Class Consciousness*. By 1922, then, it was, in an obvious sense, superfluous.

Yet, it also contains some far-reaching and subversive implications in relation to the then emerging Bolshevik ideology.

This essay could be considered as no more than a document of historical interest revealing the extent to which Lukács' initial Marxism was infused with philosophical idealism and a bourgeois "culture criticism" outlook, and its function in 1920 was seen as an appeal to anti-bourgeois intellec-

---

5. The "young Lukács" was thirty-eight when he wrote *History and Class Consciousness*. The literature relating to the "return" is too extensive to cite in one space; relevant sources appear throughout these footnotes. Regarding an overview of the significance both of the book and of Lukács' initial Marxism as a whole, as well as the significance of the official Communist opposition to it, we agree with Joseph Gabel that it is not really as an idealist that Lukács came under attack, but as a "dialectical theorist of false consciousness within a political system which could not admit the legitimacy of the problem of false consciousness without undercutting the ideological basis of its own existence." Joseph Gabel, *La Fausse Conscience. Essay sur la Reification* (Paris, 1962), I.

6. Some important notes on the underground circulation of *History and Class Consciousness* in the late 1920s and 1930s appear in Gabel, "Korsch, Lukács, et le probleme de la conscience de classe," *Annales*, Vol. XXI, No. 3 (May-June, 1966), pp. 668-680. Maurice Merleau-Ponty, *Les Aventures de la Dialectique* (Paris, 1955), is the main restoration of *History and Class Consciousness* and remains, perhaps, the most brilliant commentary on the book. Lukács and the French CP were quick to reply. See Lukács' letter on Merleau-Ponty in R. Garaudy, *et al.*, *Les Mésaventures de l'Anti-Marxisme* (Paris, 1956), pp. 158-159. The French neo-Marxist journal, *Arguments*, published in the late 1950s, contains numerous articles reviving and developing the work of the early Lukács, along with the first (and illegal) translation of *History and Class Consciousness* in serial form, plus Lukács' own complaints over the venture. A pirated edition was published and circulated in West Germany in 1966.

tuals and artists to break with their class and join the proletarian revolutionary camp. But the essay is peculiarly not susceptible to such treatment. For example, it evades categorization as a piece of either political, philosophical, or cultural criticism. In fact, the essay is fundamentally about non-life (capitalism) and life (communism): the concrete terms in which communist revolution will be the beginning of human as opposed to economic history and thus the realization of humanity's telos—freely associating men and women in a world in which they are "at home" with themselves, each other, and nature. This viewpoint has incendiary political implications which, we believe, Lukács then and later preferred neither to deny nor follow. Unlike many of the other essays from the same period which present *specific* political and strategic criticisms of the Bolsheviks from the "left-wing communist" position Lukács held at the time (his rejection of electoral activity, his defense of the "offensive tactic," etc.), this one, in its clear and overt opposition to economistic definitions of man and socialism-communism, offers the beginnings of a *generalized* critique of the Bolshevik perspective and program.[7] The essay's implicit negative thrust is a fundamental statement of opposition to the "reified" conception of socialism-communism that quickly surfaced and came to prevail in the Soviet Union: socialism-communism as a new stage in the economic-structural development of society (a view which, like capitalism itself, takes man as a function of the economy), not as a qualitative break with and surpassing of the capitalist system of social production and reproduction carried out and developed by the conscious, self-determined praxis of the working class. "The Old Culture and the New Culture" is simultaneously a radical (reaching to the human roots), positive conception of socialism-communism and the foundation of a radical critique of the "antinomies" of Soviet Marxism.

No attempt to examine the whole genesis of Lukács' Marxism can be made here; rather, our intention is to delineate some of the sources and implications of "The Old Culture and the New Culture" by viewing the essay through the lens of the *present* project to which it has definite if mediate links: the project of cultural or total revolution. Although in a form that is necessarily implicit, underdeveloped, and filled with internal tensions, this cultural revolutionary project is latent in Lukács' pre-Marxian work; pervades the initial phase of his Marxism (1919-1923); and immediately thereafter becomes the underlying object of his self-critical labors.

---

7. In the form of warnings Lukács, in the early 1920s, did bring the cultural revolutionary critique of reification perspectives to bear on specific developments in the Third International and the Soviet Union. See, for example, his dissection of the growth of a "soulless bureaucratism" and the triumph of the organizational apparatus over revolutionary will within the emigré Hungarian CP, in "Noch Einmal Illusionspolitik," *op.cit.* In this context what awaits analysis is the social-political origins of Lukács' theory of revolutionary organization, especially that presented in the essay, "On the Methodology of the Organizational Question," in *History and Class Consciousness*; how it relates to and differs from both Leninism and Luxemburgism; how Lukács attempted to bring his general theory of social being, consciousness, and action to bear on the actual political situation; and the extent to which his final acceptance of Leninism-Stalinism is anticipated in his initial positions. On these questions see the recent analyses of G.E. Rusconi, *La Teoria Critica della Società* (Bologna, 1968), pp. 68-85; and G. Vacca, *Lukács o Korsch* (Bari, 1969), *passim.*

Within the context of the links between the trajectory of Lukács' thought and that of the cultural revolutionary New Left—the substance of these links will be suggested in the following pages—the outcome in Lukács' case may be useful to present reflection and activity. [8]

By the early 1930s Lukács proposed this interpretive schema of his own thought: *History and Class Consciousness* marks the turning point in his development from an "immature" stage characterized by a wild fusion of Marxism, "existential," vitalist, and "philosophy of life" ideas, objective idealism, romantic anti-capitalist culture criticism, and crypto-syndicalism, to a "mature" stage grounded in historical materialism and Marxism-Leninism. [9] The schema is accurate, its main flaw being Lukács' contention that it entails an advance.

In our own schema, Lukács by the mid-1920s had begun to de-totalize and de-radicalize his thought, allowing it to pass over into its alienated, ossified opposite: Leninism-Stalinism. Regarding the parallels between Lukács and the present movement, the evident question is whether phylogeny will recapitulate ontogeny. In both instances the critique of capitalism originates in a "subjective" revolt against the universal poverty of existence (defined in cultural more than material terms). Yet, in the case of the New Left, the "hedonist" movement is far more "materialistic" than the abstract "objective conditionism" of orthodox Marxism. Initially defined and elaborated in idealist, existentialist, culture criticism concepts, consciousness in both cases pushes toward a new, coherent totalization of modern society; both move out against "Old Left" dogma and categories long surpassed by actual historical developments. Likewise, in Lukács and in the New Left, one notices (and *experiences*) a spontaneity of thought that is linked to a "spontaneity" of social movement and revolt. The historical situation in each case is characterized by organic crisis and motion within the existing order; at least for those with their eyes and ears open, status quo orthodoxies and habits are in a state of rapid dissolution. In the years surrounding World War I as in the 1960s world history itself has broken through an immmediately preceding revisionist and reformist period; class struggle and social contradictions have passed from latent to manifest expression; society is visibly dialectical and consciousness hurries to catch up. With Lukács in the early 1920s and the New Left in the 1960s historical-theoretical consciousness is critical and self-critical, prospectively revolutionary theory (knowledge of society as a whole and simultaneously

---

8. On the relationship of Lukács' thought to the main philosophical and social-theory currents in Europe, see Pietro Rossi, *Storia e Storicismo nella Filosofia contemporanea* (Milan, 1960), pp. 186-215; Morris Watnick, "Relativism and Class Consciousness," in L. Labedz, ed., *Revisionism. Essays in the History of Marxist Ideas* (New York, 1962), pp. 142-65; Lucien Goldmann, "The Early Writings of Georg Lukács," *Tri-Quarterly* 9 (Spring, 1967), pp. 165-81. On Lukács' Hegelianism, see Iring Fetscher, "Vom Verhältnis des Marxismus zu Hegel," in *Karl Marx und der Marxismus* (Munich, 1967), pp. 85-122. See also Kettler, *op.cit.*, and Merleau-Ponty, *op.cit.*, esp. pp. 1-99.

9. "Mein Weg zu Marx," *Georg Lukács zum 70. Geburtstag* (East Berlin, 1955), pp. 225-31. Following the Nazi seizure of power Lukács undertook an immense reexamination of his whole early development in light of the thesis that the German philosophical-cultural tradition from which he came had made decisive contributions to Nazi ideology. See Lukács, *Zerstörung der Vernunft* (East Berlin, 1954).

the self-consciousness of world-transforming praxis) as opposed to "revolutionary" ideology (which seeks to legitimize a particular organization, sect, or state power). As mentioned above, Lukács, under the pressure of changing circumstances, chose to renounce theory for ideology—Stalinism, a separate non-dialectical body of ideas whose function was to offer theoretical resolutions to actual contradictions. In our view, the idealist, subjective, existential, culture criticism beginnings of revolutionary theory and activity stand, in both instances, as a vital stage in the life of the revolutionary spirit. That this stage contains inadequacies which need to be overcome is clear, even if how they can be surpassed without obliterating the essentials of the initial stage is neither clear nor simple.

Lukács came to Marxism out of a Central European milieu of aesthetic-cultural philosophy and sociology containing a definite if "supra-political" anti-capitalist thrust. Even before World War I there had been a trend away from the bourgeois way of life, the city, "culture," instrumental rationality, quantification, scientific specialization, etc. Lukács' own politics prior to World War I had consisted of militant opposition to the "bourgeoisie, liberalism, the constitutional state, parliamentarism, revisionistic socialism, the Enlightenment and individualism."[10] Philosophically, in the pre-Marxian period, the heart of his subsequently infamous idealism was neatly expressed in his remark on Georg Simmel who, Lukács wrote, was one of the great "outsiders" of the turn of the century years, standing "without roots and impotent in a tidal wave of the most dull and soul-less materialism and positivism."[11] Likewise, in his aesthetic and cultural studies, he was engaged in perpetual opposition to methodological approaches that entailed socio-economic reductions of cultural phenomena or intrusions of the methods of the natural sciences into the human-cultural sciences.[12]

---

10. Paul Honigsheim, *On Max Weber*, translated by Joan Rytina (New York, 1968), pp. 79, 24.

11. Lukács, "Georg Simmel," in K. Gassen and M. Landmann, eds., *Buch des Dankes an Georg Simmel. Briefe, Errinerungen, Bibliographie* (Berlin, 1958), p. 173. Written in 1918 on the occasion of Simmel's death, the essay makes clear the central importance of Simmel for Lukács and reveals the latter's sense that he was pushing toward the total theory that Simmel had prepared the way for but was not capable of realizing. Lukács' friend and fellow agitator in Simmel's seminar in the pre-World War I years, Ernst Bloch, expressed a similar view in 1913. "Simmel, the best head among his contemporaries, is beyond this utterly empty, a man without goals, who wants everything but the truth; he collects his many standpoints which float around the truth without ever wanting or being able to possess it." Ernst Bloch, "Schulphilosophen heute," in *Durch die Wüsste* (Frankfurt, 1964), pp. 91-92. Later, Lukács would radically revise his appraisal of Simmel. He would quote the latter: "The 'fetish character' that Marx attributes to economic objects in the epoch of commodity production is only a particular, modified case of the general fate of our cultural situation" and then attack him for this hypostasis of, in Lukács' words, a "specific moment of the imperialist epoch into an 'eternal' tragedy of culture as such." In this view Simmel's thought stands as the point of open bankruptcy of a tradition begun by Schopenhauer and Nietzsche which "defends the capitalist system by revealing and emphasizing its bad sides and simultaneously inflating them into cosmic contradictions." *Zerstörung der Vernunft*, p. 400. This argument recapitulates the attacks levelled against *History and Class Consciousness* by the "orthodox" Marxists, a fact which suggests other, though perhaps not eternal, tragedies.

12. See, for example, Lukács' "Soziologie des modernen Dramas," *Archiv fur Sozialwissenschaft und Sozialpolitik* 38 (1914), pp. 303-45, 662-706; "Die Subjekt-Objekt Beziehung

Partially conscious and explicit in Lukács' perspective in this early period is the perception that a central component of capitalism—as distinct from previous stages of civilization—is the increasing domination of the economy and economic relations over social and spiritual life. As early as 1908-9 he wrote that social and cultural forms are shaped by the fact that "the main economic tendency of capitalism is...objectification of production, its separation from the personality of the producers. Through the capitalist economy an objective-abstract force, capital, becomes the real producer and capital has no organic relation to those who happen to own it; indeed it is often utterly superfluous whether or not the owners are personalities at all (e.g., joint stock companies)." 13 The philosophical idealism and romanticism of his work amounted to a revolt against the "primacy of the (economic) base," an attempt—still at the level of philosophy and culture in the strict sense—to liberate human subjectivity and spiritual creativity from their abstract-objectified fetters. In the pre-World War I years Lukács thought little of the Marxism of German social democracy, which he considered an integral part of the prevailing mental and social economism. He believed that human subjectivity and inter-subjectivity had been liquidated (reduced to functions of the economy) in Kautskian Marxism as they were in danger of being liquidated by industrial capitalism. Lukács' theoretical liberation of the "subjective factor"—the sensuous, active human base of social life and its historical self-consciousness in proletarian class consciousness—in *History and Class Consciousness* is decisively anticipated and formed in his pre-Marxian work.[14]

These themes can be clarified by a somewhat closer if schematic glance at his "culture criticism." Until his sudden entrance into the Hungarian Communist party in February, 1919, Lukács was a leading figure in the Budapest branch of what David Kettler has recently called the "revolutionary cultural movement."[15] The *general* character of Lukács' perspective was not unique; as suggested above, it was linked to the pervasive revolt against industrial society that unfolded among European intellectuals and youth at the turn of the century. A central theme of this revolt was its contraposition of *Kultur* and *Gemeinschaft* with *Zivilization* and *Gesellschaft*, the former concepts suggesting the sought after natural,

---

in der Asthetik," *Logos* 7 (1917), pp. 1-39; and "Zum Wesen und zur Methode der Kultursoziologie," *Archiv* 39 (1914), pp. 216-22.

13. "Soziologie des modernen Dramas," pp. 665-66. Originally written in Hungarian in 1908-09; translated (presumably by Lukács) and published in German in 1914.

14. Lukács had studied Marx prior to his own Marxism. He comments on the significance Marx's work had for him at that time in "Mein Weg zu Marx," pp. 225-227.

15. Kettler, *Marxismus und Kultur, passim.* Kettler quotes from interviews with Anna Lesznai and Arnold Hauser, both of whom had been members of the Budapest circle. Lesznai: "Lukács' appearance as a Communist came as a complete surprise to his friends.... His conversion took place between two Sundays: Saul became Paul." Hauser: "When Lukács announced his conversion to Communism, no one knew what it meant." Kettler also mentions that the Bolshevik revolution of 1917 exerted little impact within Lukács' circle in Budapest and refers to Lukács' first thoughts on the event in 1918, in a lost article, where he condemns the despotic character of the revolution. Another of the many central themes in Lukács' pre- and Marxian thought not discussed here is his preoccupation with ethics and the possible grounds on which ethical norms may be violated. See his 1919 article, "Taktik und Ethik," in *Werke: Frühschriften II*, pp. 45-54.

face to face community that would truly meet man's spiritual and creative needs, the latter concepts defining the existing "society"—mechanized, alienated and destructive of the essential vitality and fullness of human life.[16] Lukács gave expression to this position in his *Theory of the Novel* (1916, 1920) which, in the course of presenting an aesthetic-philosophical analysis of the relations between literary forms and historical-cultural epochs, points to the organic "wholeness" (*Geschlossenheit*) of classical Greek and medieval cultures, on the one hand, and on the other, the complete fragmentation and alienation (*Zerissenheit*) of late bourgeois culture.[17] This conception—clearly carried over into "The Old Culture and the New Culture"—maintains that in the bourgeois epoch subjectivity and the world, the soul and action, spirit and nature, feeling and reason, form and content are torn asunder; art is ripped from the totality of social life and the possibility of a culture that is originally (in Lukács' terms, sensuously and immediately) linked to social being rapidly diminishes. Indeed, the possibility of unified, *authentic* being as such is progressively liquidated. Following the dissolution of the unity of medieval society and its worldview, there simply "no longer is any totality of being (*Seinstotalität*)." This development is expressed in the increasingly intellectualist character of art by the late 19th century. During this period creativity becomes a project in reflection on the problem of creativity and artistic forms themselves; the typical main character in both fiction and drama is marked by almost pure passivity and interiority.[18]

Not accidentally, Lukács in this period adopted as his own Novalis' definition of philosophy as "nostalgia, the impulse to be everywhere at home in the world."[19] The pages of his early writings are literally suffused

---

16. Here one clearly sees the origins of Lukács' "anticipatory rediscovery" of Marx's *Paris Manuscripts* (not published until 1932). Not only does Lukács already grasp human history as the story of alienation, but in numerous critical aspects he is passing through the same moments of consciousness as did Marx (and Hegel in the latter's *Jugendschriften*) on his way to the revolutionary theory of an end to alienation. As is well known, the social and cultural theories based upon the *Gemeinschaft-Gesellschaft, Kultur-Zivilization* distinction amount to a pervasive phenomenon in modern industrial society, one whose consequences, not to speak of the literature, can hardly be touched on here. It may be mentioned that this tradition is generally linked to politically conservative thinkers and movements, a "fact" which since the 1930s has led most Marxists and liberals to view the traditions through a mechanical, *reductio ad Hitlerum* lens. This is by and large what Lukács himself does in his *Zerstörung der Vernunft*, hoping to bury his earlier attempt to unfold the radical implications of the "conservative" critique. More dialectical analyses can be found in Herbert Marcuse, "The Struggle Against Liberalism in the Totalitarian View of the State," *Negations*, trans. J.J. Shapiro (Boston, 1968), pp. 3-42; and Theodor W. Adorno, "Spengler after the Decline," *Prisms*, trans. S. Weber (London, 1967), pp. 53-72.

17. *Theorie des Romans. Ein Geschichtsphilosophischer Versuch über die Formen der grossen Epik* (Neuwied and Berlin, 1962), esp. pp. 22-33. Lukács' theory of aesthetic forms is central in the genesis of his social theory. Forms are the medium through which the artist puts questions to life, and poses the questions of life. The critic moves from the formed life of art and poetry to the experience and existence that is given form—from, to borrow the title of Lukács' earlier book, forms to the soul.

18. *Theorie des Romans*, pp. 32, 115. In the Preface to the 1962 edition, Lukács argues that the "life-feeling" (*Lebensgefühl*) expressed in the idea of an absence of "totality of being" is basically a pre-fascist attitude.

19. Quoted and discussed in Lukács, *Theorie des Romans*, p. 22. See also the references to Schiller in the same section.

with the yearning for a lost unity, totality and authenticity of being, glimpses of which, according to Lukács, appear in the infrequent "great moments" when knowledge and action merge and momentarily pierce through the *durée* of alienated bourgeois existence.[20] Georg Simmel, with whom Lukács studied and by whom he was deeply influenced, had raised the phenomenon of alienation and the loss of man's being and spirit in his objectified creations to the level of a theory of "the great tragedy of culture." In 1911, Simmel wrote: "The great enterprise of the spirit succeeds innumerable times in overcoming the object as such by making an object of itself, returning to itself enriched by its creation. But the spirit has to pay for this self-perfection with the tragic potential that a logic and dynamic is inevitably created by the unique laws of its own world which increasingly separates the contents of culture from its essential meaning and value."[21] But what in Simmel ultimately issued in ontologization and resignation appeared in Lukács as a quest for a dialectics of cultural renewal that might break the eternal, tragic chain. Prior to his entrance into Marxism, Lukács had historicized and sociologized the analysis of culture and its crisis, interpreting the latter, still in cultural terms, as a product of capitalism and bourgeois society. His *Theory of the Novel* closes with a brief commentary on Tolstoy and Dostoyevsky in which Lukács glimpses links between cultural renewal and social transformation. Remarking on this point in 1962 Lukács says that among other problems "at that time there was no mediation between my subjective attitude and objective reality," no conception of the concrete historical subject of renewal. [22]

20. Lukács, "Von der Armut am Geiste," *Neue Blätter*, Vol. II, Nos. 5 and 6 (1912), pp. 67-92. In the opening pages of *Theorie des Romans* Lukács speaks of those "blessed [*selig*] eras," such as that of Homer, which "have no philosophy or, what means the same thing, all men of these eras are philosophers, possessors of the utopian goals of every philosophy." Here Lukács repeats both Hegel's and the early Marx's idea that philosophy originates out of alienated existence and is the ideal expression of the impulse to abolish alienation, by actualizing philosophy. In this discussion Lukács accords to culture (art) the same significance and meaning in the structure of human experience although neither then nor in his subsequent work did he elaborate on the theoretical and practical prospects of the abolition-relation of cultures.

21. Georg Simmel, "On the Concept and Tragedy of Culture," in K.P. Etzborn, ed. and trans., *Georg Simmel: The Conflict in Modern Culture and Other Essays* (New York, 1968), p. 46.

22. "Vorwort" (1962), in *Theorie des Romans*, p. 6. Lukács and the Budapest circle had no "program" of disseminating their perspectives on cultural crisis and renewal; their "Free School of the Spiritual Sciences" was open only to a select few and in the usual sense of the term appears to have been opposed to any organizational-educational mediations between itself and "the people." The associates explicitly rejected any idea of popularizing their views. Yet, as David Kettler suggests, the group's refusal in this regard was based on a very definite theory of dissemination and mediation: the idea of the "rebirth of spirituality" as such. There is no need for a large group or mass constituency, but only for those "goal conscious" few who are instilled with the "mission of cultural renewal." Kettler, *Marxismus und Kultur*, pp. 20-21. This perspective is of great interest both in its formal and social-structural parallels to Lenin's theory of the vanguard party and in its being entirely typical of the conception held by many "Left intellectuals" in the period around World War I for whom "the power that would propel social action toward the sought-after new world was the '*Tatige Geist*' (active spirit)." Jeno Kurucz, *Struktur und Funktion der Intelligenz wahrend der Weimar Republik* (Cologne, 1967), pp. 74 ff. A plethora of *Räte der geistigen Arbeiter* (Soviets of Mind Workers) sprang up

Bang! Enter the revolutionary proletariat. In fact, the story is not so neat. There is a decisive inner coherence but no logical necessity between Lukács' pre-Marxian and Marxian works. However, the oft-made claim that he latched onto Marxism and the proletariat as a vehicle for preserving high culture and elite aesthetic values is philistine nonsense.[23] Such claims overlook the radicalism and totality, as well as the internal tensions, of Lukács' concept of culture—both in itself and in its relation to his Marxism.[24] In this context, "The Old Culture and the New Culture" marks a key transitional point by revealing the mode in which he carried the culture criticism standpoint into Marxism and by clearly suggesting the culture criticism origins of his critique of reification. Even in the initial phase of his thought, when he lacked the categories for fully thinking it through in social-historical terms, Lukács sharply perceived the essential fact of capitalism: *le mort* has taken over *le vif*. He saw that, not only within late bourgeois literature and drama, but on the streets and in the offices and shops of late bourgeois society, men were being reduced to passive objects of productive-instrumental forces and rationality. In a word, the radical and dialectical character of Lukács' early work lies in the fact that in it *cultural crisis is simultaneously a crisis of culture* (in the strict sense of creations of the spirit) *and a crisis of "man," of human existence.* "The Old Culture and the New Culture" brings what is implicit in Lukács' initial thought to the explicit and conscious level: a social theory that grasps and is anchored in the concrete human-social relations which, in bourgeois society and ideology, appear as reified, commodified relations among things. Cultural "supra-politics" and political politics are superseded by the idea of *total revolution.*

The core—the leap and the inner links between the poles—within

---

in Germany in the years immediately following the War's end. Those with more or less Marxian perspectives saw themselves as paralleling the emerging workers' and soldiers' soviets. A particularly wild example in this context was a group, including Martin Buber, Romain Rolland, Gustav Landauer, Max Scheler, and Walter Rathenau, that was to meet in Forte dei Marmi, Italy, in the summer of 1914 in an effort to avert impending war. The premise of the "Forte-Kreis" was that the spiritual energy generated by the coming together of potent minds would be able to transform the real situation. Paul Breines, "Mysticism and Revolution. Gustav Landauer Against his Times," unpublished M.A. thesis (University of Wisconsin, 1967), pp. 105-107. The experiment went untested as the group never got beyond preparatory discussion due to the outbreak of the War. Two additional things may be mentioned regarding Lukács' position in this context. First, his thinking in this period cannot be fully understood in isolation from the "identity crisis" of intellectuals, particularly radical intellectuals at the time (though not only then). In turn, this crisis is closely linked to the "identity crisis" of Marxian theory in the early 1920s, that is, part of the continuing crisis formulated by Marx as that rising out of the necessary simultaneity of philosophy's pressing toward philosophy. The clear parallels between the ideas Lukács held in the pre-War years and his post-1924 Leninist vanguardism need to be examined in light of the intervening project at discovering—through the workers councils and the theory of radical action as the initial liquidator of false consciousness—the theoretical and practical means of breaking through the crisis.

23. Most recently, Neil McInnes, "Georg Lukács," *Survey* 72 (Summer, 1969), pp. 122-140.

24. Although the more sympathetic accounts by Kettler and Morris Watnick avoid the crudeness of McInnes, they (especially the essay by Watnick) suffer from their greatest strength: genuinely honest and detached "history of ideas." Our own crudeness derives from our methodological assumption that none of this is history at all, but a very much alive earlier moment of our own consciousness.

Lukács' thought at this point is comprehended more adequately than in any other commentary by the following remark of (the "young") Herbert Marcuse: "The unerring glimpse into the essence of man becomes the inexorable impulse for the foundation of radical revolution. That the actual situation of capitalism is not only a question of an economic or political crisis, but a *catastrophe* of the *human essence*—from the outset this insight condemns every merely economic or political *reform* to futility and unconditionally demands the catastrophic *Aufhebung* of the existing conditions through total revolution." 25 As in the case of the genesis of Marx's own thought, so in that of Lukács (and Gramsci, and Marcuse, and Merleau-Ponty, and Sartre, and, on a mass scale, the "New Left") a philosophical "idealism of the human essence," that bane of "scientific Marxism," appears as the theoretical starting point of dialectical, revolutionary theory. In each of these instances an "idealism of the essence" is simultaneously a dialectical theory of essence and appearance which, when transformed into social theory, has as its life blood the idea of human practical-critical activity or praxis.

The total or cultural revolutionary substratum of Lukács' initial Marxism is most clearly summarized in "The Old Culture and the New Culture" in the idea of communism as *liberation* from capitalism which means "liberation from the rule of the economy." Communist revolution means the conscious, human expropriation and free development of the human-social relations that under capitalism are forced into sedimented and alienated commodity relations, relations of wage-labor and capital. This moment is preserved when, between 1920 and 1922, the essay's "cultural standpoint" is *aufgehoben* in Lukács' critique of reification, that is, in the essay on *Verdinglichung* in *History and Class Consciousness* where the "thingification" of human life is grasped as the fundamental component and the basic contradiction of capitalist society. Some of the main *recent* theoretical formulations of the idea of cultural revolution and the idea of a critique and transformation of "everyday life" contain decisive connections to the young Lukács' work. As mentioned earlier, Lukács' own thinking entered a phase of de-totalization after 1923-24 and the radical thrust of his early work has necessarily been developed by others—as well as by the subsequent development of modern society. It is not surprising, for example, that a student of Lukács has recently written an essay entitled "The Marxian Theory of Revolution and the Revolution of Everyday Life," arguing that the latter, as a total structure at once external-objective and internal-subjective in relation to individual experience, is the arena and object of revolutionary struggle; 26 or that Henri Lefèbvre's critique of everyday life (*la vie quotidienne*) and his concept of cultural revolution, as well as the Situationist's theory of "the spectacle," are directly linked to the

---

25. Herbert Marcuse, "Neue Quellen zur Grundlegung des historischen Materialismus" (1932), in *Philosophie und Revolution. Aufsätze von Herbert Marcuse* (Berlin, 1967), pp. 96-97. The essay is a review of the first publication of Marx's *Paris Manuscripts*; it contains no mention of Lukács.

26. Agnes Heller, "The Marxist Theory of Revolution and the Revolution of Everyday Life," *Telos* 6 (Fall, 1970), pp. 212-223.

initial project of Lukács' Marxism. 27 For what Lukács formulated in the early 1920s is the dual perception that (1) it is a universal tendency of modern capitalism to make the *totality* of social life and existence into an object of domination with the "intention" of transforming all subjectivity and activity into reified objectivity, all human subjects into passive *spectators* of their own existence; and (2) the theoretical and practical critique of modern capitalism will be a critique of the *whole* or it will be nothing but a repitition of the whole. 28

Needless to say, a huge gap separates not only the late but also the early Lukács from the present cultural revolutionary project. Nevertheless, the thrust and immanent meaning of his initial work has returned at a new level of vigor, clarity and concreteness in the vortex of the student-youth revolt. In the words of one participant: "Cultural revolution is no aesthetic ersatz for revolution; it is not a putsch in a museum, nor an attack on a part, nor a scandal in a theater. Such applications amount to leaving culture in the ghetto to which capitalism condemned it in the first place. Cultural revolution in the period of late capitalism is far more *impatient*, more *encompassing, less easily satisfied* than economic-political revolution. It entails not only the *Aufhebung* of the relations of capital, but also the transformation of all relationships in which men have become commodities and commodities have become the subject of social life: relations between the sexes, between parents and children, between neighbors..."29 This, in our view, is the legitimate historical echo of "The Old Culture and the New Culture," an echo that sharpens the original call and makes it conscious of itself. 30

The concept of culture and the idea of cultural revolution as formulated in "The Old Culture and the New Culture" are beset with tensions, both internal and historical-political. In the latter dimension, as Lukács quickly (indeed, too quickly) recognized, the end-goal articulated in the essay—communism as man's return to himself and his nature, the end of prehistory or alienated history—far outstripped the historically possible in

27. See among other of his works, Henri Lefèbvre, *La vie quotidienne dans le monde moderne* (Paris, 1968). A brief statement of Lefèbvre's criticism of Lukács' theory of reification is in his *The Sociology of Marx*, trans. N. Guterman (New York, 1969), pp. 48-49. The impact of Lukács' perspective can be found throughout Guy Debord, *The Society of the Spectacle* (Detroit, 1967).

28. The category of *Zuschauer* is central in Lukács' essay on reification in *History and Class Consciousness*. It refers to the condition of existence to which all members of capitalist society are reduced and is a dialectical category in that it is not only descriptive but intentional. It shows that men *appear* (to themselves) to be spectators at the "drama" of their own lives while in actuality, they *are* not-yet-conscious actors and producers of the drama. How central this category is today can be seen in any of a million advertisements such as a recent one for CBS News. It contains a list of recent campus uprisings around the world, and shows a picture of the globe bursting apart, while announcing in bold print: "Watch the World Watchers Watch the World—CBS NEWS." The imposed spectatorship is now mediated by technological media: one is instructed not merely to watch the world (his own) but to watch the media watch it. And since it is his own world and life, the viewer surely won't want to miss the show.

29. Peter Schneider, "Die Phantasie im Spätkapitalismus und die Kulturrevolution," *Kursbuch* 16 (1969), pp. 3-4.

30. Though still more distant from Lukács, the present rock line, "break on through to the other side," likewise reflects the thrust of his initial project.

the post-World War I context. At the very moment of the essay's publication Lukács had already undertaken the task of adjusting its aspirations to the actual circumstances. Internal to the essay lies a second and related tension that provided a means of carrying out the adjustments and also contributed to Lukács' capitulation to circumstances. This internal tension appears in the fact that Lukács' cultural standpoint—the basis of the idea of total or cultural revolution—simultaneously contains a general imperative of, and a particular way of conceiving, *cultural* renewal in the strict sense. The essay's explicit theme is the meaning of communist revolution for culture. The revolution, by transforming the relations of consciousness and social being, art and social organization (the artist, his material, the public), and the crisis of form and content that exists under capitalism, would restore the essential organic unity and wholeness of culture. In the essay the aesthetic and social-political (or "life") moments are inextricably linked. When, by late 1922, Lukács began to reorient his thought in conjunction with a more "realistic" evaluation of the pace and tempo of revolution and, shortly thereafter, in line with the dissolution of revolution in Europe, the "temporary stabilization" of capitalism, and the fact and theory of socialism in one country, the aesthetic moment in the concept of culture began to predominate—a token of an emerging fragmentation in Lukács' thinking and in the revolutionary movement itself.

Actually, Lukács' attention in the 1921-24 years was focused entirely on the philosophical and political (strategic-tactical) questions then dominating the activity of the Third International. With the book on *Lenin* (1924) and the lengthy essays criticizing the "idealist dialectics" of Moses Hess and Ferdinand Lassalle, Lukács began the immense labor of self-criticism in which he remained engaged until his death. He did not want to be the Hess or Lassalle of 20th century socialism.[31] For nearly a decade following the publication of "The Old Culture and the New Culture," Lukács' writings hardly touched upon strictly cultural, let alone "cultural revolutionary," questions.[32] In 1926, however, Lukács published an essay that is an exception to this development. It is a bibliographically obscure but substantively very important piece that vividly illuminates the changes in position he made regarding the idea of cultural revolution. The essay, "*L'Art pour l'Art* and Proletarian Poetry," stands as a companion and direct reply to "The Old Culture and the New Culture"; it is also a capsule analysis of the crisis of a generation of revolutionary intellectuals.[33]

---

31. "Die neue Ausgabe von Lassalles Briefen" (1925), in *Werke: Frühschriften II*, pp. 612-40; "Moses Hess und die Problem der idealistischen Dialektik" (1926), *ibid.*, pp. 643-86.

32. With major revisions, though basic continuity as well, Lukács' attention returned to cultural matters by the early 1930s when he had emigrated to the U.S.S.R.

33. "L'Art pour l'art und proletarische Dichtung," *Die Tat*, Vol. XVIII, No. 3 (June, 1926), pp. 220-23. Highly significant that Lukács published the essay in *Die Tat*. Its editor and publisher was Eugen Diederichs who "considered himself the leading publisher of the New Romanticism, which he traced back to Nietzsche and Lagarde." Before, during and after the war it was indeed the organ of the more far-out theorists of the Youth Movement and a wild mixture of New *Geist*, New *Gemeinschaft*, New *Eros*, ideas. After the war it was hostile to the Weimar Government and bourgeois constitutionalism generally. Though he never published in its pages earlier, it is quite possible Lukács presented this essay to *Die Tat* in an effort to woo

Despite some shifts in emphasis and a few new specifics, the 1926 essay is largely a restatement of the theses presented in 1920. For example, the "art for art's sake" school is viewed as the aesthetic expression of the desperation of the bourgeoisie over its own existence, over the impossibility of genuine life and culture in bourgeois society—the bourgeois character (*Bürgerlichkeit*) is itself in contradiction with late bourgeois society. The "purely artistic" imperative is seen as a mask for the artist's hatred of his own class, yet the artist himself is pressed into a tragic situation: genuine art requires a "sensual-naive immediacy" and precisely this is liquidated by capitalism which transforms all of social life (the material in which art must be in immediate relation) into abstract, reified appearances. Thus, art can only be a critique of the era (*"Kritik der Zeit"*). Capitalism worsens the situation by tearing the artist from a social base and public as the artist, his works, and the public are subsumed in market relations. Honest artists, as Lukács calls Flaubert, recognize that elevating this rootlessness into a theory is nothing but a "desperate self-stupefaction," others, e.g., Oscar Wilde, Hugo Hofmannstahl, Gabriele d'Annunzio, end up in a "corrupt self-betrayal." Bourgeois society destroys the material of art and thus the possibility of aesthetic forms as such. The artist can only generate forms out of himself, which is "art for art's sake." The "abstract-romantic utopias" of politically oriented art (*Tendenzkunst*)—Lukács refers here to the expressionism of the late Ibsen, Ernst Toller, Georg Kaiser—are equally hopeless. For the aesthetic crisis is itself a moment in the larger crisis and is symptomatic of the fundamental inability of the bourgeois class to perceive the social basis of its own existence and crisis.[34]

The decisive shift in Lukács' perspective, however, lies in the following question and answer posed by Lukács: "What can proletarian revolution offer to the development of art? Initially very little."[35] With his own earlier position in mind, Lukács adds that the revolutionary Marxists ought not engage in utopian overestimations of the actual prospects. For, he argues, not only has capitalism not been globally abolished, but in the Soviet Union capitalist structural forms continue to exist in the "first phase" of revolution. Then, in a graphic statement of self-criticism, Lukács writes that: "The immense transformation we are experiencing [developments in the Soviet Union], the transformation being carried out by the revolutionary proletariat, finds expression in the immediate, sensual reality (i.e., in the material and form of poetry) far less rapidly than a superficial glance would have led one to expect. This explains the 'disillusionment' with the Russian Revolution on the part of many of those intellectuals who expected it to provide an immediate solution to their special problems." He concludes on

---

segments of its coherently anti-capitalist writers and readership. It is worth mentioning that most of Karl Korsch's pre-World War I essays were published in *Die Tat*, though his perspective had nothing at all to do with the predominant views of the journal. Diederichs did in fact open his pages to a variety of positions. On *Die Tat*, see Harry Pross, *Literatur und Politik. Geschichte und Programme der politisch-literarischen Zeitschriften im deutschen Sprachgebiet seit 1870* (Freiburg, 1963), pp. 94-97.

34. "L'Art pour l'art," pp. 220-22.

35. *Ibid.*, pp. 222-23. In his revised view Lukács cites Trotsky's *Literature and Revolution* as a supporting work.

the properly subdued note that as long as one does not expect this immediate solution, great progress is visible. Artists in the West who have joined the proletarian revolutionary movement have been able to break out of the "antinomies" of bourgeois art and create great realistic novels of description while, in addition, a genuine proletarian art is beginning to emerge in the Soviet Union. [36]

What Lukács expresses in the form of a de-escalation of expectations is, in fact, a de-escalation of critical thought—specifically, a flight from the "antinomies" of Leninism, the Bolshevik Revolution, and Stalinism. The elements in "The Old Culture and the New Culture" which were subversive to the Soviet Union have been repressed by Lukács in a mode that resembles the non-dialectical, "Bernsteinian" separation of the end-goal from the daily struggle—a separation whose most profound philosophical critic had been Lukács himself. [37] The 1926 essay brings into sharp focus a crucial aspect of Lukács' whole perspective on culture and literature, one which he has held from the beginning: a dogmatic classicism and a corresponding hostility to avant-garde and modernist art. This issue in its entirety cannot be broached here.[38] It may suffice to point out the ironic fact that this aspect is (in 1920 as well as later) accompanied by "counterrevolutionary" ideas on culture itself. For example, in "The Old Culture and the New Culture" it is clear that for Lukács art that is a *Kritik der Zeit* is barely art, since it is necessarily increasingly less realistic, increasingly formless. [39] Thus, on the one hand, Lukács bars himself from immanent analysis of the projects and internal structures of avant-garde literature and, on the *same* hand, emerges as a leading spokesman of the kind of "old culture" writing that Roland Barthes has aptly criticized as follows: "Communist writers are the only ones who go on imperturbably keeping alive a bourgeois writing which bourgeois writers have themselves condemned long ago, since the day when they felt it was endangered by the impostures of their own ideology, namely, since the day when Marxism was thereby justified."[40] Thus, in reading Lukács' work one is struck by the

---

36. *Ibid.*, p. 223.

37. Lukács' rather well-known critical review of Bukharin's *Historical Materialism* (1922) is also revealing in this context. The review, published in 1925, is generally considered an exemplary historical and dialectical materialist critique of mechanistic materialism and technological reductionism in Marxist garb. Lukács demonstrates concisely how human-social relations, conscious activity, and the dialectic of social being and consciousness vanish from Bukharin's book. Significantly, Lukács does *not* raise the question of how adequately Bukharin's thought expresses the actual situation in the Soviet Union. He refuses to subject Bukharin's work to the same type of dialectical "ideology critique," attempting to unfold the social sources of the natural scientific and mechanistic tendencies in Bukharin, which he so brilliantly brought to bear on bourgeois thought and its antinomies. An English translation of the review appears in *New Left Review* 39 (September-October, 1966), pp. 27-34.

38. The primary and secondary literature on this question (Lukács and realism) is massive. A recent statement of Lukács' views is in his *The Meaning of Contemporary Realism*, trans. J. and N. Mander (London, 1962). There is also an American paperback edition.

39. By accident, Lukács is right. That is, the conscious intention of the creations and lives of the Dadaists and Surrealists, for example, is precisely to hasten the death of a too-long-in-expiring art in the name of liberating phantasy, imagination, the unconscious, desire, life.

40. Roland Barthes, *Writing Degree Zero*, trans. by A. Lavers and C. Smith (New York, 1967), p. 73.

breathtaking absence of even a reference to the most important artistic and cultural-political developments underway around him: cubism, dada, surrealism, futurism (Russian and Italian), constructivism, formalism, De Stijl, Bauhaus, atonal music, let alone a discussion of the relationship between these developments and the general theory of the crisis of culture and life he formulates.

Finally, Lukács' critical reference in the 1926 essay to "those intellectuals who expected [the Russian Revolution] to provide an immediate solution to their *own special problems*" (emphasis added), is important both in his own case and more generally. This remark is indicative of a phenomenon that is particularly pervasive within the history of the Left; one which found concentrated expression at the Fifth Congress of the Third International in 1924. There, the works of Lukács, Korsch, Fogarasi, Graziedei, and others were officially condemned by Zinoviev, speaking for the Comintern Executive. An underlying thrust of the attack was that these "idealist deviationists" were all "professors," "intellectuals." [41] As is well known, Lukács tended to accept the theoretical criticisms levelled at his work at the time; here he reveals (for tactical reasons) his acceptance of the related attack on intellectuals who supposedly poison the working-class struggle with their "own special problems." He admits, that is, that what he formulated in 1920, and in *History and Class Consciousness*, as a *universal* critique based on the needs and *telos* of "man," is no more than the ideological expression of the private and peculiar needs of intellectuals. [42] Within the socialist and communist movements the party functionary's hostility to intellectuals is notorious; [43] the worker's hostility to intellectuals is supposed to be equally notorious and, according to party functionaries and intellectuals, is also supposed to be healthy; the simultaneous caste narcissism and self-flagellation of intellectuals is, at least, doubly notorious. Lukács' remark gives expression to all these positions at once—as only an intellectual caught in a deep social-theoretical-personal crisis inside a revolutionary movement enmeshed in a crisis of its own, could.

---

41. Relevant excerpts from Zinoviev's speech are in Watnick, "Relativism and Class Consciousness," *op.cit.*, p. 146.

42. Bertolt Brecht speaks of the "type of intellectual revolutionary of whom the proletarian revolutionary is suspicious: this is the type who expects a thoroughgoing improvement from the revolution. In no sense standing under unbearable pressure, but freely selecting and choosing what is better, he opts for revolution." *Gesammelte Werke*, Vol. XX (Frankfurt, 1967), p. 64. Remarks of this type are hardly as insightful as they sometimes appear. Demanding only a "thoroughgoing improvement," let alone demanding less, enables one to accept virtually anything, such as accepting the state bureaucracy of the Soviet Union as a proletarian revolutionary regime. Cf. Lukács, "Zur Organisationsfrage der Intellektuellen," *Komm.*, Vol. I, No. 3 (Feb. 8, 1920), pp. 161-72. Here Lukács undertakes a critique of numerous theories which claim that intellectuals as a group have revolutionary interests. He argues that "The intelligentsia is today *as a class* not revolutionary and cannot be because the proletariat *as a class* is revolutionary." In this context he also asks "how can the student *as student* be a socialist when the essence of studentism (and the 'rights of self-determination' it defends) is based on the contradiction between those who are studying and those who are not, that is, on privilege—in other words, on that structure whose dismantling is the very meaning of socialism?"

43. See, for example, the remarks on Lukács in Jozsef Lengyel, *Visegrader Strasse* (East Berlin, 1959), pp. 139 and 248.

Thus, by the early years of World War I Lukács, with his critique of the crisis of culture and his concept of cultural renewal, had elaborated the foundations of a Marxianized theory of "culture revolution" which, some four decades later would reappear in the consciousness of a generation and mass movement in revolt against a world of reification. Lukács subsequently viewed his own early work as lacking any mediation between the subjective attitude and objective reality—a dilemma that has not entirely vanished for the "heirs of the young Lukács." By 1926, Lukács appears to have come full circle; but the circle itself is transformed. The subjective attitude has "matured," become "more realistic," more self-critical; while, in Lukács' view, it is grounded in the proletarian revolutionary movement as the mediating force. However, this apparent breaking of the circle is nothing of the sort. The de-eschatolization and adjustments of Lukács' thought to changing (de-eschatolized) reality entailed a decisive de-radicalization; the subjective attitude (is it also the attitude of *theory*?) suffered a loss, a diminution, while at the same time, it subjected itself to a mediation that was at once mythical and repressive—the Bolshevik party. Finally, the combination of political radicalism and classicist cultural conservatism reflected in "The Old Culture and the New Culture," and the subsequent (and more important) critique of reification, make Lukács stand as a giant among the progenitors of the present cultural revolutionary project while he himself was anything but a cultural revolutionary.

The Old Culture and the New Culture

Georg Lukács

1.

The development of society is a unified process. This means that a certain phase of development cannot take place in any area of social life without exerting an impact on all other areas. Through this unity and coherence of social development it is possible to grasp and achieve an understanding of the same process from the standpoint of one social phenomenon or another. Thus, one can speak of culture in its apparent isolation from other social phenomena, for when we correctly grasp the culture of any period, we grasp with it the root of the whole development of the period, just as we do when we begin with an analysis of the economic relations.

In bemoaning the collapse of the capitalist order, the bourgeoisie most often claims that its real concern is with the perishing of culture; it formulates its defense of its class interests as if the basis of these interests were the eternal values of culture. In contrast, the starting point of the following set of ideas is the view that *the culture of the capitalist epoch had collapsed in itself and prior to the occurrence of economic and political breakdown*. Therefore, in opposition to the anxieties [of the bourgeoisie], it is a pressing necessity, precisely in the interests of culture, in the interest of opening the way to the new culture, to bring the long death process of capitalist society to its completion.

If one views the culture of two epochs scientifically the key question is: what are the sociological and economic conditions for the existence of culture? The answers to the question with which one would then ultimately have to begin arise out of the relationships between culture and its social preconditions. What actually is culture? Briefly condensed, the concept of culture (as opposed to the concept of civilization) comprises the ensemble of valuable products and abilities which are dispensable in relation to the immediate maintenance of life. For example, the internal and external beauty of a house belongs to the concept of culture in contrast to its durability and protectiveness. So when we ask: what is the social possibility of culture? we have to answer: it is available to those societies in which the primary necessities of life can be met in such a way that in meeting them one does not have to engage in the strenuous labor that consumes all his energy; where, in other words, free energies are at the disposal of culture.

Every old culture was thus the culture of the ruling classes; only they were in a position to place all their valuable abilities in the service of culture, independently of concern for subsistence. Here, as everywhere, capitalism has revolutionized the whole social order. In surpassing the privileges of feudal estates, it also surpassed the cultural privileges of estate society. Specifically, *capitalism drove the ruling class itself, the bourgeoisie, into the service of production*.[1] The essential differentiating feature of

---

1. Engels, *Zur Wohnungsfrage*, p. 17.

capitalism, in contrast to earlier social orders, is that in it the exploiting class itself is subjugated to the process of production; the ruling class is forced to devote its energies to the struggle for profit just as the proletariat is forced to devote itself to subsistence. (For example, compare the factory director under capitalism to the lord during the period of serfdom.) This claim is apparently contradicted by the plethora of idlers produced and supported by the capitalist class. Yet our attention should not be diverted from the essence by superficial appearances, for when it comes to culture, only the best forces of the ruling class should be considered. In precapitalist periods these forces were situated in relations which enabled them to put their abilities in the service of culture while capitalism, in contrast, has made these forces into slaves of production just as it has the workers (even though, in material terms, their slavery and that of the workers is quite different).

Liberation from capitalism means liberation from the rule of the economy. Civilization creates the rule of man over nature but in the process man himself falls under the rule of the very means that enabled him to dominate nature. Capitalism is the zenith of this domination; within it there is no class which, by virtue of its position in production, is called upon to create culture. The destruction of capitalism, i.e., communist society, grasps just these points of the question. Communism aims at creating a social order in which everyone is able to live in a way that in precapitalist eras was possible only for the ruling classes and which in capitalism is possible for now class.

It is at that point that the history of mankind will actually begin. Just as history in the old sense began with civilization, and men's struggle with nature was placed in the "prehistoric" epoch, so will the history writing of the coming epoch begin the real history of mankind with developed communism. The rule of civilization will then be known as the second prehistoric period.

2.

The most decisive feature of capitalist society, then, is that economic life ceased to be a means to social life; economic life placed itself at the center, became an end in itself, the goal of all social activity. The first and most important result was that the life of society was transformed into a grand exchange relationship; society itself became a huge market. In the individual life experiences this condition expresses itself in the commodity form which clothes every product of the capitalist epoch as well as all the energies of the producers and creators. Everything ceases to be valuable for itself or by virtue of its inner (e.g., artistic, ethical) value; a thing has value only as a ware bought and sold on the market. No deep analysis is needed to show how destructive this has been of every and all culture. Just as man's independence from the worries of subsistence (the free use of his powers as an end in itself) is the human and social precondition for culture, so all that culture produces can possess real cultural value only *when it is valuable for itself*. The moment cultural productions become commodities, when they are placed in relationships which transform them into commodities, their autonomy—the possibility of culture—ceases.

Capitalism has radically attacked the social possibility of culture at still another point: its relationship to the production of cultural products. We have seen that from the standpoint of the product, culture is not possible when the product does not carry its aim within itself. Now, from the standpoint of the relation between the product and its producer, culture is possible only when production is a unified and self-contained process; a process whose conditions depend upon the human possibilities and capabilities of the producer. The most characteristic example of such a process is the art work in which the whole genesis of the work is exclusively the result of the artist's labor and each element of the work is conditioned by his individual qualities. In the precapitalist eras this artistic spirit dominated the whole industry. At least in regard to the human character of the process, the printing of a book was as little separated from its writing as the painting of a picture was from the preparation of a table. Capitalist production, however, not only wrests property in the means of production from workers, but also, as a result of the always expanding and increasingly specialized *division of labor*, it so fragments and divides the developmental process of the product that no part is in itself meaningful or self-contained. No individual worker's labor is in immediate and perceptible linkage with the finished product; the latter has meaning only for the abstract calculation of the capitalists, that is, only as a commodity.

The inhumanity of this relationship is intensified by the expansion of machine production. In the division of labor which arose out of manufacturing—where the preparation of the product was highly divided and dismembered—the quality of individual parts was nevertheless decisively conditioned and shaped by the physical and spiritual capacities of the worker, whereas in the developed machine industry every link between the product and producer is abolished. Production is exclusively conditioned by the machine; *man serves the machine, he adapts to it*; production becomes totally independent of the human possibilities and capabilities of the worker. 2

Next to the culture-destroying forces—which so far we have observed only from the standpoint of the individual, isolated product and producer—other similar forces are also operative in capitalism. We notice the most important of these when we grasp the relationship of the products to each other. The culture of precapitalist periods was possible because the individual cultural products stood in a continuous relation to one another—one developed further the problems raised by its predecessor, etc. Thus, the whole culture revealed a certain continuity of gradual and organic development. Thus, it was possible that in any area a coherent, plain, and yet original culture arose, a culture whose level went far beyond that of the highest achievement of isolated, individual capacities. By revolutionizing the process of production, by making the revolutionary character of produc-

---

2. Many place this process in the context of the technical division of labor of mechanized industry and pose the question as if such a situation must continue to exist even after the collapse of capitalism. This issue cannot be fully discussed here. Suffice it to say that Marx viewed it differently. He perceived that the "efficiency of labor within the factory and the division of labor within society" stand in inverse relation to each other and that in a society where one is developed the other regresses and vice versa" (*Elend der Philosophie*, p. 120).

tion permanent through the anarchy of production, capitalism dissolved the continuous and organic aspects of the old culture. For culture, the revolutionization of production means, on the one hand, that the production process continuously introduces factors that decisively influence the course and art of production without, however, relating in any way to the essence of the product—a work as an end in itself. (Thus, for example, the purity of materials vanishes from industry and architecture.) On the other hand—as a result of production for the market without which the capitalist revolutionization of production would be unthinkable—the novel, the sensational, and the conspicuous elements assume an importance irrespective of whether or not they enhance or detract from the true, inner value of the product. The cultural reflection of this revolutionary process is the phenomenon known as fashion; a phenomenon which denotes a concept essentially different from that of culture. The dominance of fashion means that the form and quality of the product placed on the market is altered in short periods of time independently of the beauty or purpose of such alterations. *It is of the essence of the market that new things must be produced within definite periods of time*, things which must differ radically from those which preceded them, and which cannot build upon the previously-collected experiences of production. Either, as a result of the speed of development, they cannot be gathered and digested; or, no one wants to base himself on them since the very essence of fashion requires complete deviation from what preceded. Thus, every organic development vanishes and in its place steps a directionless hither-thither and an empty but loud dilettantism.

3.

The roots of the crisis of capitalist culture reach still deeper than this. The foundation of its perpetual crisis and internal collapse is the fact that ideology on the one hand and the production and social order on the other enter into irreconciliable contradiction. As a necessary result of capitalism's anarchy of production, the bourgeois class, when struggling for power and when first in power, could have but one ideology: that of individual freedom. The crisis of capitalist culture must appear the moment this ideology is in contradiction with the bourgeois social order. As long as the advancing bourgeois class—in the 18th century, for example—directed this ideology against the constraints of feudal estate society, it was an adequate expression of the given state of class struggle. Thus, the bourgeoisie in this period was actually able to have a genuine culture. But as the bourgeoisie came to power (beginning with the French Revolution) it could no longer seriously carry through its own ideology; it could not apply the idea of individual freedom to the whole society without bringing about the self-negation of the social order that brought this ideology into being in the first place. Briefly, it was impossible for the bourgeois class to apply its own idea of freedom to the proletariat. The unsurpassable dualism of this situation is the following: the bourgeoisie must either deny this ideology or it must employ it as a veil covering those actions which contradict it. In the first case the result would be a total "ideal-lessness," a moral chaos, since by virtue of its position in the production system the bourgeoisie is not capable of producing an ideology other than that of individual freedom. In the second case, the bourgeoisie faces the moral crisis of an internal lie: it is forced to act against its own ideology.

This crisis is intensified by the fact that the principle of freedom itself ends up in irremediable contradiction. We cannot enter here into an analysis of the era of finance capital. We need only mention the fact that the immense "organizedness" of production which emerges from this stage of capitalism (cartels, trusts) stands in complete contradiction with the dominant idea of early capitalism: free competition. In the process of social development this idea loses all basis in reality. As the upper sectors of the bourgeoisie, following the essence of finance capital, became the natural allies of their former enemies—the agrarian-feudal classes—so did these sectors of the bourgeoisie look to their new allies for a new ideology. But this attempt to bring ideology back into harmony with the production system has to fail. The real foundation of conservative ideologies—the feudal estate divisions and the corresponding production order—was decisively eradicated precisely by capitalism's revolutionization of production (which reached its peak in the era of finance capital). Feudalism once possessed a culture of great value and achievement. But this was in a period when feudal estate society prevailed; when the whole of society and production was ruled according to its principles. With the victory of capitalism this social formation was annihilated. The fact that a substantial portion of economic and social power remained in the hands of the once ruling estates did not halt the process by which these estates were capitalized, i.e., assumed capitalist form. The result, for the feudal sectors, was the same contradiction between ideology and production order which emerged with the bourgeoisie, although the expression of this contradiction differed. Thus, as the bourgeoisie in the age of finance capital sought the waters of renewal, it looked to a well-spring that it had itself filled with sand.

From the standpoint of culture, this opposition between ideology and production order means the following: the foundation of the greatness of old cultures (Greek, Renaissance) consisted in the fact that ideology and production order were in harmony; the products of culture could organically develop out of the soil of social being. If the greatest cultural works were some distance from the inner world of the average man, there was nevertheless a contact and coherence between them. But more important was the fact that the harmony of ideology and the production order made possible the obvious harmony between ideology and the then existing way of life. (That each specific human way of life depends on its position in production requires no detailed discussion.) In every social order, however, where the way of life and its ideological expression are in natural and self-evident harmony, it is then possible for the forms assumed by ideology to find organic expression in the products of culture. This organic unity is possible only under certain conditions. For the relative autonomy of ideological elements from their economic foundations means that as *forms* (i.e., according to their formal values and formal validity), these ideological elements are independent of the "givens" that are formed by them; the forms of human expression are, in other words, independent of that which is presented to them by the economic and social order prevailing at the time. *The material that is formed by these forms can be nothing else but social reality itself.* Thus when a fundamental opposition emerges between ideology and the economic order, this opposition appears as follows in relation to our problem: *the form and content of cultural expressions enter into contradiction with each other.* At this point the organic unity of individual works—the harmonious, joy-imparting essence of particular works—no longer signifies an organic cultural unity for those living within the culture.

For this reason, the culture of capitalism, to the extent that it truly existed, could consist in nothing but the ruthless critique of the capitalist epoch. This critique frequently reached a high level (Zola, Ibsen) but the more honest and valuable it was, the more it had to lose the simple and natural harmony and beauty of the old culture: culture in the true and literal sense of the word. The contradiction between ideology and productive order, between the form and content of culture, appears in all areas of human expression in the entire realm of cultural material. In this way, capitalism—to mention but one very evident example—necessarily produces out of itself, out of its very freedom ideology, *the idea of man as an end in himself.* It can safely be said that this great idea never received such pure, clear and conscious expression as in the immediately precapitalist years—the period of classical German idealism. Yet no social order has so thoroughly trampled on this idea as has capitalism. For example, the commodification of everything did not remain limited to the transformation of all products into commodities; it also passed over into human relations (one thinks of marriage). Within this context, the inner necessity of the direction of ideology and culture requires that all cultural products proclaim man as an end in himself. On the other hand, the material—that which is formed by the ideological-cultural forms—is a living negation of this very idea. The best poetry of capitalism, for example, could thus not be a simple reflection of its period—as was, for example, Greek poetry whose eternal beauty sprang precisely from this naturally uncritical mirroring— but only a critique of the existing order.

4.

We now turn to the meaning of the communist transformation of society from the standpoint of culture. It means, above all, the end of the domination of the economy over the totality of life. It means thereby an end to the impossible and discordant relation between man and his labor in which man is subjugated to the means of production. In the last analysis, the communist social order means the *Aufhebung* of the economy as an end in itself. But because the structure of capitalism has so deeply penetrated the mental world of everyone living within it, this side of the transformation is only faintly perceived. This is all the more true because this side of the transformation—the *Aufhebung* of the economy as an end in itself—cannot express itself in the surface appearances of life after the seizure of power. Domination over the economy—that is what socialist economy is—means the *Aufhebung* of the autonomy of the economy. Previously autonomous, a process with its own laws—perceived by human reason but not directed by it[3]—the economy now becomes part of state administration, part of a planned process, no longer dominated by its own laws. Yet the final moving force of this unified social process can no longer be of an economic nature. Indeed, appearances seem to contradict this claim. For it is clear that the reorganization of production is theoretically and practically impossible on other than economic grounds, with economic organs, and through economic thought. Beyond this, it goes without saying that, corresponding to the essence of class struggle in the phase of the dictatorship of the proletariat—which means the high point of class struggle—questions of economic struggle, of reorganizing the economy, are questions that stand in the forefront. But this in no way means that the basic foundation of this process is also of an economic nature. The functional change which the proletarian dictatorship brings to every realm also enters here. During capitalism every ideological moment was only the "superstructure" of the revolutionary process which ultimately led to the collapse of capitalism. Now, in the proletarian dictatorship, this relationship is reversed. I do not mean that the reorganization of the economy becomes merely "superstructural" (this expression was not the most adequate even in relation to ideology, since it led to countless misunderstandings), but simply that the priority of the economy dissolves. What speaks against this claim on the surface, speaks for it if only we take a dialectical view of the situation.

In the crisis of capitalist society the ideological component always stood in the foreground of social consciousness. This was not accidental but a result of necessity; the basic motor forces of development could never entirely enter the consciousness of the masses moved by these forces. The socialist "critique" had an unveiling character in relation to these crises and revolutions: it pointed to the real, fundamental moving forces—the economic process. Thus, nothing is more natural than that the standpoint which previously functioned as a critique should remain in the foreground with the collapse of capitalism. The question is only whether or not this functional change has negated and superseded that which, in the earlier function of the socialist critique and historical materialism, had the character of "final" motive. That such a negation and supersession does occur is natural in light of what preceded it. For the economic motive can only be the final motive in the case of a disorganization of the whole productive system. Only the moving forces of disorganized production can function as natural forces, as blind forces; and only as such can they be the final movers of everything. Every ideological element either adapts itself to this process (becomes superstructural), or vainly opposes it. Thus, in capitalism every non-economic factor is purely ideological. The only exception is the socialist critique of the whole of capitalist society, since it is neither a positive nor a negative ideological retinue of individual processes but an unveiling of the whole; it is simultaneously an unveiling of the

---

3. This situation is reflected in the emergence of the school of "political economy" as an independent science. Preceding its emergence, economic science in the modern sense was impossible; and when the autonomy of the economy is ended, "political economy" as an independent science also dissolves. It is thus pure capitalist ideology to view the laws of political economy as eternal, natural laws.

totality of the economic process and an effective action toward its transformation. Yet what is transformed is not only economic disorganization but also the accompanying autonomy of economic life—life under the hegemony of economic motives. When economic life is organized in the direction of socialism, those elements which previously were accouterments at best now come to the fore: *the inner and outer life of man is dominated by human and no longer by economic motives and impulses.*

As we have seen, it is not surprising that the transformation of economic life is more vividly in the forefront of revolutionary consciousness than is that ideological moment through which it is ultimately moved. The process of functional change necessarily enters the consciousness of the proletariat only with its victory. Indeed, among the masses of the proletariat this new consciousness is no more than the continuation of conscious class struggle. Previously, the essence of class consciousness consisted in the entrance of economic interests into consciousness. The mere transition to the work of socialist construction—whose end result is the functional change analyzed here—does not touch the proletariat's consciousness of immediate class interests; it is, so to speak, "sub-conscious" (*unter dem Bewusstsein*). Only full class consciousness—which, beyond immediate interests, is conscious of the proletariat's world-historic mission—brings the functional change into the consciousness of the proletariat.

This functional change introduces the possibility of a new culture. *For just as civilization is man's external domination of his environment, so is culture man's internal domination of his environment.* As civilization creates the means for the domination of nature, so, through proletarian culture, the means are created for the domination of society. For civilization, and its most developed form, capitalism, has brought to its peak man's slavery to social production—to the economy. *But the sociological precondition of culture is man as an end in himself.* This precondition, which was present for the ruling classes in precapitalist societies and which capitalism removed from everyone, is created for all with the final phase of proletarian victory. The transformation, this radical reformation of the whole social structure, affects all those phenomena whose culture-destroying effects we analyzed above.

With the socialist organization of the economy, its revolutionary character ceases. In pace of the anarchic succession (resulting from conjecture), which we characterized by the term fashion, there enters organic continuum, genuine development. Each individual moment follows necessarily out of the substantive preconditions of the preceding moment; each moment carries with it the solution to the previously insoluble problems while simultaneously placing a new problem before the moment to follow. The necessary cultural result of such an organic development, one which flows from the essence of things (and not from conjecture), is that the level of culture can again supersede the capacities of single isolated individuals. The linkage to another's work, the continuation of another's work—the second sociological precondition of culture—again becomes possible. In

---

4. Cf. the article "Klassenbewusstsein," *Kommunismus*, Nos. 14 and 15. [This article is reprinted in *History and Class Consciousness.*]

addition, both cultural products and human relations lose their commodity character. The *Aufhebung* of commodity relations enables men and cultural products, which under capitalism functioned entirely or primarily within economic relations, to recover their autonomous character. But the possibility of culture requires that an always greater number of forms of human expression become more deeply and sharply autonomous or, what amounts to the same thing, that they become determined to serve the human essence of man. For the "being ends in themselves" of culture and man are not exclusive; on the contrary, each reciprocally serves and deepens the other. To say that a particular product, a house, a piece of furniture, etc., is produced not as a commodity but in such a way that its own possibilities of beauty attain the highest possible fulfillment, is the same as saying that the house or piece of furniture is in the service of man's "humanness" (*des Menschseins des Menschen*), that it complies with man's demands. Cultural products are no longer produced through an economic process that operates independently of each man—a process in which products are abstract commodities and men are mere buyers and sellers.

At the same time, the unhealthy specialization of capitalism has to stop. And, in fact, the moment man's interests in production are ruled no longer by the abstract effort of buying or selling on the market, but by the unified process of production and by the enjoyment of the now autonomous product—a process that *encompasses the totality of man*—at that moment specialization also undergoes a functional change. In the proletarian society, specialization loses not only its class character but also its alien character in relation to the essence of human life. With the emergence of the product as an end in itself, it will naturally fit into the totality and the final questions of human life. With the *Aufhebung* of human isolation and of anarchic individualism, human society will form an organic whole; its parts—individual members and products—will support and magnify each other in the service of the common goal: the idea of further human development.

5.

By posing this goal we reach the essence of the question. If the goal of the new society consisted in the enhancement of mere satisfaction, of man's well-being, none of the functional changes would enter the picture; that is, their meaning would be scarcely noticeable. In this case the task of the proletarian state could be fulfilled in the organization of production and distribution; economic life—with quite different aims, of course—would continue to dominate the human principle. In this case the new development would naturally reach its goals more rapidly and unilaterally; the ends would be achieved with the correct and just organization of production and distribution. Actually, however, in reaching this point the proletarian state has only established the *indispensable preconditions* for the achievement of its goals. Humanity must still struggle for their *realization*.

The reorganization of the economy is an inescapable requirement in the setting of final goals. And this is so not only for the above sociological reasons; that is, it is not as if only contented men are capable of receiving culture. The reason an economic reorganization is absolutely necessary is that because of the unique structure of human consciousness, immediate evils and miseries—even though they are on a much lower level than the ultimate questions of human existence—nevertheless (with few exceptions), block the ultimate questions from consciousness. These immediate evils and miseries are not, by themselves, capable of bringing to consciousness the final questions of existence. We can clarify this with a very simple example. Someone is racking his brain over a complex scientific problem; during his work he contracts an unrelenting toothache. Clearly, in most cases he would be unable to remain in the stream of his thought and work until the immediate pain is relieved. The annihilation of capitalism, the new socialist reconstruction of the economy means the healing of all toothaches for the whole of humanity. Everything which prevents men from dealing with the truly essential problems vanishes from human consciousness; consciousness now stands open to the essential. Our example also reveals the limits of the economic transformation. Obviously, the toothache must be relieved in order for the work of the mind to be resumed. But it is equally obvious that this work does not resume automatically with the elimination of the pain. For this a new spurt of energy, a new state of mind, a new vitality is required. Even when all economic misery and pain has vanished, laboring humanity has not yet reached its goal. It has only created the *possibility* of beginning to move toward its real goals with renewed vigor. Culture is the form of the idea of man's humanness. Thus, culture is created by men, not by external conditions. Every transformation of society is therefore only the framework, only the possibility of free human self-management and spontaneous creativity.

Sociological research must be limited, then, to analysis of the framework. What the culture of proletarian society will be—that is, what it will be substantively, how it will be essentially constituted—is exclusively determined by the powers of the proletariat as they become free. In regard to this process, any attempt to say anything in advance would be laughable. Sociological analysis can do no more than show that this possibility is created by proletarian society and that *only the possibility is created.* Further details are beyond the frame of what is presently possible in the way of scientific research; at best, one can speak of those cultural values from the old society which may be appropriate to the essence of the new framework and thus which can be adopted and developed further by it. For example, the idea of man as an end in himself—the fundament of the new culture—is the legacy of classical 19th century idealism. The real contribution of the capitalist epoch to the construction of the future consists in its creating the possibilities of its own collapse. In its ruins, it even creates the possibilities for the construction of the future. As capitalism produces the economic preconditions of its own annihilation, and as it produces the intellectual weapons for the proletarian critique that helps annihilate it (e.g., the relation of Marx to Ricardo), so in philosophy, from Kant to Hegel, capitalism has produced the idea of a new society whose task is to bring about the destruction of capitalism.

Dialectics of Nature

Michael Kosok

Introduction

Impossible! This is the general reaction of most people familiar with dialectics (either as Hegelians or as Marxists), or of those studying nature (i.e., the scientists). As a dialectician, so runs the argument, you are dealing essentially with a subjectively constituted schema that has validity for the conceptual process, but not as such for nature "out there." Thus, Hegelians remain abstract, while most Marxists regard dialectics as an ideology or, at best, as a methodology to be "used." The scientists, on the other hand, see nature as an objective process not intrinsically reflective of any such "subjective" logic as dialectic, and, at most, regard the dialectic as a curiosity giving "intuition" but not real insight. All miss the *concrete immediacy* of the dialectical process, i.e., the way in which dialectic expresses the *dynamics* of *whatever* is immediately present, be it thoughts, feelings, sensations or intuitions in the shape of objects, equations or people.

Hegel, first and foremost, is the philosopher who regarded dialectical movement as his "object" of knowledge—winding up with the absolute. However, having discovered the dynamics of dialectic, Hegel tried to "distill" the essence of this dynamics out of the immediacy of the world-situation *from* which dialectics emerges into awareness. Thus, the *philosophic* insight of Marx lies precisely in his intuition that the *logic* of dialectic and the immediacy of the world-context must *themselves* be in a dialectical relation, lest dialectic be reduced to a mere empty form, and immediate existence reduced to a blind play of forces. Hence, "dialectical materialism," regarded *not* as a party slogan or as an ideology, is but a way of giving expression to the concrete immediacy of "existence" displaying its "essence" as lying in a dialectic of relations, such that "reality" is at once immediate and dialectical (i.e., a "mediation" of relations).

Therefore in order to present a meaningful "dialectics of nature," and a "unified field theory of the sciences"—which includes *all* sciences (both "natural" and "humanistic")—Marxist dialectic must be reconsidered as its basis. However—and this is essential—precisely *because* Marxism as concrete dialectic is a philosophy *of* dialectic and therefore a philosophy of transformation, creation and movement, Marxism *itself* must be a *dialectical* philosophy, and not an abstract "position" or ideology forcing the world around it to conform to a given pattern. Any perspective *of* dialectical movement must itself be *within* that movement, lest the dialectic turn out to be only a partial and abstract account of the world, ignoring the fact that any perspective outlined by an individual or a society is paradoxically *within* the very world it is "describing."

This paper is divided into three sections. The first section outlines the philosophic basis necessary to present a dialectic of the sciences as a possibility. The second section then considers the revolution of perspective necessary for such a dialectic to manifest itself as an integral aspect of scientific practice. This revolution is a revolution of consciousness, and thus part of a fundamental change in both personal and social awareness and modes of being—i.e., in both subjective and intersubjective orientations. Finally, in section three, a concrete presentation of a dialectics of nature and a unified field theory of the sciences is given—detailing what such a perspective means for the major natural and social sciences, and indicating how such a perspective can itself become a science—with its own principles and theories subjected to the test of history for validation and modification. In concluding this section, I briefly outline a new theory of relativistic quantum mechanics based upon a dialectics of nature, and present it as a concrete example of what can be done in one field, i.e., physics.

1. The Philosophical Basis

"The chief defect of all previous materialism (including Feuerbach's) is that the object, actuality, sensuousness, is conceived only in the form of the *object of perception,* but not as *sensuous human activity,* practice [*Praxis*], not subjectively. Hence in opposition to materialism the *active* side was developed by idealism—but only abstractly since idealism does not know actual, sensuous activity as such. Feuerbach wants sensuous objects actually different from thought objects: but he does not comprehend human activity as *objective.*"

We find here, in Marx's first thesis on Feuerbach, a singular formulation of what one can call the "vital core of Marxism"—and consequently that which any living and *relevant* Marxism must explicitly express in order for it *not* to degenerate into an abstract ideology. For Marx, praxis is at once subjective and objective and never one *or* the other. It is that specifically *human* state in which each act is directed towards an *object*-of-action (i.e., it is a sensual act and not an "empty" thought process), while at the same time, every object is always an object-of-*action* (i.e., expresses an active state of awareness and not a passive datum of "blind" given). Paraphrasing a famous Kantian insight: subjective awareness without objective content is "empty," while objective content without subjective awareness is "blind"— to which one can add the Hegelian intuition that abstract subjectivity, as an empty *nothingness,* and abstract objectivity as blind *being,* can show no *becoming* whatsoever. This means, however, something quite radical and is more disruptive to one's usual categories of behavior than would be expected from a mere casual reading of Marx's first thesis. It means, specifically, that subjectivity is an act whose content is *always* objective, while objectivity is a content whose form is *always* subjective. This circular mutuality of interdependency is *precisely* what needs to be clarified in order to understand both Marxism in general, and the meaning of a dialectics of nature relevant for modern science in particular. A non-critical intuition of subjectivity and objectivity (or in their localized forms, thinking mind and sensed matter, feeling soul and physical body, etc.) not only tends to regard subjectivity and objectivity as *separable* states of being, but any mutual or *circular* interdependency between such separable states in turn seems to give rise to paradoxes and confusions as to just what is real and what is not.

Marx's *Economic and Philosophical Manuscripts of 1844* abound in such circular interdependencies between the subjective humanism of man and the objective naturalism of nature—i.e. "[thru praxis]...man has become...the being of nature, and nature...the being of man." Elsewhere: "natural science will in time subsume under itself the science of man, just as the science of man will subsume under itself natural science: there will be one science." Thus a dialectics of man *implies* a dialectics of nature and vice versa.

To understand the *eidos* of Marx's first thesis therefore requires recognition of both the *phenomenological* inseparability of subjectivity and objectivity, and their intrinsic *circular dialectic* relation. Marxism must be seen as a *dialectic-phenomenology*. Subjectivity, phenomenologically, simply refers to a *field of presence*, i.e., an immediate non-localized gestalt, "opening," or "awareness" whose content is constituted by *events* of mediation or determination—by "objects" of awareness—such that the field is always a field *of* events and never an abstract field of "consciousness-in-itself." The events in turn are always events *within* a field, context, or gestalt of presence and never abstract or detached "things-in-themselves." Subjectivity as a non-localized field of presence is nothing but concrete immediacy, i.e., experience as an *on-going-process*, in which the events or event-complexes present are any objects, products or structures appearing out of the field and thus coexisting with it, be they symbolic systems, physical objects or egos. Ego-awareness is, therefore, a special form of subjectivity and *not* prior to subjectivity as a *pre*-ego field condition —such as infancy, pre-man or natural evolutionary processes.

It is precisely this *phenomenology* of awareness between field and events which at the same time expresses itself as a *dialectic* of inseparable distinctions, or what in modern science is called a *non*-linear field of relations. In a dialectic relation, all elements are grasped as elements-*of*-relation and never simply as elements-*in*-relation. It is relation, interaction and transformation which constitutes the nature of elements or objects, any element or object "in-itself" being but a one-sided abstraction and alienation from its context within a total process of interaction. Dialectic is but a way of giving expression to the nonlinear totality of inseparable distinctions that constitutes one's awareness, in which any distinction focused or linearized into consciousness as a posited presence (or "thesis") by observation, definition, measurement, conceptualization, or for that matter by *any* activity, is mutually conditioned by its context-of-presence, which *qua* context, functions as a counter-posit or negation ("anti-thesis"). Neither exists as an already well defined entity outside of its mutual boundary relation, and consequently the so-called synthesis or unity of opposites is *not* a construction *of* opposites but rather the opposites are nothing but the inseparable sides of a *singular boundary* state of determination.[1] Dialectics is a logic of transitional relations and transformation states in which the formation of any element, object or structure out of a pre-formed

---

1. See Michael Kosok, "The Dynamics of Paradox" and "The Dialectical Matrix," in *Telos* No. 5 (Spring, 1970).

immediacy of presence is at the same time experienced as its transformation into a relation between its form and its contextual counter-form. This means that dialectical activity, while productive of "syntactical" structures and relations of forms, is *not a structuralism* of forms, for the weakness characterizing structuralism is its lack of any reference to the boundary-condition of transformation *between* objects or forms set into a pattern: forms are given and never experienced in a state of immediacy, subjectivity and objectivity, for example—must express itself as a dialectic *within* both elements. Any *singular* boundary of transition between any two inseparable sides or elements makes *each* element "itself" a transition-relation between the two elements (in effect each element expressing the singular transition-state relative to its own modality), lest they are separable into isolated (i.e., "linearized") elements whose relation is merely external. In this case, each element would appear isolated from the others without its *own* frame of reference, which serves to relate any one element *to* all the others and which *co*-ordinates elements into gestalts of contrast and/or comparison. Indeed, any *one* frame of reference is a *co-ordinate* system par excellence.

It is this mutual interpenetration of relation (*between* any elements X and Y appearing *within* X and Y) which we shall unambiguously refer to as *dialectic necessity*. The so-called content *of* any one element is, therefore, precisely the "form" of its relation and activity *to* its co-functioning context of other elements—i.e. its "properties." It also means that, as a result, the primary consequence following from "dialectic necessity" is self-determination. All elements are circularly self-referential—each element being a function of itself *through the mutual* determination it has with its context of other elements. [2] Every element *formed* (i.e., making a determined appearance) within a state of immediate presence is thus not only *transformed* through its context, but appears as a *self*-transformation, all self-relation or self-reflection being self-transformation. Undialectic theories reduce all relation to either a mechanical and *deterministic external* relation of cause and effect (behaviorism) with a formal combination of terms (formalism) or vitalistic or voluntaristic *indeterminism* of *immediate* self-reference without contextual relatedness, producing arbitrary incoherence. Neither position gives expression to an explicit state of *self-determinism* which is neither rigid nor chaotic, but subtle, fluid, flexible, and *living*—i.e., dynamic, Actually, rigid determinism and chaotic indeterminacy are the two *limiting* cases *of* fluid self-determinism, and they appear as alternatives within any complex state of self-determinism in which the complimentary aspects of unitary field coordination and individual event localization can well appear as separable and opposed dimensions.

In modern science, the dialectic state of inter-determinism is not only expressed by the notion of non-linearity itself, but is the essence of all field theories in which particles, objects or elements are determined through their properties or "modes of behavior" (i.e., their field) and not considered as "things in themselves." The distinction between in-itself and for-another, or potentiality and actuality, particle and field, substance and attribute, is

---

2. If X is a function of Y, and Y is a function of X, then X is a function of itself through Y.

consequently relative. One discovers *degrees* of interrelatedness ranging from relative independence to relative cohesion, the uniqueness of all elements, and the universality of their mutual field always being *co*-relatively determined through each other. Both relativity and quantum mechanics, as we shall see, are complementary expressions of precisely this condition. Indeed, the principle of "indeterminacy" expresses this condition as a fundamental axiom by stating that the very act of observation (in physical measurement or conceptual formulation) transforms both the observer and the observed, neither being meaningful if isolated. One cannot "stop the world and get off," even for a moment; *all* activity—thinking, feeling, acting, meditating, making abstractions and so on—is part of a concrete immediacy of interrelatedness.

Turning specifically to the problem of subjectivity and objectivity, a dialectic phenomenology would demand—by virtue of what we have called "dialectic necessity"—that any "self" or subject in its relation to the "world" or object must *itself* function as a *world-conditioned self* and never as a simple detached spirit contemplating abstract mental or spiritual forms. Subjectivity, phenomenologically perceived, must express *itself* as an intrinsic subject-object dialectic and cannot be the pure domain for a one-sided idealism. Thus, *every* subjective act is a bodily act, an act that is sensual and practically related to the world as a condition for its very existence. The self is always a body-self, functioning through its physical relatedness in an environment, and the elaborate structures of so-called pure thought or syntactical structuralisms—such as logic and mathematics for example—must at the same time be expressions of this material condition. Physiologically speaking, it is interesting to note that the skin and the brain, or the organ which "senses," and the organ which coordinates and "thinks," are actually self-differentiations of the same basic tissue—namely the ectoderm. Thus, the singular process expressing itself through a dialectic of opposition is a chemical-electronic nerve complex in which the "sensory end" relating the body to its physical functions in an environment, and the "thinking end" coordinating the various modalities of sensation into a totality, are but two inseparable sides. One literally *feels* with one's brain and *thinks* with one's skin. Sensory feeling and mental thinking are two aspects of a singular organic neurological process and not two compartments of a composite structure. Sensing is at once mental interpretation of some kind, and mental interpretation, no matter how "subtle," is also a sensual activity. (Thus, thinking or speaking words and symbols are known to co-appear with minute muscular-nerve activity reflective on a body level of the patterns, rhythms and content referred to within the brain.) Many experiments involving eye-detection perception have verified the fact that the so-called direct perception of a given sensual pattern can result in the actual perception of a modified pattern, due to the co-relation between what the eye picks up and what the brain-gestalt expects or looks for (i.e., focuses upon). Indeed, what we sense and see is neither the outer body "as such," not our "interpretations," but the interaction state occurring between-within the systems. Also, any modification in *either* is a perturbation in the combined interacting system of *both*.

However, the dialectic between subject and object, or self and world, results not only in a world-conditioned-self—as described—but at the same time in a *self-conditioned-world*. As the experiment with eye-perception clearly illustrates, consciousness is a singular state of interdependence in which the field-relatedness, or the so-called "psychic totality" literally expressing the "*common* (universalizing) sense" and therefore "meaning" of the functioning distinct senses, is inseparably related to the various distinct events of objective existence that *are* sensed. "Perception" always involves both. Thus, not only is the self or field which perceives the world as its content itself a part of that world, but the world which it perceives is in turn conditioned *by* its being present within a field of subjectivity. This means that the instant one attempts to transcend the "mind" versus "matter" game and comes to understand their functioning unity as a field-event co-relativity and dialectic, then not only must the mind appear materialized (and the self embodied), but matter in turn must appear in "mind form" (and the world perceived in self-hood). Just as mind never functions as a detached *idealism* of non-material relations, matter never appears as an alienated *mechanism* of materiality void of subjectivity and meaning.[3] Not only is there direct or immediate consciousness experiencing in a "centrifugal" mode of a self *sensing* a world, but the dialectical necessity previously mentioned demands the inverse also. Mediated consciousness in a "centripetal" mode, in which the self-as-a-*world* experiences itself as *being-sensed* by the world-as-a-*self*, must also exist. In fact, the two mediations (of self as a world and world as a self) are mutually conditioned by each other, the self appearing objectified as a body and ego only to the degree to which the self functions within a world which acts as a subjective field relative to which the ego-body functions as *its* object. Thus, the world must appear as an externalized subjectivity or field (just as the self appears as an internalized event-structure or "ego-body"), whose most *explicit* form is society itself.

Selfhood, subjectivity or a field of presence is *not* a localization or a *property* attached to a body or thing, but rather a condition of presence—a non-linear field—within which objectifications as distinctions and localizations manifest themselves as a product of its self-activity. Thus, the ego and its body as an object, and any environmental object *with* which the ego-body is in a state of interaction, are *mutual* localizations co-determined and co-determining within a field of presence—the field of presence being *precisely* the state of *inter*action, relation and transformation taking place. Subjectivity, as opposed to ego-consciousness, is nothing but the *interactive-transitive* state of objectivity itself and not a passive presence or "mind" detached as a non-visible nothingness, or a delimited and localized object "in-itself." Consequently, this subjective field on one level can appear simply as a completely unlocalized and *immediate* field, relative to which *any* mediation, object or event (ego body or environmental body) functions as its self-mediated content. However, the state of objective interaction constituting the content of the field of presence is such that it *must* appear (by dialectic necessity) within and relative to *any* one of its localizations—

_____

3. See Kosok, "The Dialectical Matrix."

each localization reflecting the *whole* field relative to its perspective (as the theory of relativity illustrates in another way), and the field as a whole in turn reflecting *each* of its localizations *as* a total-field phenomenon (which quantum mechanics illustrates in its modality). As a result, should the state of subjectivity or interdependency of all events and patterns or rhythms of events termed event-complexes (objects) constituting the non-linear field be such that any *one* event-complex or object is sufficiently organized to localize this field in a *stable and self-sustaining way* (involving organized repetition, re-presentation, re-cognition, re-production, and self-reflection or self-determination through mutual determination on many integrated levels), this would mean the existence of a world-conditioned self or subjectivity called an ego-body. However, at the same time, the highly organized object called the ego-body *functions* as a localized subjectivity or non-linear field (displaying ego-consciousness) precisely because it is an expression of its state or interaction *with the totality* of event-complexes or objects. The richer and more complex its state of total-interaction with the whole world, the richer the ego-localization of subjectivity that exists within or relative to the ego body. Thus, a *double* dialectic occurs between the subjective non-linear field and its objective event-structure. Should subjectivity or the singular non-linear field become localized or begin to appear relative to any one particular object within its objective content of interaction in the form of an ego-body, then at the same time, the mutually co-existing contextual world of objects it is in relations with, *likewise* must appear in subjective form, reflecting the singular non-linear field relative to itself, within which or relative to which the ego-body now functions and develops as but one member-object among all other member-objects of the field.

Subjectivity or the non-linear field is either a totally immediate field within which *all* objects are equally well its self-activity (ego-consciousness itself not explicitly present, or only potentially available), or this total field appears *at once* as a self-mediated immediacy of *intersubjectivity*. This means that the field appears relative to any one ego-body as a "personal I-field," and relative to the contextual world as a "counter-personal (not *im*personal *nor* personal) thou-field." There is both the field localized in an object or "ego" that is "seeing" a world of other objects and at the same time the world of objects that is manifesting this field as a wordly "commune" or "field of presence" which causes the ego-body "to be seen," making seeing and being seen, sensing and being sensed—or I and thou— mutually conditioned. The importance of this dialectic relation cannot be overemphasized. It is only through a thoroughgoing perception of *how* the dialectic necessity between subjectivity and objectivity (making each a function of the other) automatically makes *all awareness reciprocal at all times*, that a genuine perception of both social dynamics and natural dynamics can be understood. Knowledge is never an ego-centric one-directional process of observation, but always a dialectic of reciprocal immediacy and thus subjectivity of interaction—no matter how explicit or implicit this reciprocity is perceived. Mere factual or formal knowledge always appears in the form of an *object* that becomes known, while *wisdom* is the realization that a full knowledge of awareness reveals *relations* and hence perceives *all* objects and structures in a state of mutual, reciprocal determination. Subjectivity is but this very *condition of mutual* self-determination of object appearance, and therefore is a condition not localizable into the *possession* of any *one* object or ego. Wisdom is the realization that subjectivity is always intersubjectivity and thus instead of ego-centric lust for possession, love of interaction and relation can emerge in its stead.

Intersubjectivity, therefore, *cannot* be understood on the *social* level as a simple ego-ego activity of two self-centered individuals somehow "relating," it must include within its domain *nature* and the body-body *physics* of interacting energy as the *mutual content* of genuine relation. However, this also means that *any* body or object of nature—nature being a *totality* of interacting energy—is the content of an intersubjective state of presence. Have you ever really allowed yourself to *experience* a tree or rock instead of merely observing it with projections, fantasies, or designs and then reducing it to an object-complex of feelings, forces, numbers or symbols? Nature is *not* a given or inert "in-itself," and man is not an ungiven empty "for-itself." These are only abstractions projected for the purpose of analysis. The so-called problem of the "other" or "other minds" only appears if you really think (Laing notwithstanding) that experience is private and in need of being communicated, i.e., that experience can be "owned" like a commodity. Emotional reactions, thoughts, and object modifications are *not* examples of experience, but rather *products* of experience, and *qua* product, they are indeed distinctions giving uniqueness. We are so used to regarding ourselves in terms of our *results* (past and future) that the activity of *direct* experience, and therefore the creation of forms, is eclipsed from view. Once trapped into thinking that we are defined by our products or results, the only thing left to do is to see *all* elements of the universe in terms of behavior patterns of crea*ted* structures —be they what we *call* persons, societies, mathematical equations, atoms or galaxies. The *act* of creation and genuine subjectivity is suppressed. Wisdom, and love (and therefore philosophy as the "love of wisdom" and life as the "wisdom of love") is integral and total when it ceases to succumb to its own results and products, by either identifying with them *positively* or by rejecting them and consequently identifying with them *negatively* as that which must be ignored or destroyed. Growth and genuine transcendence comes only when one can re-grasp the *relation* that exists between the process of experience and its products, realizing that products and results are neither ends (positive or posited goals), not something to be denied (negative goals) but are rather *the vehicles and means through which experience can enrich* its self-mediated state of concrete immediacy and *express* itself in visible forms.

Degeneracy, however, sets in when the reverse takes place and man defines and delimits experience and transitivity in terms of its products or results. Such is the paradoxical *challenge* of existence—not to be "done in" by the very products of its process! Thus, we can now rephrase Marx's "standing Hegel on his head," and indeed the significance of any revolutionary perspective which seeks to return experience to itself. The usual interpretation of Marx's acrobatics is that dialectic idealism was replaced with dialectic materialism. As a result, a thought-centered, mind-oriented dialectic making all matter a function of mind was replaced by a matter-centered dialectic making all thinking and mind a function of matter. Such a simplistic interpretation of subjectivity and objectivity is directly *denied* by Marx's first thesis on Feuerbach. The significance of the reversal of Hegel lies in another dimension. It is *not* a question of unsettling the *reciprocal phenomenology* between subject and object, mind and matter, or ego and environment, which actually *both* Hegel and Marx never departed from. In this sense, a critical reading of both reveals that neither ever reduced anything to an abstract one-sided element. The difference lies in the fact that Hegel's dialectic of mutual mediations and continual negations and negations of negations represents only *products* of concrete immediacy in its state of direct-presence and not the process of immediacy itself. As products, dialectic relations appear as objectifications, idealizations or abstractions *of* becoming—presented as an atemporal logic of relations—instead of revealing the actual dynamics of becoming. In Hegel, the *concept* of becoming and not becoming itself as an immediate experience (e.g., through the *act* of reading, thinking, feeling, doing) is one's concern, and therefore his "application" or "manifestation" of this becoming in nature is unconvincing and incomplete, having *left out* nature, space and time from the *logic* of becoming as originally presented. Genuine dialectic, however, is always both concrete-immediate *and* reflective-mediated; both an immediate state of objective interaction (defining for us the *field* of subjectivity!) *and* the idealized objectifications and products of that interaction. Thus, Marx stood Hegel on his head not by making the subject or ego-states only a function of the object and matter, but rather by seeing that their *mutuality* as an objective-*interaction* state of concrete immediate experience must be prior to their appearance as products of experience, manipulated in an atemporal state of suspension. Experience does not derive *from* its objectifications and concepts, but the other way around. This is the *philosophic* ground of Marx's ideas on fetishism and alienation.

We can, in fact, summarize the fundamental position of dialectic-phenomenology as a concrete working philosohy in terms of two mutually related "principles": the principle of "concrete presence" and the principle of "dialectic necessity." The first principle gives expression to the reversal just mentioned, i.e., to the need to regard the immediacy of concrete presence and experience as a non-localized field and process, *within which* events, mediations, objectifications, abstractions and concepts appear. Thus, the process of experience is prior to its products. This field or subjectivity, itself not localized, is the *condition* of its own localizations. The second principle then expands upon the relation between any field and its localizations, showing that by dialectic necessity, the mutuality between context and objects—or any elements mutually conditioned—must *reflect* this single mutuality (of concrete presence and immediacy) relative to *each* element. Thus, any relation between two elements, X and Y, is productive not only of a *direct* relation between them, XY, but of a *counter*-relation: the Y within X relating to the X within Y. This will generate levels of oposition between terms, and between *relations* of terms which become higher order terms for higher order relations giving birth to the dialectic matrix. It also gives expression to the mutual co-determination between all elements of a field such that each element is a function of the *whole* field, and the whole field, in turn, a function of *each* element. Together, these two principles give a "working definition" or perspective to phenomenology and dialectics respectively, making it possible to *practice* dialectical phenomenology within any situation without requiring a complex "rule structure" to which one "fits" in experience. Dialectic phenomenology is a way of experiencing both immediate experience and the reflection or mediation *of* experience as a single self-mediated immediacy. Experience, then, is not a mere passive happening or an arbitrary *active imposition* from the standpoint of reflection, but an integrative state of *inter*action and self-development in which both the *"being* of knowledge" and the *"knowledge* of being"—immediacy and reflection—mutually co-determine each other as a single dialectic phenomenology.

Concluding our philosophical introduction to the dialectics of nature—our particular analysis of intersubjectivity—we can see that precisely *because* subjectivity is beyond any objectification or product, it *must* appear as a mutual and universal field of seeing and being seen. Thus, it must appear as intersubjectivity. Subjectivity must be objectively self-reflective and self-referential lest it appear objectified into the *possession* of an exclusive owner (called Ego, Society, God, or the Devil) thereby de-subjectifying both owner and that which it owns—both Master and Slave. It is only through the dialectic of self-world interpenetration that a self achieves *genuine* self-determination or self-consciousness (i.e., self-seeing) through the world it is in resonance with, in the form of a co-relative circular state of "seeing and being seen" when this mutual state is explicitly experienced as a singular non-linearity. This is *not* to be confused with a mere *sum* of two linear acts (as Sartre would have it) in which first I see (and objectify) the world, and then the world or the other-in-the-world sees and objectifies me: "two looks do not a *mutual-looking* make...nor a single look, a look at all." A single look "as such" is merely a linear, one-dimensional relation. Hence, it is an abstraction and an alienation from the mutuality of interrelation. Two, three, four and so on, looks are merely a *collection* of linear acts (productive of paranoid vision). A mutual looking, on the other hand, is a singular, paradoxical, non-linear experience of subjectivity in a process of creativity, whose products and results are event-complexes or objects within and among the ego-bodies and natural bodies constituting its content.

From a dialectic phenomenological viewpoint, therefore, nature, or the world, is never a mere object of contemplation or perception—as Feuerbach formulated it—but is always *co-active with* man as a functioning totality or *Lebenswelt* in which a *dialogue* of mutual interaction and communion is established. It is this co-active relation between man and nature which Marx in his first thesis called "sensuous human activity, practice [*Praxis*]" and subjectivity. Man, as a subject, relates subjectively with his environment in the *Lebenswelt* and is not born *out* of it as a conquering agent that has to fight against the forces of nature and society in order to *maintain* his distinct individuality—reducing both to a mass of blind irrational forces and himself to an arbitrary "chance-event" detached from the origin and context that not only bore him but continually re-creates him through mutual interaction. All event-complexes appearing objectively—be they so-called given matter in the form of photons, atoms or stars; living matter in the form of plants and animals; thinking matter in the form of humans; or culture in the shape of tools, institutions or expressed ideas— are dynamic expressions of non-linear field activity capable of resonant response *with* man. They are not just a collection of "things" aggressively consumed and manipulated or observed in a detached manner. The *difference* in the intersubjective component between man and the various forms of objectivity lies precisely in the scope and depth of the "I and thou" resonance that *can* be established in the nonlinear state of affecting and being-affected or seeing and being-seen. As Marx put it in the *Economic and Philosophic Manuscripts of 1844*, reality "as fully developed naturalism equals humanism, and as fully developed humanism, equals naturalism; it is the *genuine* resolution of the conflict between man and nature and between man and man—the true resolution of the strife between existence and essence, between objectification and self-confirmaion, between freedom and necessity, between the individual and the species."

2. Revolution in the Sciences

Having established dialectical phenomenology as the basis of our conception of consciousness, we can proceed with an analysis of the revolutionary perspective required to develop a unified field theory for the sciences. Because the dialectical relation between subject and object constitutes the content of the subject as an objective person and the form of the object as a subjective environment, *all similar* pairs of oppositions appearing within consciousness manifest the same dialectic. For example, the subject *qua* universalizing thought form giving meaning and expressing "intention" is at once the reflection of objective interaction and "extension," and vice versa, any extended objectivity encountered in the world is reflective of a meaningful world. ("The rational is real, and the real is rational" *can* be interpreted in this way as a phenomenological condition.) No "epistemology" is needed as a separate structure to relate mind to matter, soul to body, or mental events to physical events because—as Marx puts it in his *Economic and Philosophical Manuscripts of 1844*—"Thinking and being are thus no doubt *distinct*, but at the same time they are in *unity* with each other... Feuerbach wants sensuous objects actually different from thought objects: but he does not comprehend human activity as objective." Mind and matter are but two sides of a single human praxis, which cannot be compartmentalized without destroying it. Consequently, as a foundation for a universal field theory of the sciences we can note that all mental activity of universalizing forms is grounded in the physical and practical activity of its *content*, namely the body-in-the-world, while the world with which the body is inseparably correlated is a knowable meaningful world revealing its *form* to be none other than the universalizing activity expressing itself mentally and theoretically.

This means that a dialectic of the cosmos—a dialectic of nature revealing the objective status of nature through its intrinsic subjectivity or form *to* the subjectivity of man who is objectively *within* nature by means of an "intersubjective dialogue" between man and nature—is not only possible but necessary. The problem remains, however, of *how* to transform this phenomenology of intersubjectivity and the dialectics of nature into consciously directed practice, and how to recognize it as actually manifesting itself within the present forms of scientific praxis, even though obscured by the alienated state of consciousness of modern scientific culture. The ancients used to relate to the world in terms of an elaborate mythology which some took literally, but which most regarded as a schema giving expression to the intersubjective state that exists between man and the universe. Of course, the ancient as well as the medieval mythologies and religions eventually reified these myths into deterministic patterns of superimposed authority, consequently de-subjectifying them into alienated structures. However, the subjective content expressing itself through these myths was never far from the surface. On the other hand, science in the modern world has replaced ancient and medieval mythology with a view of the cosmos that is, at best, *ambiguous*, and in its more usual presentation *destructive*, to the intrinsically intersubjective state of the universe. Scientific technology and thought patterns together with a network of human relations among scientists productive of rituals and ideologies that tend to automatically channel all human awareness along narrowly prescribed paths, have collectively contributed to an overall impression that nature and the universe is an illusive object of conquest which man must confront as alien. As a result, the infinite and the infinitesimal appear more and more complex, strange, ungraspable, formidable and hyper-formal in their mathematical description, until its immediate relevancy for *human* praxis as a whole indeed looks nonexistent. Except for a few creative men of genius in the sciences, the world of science "out there" appears cold and void of spirit.

However, all this "cold objective reality," either in the form of scientific "structures" describing nature by means of impersonal "energy transformations" using abstract mathematical symbols, or ideological structures describing society in terms of impersonal movements of economic and political forces—dehumanizing both nature and society—are *myths* (or *models*, to use the deceptively neutral terms employed by the sciences), generated by abstracting elements-of-experience *from* the dynamic of experience and hypothesizing them into ideal forms. This process is the first stage of alienation, which, as such, is not destructive if one can remain aware of them *as* idealizations. In fact, abstraction and highlighting distinctions out of an immediate context are essential for the development of the defining and measuring processes of consciousness. However, the suppression of context necessary in order to achieve such a clarity, must continually be transcended such that all mediation and formations (e.g., mathematical principles of physical processes), appear as *self*-mediations and transformations *of* the dynamic immediacy of subject-object interaction continually present, and so that they do not *replace* it with an artificial world and a pseudo life principle. Knowledge is based upon limitation and ignorance, i.e., the ignoring of context. Wisdom only comes with the recognition of the limitation of limitation, and with the recognition of pre-limited immediacy. Wisdom only comes by experiencing the active and *always on-going dynamics* of awareness within which the accumulating mythology of isolated facts and theories has *meaning*. Wisdom only comes through recognizing the dialectic of *mutual* limitation between any focused form and its codetermining context. If no integrated *experience* exists within which the immediate mutuality of subject and object is felt *directly*, then the alienation of subject from object hardens and the subject-object paradox becomes a contradiction. In capitalist societies (and their variations in the form of "state-capitalism"), this hardening takes the form of the institutionalized separation of the subject as producer from his object of production, reducing both to commodities in an external exchange relation in which price (externalized value) replaces value (intrinsic worth) with objectified role-playing replacing the importance of genuine subjective experience—subjectivity being regarded as a mere *private* counter-position to the so-called *public* domain. In philosophy, the hardening first takes the form of an opposition between objective "scientism" (positivism, behaviorism) and subjective existentialism. In both of these positions, subject and object stand as intrinsically "other" to each other. There is no dialectic interdependency manifesting itself through a *transformation* in which each becomes a function of the other and each a function of itself through the other *as inseparable distinctions* without *reducing* the two to each other to form an inseparable indistinction and hence inconsistency, or *splitting* the two *from* each other to form separated distinctions and, consequently, incompleteness.

Recently, a more insidious hardening of alienation has taken place. As R.D. Laing's psychological investigations point out, today one not only suppresses, forgets, or becomes alienated from the totality or reality, but one also becomes alienated, forgets, and suppresses the alienation itself. As a result, self-alienation, self-forgetting, and self-suppression set in, and once one forgets that he has forgotten, no problems seem to have existed in the first place.[4] Consequently, the so-called normal life in stabilized societies is in reality a double-insanity—an insanity or condition of separation and dissociation which has itself become dissociated from general awareness. The horror today consists not in the *appearance* of violent conflict or the *expression* of madness or alienation, but in the *normalization* of psychosis and the acceptance of mythological structure as reality without any awareness of there being any conflict or tension between myth and reality. First order alienation is the *felt* separation between subject and object, man and nature, mind and matter, culture and science. However, if this separation itself is not transcended, then a self-degenerating process of further separation occurs. Thus, the very experience of an initial separation *between* subject and object or man and nature objectifies *both* into structures and images, i.e., into opposing mediations and delimited opposites.

---

4. R.D. Laing, *Politics of the Family* (Toronto, 1969), p. 28. He writes: "We forget something. And forget that we have forgotten it. So far as we are subsequently concerned, there is nothing we have forgotten. It is very effective."

This means that the genuine subjectivity *experiencing* the painful separation between subject and object—if not successful in resolution—becomes more and more eclipsed from view. The *active* subject of experience, in order to escape from his unresolved predicament as a responsible agent in the alienation process, permits himself to become more and more replaced in his own awareness by the *passive* image of himself *within* his own (and society's) experience. Thus, subjectivity either becomes but another describable structure or an object among other describable objects (resulting in various forms of "structuralisms") and hence impotent to really *effect* anything, to bring about meaning, or to create, or it vanishes from sight. Either man becomes reduced to a blind being or structure of scientism and formal behaviorism, or man is reduced to the empty nothingness of existentialism and becomes *but* the lack of being. The initial *conflict* between scientism and existentialism is now *accepted* as a necessary one and hence no longer as a *real* conflict that can be transcended. Thus, subjectivity *must* either be taken as a given thing or as an empty absence. In neither case is man himself—or subjectivity—directly experienced as the *becoming* and creation of being, whose being "consists" of *being* and *creating*.

This situation is a condition of *total* madness, for it tends to express a perfect crime. There is no murder of subjectivity or man, no myth of alienation, precisely because no murderer or myth maker is present as an active, *creative* subject in the first place. Myth is reality, and reality is myth. Man has not only created an alienated structure, but now he has succeeded in redefining himself within it, thereby expressing himself as the alienated product of an alienated process. Frankenstein's monster has finally recreated Frankenstein the man in the monster's image. Man is *but* the image-of-an-image, the negation *of* a negation and thus, he is totally devoid of reality, assertiveness and immediacy.

The only way to prepare for a genuine transformation of consciousness—a revolution in the *mode* of subject-object behavior (both in man's relation to man, giving expression to a true dialectic of society, and in man's relation to nature, bringing about a genuine dialectics of nature)—is to both uncover the subtle ways in which objectification and alienation occur, and to allow oneself to *experience* the way in which alienation feeds upon itself, rigidifying simple alienation into self-alienation and blindness. This means that the task of a revolutionary in any area (in science or society) cannot consist in merely exposing alienation, objectification, exploitation, violence and discontent in all their explicit and hidden forms. Mankind can adapt himself all too well to alienation and exploitative situations, Mankind finds security from the ambiguity of change inherent in the dynamic and transforming nature of subjectivity and immediacy by dehumanizing himself into a non-responsive object. The revolutionary must go deeper, and this is our concern here, regarding the state of alienation in the sciences.

In any stabilized consciousness—whether in the form of ego consciousness or social consciousness—it is the *adaptive norms* projected by that consciousness which function to contain and defuse the spontaneous and unpredictable dynamics of immediate subjectivity. This is accomplished through alternating cycles of coherent suppression and incoherent explosion, neither of which produces the necessary insight needed to transform consciousness into an active state that is neither passively inactive nor blindly reactive. Normalcy functions precisely by institutionalizing the subtle dialectic *between* asserting the given and rejecting the given (a dialectic expressing the given as that which is always in a transitive mode of "being given" and consequently neither assertive or rejective), into a rigid pattern of alternating assertion and negation or *conformity and rebellion*, each being the mirror image of the other. Neither conformity nor rebellion questions the function of norms and rules which delimit the dynamic of immediacy of the universe into a pattern of given structures. Conformity means simple acceptance of the given while rebellion means simple rejection of the given; both are therefore reactive mechanisms to the given. The function of myth or abstraction—in science as well as in society—which alienates a product from the process of experience is, therefore, to delimit all actual and conceivable experience as expressions of that product. Thus, language, perspectives, and formulations of consciousness become centered around either accepting or rejecting the given, but never *transforming* it, never grasping the given or the product as but one element within a dynamic immediacy of events being-given, formed, unformed, reformed, and transformed. Consequently, one becomes trapped in a double bind centered around the given system, making it impossible to transcend or transform the level of awareness present. One either functions *within* the system, accepting it, or one functions *outside* of the system, rejecting or attacking it, but the system *itself* remains un-transformed, even though it *appears* at times to be "replaced" by other forms—these other forms being but mirror images of the original system. How many "revolutions," "revelations," or "insights" have either degenerated or only partially succeeded by failing to completely grasp the double-edged sword of dialectic negation? Mere change, negation, simple dispossession and reversals of power are linear reactions to what is present and not a non-linear transformation with what is present by expressing the mutuality and interdependency of all negation and change. The function of a myth in a thoroughly alienated consciousness is to keep consciousness tied to that myth by the very oscillations which occur between its acceptance and its rejection, its praise and condemnation, its preservation and destruction (leading to a recreation of that myth or system in a new form and its redestruction). Such a constant shift between opposites is not an expression of genuine freedom or "choice." Freedom is not a matter of simply choosing among "alternative paths," for *all* such paths are already mediated, determined and mutually conditioned.

Indeed, the highest form of normalcy functions by *simultaneously* permitting both acceptance and rejection, conformity and rebellion, playing one off against the other without transcending either. Thus, in the modern world of computerized commodities, the worker *qua* producer exists in a *public* world as a robot controlled by his alienated products, displaying no meaningful subjectivity or control over the production of his own products. He conforms and accepts his inhumanity as long as he does indeed produce.

This is true of both material production and the production of ideas in academic institutions. Ideas and objects alike become divorced from their creators and take on an autonomous life in the public domain. On the other hand, the worker *qua* consumer exists or imagines himself to exist in a totally private world that is indifferent to the problem of public production. He is indeed encouraged directly or indirectly to rebel from the concerns of public interaction whenever they are involved with "bread and butter" issues concerning the various ways available to heighten the pleasures of private consumption and autistic self-expression, which includes autistic self-expression through ideas, art for art's sake, and so-called religious gratification. (Superficial "political" concern by merely voting among choices whose most *probable* outcome is already determined by the myth-making, consciousness-controlling organs of the given power structure only *adds* to the alienation of individuals from society by sublimating the "public conscience" along essentially harmless channels.) It is thus not only proper but necessary for a normal consciousness to respond so *completely* to the given that two well-separated compartments emerge, expressive of the *statics* of the given. The subject as producer sells himself and his energy to the system (and the given) without care or concern for the products which somehow have their own life, prostrating himself as a slave to their production, while the worker as consumer *buys and takes* the products from the system (and the given), telling the system to "go screw itself." Alienation as self-alienation takes the form of setting one aspect of consciousness against the other, giving rise to a dynamics of alternately using and being used, exploiting and being exploited, seeing and being seen, objectifying and being objectified.

Consequently, in a normalized consciousness (both within the ego and society) no genuine subjectivity responsible for, or to, integrated behavior exists and exploitation, violence and discontent, i.e., alienation, appear *universal*. Alienation becomes eclipsed from view as a condition that can be changed: alienation, contradiction and negation of subjectivity appear as the external imposition of fate. Like the "music of the spheres," this very omnipresence turns into an omniabsence by virtue of any lack of contrast. Consciousness sinks into unconsciousness and automatic response. Subjectivity, both in its relation to nature and the sciences and in its relation to man in society, becomes dissipated into separated conflicting structures existing within an external space that nowhere reveals subjectivity in its genuine mode as a creative and active process of transformation. In the normalized world of the given, there is only the "cunning" of the structures to which there is no appeal, and with which there is no dialogue (i.e., a James Bond movie). Dialogue is reduced to a mere exchange of inert information or is replaced by manipulative tactics designed to bring about positive or negative (conformist or rebellious) compliance to a mythological structure.

One can therefore formulate the task of the revolutionary as the initiation of dialogue in its most profound sense and on all possible levels. The revolutionary is one whose subjectivity as an active agent sees the necessity of giving depth and scope to genuine action through its objective condition of appearing as interaction, intersubjectivity, dialectic, dialogue. The revolutionary must always attempt to overcome one's continual tendency to simply react passively and one-sidedly in the static and contradictory modalities of mere acceptance *versus* mere rejection, or the mechanical game of either conformity or destruction, of judging either true or false. A revolutionary transcends judgment as an end in itself and is concerned with transformation, conversion, salvation and resurrection in the deepest sense—seeking neither to accept masks, nor to "rip" them off, but to dissolve them—recognizing that any one-sided action is always a passive reaction to a given and never a single active state of immediate subjectivity in which all opposition is at once mutual, transformative and revolutionary. Freedom—the life of revolution—is then not a mere "choice" of paths or possibilities, each of which is, as a *particular* path, mediated and mutually *conditioned* by all the other paths. Freedom is the "pathless path," the transcendence of being limited to any one product or path of experience by *experiencing* the mutuality of all mediations and identities, through an all-embracing, open dialogue, as a singular self-mediated activity or immediacy. It is experiencing oneself as self-determined through the mutuality of all determinations. Freedom is then the power of immediacy which creates and continues to create mediations and paths, and not itself any one path or choice, which by compulsive "adherence" becomes a rigid response rather than a living force. Violence, "evil," "bad faith," "terror," "anxiety," or "falsity" is *not* an intrinsic property of any object or ego but rather an expression of the rigidification, fetishization and ossification of relation and the creative act. Consequently, it is precisely the de-ossification of any relation which is hence automatically an expression of freedom and genuine consciousness, i.e., consciousness not alienated into self-separation. Man is so frightened of freedom that he confuses it with "license"—which, ironically enough, is but a negative reaction to and hence expression of conformity, law and legal license. Freedom is beyond license in any sense of the word, all license being an ossification of relation.

Furthermore, a dialogical state of genuine intersubjectivity and inter-action between and among all forms of objectivity—in society and nature—is not a *means* to a revolution, but the revolution or end itself, i.e., the revolution of transformation as it is taking place. The point is to expand the depth and scope of this dialogue, to make it more and more visible on more and more dimensions, both within individuals, among them, and between individuals and their objective natural state. A revolution and genuine dialogue does not and cannot mean either a mere "confrontation" in which anger, violence (both against man and against nature) or alienated reaction-mechanisms are displayed and dissipated (only to build up again) or a mere "liberal discussion" or "abstract contemplation" in which anger, violence, unintegrated need and alienated reactions are *suppresed* and reinforced. Dialogue and revolution mean a transformation and liberation of energy by dissolving the contradictory frictional oppositions which are draining creative energy into dissipated energy. It means a transformation of destructive frustration and anger into constructive passion and compassion. It means the appearance of a *telos* that is grounded and continually re-grounded in the dialogue taking place—and not in the projections, memories and myths generated through dialogue—namely, the mediations, judgments, formulations, ideals and goals continually arising in awareness, and constantly serving as a potential threat to the dialogue and the subjectivity from which it emerges. Man continually generates an idealism of static and quasi-static structures, patterns and descriptions about reality. The point is to utilize these as means and not to become trapped in them, converting yourself into the means and the structures into an end. So-called "false" and inauthentic consciousness is simply the product of "true" or authentic consciousness, instead of being the process. "Evil," rigidification and dissociation is but the "good" localized; falsity is but truth repeated and identified, and ugliness only appears when the beautiful is possessed and owned. Gramsci, more than any other Marxist in recent times, understood the dynamics of intersubjectivity, dialogue (e.g., his notion of workers' councils), and the necessity to regard the "preparation" for revolution as inseparably connected with any particular dramatic act of revolution or power take-over. Revolution and dialogue, like subjectivity, is *not* an isolated event (whose opposite is "evolution"), but rather a condition of presence. Revolution—as consciousness itself—degenerates when its transforming process is reduced to a packaged product to sell.

Now, precisely because a genuine intersubjective dialogue is the "end" and not itself an objectifiable means, subjectivity as the dynamic *condition* or field of any objective presence arises through such a dialogue. Alienation, contradiction and violence, then, are not seen as an externally imposed fate, but as issuing out of subjectivity and awareness as its product. One experiences contradiction as self-contradiction and consequently rediscovers his own form of subjectivity as a power for creating good and evil. No motivation for changing contradiction and alienation can appear until this contradiction and alienation is experienced as self-contradiction. Motivation will appear only when one can literally see *how* it is one's own attitude that is "screwing" himself up (when one sees how he plays one part of his awareness against another through unconscious but socially validated conditioning). Until such self-awareness is realized an individual will merely hold "the others" or "fate" responsible for what exists and simply react to the given (conforming or rebelling), but not act-with the given, transforming it into a dynamic reality and being responsive to and with this state of dynamic creation. Force, as an external display of unintegrated energy, and inertia as an internal withdrawal of energy appear to the unaware as reactions to alienation. However, it is only the power of creativity which can express itself as an integrated mutuality of interacting forces and oppositions and which can be experienced as growth. To the degree to which a person is powerless and impotent, force (or inertia) appears to an alienated consciousness as a "way out." The revolutionary "party," or agent, cannot be a force acting on the masses (of inertia), but must be a power of interaction, revealing authentic consciousness to be the intersubjective state of dialogue—and consequently revealing a particular subjectivity to be simultaneously both the author (i.e., the authentic creator) of his own state of subjectively-felt alienation, and a coauthor with the intersubjective state of existing alienation and contradiction. Unfortunately, any hypothesized, and therefore idealized pattern of revolution, lifted out of the historical immediacy of dynamic process as a product, which attempts to "combat" alienation and exploitation with the products of awareness and not with awareness itself, must itself degenerate into counterrevolution merely creating more alienation and contradiction. The world of alienation is a madhouse of commodities and products run wild—this includes material products, scientific products, ideal products and revolutionary products. Life is then merely a matter of automatic production and autistic consumption, public service and private compensation, with the producer but a product of his product and the image of an image.

Turning specifically to the revolution in the sciences, and the task of giving expression to a genuine dialectics of nature, one must carefully distinguish (not separate and thus produce more alienation) between the process of man's interaction with nature, and the products of that process. The process is the immediate state of existing interactivity, in which neither observer nor observed exists as such (as imaged products or objects), but rather the state of *observing* in which both appear as interdependent sides of a singular activity. In this state, not only so-called facts are the events or objects of the process, but likewise "definitions," theories and intuitive-emotional responses are likewise events and objects of the process. As previously discussed, such an interaction state between man as an ego-body and nature as his contextual environment is subjectivity as a nonlinear field-phenomenon expressing itself intersubjectively. In the actual state of direct relation with nature, the scientist does not first regard nature as an already given and passive object to be investigated, or himself as an already localized ego ready with fixed definitions and principles to "capture" the illusive object in image-form. In the actual situation, man and nature mutually co-confront each other. A dialogue of simultaneous action and reaction, "sponse" and "re-sponse" and therefore "co-response" is generated, and the language of this dialogue is the appearing patterns of interaction. Thus, perception and conception in the brain-body complex of an individual result in patterns which are neither just images of the environment, nor just images of man's reaction to the environment, but "reflections" of the man-environment state of interaction now localized as a product and process relative to the one inseparable aspect of a mutual process. Consequently, any perturbation either within the body-brain complex (by means of altered metabolism, drugs, meditation exercises, operations, etc.) or within the environmental object (altering its appearance, properties, composition) will result in a different perceptual-conceptual interaction pattern, which is as "valid" as any other pattern (the so-called normal state patterns), for it must not be forgotten that any state of the body-brain is always a particular state of electronic-chemical-biological (socially conditioned) organization and, therefore, biased relative to that particular modality. The point is not to divide perception or conception into "real" (objective, lasting, permanent) and "imaginary" or "hallucinogenic" (subjective, passing, and the result of "distortions"). All perception and conception is dynamic and in a state of transformation; that is the nature of objective action. Objectivity is not permanency. It refers to the event-process and structure which appears within any field of presence or subjectivity. It is precisely the subjective field of interaction, however, which expresses objective patterns and rhythms that have varying degrees of "permanency" and are therefore capable of action as "gestalts" or "frames of reference" for the more temporary ones. There are, however, no ultimate objectifiable patterns which *themselves* are not within a transformation process. Vice versa, that which appears "imaginary" and fleeting within any one state may be but the beginning of a patterned response that will become more and more "normal" and stabilized in time—that is, as *relatively* established as any normal structure.

Alienation sets in when these internalized products called "normal" patterns of interaction are used as a framework or end to which the continually on-going process of objective interaction is subordinated. All the various conservation principles, symmetry conditions, closed systems-analyses, invariant relations—the models and myths employed by the sciences—appear as reality, while the *actual* dynamics appear as myth. Nature then appears as a remote, given "stage" or a "cold objective reality" against which man must pit his power in order to wrest from her her secrets. Knowledge without wisdom is rape, both man and nature appearing as alienated structures without meaning. A revolution in the sciences means that scientific theories and technical approaches must be reviewed and recognized for what they are: moments and products of an immediate dialogue continually taking place (in varying tempos and rhythms) between man and nature (and taking place, by dialectic necessity, within each). Nature can then reemerge into view as the coauthor with man of the inter-active state of subjectivity mutually defining the objective forms or events of both. What remains to be investigated now, is the nature of the language that exists in this dialogue between nature and man. Once we know the language, we can formulate through that language of intersubjectivity a "dialectics of nature."

Tran Duc Thao has recently given an excellent account of the origin of both man and language from the state of mutual interaction between what can be called "pre-man" and nature. Language, he points out, is not an expression of consciousness or "subjectivity," but is this consciousness itself, which in turn is nothing but the form of natural interaction taking place. Pre-man begins to evolve into man when the objective state of interaction between pre-man and nature gives rise to socially validated "sign" behavior, i.e., to a process of socially recognized pointing and signifying among pre-men expressing the emergence of a new state of objective activity. Instead of directly consuming food from nature as animals do, the appearance of mediating tools causes man's center of attention to be gradually focused upon the tools themselves as instruments for production, consumption consequently appearing as a delayed goal or ideal. As a result, an inheritable culture of activity begins to emerge, together with an ideational process of goal-formation expressing this activity. "Natural pre-man" begins to also be "social-man." However, both the physical tool-making process and the mental ideational process of goal formation are two sides of a singular state of man-nature interaction in which language emerges as a unifying field between man as a signifier, pointer, or "goal maker," and any object (nature, tools from nature, other men, himself) as that which is signified and pointed to in a goal-oriented process. Language is thus not just a sign-sign syntactics or semiotics expressing an "internal" state of consciousness about objective or "external" interaction, but is rather an *immediate* sign-object dialectics in which any "unsigned" object or event complex in its state of immediate interaction, becomes signed, focused, identified and mediated relative to a specific field of presence. The sign itself is not an object (just as subjectivity is not a localized event) but rather expresses a particular type of self-mediated object relation between man as an ego-body and his environment. Signification is thus a complex objective process expressing a state of objective interaction which, *qua* interaction, is both the state of intersubjectivity present, and the language process itself. The dynamics of language (and not its statics as a collection of terms) is thus automatically the dynamics of object-interaction. However, just as subjectivity can become objectified, sign-behavior can become reified and, as a result, a particular object (gesture, activity, sound, symbol) appears singled out as the sign for another object as the signified (productive of a "semantics" of sign behavior). Should the signification process, continually producing products of activity such as sounds, words, ideas, objects of attention, etc., then become obscured by the products themselves, the active state of generative subjectivity present becomes eclipsed, and man becomes alienated from his dynamic codetermining environment of nature and other individuals. Language in turn appears mystified either as an intuitive, mysterious manifestation of a hidden subjectivity or "intention" expressing an eternal and ideal Logos world of invariant forms (e.g., a mathematical world), or as a mechanism and behaviorism of objectivied products in external space-time relation, void of any "inter-subjective meaning."

This "either-or" condition of language appearing divided into abstract idealized formalism on the one hand and positivistic behaviorism on the other hand—language expressing either "mathematical-logical truth" or "empirical-factual truth"—is precisely the state of alienation characterizing the sciences today, preventing a genuine dialectics of nature from explicitly manifesting itself. Indeed, formalism is a form of behaviorism (and vice versa) in that both are different expressions of the phenomenology of subject-objectivity being reified into identity-structures whose only relation is external juxtaposition: genuine emergence or becoming is lacking. In order to revolutionize scientific activity, therefore, one must become "radical," i.e., return to the root as the basis of scientific activity and discover how in fact it does function—as a process—cutting through the accumulation of myths called "empirical facts" and "abstract theories," discovering that it is the scientist himself who is the source of these myths and the contradictory nature of these myths. The key phenomenon in the creative process of scientific praxis is the integral activity of "model building" which in science is the practical way the phenomenology of subject-objectivity expresses itself.

Man as a scientist cannot start to "make observations" or "take measurements" in the world he is in without approaching it with a theory of observation or measurement, i.e., without a certain pragmatics or "model of nature" which functions as a gestalt or frame of reference which allows him to discriminate between that which is relevant and significant and that which is not. Directly in contact with nature, man is in a state of immediate and total involvement—all events near or remote, clear or confused, form a singular nonlinear field of presence. In order to focus out of this fabric of presence particular data or information, some notion of what is relevant or significant must already be present, for everything in its immediate state offers itself as a possibility of significance. In measuring the temperature of a gas, not only must a certain already standardized scale and measuring instrument be available, but likewise one must have a notion as to the interpretation that one will use in utilizing the measurements taken. Thus, it takes nature to measure nature (either one's own natural biological equipment, or artificially produced instrumentation), which in turn implies that the nature used in measuring the nature present-for-observation has already been judged and categorized as functioning in a certain way. Otherwise, the nature used in measuring would not function as a tool but as part of the immediate natural complex happening.

There are two necessary assumptions that the scientist needs as part of his theory of measurement in order to even take down one piece of information. Both assumptions amount to a linearization and compartmentalization of nature. The first consists in the assumed constancy or "reliability" of the measuring instrument itself, since any object-complex of nature, being codetermined with the immediate context it is in—and the instrument is an object complex itself—changes its nature and characteristics whenever there is any kind of change within the context. Thus, a measuring rod initially calibrated to be of such and such a length under one set of conditions (i.e., during its production as a measuring rod) may or may not actually exhibit the same length under a second set of conditions—namely, the very first experiment it is used in. Pressure, temperature, moisture conditions, etc., can affect the length. The second assumption lies in what the object-complex being measured by the instrument consists of. Thus, measuring a length or a temperature of a steel rod placed at a certain position is strictly speaking not only a measurement of the steel rod, but of the entire objective complex within which the steel rod is but one member. One has to decide or know in advance which contextual influences are relatively "ignorable." If one takes one measurement of temperature when the steel rod is at point X, and another when the rod is at point Y, should the location be included in the data representing temperature? How many environmental conditions should be noted along with any one observation? The number possible is indefinite. Our information may only appear to be about the temperature of the rod. If this temperature is to be a referable quality, having therefore a quantitative measure, then one has to be sure that what is called the temperature of the rod in case X is the same kind of temperature in case Y, if case X and Y are to be regarded as but two instances of one kind of measurement. Thus, at point X, a strong electro-magnetic field might be present, while at point Y, a weak one, and consequently, the temperature measured at point X may not be just the temperature of the rod, but the temperature of the rod in a strong electro-magnetic field, while the temperature at point Y may be the temperature of a *different* complex, the rod in a weak electro-magnetic field. Consequently, any equation containing the temperature of the rod is not only an equation about the rod as such, but about the rod in its various contextual states. If we were to generalize or abstract the context from the rod and assume that the data relations obtained speak only about the properties of a rod, then one would be assuming that the objective-complex measured can be delimited to the rod itself, and that the environmental influences are essentially irrelevant and non-significant. Even repeating the same measurement at the same place actually amounts to a shift of context, for new contextual influences could have intervened.

The point is simple. Any measurement is actually a measurement of the interaction between an instrument and its immediate object, and the interaction between the instrument-object complex and the total environment it functions in. Therefore, before one can lift out any one piece of information, one has to already have a gestalt in mind as to what is relatively constant and ignorable and what is variable and significant. This, however, implies that man as an observer of nature must approach nature as already nature-conditioned, expressing empirical idealizations accumulated through his history as a natural-complex within nature. Indeed, man as a body is the primordial measure of things in nature, and any tool he is sensitive to becomes an extension of his interaction with nature. This means that man does not approach nature as an abstract subjectivity in possession of ready-made (non-natural) formal rules of manipulation (a "mathematics") which he then utilizes to give structural expression to a barrage of isolated sense-data coming from nature. Rather, man, as an integral part of nature, becomes sensitive to objective rhythms and patterns that flow between and within the man-nature complex—patterns and rhythms which then become idealized and linearized into formal structures and principles (such as number, space-time, the four essences of earth, water, air, and fire)—if these structures are sufficiently repeatable and hence recognizable as part of the objective state of interaction that is present, at least for a certain time. This formalization is the first primitive "model" of nature made by man as nature, within nature. With time, these empirical idealizations become more and more refined. Newton's three laws of motion are a beautiful example of such a model. However, at no point can one say that these empirical idealizations are *simply* abstract logical idealizations or empirical facts. They represent a functioning image of man-in-nature that is reflective of a certain state of inter-communication between man and nature. According to Charles Peirce's triadic philosophy, logical idealization ("firstness") follows from simple "subjective" deduction; empirical generalization ("secondness") follows from simple "objective" induction; but empirical idealization ("thirdness") comes from the integral and creative subject-object acts of abduction—abduction being a process by which men can grasp ideal and universal relations within and through concrete particulars. Only through such empirical idealizations does one learn the language of nature and the logic of its relations. However, such subject-object communication is only possible if we recognize that any experience is both subjective and objective, i.e., reflective of a non-localized field of presence and localizing events, making each experience universal and concrete, i.e., a concrete universal.

With growth of specialization, and the refinement of instrumentation, man makes more and more diverse measurements of the interactive man-nature complex while at the same time accumulating a history of theoretical models. This, then, entails the development of an explicit feedback dialogue between man and nature which takes the following form. Man, in conscious possession of a particular complex of patterns and rhythms which have emerged out of a state of interaction with nature and been linearized and formalized into mathematically expressible relations, confronts nature (or rather nature as man-in-nature), with its own pattern as a refined gestalt or frame of reference which he then uses as a means of taking significant measurements, i.e., measurements that have relevance to the pattern that has already emerged. These measurements in turn reveal additional patterns which are fed back into the observing pattern to form a still more complex pattern—a new total pattern or gestalt within which both the previously accepted patterns and newly generated ones become moments.

Thus, a genuine dialectics of nature develops from the initial nonlinear and immediate state of pre-reflective patterns of objective interaction. In the terminology developed to express dialectical logic, any initial immediacy or "element" such as this state is referred to as e. This initial state of totality or immediately appearing patterns and rhythms of man within nature, e, becomes self-negated into a new gestalt of patterns or totality, e', in which the previous immediacy becomes mediated into organized observing and self-integrated structures, $+e$, in opposition to or confrontation with other observed patterns or structures as yet unintegrated, $-e$, such that both become preserved but transformed as mutual moments, $+\text{-}e$, of a higher order pattern which is now capable of being immediately present as a new totality, e', ready for further states of self determination, expressing the dynamics of a continual process of "e-ing": e, e', e'', e''', or a dialectical self-relational expansion. However, because of the nonlinear nature of the "e-ing" process, the results or linear products of any particular stage of immediacy cannot be predicted or determined as necessarily "progressive" or "regressive." A dialectical process cannot be a "progress theory" with linearized "iron laws" of necessity—any such determination being a "final judgment" standing outside the historical immediacy of existence. The objective state of man in nature is always an immediate totality of patterns such as e, e', or e'', within which two submoments continually emerge and reintegrate back into that totality, transforming it—these submoments being the $+e$ observing patterns and $-e$ observed patterns. Man, in effect, is objectivity or nature *qua* observing pattern, interacting with nature *qua* observed pattern to express, finally, man as nature or objectivity in a continual state of self-observation and self-reflection. Thus, nature comes to know itself through man and the dialectics of nature is the dynamics of nature in a state of self-reflection, self-observation and self-relation through man who is this "self-observer" as its active agent. Nature, as man, has explicated its intrinsic state of subjectivity, causing it to appear as concrete subjectivity. Thus, it is not only that man is in "dialogue" with nature, but that—just as subjectivity is objectivity in its interactive state—man is actually nature itself in a state of self-relatedness. What you are observing as "nature" is therefore equally well you in a state of self-relation, just as you are a form of nature in a state of self-relation. Self-relation, as a result, manifests itself through an elaborate dialectics of inseparable distinctions in which each distinction of objectivity (and this includes you as an ego-body or any other event-complex) becomes a function of itself (exhibits self-relation) only to the degree to which it becomes a function of its contextual relatedness and vice versa. The distinctness of self-relation or uniqueness increases with the interrelatedness or inseparability of universality, which is but a way of saying that the more "properties" or defining characteristics any distinction has, the more it expresses a complexity of relations. Thus, there is no "thing-in-itself" in any way whatsoever. The more an element is remote in its state of relation, the less that element exhibits any definable characteristics, such that in the "limit," any isolated fact or state would be *void* of any properties whatsoever, i.e., it wouldn't exist. Conversely, therefore, it is precisely the development or intensification of the interactive state of objectivity—its subjectivity—which illustrates the function of subjectivity and its form as consciousness in the shape of man. The greater the depths and scope of genuine interdependency and dialogue, the greater the functional integrity (self-identity and uniqueness) of all its mutually conditioned elements. The greatest uniqueness comes only through the greatest universality and vice versa. This holds for all levels of objectivity, including the human and natural dimensions. The development of subjectivity through human awareness will only achieve richer states of integrity to the degree to which that subjectivity is capable of living as a functioning element within the whole of the universe.

3. A Unified Field Theory of the Sciences, and the Dialectics of Nature

The unified field theory of the sciences emerges in three stages. Stage one is an analysis of the immediate states of consciousness, which we have already seen to be both a phenomenology of awareness and a dialectic of relations. What develops out of this basis is a fundamental "rhythm" of dialectical movement. Any immediate pre-reflective presence or state of nonlinear subjectivity becomes posited or determined ($+e$) by appearing in contrast with a counter-position or negation ($-e$), both of which are mutual co-defining aspects ($+-e$) of the original state of immediacy, now appearing developed as a self-determined and self-mediated immediacy (e'). Thus, immediacy or subjectivity is a state of totality which develops all objectifications, oppositions and mediations as mutual relations and self-transformation, i.e., as self-mediations. At this stage, an *implicit* dialogical relation already exists between any one state of presence and its objectifying context or negation, both of which simultaneously co-determine each other. Stage two then develops this dialectical phenomenology into an explicit dialogical relation. Here the fundamental oppositions are immediacy or presence in the form of subjectivity or "self," and its mediation and negation as objectivity or the "world." All subjectivity as an immediate nonlinear field of presence develops its dialectic as a self-world interaction through self-mediation. This gives rise to both a world conditioned self (man), and a self conditioned world (nature) by what was called "dialectic necessity." Thus, any subjectivity, in revealing a world, in turn appears as a world or body revealing a world of subjectivity with which it is in a state of intersubjectivity and mutual dialogue. By analyzing this dialectic complex of self-world mutuality—or man-nature interaction—subjectivity as a nonlinear field expresses itself both as a process of inseparable distinctions, and as a process of products—distinctions singled out of context and linearized, producing alienated subjectivity. Consequently, a revolutionary perspective is needed in order to reintegrate at any stage, the products of subjectivity with its own process.

The fundamental "variables" or distinctions in dialectic phenomenology are: (1) the subjective field of immediate presence (e, determined as $+e$), (2) the objectifying events of mediation, negation and determination ($-e$), and (3) the self-mediated and self-determining co-relative mutuality of field-event resonance and feedback ($+\text{-}e$ which leads to e'). However, all three are inseparable distinctions, and by dialectical necessity any one of the variables must exhibit all three within it as part of its intrinsic nature. On the other hand, one can and does linearize these distinctions into three different modalities of presence. Hegel's *Encyclopedia* represents such a linearization of a dialectic phenomenology (i.e., *Phenomenology of Mind*), and we shall in effect be developing a unified field theory of the sciences (i.e., an encyclic-totality or encyclo-pedia) as a modern version of Hegel's initial attempt. Thus, Hegel's division of the sciences into logic, nature, and spirit reflects, respectively, the division of subject-objectivity into (1) the subjective field of presence as a nonlinear *essence* or frame of reference (a logic) relative to which (2) existential events in objective space and time appear (nature) such that both together express (3) a logical-nature or a natural-logic in the form of spirit, i.e., reality or totality as that which explicitly functions simultaneously as a subjective field and as an objective event-complex, namely the appearance of nature, self-reflected or "spiritualized" as the emergence of humanity. Reality as humanity is thus concrete subjectivity or self-reflecting objectivity.

However, from our perspective, Hegel's initial attempt was phrased and developed within an idealistic gestalt, the development of the initial stage called logic or the subjective field taking place as a thought-process independent of its co-determinate opposite called nature: subjectivity is not immediately grasped as inter-objectivity and inter-action. Thus, when nature, or the stages of specific objectification, appears in opposition to logic, it appears only as self-estranged thought—or thought in its pure "otherness," which returns to itself as spirit without really integrating both logic and nature into an explicit totality in which neither has any reality without the other. As a result, the dialectic dialogical interrelatedness among logic, nature, and spirit is lost from view and each section appears as a complete totality independent of the other, even though the intention expressed is one that attempts to go beyond such a simple linearization. For a concrete unified field theory of the sciences (based upon the self-development of the nonlinear field of objective inter-action called subjectivity, through an $e, e', e'' \ldots e$-ing process or dialectic), and therefore a genuine dialectic of logic, dialectic of nature, and dialectic of spirit or humanity, it is essential to develop the "content" of each domain as an explicit expression of its relation to the whole triad or totality. In this way, logic, nature and humanity, or the sciences of "essence," "existence" and "reality" are but three distinct perspectives of an inseparable whole, each perspective expressing the whole relative to its particular nature making whole and part co-relative. Consequently, logic as the science of essence must display (1) the essence of essence (essence qua essence), (2) the existence of essence, and (3) the reality of essence, while nature revealed through the sciences of existence must reveal (1) the essence of existence, (2) the existence of existence (existence qua existence), and (3) the reality of existence. Finally, humanity revealed through the sciences of reality must involve (1) the essence of reality, (2) the existence of reality, and (3) the reality of reality (reality qua reality). Since the "being" of phenomenology is not "ontic" or identifiable but rather dynamic and in transition, there are naturally levels or gradations of essence, existence and reality. Reality, being the integrated totality of essence and existence or subjectivity and objectivity would be expressed in greater degrees by those inter-action patterns which explicitly display the greatest unity and inseparability (subjectivity) of the greatest diversity and distinctness (objectivity) present. And to date, humanity (what Hegel calls spirit) is taken to be the most integrated totality of subject-objectivity known—and thus the bearer of what is most real, despite its modalities of alienation—in which subjectivity and objectivity, or its essence and its existence, appear in self-opposition instead of self-integration.

If we look at our dialectical analysis of the sciences of essence, existence and reality, we see not only a major triad (of logic, nature and humanity) generated by the dialectic between the subjective of immediate field of presence and its objectifiable events (a formalization of our "first principle" called the "principle of concrete presence"), but also a triad within each of the elements of that major triad, producing nine elements in relation (and generated by our "second principle," that of "dialectic necessity"). What this leads to is a non-ending, self-generating dialectical phenomenology of triads within triads or cycles within cycles called the "dialectical matrix" (i.e., the $e, e', e'' \ldots e$-ing process producing a power series of terms: 1, 3, 9, 27, 81 ... based on a continual recycling of triads and hence more complex modes of dialectic necessity). This shows that a indefinite number of levels or cycles of relations can exist, and consequently that "essence," "existence" and "reality" are in no way regarded as separable "domains" of being. They are rather elements of a dynamic phenomenology of science, to which we shall now turn. For our analysis here a nine term linearization will be investigated as the simplest example of triadic or dialectic necessity in a unified field theory of the sciences, laying the foundations for more complex transformations to take place (see diagram). This represents the encyclopedia as a field theory of nine sciences which shall be explicated in the remaining pages of this article, paying particular attention to the dialectics of nature appearing within the encyclopedia.

The immediate state of interaction between man and nature has been described in terms of the ego-body and contextual-environment complex, generating a dialectic of self-emerging patterns and rhythms. Here the primordial "model" or "image" of this interaction complex appears through the natural language of patterns and rhythms which flow between man and nature as they function in a common system of co-determination. Thus, any partially stabilized repetitive and recognizable pattern or rhythm appears as a relative invariant field, perspective, gestalt or frame of reference relative to which distinctions and events (variables) appear. Experienced as a universal or universalizing field of presence, subjectivity appears in the form of a common "ground" or "essence," to whatever distinctions appear within it. This "common essence," relative to man as a subjective presence—indeed, relative to the man-nature complex as an intersubjective totality—is perceived as a syntactic or "pure logic" of relations, i.e., as the dialectic of patterns and rhythms intuited, felt, explicated

A UNIFIED FIELD THEORY OF THE SCIENCES
in the form of a modern version of Hegel's Encyclopedia of the Sciences

1st order division / 2nd order division	LOGIC and the sciences of *essence* for the universal *field* of presence	NATURE and the sciences of *existence* for the differentiated *events* present	HUMANITY and the sciences of *reality* for self-differentiated *field-events*
The *essence* (es) or universal field nature of	(the es of es) SYNTACTICS The "pure dynamics" of dialectic interaction, or subjectivity as a non-linear field	(the es of ex) PHYSICS The "pure dynamics" of matter in motion in space-time, or the concrete events of the nonlinear field	(the es of re) PSYCH-OLOGY The "pure dynamics" of concrete subjectivity—the field-event "psyche"
The *Existence* (ex) or differentiated event form of	(the ex of es) SEMANTICS mathematics and the particular levels of objectified syntactics	(the ex of ex) NATURAL SCIENCES the particular levels of material objectification [fundamental nonlinear units of existence]	(the ex of re) SOCIAL DYNAMICS the particular levels of social objectification and relation
The *reality* (re) or self-differentiated field-event form of	(the re of es) PRAGMATICS Linguistics and self-referential evolution of syntactical relations	(the re of ex) COSMOLOGY self-referential evolu- of material interaction	(the re of re) CONCRETE PHILOSOPHY self-referential evolution of concrete subjectivity: the nonlinear field as a self-reflecting totality in concrete form

and formulated as a functional syntactic of mutual inter-connectedness. However, relative to nature, and indeed relative to the man-nature complex as an objective state of interaction, this same "common essence" appears as an "objective syntactic" of relations. Thus, nature not only reveals particular events, but a nonlinear field or condition of interaction appearing through these events. Space and time (the condition and gestalt for the appearance of patterns and rhythms), sets and sequences, symmetrical co-appearance and asymmetrical ordering appear. This space-time kinematic topology or nonlinear field seen as a function of the objective events is the "objective syntactic" of nature. Furthermore, this space-time kinematics or motion is also a space-time dynamics involving "matter in motion"—the notion of "mass" or "inertia" being but a general way of referring to any element or distinction of space-time. Thus, the objective syntactic of nature —as a dynamics of matter in motion—forms the essential content of physics, regarding physics in its broadest sense as being the "philosophy of nature."

Consequently, the "common essence" of man-nature interaction, relative to the subjective pole or the "essence of essence" (essence *qua* essence of subjectivity) is a "pure logic" or syntactic relation, while relative to the objective "pole," or the "essence of existence" (essence *qua* existence or objectivity), it appears as a space-time dynamics or "pure physics." Actually, both function together, such that the "essence of reality" (or essence *qua* reality of subject-objectivity, i.e., the "common essence" seen relative to the mutuality of man in nature) is the non-localized or immediate state of concrete-subjectivity or the immediate state of the consciousness process itself. The "essence of reality" is the emergence of an increasingly more integrated and integrating (i.e., total and real) subject-objectivity in whatever form it might take (which is not to make its actual appearance in any particular form—such as humanity as a concrete subjectivity—a "necessary" and "derivable" fact). The "essence of reality" is therefore a combined "pure logic" of relations and an objective space-time dynamics functioning as an integral unity. This integral unity is what is often referred to as the "pure psyche" of a concrete subjectivity, i.e., the so-called *anima* or soul of consciousness which, *qua* essence, is a state of being whose specific existence and realizations have yet to "unfold." The "psyche" is thus both a sign creating activity, or logic, and the objective structure involved with and referred to by the sign creating activity. At this stage, the "pure psyche" is not an individual "id" or developed ego, but rather the body-environment complex of objective interaction seen as a ground-condition for the emergence of its subjectivity as an explicit ego consciousness— an emergence which will have to take explicit intersubjective form, but whose intersubjective nature in order to become a "social" being is nevertheless objectively present as an existential potentiality. We have, therefore, developed briefly the first of three stages for the science of logic (as the essence of essence of the science of pure logic and syntactic), the science of nature (as the essence of existence, or the science of space-time physics), and the science of humanity (as the essence of reality or the science of the "psyche" or "psych-ology" taken in its broadest sense).

We can now briefly turn to the second of the three stages which must appear throughout the entire triad of logic, nature and humanity (and which, by dialectic necessity, is also mirrored within the first three stages relative to its modality, but only explicitly revealable in a higher order 27 term analysis). Returning to the immediate state of interaction between man and nature, and the common essence of patterns and rhythms, we find that the function of such a common essence is not to appear as an abstract or isolated "given," but rather as a frame of reference or field, relative to which particular distinctions and events appear, productive of new patterns and rhythms, such that their mutuality makes both the immediate essence of a "viewing-pattern" or "governing-gestalt," and the mediated existence of newly arising patterns and rhythms into moments of a larger gestalt. Thus, essence continually becomes redefined through existence, reality being their mutuality as a process but never as a product. Thus, in the state of interaction between man and nature, the various particular events, complex of events (or "objects") and complex of complex-of-events serve to give specification and determination to the universalizing perspective of common essence. Seen relative to the subjective "pole," such events and objects give expression to the existence of a "semantics" of syntactical relations. A semantical relation is a relation of objectification or localization. Any element within a structural pattern or rhythm, upon being identified, can become an object of signification. Consequently, within the science of logic, the "existence of essence" or the objectified modality of a syntactic totality introduces semantical activity, the most developed and systematically formulated modality being the science of mathematics. Mathematics is not a "pure syntactic" in that a definite and determinate quantification of syntactic quality occurs. Algebra deals with linearizable and hence arithmetizable elements within sets; geometry, or topology, deals with another kind of presence called spaces; analytics, or calculus, deals with the "limit-relations" between elements or points in a space (the "mirroring" of the space within each point or element); "synthetics," or probability theory, deals with the "measure" each element or point has throughout an entire space (the "mirroring" of each element throughout its space as a total-space function). Indeed, topology is to algebra as nonlinear fields—or subjectivity—are to linearizable events or objectivity, such that analysis represents the fields or spaces mapped into each of the events, while synthetics represents each of the events mapped out onto the fields or spaces, thus mirroring the entire phenomenology of subject-objectivity within the mathematical modality of logic or the science of "essence." Mathematics is, however, not based upon a fixed essence structure, but is rather a semantics of objectification emerging out of a dynamic syntactic, that is, out of a dialectical logic of relations, reflective relative to the subjective pole, of the objective state of interacting patterns and rhythms perceptually present at any stage in space-time existence. Thus, the concept of number is not a given object but is defined through the type of recognizable operations encountered. Take, for example, addition or powering: the notion of number itself has evolved and continues to evolve through natural numbers, rationals, irrationals, reals, complex, hypercomplex matrices, vectors, tensors, etc.

If we now view the state of objectifiable interaction between man and nature relative to the objective "pole," (existence *qua* existence) then the various particular determinations continually appearing as specific localizations or as specified events and complexes of events, give expression to the existence of a "determinate physics." Physics now appears pluralized and quantified into the various particular objective sciences such as electrodynamics, chemistry, biology, and even the social sciences in so far as they can be viewed as objective space-time complexes. Thus, the science of cybernetics—dealing with feedback theory—covers not only the so-called natural sciences, but is also applicable to bio-psychological systems and economic-social-political structures, when viewed in terms of interactive systems theory.

Finally, one can study the existential and deterministic state of man-nature interaction relative to the total field of subject-objectivity; that is, relative to the "existence of reality" (or existence *qua* reality). If the "essence of reality" is the "psyche" as the undeveloped and immediate state of consciousness itself, then the determinate "existence of reality" is mediated-consciousness, or consciousness as an explicit intersubjectivity of inter-psychic reality. We thus pass from "pure psychology" to "social dynamics," i.e., to the dynamics of groups and class structure, since consciousness develops its potentialities only within the context of an explicit and determinate social process. Thus, the three second moments within the overall sciences of logic, nature and humanity give rise, respectively, to the three determinate or existential modalities called (1) semantics (or mathematics as its most systematized modality) which functions as the "existence of essence," (2) the particular objective sciences as "the existence of existence" (or existence *qua* existence), and (3) social dynamics as "the existence of reality." Looking at the encyclopedia as a whole so far, one can state that the "mathematical sciences" deal with levels of structure, the individual "physical sciences" deal with levels of material interaction, and the "social sciences" deal with levels of human relation covering the mediated and determinate modalities of a unified field theory of the sciences. The immediate and non-determinate (universal) modalities are respectively, "pure logic" or syntactics, "pure physics" or space-time dynamics, and "pure psychology" as a study of the syntactic-dynamic nature of immediate consciousness.

We can now turn to the man-nature state of interaction, and study the totality, or reality, of this interaction. This totality, relative to the subjective "pole," would involve a study of the functional unity of syntactics and semantics—namely, "pragmatics" or "linguistics" as the "reality of essence." In syntactical relations, forms of patterns and rhythm forms appear as a universal (non-localized) presentation or dialectic of relations (capable of formalization into theories of syntactics) without any specification as to objects of identification. In semantics the objects of specification appear as localized linearizations within the overall syntactical field (as "poles within a field"). However, the mutuality between any qualitative syntactical field, giving expression to the forms of relation, and the quantified objects specified by that form (the semantics of the field), is nothing but the activity of a concrete language seen as a continual evolution of qualitative form and relation through the localization of this form in particular objects or "terms." In concrete language, syntactical relations explicitly express a dynamic of evolution. As a result, objects, terms, symbols, words or gestures no longer remain a fixed semantics in which each object or term has a definite designation (or "truth" value), instead they interact with each other to give expression to a concrete semantics that exhibits syntactical significance. Thus, a meaning-structure, pragmatics, and organizational pattern continually redefines the terms, elements or objects that appear and have appeared from diverse event-sources, so that they manifest a functional "organicity." Naturally, as the "elements" transform relative to the meaning-structure, the meaning-structure is likewise continually redefined through the elements.

As a whole, the science of logic displays three subdivisions in which the following dynamic appears. "Syntactical" relations "as such" are prior to any semantical designation of being "true" or "false." They express patterns or rhythms of relation. Then, "semantical" relations localize the overall patterns and rhythms into determinate terms, any combination of which can be given a definite "truth value." Finally, in pragmatics or linguistics, we move beyond the designations of what is true or not. Every determinate object, or form, is itself in a state of continual transition, redefinition and reformulation with its co-determinate forms. As a result, a dynamic syntactic-semantic language is the reality of any relational structure of subjectivity, and is pragmatically (contextually) determined by the specific conditions of subjectivity present, and not by any fixed rule that is singled out, subordinating a meaning-structure to a predetermined semantics or rigid syntactics.[5]

If we now view the objective "pole" of the state of interaction between man and nature, we can see that a functional unity must likewise exist between pure physics as a nonlinear space-time dynamics, and its linearizations into determinate event-complexes. Thus, within nature, not only must there be the physical space-time field as a universal presence, and particular levels of space-time interaction (such as electronic-chemical-biological and social manifestations), but these levels in turn must reflect the totality of the nonlinear field as a singular process of space-time evolution. Thus, we pass to cosmology as the "reality of existence," or as the study of all of nature, now seen as an emerging totality, and as a space-time structure determining its modalities through its appearance in particular

---

5. Indeed, one can mention that a genuine dialectics of logic has to move beyond the simple presentation of "assertions" in the form of statements or sentences. The role of a genuine subjectivity must be developed in which the logical status of questions must be given a place. A question cannot be written in a simple assertive manner as a sequence of forms without transforming that question into a statement or assertion. Thus, the dialectic between observing patterns and observed patterns involves a dialogical logic between questioning patterns and responding patterns to form a genuine dialogue that expresses terms or objects in their state of being-formed (reformed, unformed, transformed). The activity of questioning is the activity of de-localization—the activity of subjectivity which is a field of presence, but not itself a term, element or object-present. This, of course, implies that without any terms, objects, or events present, the question and subject would be empty, just as the statements or events present without question and a field would be blind and irrational: non-relational, non-effective and consequently, nonexistent.

forms. From this perspective, the various localizations of nature into specified event-complexes, patterns, and rhythms (such as electrons, atoms and cells), must be re-grasped as a singular cybernetic feedback structure, expressive now of a concrete physics of evolving and transforming objects, whose subjective counterpart is the evolution of language as a dynamics of evolving and transforming signs of signification.

We can now pass into a consideration of the totality of interaction between man and nature, relative to that totality; that is, to the reality of reality or reality *qua* reality. In the science of humanity, its essence was seen to be the immediate field of consciousness as a "pure psyche" of body-environment interaction. The "soul" or *anima* is literally the dynamics or animation of one's body-context system, or the body-environment complex experienced as a singular and immediate state of subjectivity or awareness. Now its existential form is none other than its appearance as a social-dynamics of "ego-ego" interaction and class structure. Thus, the various "social sciences" appear in this domain, not as a natural space-time complex of social behaviorism, but rather as a state of social-experience—a state of interpersonal "seeing and being seen"—involving us with the dynamics of both authentic process consciousness and alienated product consciousness, and consequently with the dynamics of revolutionary praxis. Social dynamics views immediate consciousness as a mediated-social structure of interacting levels of awareness as the essence, or condition, for the very presence of consciousness, and its existence through mediated particular forms of intersubjective societies, in turn are but two moments of a self-mediated totality. In self-mediated awareness, concrete subjectivity experiences itself both as a universal field of "ever-present" immediate awareness, and as a mediated presence which transforms itself socially and historically into changing levels or perspectives of awareness. It is this very transformation of consciousness through history and revolutionary praxis (through its authentic expression as a process and never as a product, isolated goal or end) that expresses the reality and being of consciousness as a dynamic immediacy. Self-mediated consciousness is the state of true enlightenment; the state in which the opposition of immediate being (being as such) and mediated becoming (becoming or revealing something other) appear united into a singular state of self-becoming, self-determination and freedom. Self-mediated awareness is the subject matter of the sciences of "concrete philosophy"; not philosophy idealized into a given set of rules, norms, or patterns (academic philosophy), but rather philosophy experienced as the "love of wisdom," as a total praxis of integrated humanism and naturalism whose being is precisely that which is ever in a dynamic state being-given or being-made. To experience your identity as lying in the very "transcendence of identity," to experience the philosophical trinity of the "beautiful, good, and true" as the becoming of truth and never as the possession of truth, is to become free of the alienated states of mediated consciousness that merely defines itself through its own products. The positive nature of religion, insofar as it is directed towards the notion of transformation and transcendence rather than passive submission and the denial of the objective interactive nature of subjectivity, is an integral aspect of concrete philosophy.

Thus, "the essence of reality" as psychology, the "existence of reality" as social dynamics, and the "reality of reality" as concrete philosophy reflect the state of man-nature interaction relative to the phenomenological totality. At the same time, linguistics, or natural language as the "reality of essence," and cosmology as the "reality of existence" can likewise be seen as culminating in concrete philosophy as the "reality of reality." The evolution of concrete language as the subjective "pole" of reality, and the evolution of the cosmos as reflective of the objective "pole" in its dynamic state, together define concrete philosophy as a subjective-objective totality in which the evolution of language (the evolution of the dialogical state of intersubjectivity) is but the very form of the evolution of cosmic objectivity, which in turn is but the content of interaction for intersubjectivity. When what one "speaks" is at one with what there "is"; when language is not used to hide existence and the sensual world of objective existence; and when objective existence in turn gives birth to its own form of communication; then one has transcended both empty verbalism and blind facticity. Philosophy as concrete wisdom is the living unity of Logos and Cosmos, and this living unity is life lived as a permanent revolution in which all being is being, and all formation at once trans-formation.

Finally, one can look at the entire nine sciences and examine the "diagonal" triad which cuts through the triad of essence, existence and reality along both triadic directions at the same time (through the major triad and the sub-triad within each member of the major triad). Pure logic, or syntactic, is essence *qua* essence; the particular physical sciences represent existence *qua* existence; and concrete philosophy is reality *qua* reality. The unified field theory of the sciences regards the "aesthetics" of dialectic as a dynamic syntactic of transitional relations to constitute "pure subjectivity" which, however, is nothing but the mutual co-determinate of "pure objectivity," i.e., the existence of a diversity of event-complexes and complexes of event-complexes in space and time. Pure subjectivity as the "universal," and pure objectivity as the "concrete" aspects of phenomenology, give us pure subject-objectivity, or "concrete universality" (the concrete universal), as their reality, or "reality *qua* reality." Thus, concrete philosophy now appears as the dialectical unity of pure essence as "logic" and pure existence as "facticity." Pure (*a priori*) syntactic and wordly (*a posteriori*) objects. This would be a contradiction in terms were it not for the fact that all logic is a natural logic, and all nature, a logic of interaction, alienated consciousness reducing the necessary distinction between them into a suspended separation. The point of this encyclopedia has been to dissolve the separations such that the distinctions can become heightened to express each science as a universal "monad" and a unique modality of all states of the universe, instead of as a simplistic expression of a narrow field, whose boundary states are at best ambiguous, but most generally productive of contradictions and distortions.

Having given a brief outline of a modern version of Hegel's encyclopedia of the sciences as the basis for a unified field theory of the sciences, we can now center our attention on the existential-objective aspect of that outline: the dialectics of nature. As already indicated, the dialectics of nature, as an integral aspect of an explicated phenomenology of subject-objectivity, must appear as an "inner triad" of pure physics, the various physical sciences in particular, and cosmology. In pure physics, one is concerned with formulating an "objective syntactic" that serves as a concrete "model" for the explication of the various specific event-complexes that appear in nature. Thus, physics as opposed to the various natural sciences, is not limited to a specific event-complex (molecules, stars, cells, etc.) but rather studies the "general laws of matter in motion common to all levels of existence." Any one state of awareness reveals both a particular event-complex as an expression of the whole of objective existence with which it exists in co-relation as previously indicated. One never merely observes a concrete object or a universal and general condition, but always a concrete universal. The point is to grasp in greater and greater detail the many ways in which each experience is a congressence of universality. In physics, general laws of dynamics have emerged, expressed in such forms as conservation principles and symmetry conditions. These terms characterize our present state of awareness of the physical universe of space and time. Central notions of momentum, impulse and force, energy, work and power, have gradually evolved into a complex pattern of "objective syntactic" which serves as the basis for the "physical models" of particular event-complexes.

Now, the nature of all such objective syntactical relations is that the particular event-complex in which they initially appear is no longer referred to as a limiting condition of the syntactical relations discovered. Newton's law of force as the "rate of change of momentum," was initially regarded as a simple empirical generalization of a particular level of chemical-mechanical interaction. In this case, Newton's law would be a particular law of a particular level. Just as the "ideal gas law," Newton's law would involve an "empirical experimental constant"; a "coefficient" that relates one set of observed variables to another set of observed variables; a constant that has to be determined (and continually redetermined) through particular experiments. However, if one is interested in the syntactical relations which connect the terms to each other, then Newton's force law has to be "idealized," which is to say that one variable or set of variables is now defined in terms of the others as part of a necessary relation—once one agrees to the usefulness of the "abduction" which permits one to idealize a particular experience directly into a universal and ideal form. This naturally explicates a condition of coherence of variables, and can only be "justified" if one remembers that in a nonlinear field, all variables are inseparable distinctions and mutually co-determinate; the point being in finding out the relative scope and depth that can be given to the co-relation and co-appearance of any two particular distinctions. In Newton's case, force as a contact-relation between two systems or "masses" and the "rate of change of momentum" of the masses were defined as mutually inseparable and "necessary." Any contact always produces a change in state of motion and vice versa. Thus, force is not simply measured as proportional to the rate of change of momentum; but as an ideal principle, defined to be always co-present with a rate of change of momentum and numerically equal to it (the proportionality constant between them being defined and not measured as unity); although the notion of force as a contact relation is still distinct from the notion of changing momentum. Force and change of momentum become extensionally equivalent.

This means that Newton's law now expresses an ideal principle of rhythm and pattern which is neither true nor false "semantically" (neither verifiable nor disprovable in any particular experiement), but only syntactically relelvant or not relevant as a general perspective of analysis. By making force into a definition, this means that a momentum change must involve a contact relation (even if as yet unobserved) and, vice versa, no one experiment or set of experiments is ever capable of uncovering all possible "contacts" or "momentum changes" in order to "ultimately" prove or disprove this idealization. At the same time, however, an empirical idealization forces scientists to continually reexamine empirical evidence in order to reveal hidden possibilities. Thus, for example, an object moving due to a single visible force, through space, not producing a change of momentum must, according to Newton, reveal, upon further examination, hidden "friction" forces in space balancing the visible force so as to not produce any net change of motion. The success of Newton's laws on the gross chemical level (in particular, celestial mechanics and present day space dynamics) lies precisely in its ability to always co-relate any force contact with a change in momentum, and vice versa. Empirical idealizations are therefore programs and projects for research, directing one's attention to nature with the intent of making explicit, implicit patterns of possible relation.

All general laws of matter in motion such as Newton's laws or the conservation principles of momentum and energy are such "pragmatic *a priori*" formulations, i.e., formulations which are neither logically derivable by deduction from pure syntactics, nor empirically derivable by induction from a specific complex of determinate events. They are rather empirical idealizations obtained by abduction, paving the way for future experimentation. Thus, the way in which they are used, and the particular meanings attached to the various distinctions contained within any ideal law (mass, space, and time, etc.) continually change. For example, in modern times, Newton's laws would not be very relevant if one could not define the existence of field momentum (field momentum not known to exist in Newton's time), the absence of which would imply the necessity of assuming the existence of unknown relations in order to keep Newton's law in operation.[6] What happens, therefore, is that an evolving syntactical structure of objective interaction appears, and through continual redefinition and reformulation, the scope and depth of the individual syntactical principles involved become increased. By not delimiting the syntactical content of co-relation to particular semantical forms, (e.g., the structure of atomic relations to only atoms) one not only achieves a more universal

---

6. This in itself would not have been "bad," for the possibility is always present that any one non-functioning law will in the future become functioning again through new discoveries, or vice versa, and indeed there might be a continual shift between the functioning and non-functioning of any particular law or general principle. The principle of conservation of energy stood violated for over a decade until the scientists discovered the neutrino, which they first "invented" in their theories before they uncovered the neutrinos in order to keep the conservation principles intact. (There are now four kinds of known neutrinos.)

appreciation of the non-localized nonlinearity involved in the dialectic of syntactical relation, but at the same time comes to appreciate the concreteness of the particular semantical forms involved. Each semantical form of particularity makes a general syntactical relation take on a certain empirically limited nature. Although no one semantical form exhausts any general syntactical relation, no general syntactical relation manifests itself except through particular forms which are bound to delimit its universality.

We now come to the modern theories of relativity and quantum mechanics. From the perspective of "pure physics" (and also that of the particular sciences of nature) both of these theories are still not in proper form. Thus, like the ideal gas law, both formulations rest on empirical constants. However, unlike the ideal gas law, both constants are taken to be universal *qua* measured (and continually re-measured) value—which is of course a contradiction in terms (even if the constants have a greater applicability and a more universal scope than that of the ideal gas law's constant). Any measured and re-measurable quantity is, by definition, limited to the time and context of the act of measurement and need not be universal in all of space or for all of time. An empirical value limited to a specific context must reflect the spatial and temporal localization of that context *qua* measure, even if the syntactical relations involved go beyond the context. Relativity is based upon the constant velocity of electromagnetic light, c. Quantum mechanics is based upon the quantum interaction, h, which is also electromagnetic in nature in that it relates electromagnetically conditioned energy and momentum (energy and momentum as a function of the speed of light, c) to its frequency and wavelength when considered in its most general form. Thus, relativity and quantum mechanics must properly be studied as part of a particular science (the science of the "electronic-level" of interaction), and must not be regarded in its present form as a generalized syntactic on the same level as the generalized equations of conservation of energy and momentum or the generalized force equations. If this is not done, then relativity and quantum mechanics in its present form can distort measured event-complexes into an electromagnetically conditioned gestalt, when in fact it might be due to a non-electromagnetic process. Indeed, present day "neutrino physics" and the study of "weak forces" in general, may eventually give a clue to the existence of sub-electronic interaction, and consequently to the possible existence of interactions not bound by the empirical constants c and h. For clarity, there should be a sharp distinction (but not separation) between the generalized "viewing patterns" which are not empirically limited, but ideal syntactical relations, and the "viewed patterns" which must come through empirical values and constants and always refer to specific manifestations and event-complexes, so that their interrelation as a dialectic of universality and concreteness can be given explicit form. The dialectic of inseparable distinctions only functions as an inseparability and unity, to the degree to which the distinctions are clearly in view; otherwise a vague indistinct inseparability emerges and contradictions appear. This is exactly what is happening today in relativity and quantum mechanics. The generality, or universality, of perspective is confused with the particular level through which this universality (nonlinearity) of syntactical relatedness appears. As a result, the genuine universality of relativity and quantum mechanics, offering insight that goes beyond the values of c and h, (having applicability in many domains, such as psychology) is confused with the dependency that is put on these limited values of velocity and interaction. Conversely, the particular level to which the concrete values of c and h belong, namely the electronic level, is regarded primarily in an abstract syntactical fashion void of specificity. One is often told that electric and magnetic fields do not "really exist" as material states, and that relativistic "changes" in electromagnetic variables are not physical but due to a non-material change in space-time relations nevertheless having physical consequences for the electromagnetic variables.

At the conclusion of this essay we shall present a theory in which relativity and quantum mechanics in their specific form are derived from the electronic level by showing what this implies for a dialectics of nature and for the present state of physics. However, one can also regard relativity and quantum mechanics in terms of their universal syntactical natures independent of the empirical values c and h (just as Newton's laws can be generalized to mean a coupling betwen any kind or degree of contact or interaction, and a change in any kind of "steady-state" motion. When this is done, an interesting aspect of the nonlinear dialectic is revealed. Thus relativity does not consider the existence of an absolute space-time whole, but only the space-time whole relative to and a function of each particular element or particle. Conversely, quantum mechanics does not consider the existence of absolutely determinate elements or particles "in themselves," but rather regards each particle relative to and a function of the entire space-time whole it functions within (as a "wave-function"). This means that whole and part, the universal and the unique are dialectically co-determined by expressing in physical terms the nonlinear field of interaction from two complimentary perspectives in which the (1) inseparable space-time whole is mapped into each distinct part, or "frame of reference," and never exists as such, as a single absolute (the condition of relativity) and (2) each distinct part is mapped out into the inseparable whole and is never a simple delimited or bounded particle (the condition of quantum wave mechanics). However, such a complimentary syntactic between relativity and quantum mechanics is usually lost sight of precisely because of the semantical localizations (c and h) which bind them in different ways to the behavior of the electromagnetic photon. Relativity expresses the determinate analytic whole-oriented aspect of the nonlinear relation, while quantum mechanics expresses the indeterminate synthetic and part-oriented aspect of this nonlinear relation. Thus, a nonlinear field is at once deterministic (each part mediated by the whole) and indeterministic (each part itself an immediate whole). It is a self-deterministic (self-mediated) totality of part-whole mutuality which is neither strictly causal or a-causal, but exhibits both within a condition of mutual causality, expressive of a reciprocal feedback, co-determination and self-interaction of all elements.

Looking at the first domain of the dialectics of nature, called "pure physics," as a totality, gives us the following syntactical structure. The overall space-time dynamics reveals a whole-part dialectic of events, event-complexes (objects), and complexes of objects in which one must distinguish between levels of material interaction. On any one level, the conservation of momentum expresses the constancy of visible movement. However, for that one level, the kinetic energy may or may not be conserved. If it is, the "collisions" or interactions are called "elastic"—which means that the internal non-visible motions within the interacting objects are ignorable or non-existent. However, if the kinetic energy of motion is not conserved for that level, then deeper levels of internal movement must exist if the overall state of energy is to be considered a constant. This means that internal energy exists either in the modality of unorganized and "random" motion or in that of "organized" potential energy (a form of organized motion). An interaction between objects or bodies is then not only an action taking place on the visible or given level, but one also taking place within the objects or participating systems and hence on a deeper level. From what we now know of object interaction, one can state that in general, all interaction is always between and within any two or more objects or event-complexes that are in mutual relation. Thus, there is no such thing as mere "external contact," and no particular "particle" of movement can itself be localized as a "simple point or event." Here we have a physical counterpart to what was called the second principle of dialectic necessity. In fact, the fundamental syntactical structure in modern physics is not a particular particle or event-object-complex, but rather field phenomena, within which particularizations and localizations ("poles") of energy appear as particles. Thus, the general field of interaction in physics is nonlinear—nonlinearity in physical interaction being expressed through the self-coupling or resonance that exists between the universal (inseparable) field and its particularizations (distinctions). A pure field "as such," as well as pure particle mechanics "as such" is essentially linear even though it can express non-linearities. It is precisely their dialectic of co-relation, in which particles are self-localizations, or products, within and of a field or process of interaction, that gives the paticular quality of nonlinearity to the field. In such a state, the "whole" is never the mere "sum" of the particles, but includes their intrinsic mode of interaction—no particle existing as an abstract isolated quantity to begin with. Here then, we have a physical counterpart to our first principle of concrete presence, in which all objectification is considered to be the product of the subjective field of presence itself not localized.

Particularization and localization within an interacting field of space-time events (gravitational, electromagnetic, strong and weak fields) represent linearizations and polarizations of a nonlinear field of inseparable distinctions (the mediation of an immediate field of presence). These localizations in turn can either disintegrate and return to the field, or become re-organized among themselves to form a higher level of nonlinear field interaction (a higher order self-mediated immediacy). Thus, we have here within the first domain of "pure physics" the fundamental transition to the second domain: physics now considered in its determinate modality of appearing as level-complexes of particular forms of matter in motion.

The second domain of physics, or nature, is to consider the various particular event-complexes that constitute existence *qua* existence. However, we have seen that the syntactical structure of relations ever-present in various forms as the ground or "essence" of these existential structures is the nonlinear field of interaction. Furthermore, the dialectics of such a nonlinear field itself can express a cycling from an immediate field or level of presence (e), through mediations in the form of localizations and polarities $(+e, -e)$, to a self-mediated nonlinear field of a higher order level of immediacy $(+-e$ or $e')$, one which functions on a qualitatively different plane of interaction, constituted now out of the previous linearizations, localizations or polarizations, reorganized into a new modality of nonlinearity in which the previous linearizations or localizations have now become a relatively stable substructure no longer disappearing into the simple nonlinear field from which they emerged. We shall therefore start our central core of the dialectics of nature, existence *qua* existence, by a presentation of the entire known universe of space and time in the form of a leveling structure of nonlinear fields. [7]

We shall start with the lowest level of immediacy that is presently known to us: the electronic level. Here, the nonlinear field is the photon-field of electromagnetic energy traveling at the speed of light, c. The linearizations or polarizations arising out of this field are charged particles whose only stable forms are positive and negative charges. In fact, the only stable particles of finite rest mass are electrons and protons. [8]

The electronic level is characterized by a charge-charge interaction system, in which the field of energy causing the charge process to manifest itself is the photon field. Indeed, not only is each charge in a state of continual ("virtual") photon emission and absorption, and not only does the acceleration of charges liberate "real" photons, but the charges themselves are nothing but "photon-complexes" in the sense that they can be completely annihilated into electromagnetic photon energy. These charges, in their state of interaction, can reorganize themselves into a trans-charged state: into atoms and groups of atoms, in which a qualitatively new form of objective nonlinear interaction manifests itself. Thus, the chemical level appears when whole complexes of atoms—in the form of galaxies of stars and planets—begin to manifest themselves as a new nonlinear field: the field of chemical matter in the form of gases, liquids, solids and plasma.

---

7. This section represents the development of ideas for a dialectics of nature initially started several decades ago by my father, the late Dr. Paul Kosok. In fact, it was his unique perspective of nature which prompted my work in dialectics to begin with, and I set as one of my major goals the validation of this view by trying to make it into an integral phenomenon of the dialectic process itself.

8. There are, naturally, other fields on a sub-atomic level, such as the strong and weak fields associated with nuclear structures and decay products, but they will not concern us directly here for they are associated with the structure of elementary sub-atomic particles in various states; structures whose constitution is still quite ambiguous and which may lead to sub-electronic and sub-charged dimensions or levels of interaction not yet known. The gravitation field is most remote in so far as its inner dynamics is concerned. It may be that, unlike particular fields associated with particular localizations, the gravitational field is a general-total-effect of all fields and localizations acting together or in some combined way—in that the field seems to depend not upon the type of matter or distinction present, but only upon the mere presence of matter or distinctions themselves. In this case, gravity would be part of both "pure physics," which deals with the universal nature of space, time and matter, and with cosmology, which deals with the overall totality of levels.

On the chemical level, atoms form a new type of interaction structure, the formation of complex compounds of atoms and molecules of atoms. Here the fundamental quality which characterizes the chemical level is the compound-compound interaction, in which the unit of energy exchange consists of atoms of organized charge (in contradistinction to the electronic level, in which the fundamental quality consists of charge-charge interaction, the photon being the basic unit of energy exchange). Inorganic and organic compounds are the polarizations and mediations on the chemical level (produced by selective coordination of atoms from a given field of atoms into singularities which differentiate them from their background) whose most complex modalities are protein structures and the DNA-RNA type organizations. Just because it is easy to "visualize" compounds as "sums of atoms," the mistake must not be made that it is a linear sum. The "addition or subtraction" of any one atom or charge to a molecular-complex causes the whole complex to reorganize its structure. Moreover, the chemical level, just like the electronic level before it, is productive of a synthesis of its linearizations and polarizations which in turn acts as the basis for a qualitatively new level of nonlinear interaction. The living cell is the most complex chemical structure, and is at the same time the basis for the development of the biological level of interaction.

On the biological plane of activity, a nonlinear cellular field of interaction occurs, in which living matter gradually develops its forms of linearizations; namely, particular organs of cellular activity in which cells are organized into tissues of plant and animal life to perform specific functions. Cellular activity produces complexes of organs and organisms of organs by self-differentiation and reproduction. The fundamental quality which characterizes biological activity is the organ-organ interrelation, in which the basic unit governing energy transfer is the cell. The biological level, like the chemical and electronic levels before it, develops its particular type of interaction producing more and more intricate forms of organ-organ interaction, until the point of complexity is reached where a qualitatively different mode of interrelations begins to appear. The organ-organ complex of either plants or animals not only expresses a particular type of cellular based energy-state of interaction within itself (metabolism) but this form of energy-relation functions through a reproduction of its entire structure. Groups of plants and animals emerge, so-called societies of organisms, in which the organisms have a different kind of affinity towards themselves than the groups or combinations of molecules on the chemical level that have not appeared as a result of organ self-reproduction. However, all of these "social" structures are essentially biological in nature in that the so-called social patterns of behavior are basically instinctually determined and biologically inherited. It is only with the emergence of man out of pre-man, that the most complex modality and organ synthesis of the biological level at the same time becomes the basis for a genuinely higher level:that of the social level of human interaction.

The characteristic feature of humanity as a nonlinear field is that of cultural interaction (by culture, we mean the existence of a definite pattern of social-inheritance). Thus, unlike so-called animal societies, man, through the development of tools of production and records of relations, produces cultural groups, families, clans, tribes and classes in which each new generation does not start from the same instinctual pattern biologically given, but rather builds upon the culture already lived as a history. Human culture exhibits a unique form of historical feedback with its own past development, and consequently with projections into the future of goals of development not yet achieved. Consequently, the fundamental quality of the social level consists of class-class interaction (or group-group interrelation) in which the fundamental unit of energy production and exchange is the human individual. Individuals are indentified by their cultural-national inheritance as a social entity and society is a complex "organism" of class and cultural (as well as subcultural) group structures. The individual is the unity or unit of interrelation within and between these class-group structures, giving them their coherence. The social level of relation is therefore a cultural group-dynamics in which the individual exists as the active agent of interaction. To the degree to which the individual is therefore merely identified with one group against another, he delimits and alienates his identity into a given pattern of class or group relation and the society in turn becomes class-fractured. The function of a truly "democratic" society is to permit the individual to express his trans-group identity as an active agent of interrelation and intersubjectivity by means of well developed feedback activity in its social, economic, political and cultural relations among all groups. This makes the society an integrated and fluid system, and at the same time, frees the individual from being class-identified or reified: belonging to only such and such a class or group, performing only such and such an activity. This class identification establishes the condition for exploitation, private property and the alienation of an individual from the total social dynamics; a dynamics which is but an outer expression of his inner potentialities to be a total self-determining agent. Social dynamics is not a question of the individual versus the "state" or "society," but rather both the individual and society versus the hardening of the group and class structures that simultaneously delimit the individual into a rigid pattern of behavior, and fracture society into an internal "civil" war of classes and groups. A little reflection will show that it is not individuals *qua* individuals which are anti-social or anti-intersubjective (individuals indeed being in need of intersubjectivity in order to develop their own subjectivity); it is rather their class, group, family and clan identification which causes them to view other individuals through the products and results of experience (their traditions, patterns of behavior and norms), instead of through the process of direct and immediate experience which is nonlinear and interactive by its very nature. Thus, out of the nonlinear field of humanity class organization appears as its linearization, and the synthesis of class structure into a funcioning unitary society of interrelating groups demands the transcendence of the alienating and separatistic character of class structure. This is not a "utopian" quest, but only a matter of spelling out the functioning dynamics of what an "efficient" society really must be. Material-physical efficiency and integrity on a total social-natural scale is actually congruent with physiological-psychological-social or "humanistic" integrity. The picture of a brutal "1984" in which technical efficiency must supplant human values is totally misleading and indeed propaganda bred by the myth-making structures of today's society. Genuine self-reproducing and self-sustaining material efficiency can only function to the degree to which the human agent can express his individuality as being free of any rigid class or group identification which fractures society as a "smoothly running" intersubjectivity . Naturally any transition from a given fractured society to one that is not fractured would necessarily seem violent, aggressive and productive of the release of hostility by virtue of the boundaries of identification that must be "softened." However, it is necessary to distinguish between the smoke produced as a result of de-localizing already existing suppressed violence (and active violence), and the flame of genuine human need which is ever attempting to give explicit expression to the intersubjective "I and thou" condition of its subjectivity. It is always possible to degenerate, as well as to generate into different modalities of nonlinearity. Stability is the greatest hoax of all time. The only genuine "stability" or "identity" possible on any level is the very process of transformation itself.

Looking at the four levels of nonlinear field relations (the electronic, chemical, biological and social levels, together with the various particular sciences that study each of these areas or combinations of these areas), we see that we have traveled from the photon to society, through a process of continual linearization (localization, polarization) and re-nonlinearization—each time producing a qualitatively distinct form of energy-interaction. In this development, the photon, the atom, the cell and the human being appear as nodal points of transition, and in each case the unit involved or evolved on one level is precisely that which becomes the fundamental unity of energy production and exchange on the next level. Indeed, a functional unit such as a photon, atom, cell or human being, is representative of the universal gestalt or nonlinear field relative to a particular level of existence. It is a functional sub-whole of the whole it is within. Therefore, should it begin to be subordinated as a part of a larger system of organization (photons or electromagnetic energy within charges, or atoms within compounds, or cells within organs, or individuals within groups or classes), then the integrity of that unit will be delimited until a sufficiently developed structure appears in which the units no longer "belong" to any one meta-unit organization, but are rather the active energy-agents between a whole series of possible organizations and hence beyond the limitations of any given organization. Thus, photons as sub-whole elements appear localized as electromagnetic energy within any one charge. However, as part of a charge-charge interaction process, they become free agents of exchange, which indeed is what gives the charges their characteristics of "charge-attraction or repulsion." Similarly, this charge-charge system, when balanced into an atom or a molecule begins a higher level of unit-activity in which at first the unit atom or molecule becomes localized within certain compounds or structures, but finally becomes re-leased as an active energy exchange unit between compounds.

The most complex structure of compound-compound interrelatedness is of course the cell (involving protein, DNA-RNA interactions, etc.). On a biological level, each cell functions within a particular organ participating in a specific activity, but also expresses its uniqueness to the degree to which it relates to the whole organism through a mode of organ-organ feedback interaction. Nerve cells, of course, have "specialized" in this interrelatedness of organic function and, consequently, play an important role in the integrity of an organism. ("Abstract thought," however, as a highly complex nerve interaction, can become an "overspecialized" generalizing activity if it is divorced from its total body integration.) Finally, on the social level, individual organisms not only function within groups and classes, but between and beyond them, and it is only to the degree to which the intersubjectivity of trans-class behavior emerges, that both the individual as a unit or unity can express itself and society as a nonlinear integration of these units. Indeed, such an integrated behavior gives explicit expression to the state of universal-unique, or whole-part co-determination. The point is in the degree to which such an implicit state can become explicit, and hence the basis for higher order interactions. Obviously, the degree of dialectic feedback is on a qualitatively more complex scale in the higher order levels of interaction, each level being a unique expression of a certain order of self-determination and dialectic "organicity."

Not only is the human social domain itself an integral aspect of a dialectics of nature, but the nonsocial levels of the dialectics of nature—the electronic, chemical and biological domains—can also in their own ways manifest the "problems of alienation" or rigidification. Thus, the functional efficiency or integrity of any system can be investigated to see if it appears overly determinate and whole-oriented, or overly indeterminate and part-oriented. Those systems which exhibit the greatest degree of explicit interrelatedness between their elements of distinctions and their field of inseparability have the greatest potentialities for growth, expansion, and hence self-expression through transformation—transformation being the essence of any element or event. Naturally, each level develops its own unique expression of the type of transition process in existence. The electronic level gives birth to the fundamental "charge-process" which characterizes the constitution of atoms. The chemical level gives birth to the "metabolistic-reproductive" process characterizing the cell. The biological level brings about brain-body "consciousness" which characterizes the human being. The social level brings about "cultural praxis" which distinguishes the dynamics of society from previous levels. Whatever is previous or subsequent to the four known levels of interaction can only deepen the many ways in which the dialectic of field-event subject-objectivity can manifest itself. It can in no way de-valuate that which has already expressed itself and that which is presently the appearing modality of dialectics.

Thus, objective reality is not a single and abstract dialectical field unity, or a diversity of plural forms, each of which reflects some particular or limited aspect of a dialectical process. Objective reality is literally the existence and explication of the entire dialectic essence of nonlinear interaction in object form. Multiple centers or units of dialectical synthesis exist in a space-time "organic" totality of levels of relation, these units determined here to be the photon, atom, cell, and the human being, as far as we know to date. Consequently, each of these units must be studied as a particular manifestation of a universal process of nonlinearity. Each of these units must be investigated in terms of its organizational nature as the synthesis of polarizations coming from a deeper level of nonlinearity. The atom, cell, human being and even "society" as a functional system (although not as yet a new self-integrated unit for a still higher order "meta-human" or "meta-social" interaction) all display a "nucleus-body" type of organization. Thus, there is the positive nucleus and the negative electronic shell structure of the atom; the nucleus and cytoplasmic structure of the cell; the organizational brain and the body of the human being; the governmental "state," and the individuals of society. All of these display both functional and structural similarities which are here regarded not as superficial similarities but as essential similarities reflective of the existential modality of a dialectics of nature.

The unit of a given level of nonlinear field activity is actually itself a self-mediated unity of the previous nonlinear field. The atom, for example, is a self-mediated unity for the electro-magnetic photon field with its continual propensity to appear and disappear as positive-negative charges (electron-positron creation and destruction). The atom is a particular kind of positive-negative synthesis of a proton (neutron) nucleus that is positive, and an electron shell structure which is negative. The nucleus, although constituted by a proton-neutron interaction field whose energy exchange unit is a meson, is nevertheless still a composite charge structure that can be disintegrated into elements on the electronic level which are light, or c, conditioned. Electrons, protons, photons and neutrinos will appear upon one form of disintegration. These in turn can be transformed completely into electro-magnetic photons traveling at the speed of light, c, and neutrinos (uncharged, but with "zero rest mass") which also appear to travel at the speed of light, but whose real function is not understood. It is this electro-magnetically constituted positive nucleus which gives the atom its basic chemical identity, the negative electronic shell being its mode of contextual relatedness to other atoms within a chemical level. However, even though it is possible for negative protons and positive electrons to exist (and conceivably—thus far—an "anti-atom" made up of a negative nucleus and a positive shell structure), our known universe functions in a definite way in which the positive charge is always nuclear and the negative one always extra-nuclear. Furthermore, from a dialectical point of view, functional opposites are not merely symmetrical, but also asymmetrical. Even positive numbers and negative numbers in mathematics do not function the same way. Self-multiplication preserves positivity but cancels negativity. Subjectivity and objectivity, self and world, female and male, center and periphery, for example, are not mirror opposites (abstractly replaceable); they complement each other to form a mutual totality. Thus, the polarity between positive and negative charges is not just a mechanical mirror symmetry, but a functional one, in which positivity and negativity on the electronic level are qualitatively different and express a certain kind of organizational activity. Positive charges become nuclear and give unit identity, while negative charges are those which act extra-nuclear and express unit interrelatedness; because of the functional interrelatedness between them each is complementary to the other but not replaceable with the other.

Turning to the cell, we see that the nucleus with its hereditary DNA-RNA structure, expresses cellular control and gives biological identity, while the cytoplasmic protoplasm serves to interrelate the cell to other cells and the environment. Within the human being, the brain is naturally the functional identity center (whose essential "memory" structure is also RNA constituted), while the body is the means of environmental interaction. Finally, within society, the particular governmental-state structure expresses the social identity present in terms of a visible and legal power apparatus, while those groups not directly involved in governing represent the body of a governed society, i.e., society itself as a living and functioning organism relating to other such organisms or nature itself in its "natural" or "extralegal" manner.

If we return to our description of the dialectic of man in nature, seeing how it is reflective of a dialectic between subjectivity, or field of presence as the observing patterns, and objectivity, or the events present as the observed patterns, and hence objectivity in a state of self-observation in which subjectivity represents the interactive state of objectivity permitting self-relatedness to appear, then one can easily interpret the significance of the "nucleus body" nature of all units of existence. Thus, the nucleus structure or system expresses the subjective aspect of a unit in its reflective mode and hence manifests "controlling or observing" patterns. The body structure of a system represents the objective aspect of a unit in its immediate modality and hence expresses those "observed or functionally present" patterns of unit environment interaction immediately present with which the nucleus must be functionally coordinated in order to act as a reflecting and controlling pattern. The nucleus "control center" is thus an objectified (reflected and mediated) subjectivity, whereas the body is a subjectified (immediate) objectivity. In a sense, it is actually the body of immediate interrelatedness between unit and environment that is the objective base and content of a unit, while the nucleus of control, order and reflection is the mediating superstructure emerging out of the objective immediacy of nonlinearity which expresses the form and direction of that content. The body is thus the immediate state of objective energy or *Eros* and the nucleus the reflected state of subjectivity, or *Logos*, which together function as a self-mediated *telos* of action, if they are not functionally degenerate or uncoordinated. Each higher level of nonlinearity is thus a qualitatively more complex expression of a telos of self-interaction and field-event unity, whose appearance as explicit ego consciousness and social interaction is the most advanced form yet encountered in terms of the complexity of field-event feedback and subject-object interdependency.

If we now look at the totality of all levels known to date, the social level naturally stands out as the most complex and self-integrated one. This means that the interaction state between man and nature is a social dynamics of man *qua* culture and nature, embedded, however, within a biological interaction state between man *qua* animal and nature, which in turn is embedded within a chemical interaction state between man *qua* chemical and nature, which in turn is embedded within an electro-magnetic interaction state between man *qua* electro-magnetic photons and nature. Furthermore, this means that man is actually, at least, a four-level natural complex functioning as a singular totality (not "reducing" the higher levels to the lower ones, or "subordinating" the lower ones to the higher ones, but rather seeing them as a singular state of interrelatedness). Indeed, man's brain is unique in the way in which all four levels are brought together as a single unit of nonlinearity (the nerve process as a socially conditioned electro-chemical cellular process) and unsurpassed in its depth and scope of subjectivity and intersubjectivity; that is, the depth and scope of the way in which the brain both expresses, reflects and self-reflects the universal state of nonlinear field interaction.

However, if we look at the known levels of particular nonlinearity as a totality, in relation to the universal nature of nonlinearity as described in the first section of "pure physics," we see that one cannot expect the photon to be the ultimate unit of existence (the "alpha point," as the atom was once thought to be), nor can we expect society in its present form or its future projection as a unified society to be the most developed unit of existence (its "omega point"). The photon itself may be but the most complex unit of energy-organization of a sub-electronic level (involving the neutrino in some way), just as society as an integral unity may be but the beginning of a meta-social level—perhaps an "interplanetary" "intergalactic" society within which the human being becomes transformed into a higher order consciousness. This means that the velocity of light need not be the "ultimate" one, but only a constant for a certain level of matter. Larger velocities of energy transfer might be discovered, revealing deeper levels of matter which at the same time could serve as a means of developing higher levels of social interaction.

At this point, the dialectics of nature becomes a cosmology of structure and evolution, for we are passing through the transition point to the third and last section of the dialectics of nature. From the viewpoint of the cosmological totality of transformation, all the particular levels of objective interaction cease to be merely determinate structures of existence, and become self-determinate structures of objective reality as a totality. Thus, we observe that not only has the social level of explicit intersubjective consciousness emerged out of a biological womb, but the biological level in turn appears to have developed out of a deeper chemical womb of intergalactic structure. It also appears that this chemical complex evolved and might still be evolving out of the electro-magnetic space-time field that pervades all of known space and time. Considered as a self-evolutionary process, objective interaction thus presents us with a dialectics of nature whose reality is the coming into being of consciousness. Indeed, scientists regard galactic structures as filled with trillions of trillions of stars and planetary formation as a very common formation (perhaps one star in every 100 or 1000). Furthermore, among the planets, the proper conditions for life and social development is deemed to be quite frequent (perhaps one out of every 100 planets). There are areas within our own galaxy and in others which are millions of years ahead and millions of years behind us, and hence there might right now be a fantastic cross-section of human-type or humanoid development in a variety of stages, from primitive cultures to more advanced ones. Life among the stars, according to present probability, seems to be developing in billions upon billions of places, with perhaps a million places in our own galaxy.

Cosmology cannot be considered apart from the phenomenology of subject-objectivity and the process of awareness, and consequently any attempt to merely picture the evolution of the various levels of matter in motion as a blind phenomenon of meaningless matter (or a tautological evolution of a pure universal mind) is to become alienated by the linearized abstractions of science that picture cosmological evolution in merely mechanical or formal terms. The status of cosmology today is but a scientific equivalent to the mythological structures primitive consciousness accumulated—clearer, more precise, but at the same time lacking the depth and profundity many of these more primitive but immediate and direct formulations of consciousness possessed. Regarded dialectically, cosmology studies the cybernetic totality of all levels of nonlinear interaction, postulating no objectified or particular beginning, or any objectified end. Dialectics refuses to postulate either the existence of an "ultimate particle" or an "ultimate and final state" of consciousness or matter (all such states involving an assumed finiteness and/or boundedness of the universe). Rather, all mediations and objectifications are seen to be either in a direct state of immediate subjectivity and nonlinearity (in which case no question arises as to beginnings and ends) or in a self-mediated state of immediacy (in which case any given level of mediation and linearization by dialectical necessity must refer to a deeper state of nonlinear internal interaction within each of the linear objects interacting). The question of beginning and end is essentially self-negative. Either experience is directly immediate without any boundaries, or there are boundaries, in which case any object or linearized beginning and end must reveal a deeper state of interaction between and within the object and its space or context. This is just a way of saying that a particular boundary cannot be an ultimate one.

Thus, "ultimate presence" can never be a particularized object-complex (such as a photon or an atom "itself"), but must be a paradoxical nonlinear state of immediacy, which always has the potentiality and essence (being immediate and not bounded) of revealing or developing sub-linearizations or meta-linearizations. This, of course, is but a way of denying the objectification of any absolute as an existent. The question as to whether the universe is "finite or infinite" in space or time is thus transcended in a dialectical cosmology, for both conceptions as isolated identifications are delimitations and objectified possibilities. As separated alternatives, moreover, they are contradictory opposites and not paradoxical and dialectical. The Hegelian notion of "true infinity," however, is a paradoxical synthesis and transcendence of both a finite cosmology predicated only upon a given and static universe, and a merely infinite cosmology predicated simply upon a universe that is ever incomplete and beyond what ever is given. A dialectically infinite cosmology based upon a "true infinity" regards the objective universe as a state in which being itself is never in any given, or identified state that can remain fixed, or become unfixed and change. All being is ever becoming-given and consequently a dialectical infinity neither converges to a given, nor diverges beyond a given, but continually "trans-verges" with what is into a new form of itself: *nothing is given!* A dialectical cosmology perceives-conceives nature as a dynamic immediacy in which all mediation is immediately self-mediation, all movement is self-movement and "growth" (positive or negative growth, generation or degeneration) and never a mere external movement or becoming leading to a mere infinity beyond any given. It is not a question of any ultimate conservation of energy or of any closed universe leading to thermodynamic stagnation on the one hand or of an open universe beyond conservation, determination and understanding on the other. The notions of complete vs. incomplete, closed vs. open, symmetrical vs. asymmetrical, finite vs. infinite, determinate vs. indeterminate, absolute vs. relative are all abstract linearizations and consequently inapplicable as a description for a dialectical cosmology. Rather, such notions are always both applicable in the presentation of any one aspect, depending upon the perspective chosen, and at the same time inapplicable in their linearized oppositional forms. A dialectics of nature ends with cosmology or the "reality of existence" as being beyond any product or "final conclusion" of abstraction, including the equally abstract notion that such an impossibility is a lack and a negative result. Nature being the very process that is happening, cannot in reality be regarded as an external frame of reference or "world" within which man moves in a container of space and time. Nature, along with space and time, is rather the very process of interaction defining the state of subjectivity and intersubjectivity man is experiencing. What have you actually experienced of that which you take to be the vast empty spaces filled here and there with stars, lumps of rock and dust, and implacable energy transformations as elusive as they are inevitable? How much of your conception of nature and science is the result of taking the models and myths of linearized products, produced by science as the pointers to reality as the reality itself, instead of experiencing yourself either as a human being in nature, or as a scientist in the act of scientific praxis?

From a scientific viewpoint, theoretical structures serve as a frame of reference with which to regard empirical observation; as a result, both observations and theoretical structures co-evolve in mutual feedback. Within any particular area of science, empirical observation is generally limited to the so-called objective component, be it facts, numbers or persons which appear as the objects in question. If a certain set of "facts" appear which do not "fit in" to a given structure, or which one wants to utilize to predict other "facts" or objectifications not yet visible, then theoretical structures in the form of "hypotheses" appear. However, it is the history of consciousness that determines the relevancy or significance of a particular hypothesis for a given state of objective interaction (with regard to its very practical side of directing human consciousness and not simply "informing" it). It is also possible to consider these hypotheses or theories "about" facts as facts themselves; that is, as objectifications appearing in the history of consciousness in its attempts to become self-conscious of its own conditioning. Thus, the dialectics of nature is a theory of subject-object phenomenology, and is part of the overall "encyclopedia of the sciences" given here as a unified field theory of logic, nature, and humanity. This means that it is in effect a "meta-science" and not a direct science or a nonscientific philosophy about science. Thus, the encyclopedia here developed, and the dialectics of nature within it, is a science which makes theories about the various sciences in their praxis of making theories:

dialectical science regards as its "factual basis" the history and development of science as part of the development of social consciousness.

The encyclopedia of the sciences as here presented regards all sciences in terms of nine major divisions—divisions and linearizations which explicitly refer to the nonlinear totality within which they function as a singular science of man in nature. Consequently, each of the various nine sciences (and the innumerable sub-sciences definable) must in some way or other reflect within their own particular theoretics non-linear relations of mutual co-determination with all the other sciences as outlined here. The sciences of syntactics, semantics, pragmatics; physics, natural science, cosmology; psychology, social dynamics and concrete philosophy form a singular nonlinear totality. The various particular theories formulated within each of these sciences must give explicit expression to this nonlinearity if the unified eneyclopedia of the sciences and the dialectics of nature within it does in fact express a meaningful and significant theory about the nature of consciousness and its evolution from the objective world. Consequently, the dialectics of the sciences can now offer a concrete program of action. It can offer a criterion of judgment about what it takes to be its "factual" basis: namely, the various particular theories emerging within the specialized sciences. If a particular science such as physics produces several hypotheses and theories, each of which is more or less satisfactory regarding the way in which it relates known empirical data, one can then regard these several theories themselves as facts to be analyzed by the dialectics of nature as a meta-science. Thus, according to the nonlinear perspective, or the meta-science of dialectics, one can then regard the various theories under consideration in terms of the relevancy these theories have as an explicit expression of nonlinearity, and represent the better of the known theories in a form that best brings out the nonlinear components involved. The dialectics of nature then regards the theory most developed in its nonlinear formulation of the facts as the theory most likely to be relevant, i.e., most likely to give the best account of both present facts and future facts not yet uncovered. As with any hypothesis in a particular science, it is the history of consciousness that determines whether or not the meta-theory of dialectic is correct in its judgment. Furthermore, a feedback structure between the dialectic in any one nonlinear form, and the actual evolution of relevant theories in the particular sciences takes place, continually transforming the meta-science of dialectic itself through the history of its factual basis: the history of the particular theories in the sciences. Thus, the dialectics of nature becomes more "efficient" in interpreting the linear and nonlinear components of nonlinearity. Nonlinearity, like immediacy and subjectivity, is a field of presence within which linearizations, mediations and objectifications appear: nonlinearity works through linearizations and hence is not a simple (linear!) negation of linearity. [9]

9. In order to proceed with such a program, an "institute of dialectic research" (or an "institute of nonlinear research") is naturally necessary, for no one individual can integrate the various sciences together as proposed by the encyclopedia. Such an integration requires a major reorientation of all the fixated categories presently employed by the various sciences. The author, being familiar with some of the problems within one of the sciences, namely physics, has proposed a particular model of electro-magnetic interaction—based upon a

Relativity and quantum mechanics are incorrectly presented as general theories of matter in motion; in fact, they are dependent in their present form upon constants of a particular level. If one is aware of the dialectical nature of levels of material interaction, one does not present a c-dependent relativity as a general theory of space and time. Instead, one explicitly shows how relativity is a function of electro-magnetic space and time. The presentation of relativity to date mystifies physics by reducing the dynamic variables of a specific kind of material interaction (which is always a function of a particular level) into a generalized abstract kinematics and geometry. Relativity makes the specificity of light-dynamics into a general dynamics, and consequently makes light-dynamics itself unexplainable while forcing the specificity of other non-light modalities into a light-frame of reference. Relativistic space-time geometry, a product of a specific kind of experience, is set up as a nonmaterial condition independent of the actual properties of photon-charge interaction. Any kind of matter—even matter having nothing directly to do with photon-charge dynamics—is nevertheless governed by that interaction process. Here we have an important example of how a model of interaction derived as a specific product from experience now inverts the order. The space-time model for a particular activity is taken as reality and used as a means for judging all of experience and possible experience relative to it. For all its aesthetics, relativity has alienated physical experience. Instead of either grasping the universal syntactics of c-dependent relativity which goes beyond any semantical localization to a specific constant called c or seeing how the electronic level actually accounts for relativistic energy transformations in a concrete way (making mass, momentum and energy changes always changes in electro-magnetic energy which is charge-photon dependent), relativity obscures the issue by replacing physical experience and intuition with the "beauty" of a purely *mathematical* model of physical interaction.

Modern physics is so used to developing its theoretics in abstract formalistic terms by stating that "physical intuition" cannot "reach" beyond a certain point (meaning that intuition, like any faculty, must be trained and sharpened in order not to become lazy), that it has become a kind of formidable idealism, stifling any kind of approach which wants to reintroduce physical models (not just mathematical ones) back into the theories of physics. A division of labor exists between the experimentalists who measure existence and the theoreticians. The theoreticians, the prima donnas of physics, bring into play gigantic patterns of formal mathematical manipulation, constructing schemas of relation which have no direct bearing upon the physical meaning of the models constructed—although with some effort, any symbolic relation can be given both a physical and a psychological meaning. For example, the electro-magnetic field is so vaguely defined that most students of physics take a long time before they realize that the formal definitions of electric and magnetic field densities and intensities actually refer to a material process of photon interaction through space.

---

dialectic analysis of the variables present—in which relativity and quantum mechanics appear directly out of the nature of charge-field interaction. See the *Science News Letter* (Spring, 1970), published by Fairleigh Dickinson University at Teaneck, New Jersey.

Relativity, abstractly developed, in turn has caused quantum mechanics to appear as an even more abstract formalism of interaction. By not seeing (indirectly through DeBroglie or directly through J.J. Thompson) how quantum mechanics follows naturally from an electro-magnetic relativity, standard quantum mechanics is presented in terms of a mysterious "Psi"-wave function. This function is a "probability wave" which is taken to be a generalized and abstract mathematical relation in space and time. In reality, the Psi-wave function is a concrete manifestation of the electro-magnetic field in resonance with its own source charges, producing a nonlinear dispersive equation for electro-magnetic wave-length and frequency which—upon analysis—gives rise to the standard forms of quantum wave mechanics.

Not only is it possible to derive relativity and quantum mechanics from electro-magnetism, but the physical model used is a direct expression of the dialectics of the electronic level of matter in motion. The fundamental model postulates a structure consisting of a "charge-field coupling" state in which the electro-magnetic field as wave-radiation is coupled with a charge or particle localization of the field, producing a particle-wave or charge-field self-interaction structure purely in terms of electro-magnetic variables. The model itself progresses in a dialectic of three stages. In stage one, any charge initially appears as a simple particle with "attached" induction fields. These induction fields act as the direct extension of the charges into space and have no autonomy from the charges. Here, the classical electric and magnetic force equations between charges and their induction fields can be defined. Stage two analyzes the properties of these electric and magnetic induction fields, and discovers that their interrelation in "free space" causes them to be continually re-induced as a wave-phenomena traveling at the speed of light c. (We now enter the stage of Maxwell's equations and relativity.) These so-called induction fields, previously thought to be mere extensions of the charges into space, can actually exist in space as free wave-radiation, i.e., as an autonomous radiation field possessing momentum and energy. Furthermore, a calculation of the energy and momentum changes undergone by light absorption and emission by charges leads directly to the relativistic expressions for energy and momentum without introducing a space-time transformation geometry. However, the space-time kinematics of the electro-magnetic field, when looked at from the invariance of Maxwell's equations, do give rise to relativistic space-time transformations of electro-magnetic space based upon the constancy of the "medium" parameters, which in turn means the constancy of the velocity of light c. This invariance, however, from our perspective merely means that the speed of any specific quantity of energy of the electro-magnetic radiation field must always have a constant value relative to the induction field attached to a sending or receiving charged particle. From this, one can calculate wave-length and frequency changes or transformations. One can interpret these as length and time changes but not necessarily as generalized changes in "space and time" as if they were self-sustaining "things" or "relations" instead of expressing interaction properties of events and event-complexes called objects.

We now have a contradiction between stage one and stage two. In stage one, the field appears as an actual dependent extension of the charged particle into space (an induction field), while in stage two, the field also appears as an autonomous wave-field independent of the particle (a radiation field). The only way out of this contradiction is to realize that a charge and its radiating field, or particle and wave, must be redifined in terms of each other as two sides of a singular paradoxical phenomenon. Thus, a charged particle sets up a field which is at once both dependent and independent of the charge. The field exists in an interdependent state of mutual coupling with the charge in a state of inseparable distinction. Thus, in stage three, particle and field once more appear "connected," but not in the simple fashion initially found in stage one. Now, by dialectical necessity, the distinctness between the field and the particle, discovered in stage two as an existential condition of field objectification (autonomy) in conjunction with their inseparability as a singular state or "essence" as formulated in stage one, makes each in reality an explicit function of the other. Consequently, the charged particle appears redefined in terms of the autonomous wave-field it sets up, and becomes a "group" wave-effect. On the other hand, the wave-field set up by such a particle, in turn is a function of the particle-localization of the wave into a self-contained topology. Thus, any wave radiation coming from such a quantized and localized wave state will display itself in the form of quantized "photons" of radiation. By using Maxwell's equations for wave-radiation in free space, and investigating the way in which such a wave-radiation interacts with the source-particle setting up this wave-radiation, the source particle in turn being but a localizaton effect of these waves, will give rise to a dispersive wave equation $w^2 - c^2 k = w_o^2$. When this is combined with a similar parallel equation for energy and momentum obtained from analyzing the way in which electro-magnetic energy and momentum changes, $E^2 - c^2 p^2 = E_o^2$, one can obtain the two fundamental DeBroglie relations of quantum mechanics, $E = Hw$ and $p = Hk$, where Planck's constant is obtained as a constant ration between rest-frequency and rest mass, $H = (m_o/w_o)c^2$, which has to be the same constant for all charge systems capable of being mutually coupled together by means of common electro-magnetic field interaction. Quantum mechanical relations as presently formulated (in either the standard way, or the approach used here), are applicable only to those systems whose energy is electro-magnetic field energy (energy in the form of $E = mc^2$). These relations also express the way in which this energy behaves when it is in a state of interaction between itself as localized particle energy and itself as nonlocalized field energy.

We have now set up a particular model or theory of electro-magnetic dynamics according to a dialectical structure of nonlinear self-interaction. This theory expresses the relation between a charge and its field as also a relation within or relative to each, and as a result obtains a reformulation of relativity and quantum mechanics. Such a formulation has definite physical consequences which can be subjected to experimental verification or invalidation. For example, the electro-magnetic model for relativity and quantum mechanics makes certain claims as to the structure and topology of charges, and to a certain relation between three important constants: the electron charge e, the velocity of light c, and Planck's constant h (or H), and their interrelation into the fine-structure contant—which must be worked out in greater detail and then submitted as a theory capable of being tested.

Summarizing the essential physics of this model, one can say that pure particle mechanics (with static field conditions) would be Newtonian classical physics; pure electro-magnetic field-wave mechanics (with particle boundary conditions) would be relativistic classical physics, and both are examples of linear dynamics. It is only when quantum mechanics is explicitly developed as a field-particle self-interaction process that a genuine nonlinear nonclassical physics arises in which pure Newtonian particle physics and relativistic wave propagation at the speed of light become special sub-cases. Then, and only then, is quantum mechanics not simply another theory imposed axiomatically upon particle and field relations, but rather the very expression of the mutual dialectic between particle and field capable of being idealized as a universal syntactics, always open to reevaluation.

Thus, the dialectics of nature is a theory and philosophy of consciousness, based upon an explicit phenomenology of subject-objectivity. However, the dialectics of nature is also a praxis and history of consciousness. It is a meta-science praxis which can be utilized concretely as a working model for the analysis of theoretical structures as they appear in the particular sciences—a model which can be subjected to the history of consciousness and through that history continually become redefined and reformulated. If this is done, the history of consciousness will itself become a more explicit function of the dialectical philosophy that is emerging from it, as a result of the concrete dialectical praxis set into motion. Thus, philosophy becomes historical and history in turn philosophical. A revolution in the sciences is necessary before this can happen, which in turn means that the culture of man and the entire social dynamics must become radicalized. The purpose of this paper has been to show what such a revolution means for the sciences within that culture. Hopefully, it can also be a small part of that revolution.

Marxism and Utopia: Ernst Bloch

David Gross

The question of consciousness is crucial to the problem of revolution. Naturally, this question cuts both ways. On the one hand, the revolutionary forces of the world are attempting to create or induce the objective conditions which make revolution possible. In doing this, they must focus on consciousness: how to move people to revolution once the objective conditions exist, or simply how to make them *aware* that such conditions exist and that those conditions imply a need for transformative action, for revolutionary praxis.

On the other hand, the ruling classes (i.e., the present-day defenders of world capitalism) are also preoccupied with the issue of revolution, but from the opposite point of view. They want to know how to suppress it, how to prevent revolutionary conditions from emerging. This leads them to the problem of consciousness as well, but it is false consciousness with which they are primarily concerned. They want to know how to keep people unaware of the real conditions of their daily lives.

The writings of Ernst Bloch relate in a general way to both these questions: revolution and consciousness. This is not particularly unusual, since the entire European Left in the twentieth century has had to confront these issues to one degree or another. What makes Bloch unique, however, is the *way* he confronts them, the *way* he deals with the problems they pose. No other modern writer, Marxist or not, set up a framework of explanation as elaborate and insightful—and at the same time as novel and *unlike* all others—as Ernst Bloch. This is partly because he managed to synthesize a number of intellectual traditions previously considered too disparate to be joined. But just as (in Lenin's words) Marx fused the three strains of French socialism, English economics, and German philosophy, so Bloch can be seen as bringing together (holistically, not as a *bricoleur*) such diverse currents as Jewish mysticism, "Left" Aristotelianism, German idealist philosophy, Romanticism, utopian socialism, and Marxism. Obviously, this makes Bloch hard to cope with, let alone to interpret. He cannot easily be pigeonholed or dealt with as a "type," which may explain to some extent why there has been a great deal of criticism, if not downright opposition, to his thought in both East and West Germany. After all, if it is order and stereotypical simplicity that is desired, how does one grapple with a man who speaks with equal facility and authority on the Cabbala, Joachim di Fiore, the history of music, townplanning, Schelling's nature philosophy, Homeric heroes, the Riemannian concept of space, the circus, the Faust legend, Hegel's *Phenomenology*, Thomas Münzer's radical Christianity, the evolution of utopian thought, and Marx's *Theses on Feuerbach*?

This essay will attempt to come to terms with only one aspect of Bloch's thought: his "utopian Marxism."

At first glance, this term may seem strange and contradictory. According to Bloch's Stalinist critics in East Germany, it is impossible to be a Marxist and an utopian at the same time. Historically, Marxism transcended utopianism. The pre-capitalistic "spirit of utopia" belongs to an "earlier stage of development," and as such is incompatable with scientific socialism. From this viewpoint, any flirtation with utopian modes of thought has to be labelled romantic, reactionary, bourgeois, and, of course, anti-Marxist.[1]

Bloch sees things differently. It is true, Marxism has surpassed utopianism, but in dialectical terms it has also taken up and preserved the living elements of utopianism, and these must be animated if Marxism is not to become frozen or doctrinaire. The orthodox communist intellectuals of the DDR saw utopianism as having been "cancelled out," but in looking only at the negative side they forgot that it was also "incorporated" (*aufgehoben*), to use Marx and Hegel's term. Bloch does not want to *return* to utopian modes of thought, as his accusers have inferred; he merely wants a *reactivation* of those utopian elements which are still alive (even if dormant) within the Marxian tradition. "There has been," Bloch writes, "a somewhat too great progress of socialism from utopia to science, with the result that not only the clouds of utopia but also its pillar of flames have been liquidated." The consequence of this is by now familiar: a gradual "undernourishment of revolutionary fantasy and a convenient schematic-practical narrowing of the totality."[2] The solution, in Bloch's view, is a rejuvenation of utopian strains *inside* the framework of Marxisn; and his vision of what this would imply is best described as "utopian Marxism."

In many ways, Bloch's philosophy is almost a "vision" in the religious sense of the word. It is often hard to perceive the radical content of his thought due to the kind of mystical, even transcendental aura with which Bloch envelops some of his most important ideas. Before discussing his Marxism, it is helpful first to touch on two other matters which should put Bloch's thought in perspective and perhaps make it more understandable. These are the role of philosophy (including Bloch's) in contemporary Marxian theory and the concept of the "not-yet" (*Noch-Nicht*), which is fundamental to Bloch's whole worldview. The first is useful in situating Bloch in relation to other Marxists, and the second points up the importance of perhaps his most pivotal concept. Both together should clarify the meaning of Bloch's utopian Marxism.

From Marx's viewpoint, Hegel both summed up and brought to an end the entire Western philosophical tradition. After Hegel, philosophy could go no further since its subject matter—reality—had already been "explained," at least theoretically. Not only the "truth" of the non-philosophical world (e.g., religion), but also the whole philosophical spirit of the past, had been assimilated and synthesized. After Hegel, according to Marx, the point was no longer to interpret reality, but to *change* it. Philosophy had to pass into action, and pure theory into concrete praxis. As Marcuse puts it, paraphrasing Marx: "Philosophy reaches its end when it has formulated its view of a world in which reason is realized. If at that point reality contains the conditions necessary to materialize reason in fact, thought can cease to

1. See Rugard Otto Gropp, ed., *Ernst Blochs Revision des Marxismus* (East Berlin, 1957). Particularly critical are the essays by Gropp himself (Bloch's former pupil), R. Schulz, and W. Schubardt.

2. Ernst Bloch, *Das Prinzip Hoffnung* (Frankfurt am Main, 1969), Vol. II, p. 726.

concern itself with the ideal. The truth now would require actual historical practice to fulfill it.... Critical thinking does not cease, but assumes a new form. The efforts of reason devolve upon social theory and social practice."[3]

In the same way that Marx incorporated and superseded Hegel, it might be said that Lenin incorporated and superseded Marx. Lenin appears at first sight to represent a total, thoroughgoing, and practical implementation of Marxian theory. For him, the essential correctness of Marx's social analysis is not disputed; the only question asked is how to actualize, in revolutionary practice, the notions *already arrived at* in the corpus of Marx's work. In other words, everything, including philosophy, seems to be reduced to a *practical issue* because there is nothing that remains to be done with Marx's thought except to transform it into strategy and tactics.[4] It appears to follow, then, that a "Marxist philosopher" after Lenin is a contradiction in terms, since the vocation of philosophy is at best obsolete and at worst counterrevolutionary. The role of the philosopher seems to wither away, since the need for theory is entirely replaced by the need for practice. By this kind of logic, the Left-Wing species of *homo philosophicus* should be completely extinct by now.

But this has not happened. Since 1917, there has been a proliferation of Marxist philosophers none of whom feel embarassed about being Marxists *and* philosophers at the same time.[5] Does this mean that they have sold out the revolution and opted for a return to thought? Under the guise of being revolutionary thinkers, have they become only thinkers *about* revolution? Have they reverted to the bourgeois, contemplative attitude towards the world when they should become men of undiluted praxis?

The answer to each of these questions must be "no," and the reason has nothing to do with Kantian arguments about the perennial value of philosophy. It has to do, rather, with arguments found in Marx himself—arguments which justify the *practice* of philosophy even in an age as revolutionary as ours. In this context it should be enough to mention just two of these arguments.

Marx once noted that no society fully passes away until all the problems it has raised have been solved. Applied to philosophy, the same point can be made: bourgeois philosophy cannot be wholly transcended until the wealth of ideas and issues it has thrown up (and made "problematic") have been thought through to completion. Bourgeois thought, particularly German classical idealism, *was* at one time a revolutionary philosophy. It opened up

---

3. Herbert Marcuse, *Reason and Revolution: Hegel and the Rise of Social Theory* (Boston, 1964), p. 28.

4. This, of course, is a far too mechanistic view of Lenin, which Paul Piccone (for one) has done much to dispel. Nevertheless, it is true that Lenin often reverted to philosophy only to settle specific organizational questions or invalidate "heretical" tendencies which diverged from his own views (such as, for example, his writing of *Materialism and Empirio-Criticism* to discredit Bogdanov and his group and expel them from the party). See Paul Piccone, "Towards an Understanding of Lenin's Philosophy," *Radical America*, Vol. IV, No. 6, pp. 9 ff.

5. Examples: Georg Lukács, Ernst Bloch, Jean-Paul Sartre, Maurice Merleau-Ponty, Henri Lefebvre, Adam Schaff, Antonio Gramsci, Leszek Kolakowski, Karel Kosik, Enzo Paci, Herbert Marcuse, Max Horkheimer, Theodor Adorno, Pier Aldo Rovatti, Louis Althusser, Galvano Della Volpe, among others.

discussion on topics such as freedom, equality and brotherhood which had never before been seriously broached. However, because of the limited and circumscribed way it handled such topics (partly due to its class perspective which prevented it from going too far), it could not deal adequately with these problems without undermining the foundation of its own existence. Consequently, some of the most important *implications* of these ideas were not—*and could not be*—drawn within the confines of bourgeois thought. There is nothing wrong with a Marxist philosopher returning to, and reformulating, these same questions—this time solving them within a Marxian framework.

Sometimes the solution will necessarily mean action, since there are intellectual problems which can be decided only by *acting them out*. Other problems, however, may need more mental labor so that "acting them out" does not lead to disaster. In such cases, philosophy is not only desirable but necessary. The question of a "cop-out" is not even at issue, since the rethinking of old themes is a prolegomena to gaining a firm grasp on what these concepts could mean in reality. Bloch, for example, does not need to be criticized for taking a second look at notions like "freedom" or "individualism" this time through Marxian spectacles. Nor was Gramsci wrong in reassessing the "state-civil society" motif and the task of the intellectual (pushing both in directions Hegel would never have foreseen). This is the way to clear a path towards the future. Just as Marx believed that the working classes "have no ideals to realize [except] to set free the elements of the new society with which the old collapsing bourgeois society itself is pregnant,"[6] so too, philosophy may have no ideals to realize *except* the very important one of bringing to fruition the undeveloped elements within bourgeois thought so they can be reconstituted in actual praxis. Obviously this is no small order!

A second argument in defense of philosophy can be found in Marx. It has to do with the notion (best expressed in "Toward a Critique of Hegel's Philosophy of Right") that philosophy cannot be realized until it is abolished, and cannot be abolished until it is realized. The first part of this statement has already been dealt with: philosophy cannot be made real until it outgrows the fetters of pure theory. Thus, it must be developed in such a fashion that it prepares the way for its self-overcoming. To "think through" the problems of philosophy so as to make them obsolete (i.e., to apprehend them from the viewpoint of radical praxis), is, in effect, to transcend philosophy and turn it towards practical activity. To a large extent this "completion" of philosophy—and therefore its abolition—is still a philosophical task. Abstract thought must *supersede itself* and bring about its own self-immolation before it can reappear as *realized philosophy*.

However, the second part of the statement—that philosophy cannot be abolished until it is realized—is crucially important. Today, philosophy is

---

6. Marx, *The Civil War in France*; cited in Shlomo Avineri, *The Social and Political Thought of Karl Marx* (London, 1969), p. 221, note 1. Ernst Bloch has always held the classical achievements of bourgeois thought in high esteem. He frequently talks about salvaging the "dialectically useable heritage" of the bourgeois world, i.e., *actually implementing* the abstract formulae of natural rights, democratic theory, human equality, and eternal peace. See Ernst Bloch, *Naturrecht und menschliche Würde* (Frankfurt am Main, 1961), pp. 151-259.

nowhere realized, and therefore by Marx's own terms it cannot pass away. Philosophy is nowhere realized because there is no society in which philosophy has "gripped the masses" (Marx) or where the truths of philosophy (rationality, freedom, etc.) have been embodied in concrete social relations. Furthermore, human alienation still exists everywhere on earth; and there can be no actualization of philosophy so long as man has not become one with himself and his surroundings. Thus, there remains an opposition between the world of philosophy and the non-philosophical world—that is, between abstract reason and the irrational reality of everyday life. Until this dichotomy is resolved, philosophy will continue to be needed. And yet, ironically, one of its chief goals must be to aid in bringing about its own disappearance as abstract thought. Philosophy's task, in other words, is to try to bring the world into harmony with itself. Its imperative is to make the world philosophical by liberating it from "non-philosophy." Thus, since the modern world persists in an "unphilosophical condition," it still needs philosophy to "enter into tension" with it, to analye it, and eventually to prepare the way for its supersession.[7] Once again, this is no small order.

All this is to suggest that the abandonment of philosophy is premature, even for a Marxist writing a half-century after Lenin. An epoch may have to be grasped in its totality in thought before it can be transformed in its totality in social practice. The modern world has not yet been transformed in reality, perhaps partly because it has not been adequately comprehended in its totality even in thought. Hegel summarized, in abstract philosophy, the bourgeois world of 1800; Marx summarized, in critical social theory, the capitalist world of 1850; but the complex age of the twentieth century still needs its synthesizers.

What form such a synthesis will take cannot be predicted, but one thing is certain: it cannot be a return to pre-Marxian categories or a "going beyond" to post-Marxian terms of analysis. Marxism, as Sartre has pointed out, *is* the "philosophy of our time," the truth of the modern age, its "regulative Idea." "There is no going beyond [Marx] so long as man has not gone beyond the historical moment which [Marx expresses]."[8] This "historical moment," even though it was first described in the middle of the last century, is still *our* moment—though perhaps it is now *felt* and *perceived* differently. Nonetheless, Marx's historical moment remains ours so long as capitalism and its accompanying alienation remain the fundamental realities of the contemporary period. Marxism, as the reverse side of these realities, points out and criticizes them. It holds up a mirror to things as they are and "explains to the world its own acts." As Marx put it most succinctly: "We merely show the world why it actually struggles; and the awareness of this is something the world *must* acquire even if it does not want to."[9]

---

7. L. Easton and K. Guddat, eds. and trans., *Writings of the Young Marx on Philosophy and Society* (New York, 1967), pp. 60-64, 255-258.

8. Jean-Paul Sartre, *Search for a Method*, trans. Hazel Barnes (New York, 1968), p. xxxiv, p. 7.

9. Easton and Guddat, *op.cit.*, p. 214.

Bloch is a Marxist with a decidedly Hegelian bent to his thinking. [10] Moreover, he is a philosopher, and would strongly defend the role of philosophy in the present age. But when it comes to defining that role—i.e., the new form and content philosophy *must have* in a revolutionary period when traditional approaches to philosophy have been overturned by events— Bloch takes a different road from that of most Marxist philosophers. Some Marxists say that philosophy in our time must, of necessity, become *social philosophy* rather than metaphysics. According to this view, philosophy can justify itself only by becoming the theoretical expression of this age of upheavals—not as an abstract formulation of purely intellectual, cognitive problems. Others, taking a somewhat different tack, argue that philosophy in the contemporary period must be that mode of thought which explains and clarifies praxis. From this perspective, there is no philosophy except that which, dialectically speaking, is the other, "reflective" side of practice: *practice aware of its own activity.* In this sense, philosophy is a "moment" within a continuing process of revolutionary praxis—a "mediation" between the problems posed by the world and their successful overcoming in action. Lastly, other Marxist philosophers say that philosophy in the modern world can legitimately be the self-consciousness of only one class: the proletariat. Only the "representations" of the proletariat can be truly philosophical in this epoch, because only the proletariat (as the universal class) can perceive and express the totality of the contemporary period. To many Marxists, this also means that proletarian thought (philosophy)—to the extent that it grasps the whole of the present—is simultaneously the de facto "negation of reality," since the acts of knowing and of transcending are one and the same. [11]

Bloch, *while not repudiating any of the above*, suggests an entirely different role for philosophy. According to him, philosophy should attempt to comprehend and express the future rather than the present, i.e., those things which are not yet materialized rather than those which are. "The presence which is usually called reality," Bloch writes, "is surrounded by a tremendously greater ocean of objectively real possibility."[12] It is the task of philosophy to explore this region of unrealized possibility which lies just beyond the horizon. Its role is to be the "light that shines out ahead of this world." For Bloch this means that philosophy has to focus not so much on what was or is, but rather on what exists as pure potentiality at the threshold of the future.

For Bloch, then, Marxist philosophy has not gone far enough. There is nothing inherently wrong with it becoming social philosophy, or the analytical-critical side of praxis, or even the theoretical expression of the working

---

10. Despite some significant differences with Hegel, there is a profound Hegelian accent in much of Bloch's thought. See Bloch, *Subjekt-Objekt: Erläuterungen zu Hegel* (Frankfurt am Main, 1951) and his *Philosophische Aufsätze zur objektiven Phantasie* (Frankfurt am Main, 1969). The section on Bloch and Lukács in Iring Fetscher, *Karl Marx und die Marxismus* (Munich, 1967), is also interesting.

11. These ideas on the role of philosophy can be found in Lefèbvre, Sartre, and Lukács, among others.

12. Bloch, "Man as a Possibility," *Cross-Currents*, Vol. XVII, No. 3 (Summer, 1968), p. 281.

class, *provided that* none of these roles (or even all of them together) is considered sufficient. The most crucial task of philosophy overshoots all these: philosophy should become an "anticipatory consciousness," an intention pointing ahead. Philosophy justifies itself best when it turns its attention toward the *plus ultra*, the ultimate and yet unrealized possibilities of life, rather than when it immerses itself in the contingent and still incomplete world of today. This notion, Bloch claims, does not represent a return to idealism or mysticism; on the contrary, it is entirely consistent with the spirit of Marx (who, Bloch feels, always stood for vision and projection, without which there would remain only a stale, flat economism). "Marxist philosophy," Bloch writes in *Das Prinzip Hoffnung,* "[is] that which ultimately relates itself adequately to Becoming and to what is still approaching.... Marxist philosophy is that of the future."[13] From this premise, Bloch asks that the tasks of philosophy be reassessed. The philosopher's vocation, he suggests, is to probe all that is not yet fully manifest but which lies half-concealed at the margin of the present. In a more poetic mood, he expresses it this way: philosophizing means "building into the blue that lines the edges of the world" and dealing with all "that-which-is-not-yet, that which is drifting and dreaming in the darkness of life, in the factual blue of the objects and ... as content of the deepest hope and awe."[14]

Even if one grants for the moment the attractiveness of these ideas, a legitimate question still needs to be raised: precisely what is it in the future that philosophy is supposed to perceive and explicate? In answering this, Bloch introduces the concept of the "not-yet," which becomes one of the central categories of his thought. For him, the mission of philosophy is to comprehend the objective content which lies in the space between the incomplete present and the unachieved future *and* to help bring the future into existence. In this way, Bloch has given the philosopher a unique task: to interpret the (as yet unrealized) world *as well as* to change it.

The "not-yet" is the *really possible* which has still not come about. It is all that which is fully present in the forward edge of the future but which remains unestablished in the actual world of the present. In a word, the "not-yet" is potentiality: the uncongealed and only partially known reality which lies waiting in the "red dawn" of daybreak. It is everything "still pending in the world-process."

Bloch sometimes subdivides the category of the "not-yet" into three parts. There is first of all the "not-yet-conscious," which is man's still unclear and undefined awareness of what he really wants. In the state of not-yet-consciousness, man remains uncognizant of what is actually present to him. He may feel hope or unspecified longing, but he has no real understanding of the origin or content of these feelings. He may vaguely experience the yearning that is at the root of existence, and still not know

---

13. Bloch, *Das Prinzip Hoffnung,* Vol. I, p. 8.
14. Bloch, *Geist der Utopie* (Frankfurt am Main, 1964), pp. 309, 345. This part of *Geist der Utopie* is included in Ernst Bloch, *Man on his Own,* trans. E.B. Ashton (New York, 1970), pp. 43, 71.

exactly what he yearns for. [15]

Secondly, there is "not-yet-being": that which, objectively speaking, has not achieved substantiality. For Bloch, there is an "ontic difference" between what man is now and what he could become. Specifically, man's true being is out ahead of him and still must be acquired. Marx tended to define man by his existing relationships; but, according to Bloch, this is not enough, since it misses the future dimension of man's becoming. Between man's current appearance and his "non-present essence" there is an apparently irreparable gulf. Man as he is can never be grasped unless his forward projection—his process of being *underway* toward his uncompleted being—is fully apprehended. In human terms, "man is still something that has to be discovered." [16] The same is true for matter and for the world at large. Both are in a similar state of "not-yet-being," since they are as unfinished as man and are equally involved in a struggle to unfold their potential (*Potenz*). Just as there is within existing man a *homo absconditus* (whose countenance has to be unveiled) within the present world of nature there is likewise a cosmic *incognito* which has yet to be uncovered. Like man, the outer world "seethes with dialectical fire" and strives to become what it is. In either case, everything that *merely* exists pushes towards a "not-yet-being" which lies at the open edge of the world process.

Lastly, the "not-yet" is occasionally described as "not-yet-become," that is, as the unrealized ideals of the past: projections which were held up as goals (or dreams) but never concretized. For Bloch, the past is virtually an "antiquarium" of unachieved becoming; consequently, it is legitimate for philosophy to glance backward to discover the future *in* the past ("all that which was always intended but never came to be"). [17] The highest aspirations of former times are not dead weight pressing on the consciousness of the living. Rather, they are reference points towards "what has not yet come to be," and ultimately towards the *still underived derivation* of all that happens." [18] Thus, the ideals of the past need to be continuously called to mind and preserved, for they say a great deal about what man wants—about the "essence" he is trying to uncover in and for himself. [19]

---

15. The "Not-Yet-Conscious" is the opposite of Freud's "No-Longer-Conscious." Freud's concept describes what has been forgotten or repressed whereas Bloch's term designates that which one has not completely apprehended. Marx captured something of Bloch's meaning in the *Deutsch-Französische Jahrbücher* when he wrote: "The world has long dreamed of something of which it only has to become conscious in order to possess it in actuality." *Writings of the Young Marx*, p. 214.

16. Bloch, *Spuren* (Frankfurt am Main, 1969), p. 32; *Das Prinzip Hoffnung*, Vol. III, p. 1520; and Jürgen Moltmann, *Religion, Revolution, and the Future*, trans. M. Douglas Meek (New York, 1969), p. 15.

17. Bloch, *Subjekt-Objekt*, p. 517; *Tübinger Einleitung in die Philosophie*, Vol. II (Frankfurt am Main, 1968), p. 165 (translated in *Man on His Own*, p. 83); and Martin Walzer, "Prophet mit Marx—und Engelszungen," in *Ueber Ernst Bloch* (Frankfurt am Main, 1968), p. 10.

18. Bloch, *Tübinger Einleitung*, Vol. II, p. 165; *Man on His Own*, p. 83.

19. Bloch is close to Marx here. In the *Deutsch-Französische Jahrbücher*, for example, Marx wrote: "There is not a big blank between the past and the future...but it is a matter of realizing the thoughts of the past." *Writings of the Young Marx*, p. 214.

So, for Bloch the task of philosophy is to probe into the "not-yet" in order to grasp its lineaments more clearly and, if possible, to help realize it. However, a problem exists here. The "not-yet" is nowhere actualized; it has no concrete substance. How, then, can one perceive it and draw out its implications? This difficulty would not present itself if the role of philosophy were to *reflect* existing social conditions or simply to express the "actuality of revolution" (Lukács). In either case, philosophy would take its starting point from the facticity of the real world rather than from what has not yet been established. However, if philosophy is commissioned to focus on what has still not arrived materially, how does it do so?

Bloch solves this problem by pointing out that the "not-yet" is *not* wholly and absolutely distinct from the world at hand. It *seems to be* when the insufficiency of the given is compared to the fullness of Being (the *totum*), of which we can now only dream. But in reality, the future is not irrevocably split from the present. It exists *in nuce* in the "now" as tendency, hope, and objective possibility. The "not-yet," therefore, also exists (or is at least prefigured) in the present, albeit as a pale illumination of the fullness of being yet to come. The philosopher need not concentrate on intangible future essences, but can focus on the traces and "anticipatory designs" of the future *within* the present. These "traces" Bloch calls the *novae* of history. The obligation of philosophy—and now not just any philosophy, but *Marxist* philosophy—is to ferret out the radical *novae* of history and help amplify their meaning (with the ultimate goal of "actualizing" them in time and through an historical dimension).

The *novum* (the new) is the real, though undeveloped, presence of the future in the given: an "epiphany," as it were, of a higher level of being into a lower. It is the intensively alive *existere* in everything. Sometimes this manifests itself obliquely in what Bloch calls the "darkness of the lived moment," but at other times it announces itself suddenly as a disruptive (and diremptive) element in the historical process. In religious terms, the incarnation of Christ would be one example of a *novum*: the introjection of the Absolute into history, where Christ represents the *inception* of a truth eventually to be realized in the "fullness of time." More importantly for Bloch, the proletariat is a *novum*, i.e., the breakthrough into social history of something radically new, something which prefigures the advent of a "new aeon." In "Towards a Critique of Hegel's Philosophy of Right," Marx wrote that the working class heralds *"the dissolution of the existing order of things."* The proletariat, he continued, "merely announces the *secret of its own existence* because it *is* the *real* dissolution of this order."[20] Lukács would perhaps argue from this premise that the proletariat, in the very concreteness of its existence, is the thorough embodiment of a revolutionary class. Bloch, on the other hand, would only argue that it is a revolutionary class *in embryo*: that it heralds, but does not yet effectively achieve, the dissolution of the existing order. For Bloch, it is the "secret" of the proletariat (its existence as a *novum*) that is truly radical, not merely its "at hand" occurence. Consequently, the revolutionary potential of the working

---

20. Marx, "Toward the Critique of Hegel's Philosophy of Law: Introduction," *ibid.*, p. 263.

class has to be *unfolded* rather than taken for granted. That implies *historical action* to convert the proletariat's "secret" into manifest truth.[21]

Implicit in Bloch is the imperative not merely to think but to act. Thought must tie itself to the radical *novae* of history, to those aspects of existence which announce the beginning of a new life. Marxist philosophers are needed both to discern the seeds of the future *and* to nurture them as best they can. Such men must attach themselves to a world in ferment—or, at least, to the fermenting possibilities *in* the world—and must try to establish what has not yet come to be. This means concrete praxis: "not only grasping a knowledge of things to come, but *willing them* and *carrying them out* against timid and short-sighted doubts" (italics added).[22] For Bloch, this activism was not an afterthought; it was an integral part of his work from the very beginning. As early as *Geist der Utopie* (1918), he wrote: "The categorical imperative must carry a gun wherever and for so long as power can be crushed by no other means."[23] And in one of his latest works, *Widerstand und Friede* (1968), Bloch still insists that thought demands action in order to fulfill it. The *vita activa*, he says, is actually within, and flows out of, the *vita contemplativa*.[24]

So knowledge must become practical and must work to spring men out of the rule of necessity. This means that philosophy is asked to unite with historical forces and tendencies to realize the latent potential within them. Quite obviously, this notion ties Bloch intimately to the theory-practice fusion of Marx, which asserts that one must not only know but *will* what one knows.[25] Bloch asks the philosopher to grasp the "not-yet" through the *novum* and then to become *engagé* in order to enlarge the sphere of the *novum* and to help ground it in the actual. As abstract as this sounds, it is a call to praxis. The purely speculative philosopher as an abstract form of alienated man is truly *passé*, according to Bloch. In the last analysis, thought justifies itself by eventually becoming "historical through and through" and by working to unfold what is objectively possible in reality. Marx thought this as well; thought needs to become concrete and practical to engender a better future out of a bad present.

Bloch's social and political thought—his "Utopian Marxism"—may now be more understandable when viewed against the background of his philosophy. Here, one finds the same attempt to introject a "not-yet" (Utopia) into a given, to fuse the dynamism of hope with a concrete, materialist orientation (Marxism), and to give the socialist movement a

---

21. The Russian Revolution was also a *novum* for Bloch, and this presented a number of ideological problems which he never solved adequately. On the one hand, Bloch felt the need to support it with "active hope" and to "keep faith" with this new beginning, on the other hand, he realized it was an incomplete revolution which deserved criticism for several reasons. Generally, Bloch was not as critical as he could have been, perhaps because he did not want to jeopardize the existence of this particular *novum*. Nonetheless, this in no way justifies his inexcusable obeisance to Stalinism even as late as the mid-1950s. See the unflattering account of Bloch's politics in Helmuth Butow, *Philosophie und Gesellschaft im Denken Ernst Blochs* (Berlin, 1965).

22. *Das Prinzip Hoffnung*, Vol. II, p. 511; *Man on His Own*, p. 204.

23. *Geist der Utopie*, p. 302; *Man on His Own*, p. 36.

24. Bloch, *Widerstand und Friede: Aufsätze zur Politik* (Frankfurt am Main, 1969), p. 110.

25. *Ibid.*, p. 57.

forward thrust into the future to prevent it from becoming a one-dimensional positivism. Bloch seems to enjoy combining and juxtaposing concepts which are full of dialectical tension. "Utopia" and "Marxism," for example, seem to be exactly opposing terms—one refers to what is "unreal," the other to an incisive analysis of the "real." Putting concepts like this together is certainly intentional and not simply a fondness for paradox. Bloch wants such concepts to interpenetrate and inform one another so that what is now called "utopian" can become more Marxist at the same time that Marxism becomes more utopian. Today, the problem of *das Ende* (the end, the ultimate goal, the future human community) still remains in Marxism, and the problem of the end has always been "the supreme utopian problem."[26] The radical longing, the "utopian intentionality" which still exists in capitalistic and socialistic societies, needs to be confronted by a Marxist methodology—but one which has reviewed itself at its beginnings and is alive again with forward projection.

Bloch considers himself not only a Marxist but a communist. At the same time, he feels there is something profoundly lacking both in Marxism as an "ideology" and in state communism as a reality. The trouble with "official" Marxism (i.e., with what Marx's thought *became* in the Second and Third Internationals) is that it turned into a narrow, impoverished dogma. It began erroneously to define man in a thoroughly deterministic way. Furthermore, it set up rigid economic laws which were said to operate outside of human volition, and it began to mistake mechanical empiricism for Marx's concrete analysis of society. The result was what Bloch calls "an excessive deprecation of the individual man" and "the idea that the world process proceeds without us and drags us on ... whether we want it or not."[27] Thus, "official" Marxism seems to stand not for the freedom of the individual *in* society, but for a new bondage of the individual *to* society. It was easy for bureaucracy, hierarchy, and statism to arise in the framework of this Marxian socialism. Similarly, it was easy for the dictatorship of the proletariat to be misunderstood as the rule of bureaucrats (*apparatchiki*) and party functionaries and for economism and opportunism to prevail wherever socialism established itself.[28] In a word, the *goals* of Marxism have begun to recede, and utopian energy has dried up to the extent that the movement has become everything and in the end nothing (E. Bernstein). Bloch was aware of this danger. "We have," Bloch writes, "no genuine socialist idea ... no scope, no vista, no ends, no inner threshold to sense and to cross, no cross and no conscience that would gather what is."[29] Marxism has become, in Bloch's opinion, too much a closed system, and in the process it has lost its inner strength (not, however, its autochthonous, irreducible "truth").

For the same reason, the practice of communist regimes is unsatisfactory to Bloch. Too often communist states represent a deathly "totality from above"; or, just as bad, they emphasize a "thoroughly organized production

---

26. *Das Prinzip Hoffnung*, Vol. III, p. 1412; *Man on His Own*, p. 160.
27. "Man as a Possibility," p. 280.
28. See Fritz Vilmar's interview with Bloch in *Ueber Ernst Bloch*, pp. 89 ff; also Bloch's *Widerstand und Friede*, pp. 66-67.
29. *Geist der Utopie*, p. 308; *Man on His Own*, p. 42.

budget" without the humanization of life that should be implied.[30] Thus, communist societies are hardly an improvement over capitalist ones. "Under neo-capitalism the old servitudes are only upholstered and painted over, whereas under state communism they are only congealed and renamed; but ... in neither case are they disposed of."[31] Bloch insists that the real content of man's longing shoots beyond *all* economic solutions: man wants freedom and spiritual wholeness, the "essence" which still eludes him. No redefinition of human needs in purely material terms will suffice for long. Men do not want things so much as they want community and a sense of being at home with themselves and their world.

What is to be done, then, given the residual heritage of "vulgar" Marxism and communism? Bloch's answer is two-fold: first, return to the *Geist* of Marx himself, to the rebellious disposition and revolutionary intention of the founder; second, re-infuse utopianism into the Marxist tradition, thus reviving attitudes prematurely abandoned since Marx.

The call for a recrudescence of the "spirit" of Marx is not unique with Bloch. The idea of renewal—of return to the original vision—has often been offered as a solution to ossification. However, the idea of injecting utopian overtones back into Marxism is something others have not called for, perhaps because it seems bizarre to ask for the revival of an outlook as seemingly out of step with the times as utopianism. In Bloch's view, however, utopianism, up to the nineteenth century, was the most radical and heretical (though unsystematic) tradition in the West. It was brought to an end only by Marx's naturalistic and scientific approach. Unwittingly, Marx foreclosed a long, rich tradition. He did so too quickly, however; for in negating the utopian fantasy of his predecessors, he paved the way for the unimaginative realism of his followers. The old dreams, the religiously construed teleologies, were done away with, but nothing replaced them except an overemphasis on productive forces and economic relations. According to Bloch, Marx should have sifted through and inherited the "utopian superiority" of his forerunners instead of abandoning it as obsolete.[32] Consequently, Bloch argues for a reassessment of the social constructions "stopped short" or "cut back too severely" by Marxism. The need is for a new look at "utopianism" as a tendency which remains latent (because inadequately transcended and preserved) within Marxism itself.

To revive the issue of utopia is to awaken in Marxism qualities it now seems to lack: explosive vision, frontal expectation, radical hope, and openness toward the "not-yet." As Bloch sees it, Marx himself possessed all these qualities; he incorporated in a single world view both enthusiasm and sobriety, consciousness of the goal and strict analysis of the given. After him, however, "Marxists" have not been able to combine these two extremes. Most have inclined towards what Bloch calls the "cold stream," i.e., blind empiricism, positivism, and *Produktionsvernunft*. Bloch wants to resurrect the opposite: the "warm stream" of passion, awareness of the end,

30. Bloch, *Ueber Karl Marx* (Frankfurt am Main, 1968), pp. 136-169, 176; and *Widerstand und Friede*, pp. 76-77.
31. *Tübinger Einleitung*, Vol. II, p. 178; *Man on His Own*, p. 91.
32. *Geist der Utopie*, pp. 301-307; *Man on His Own*, pp. 35-40.

eschatological hope, and even the "numinous element." These elements now lie *within* Marxism: the fire and the dream lie within. They need only be brought to the surface for dialectical tension to be restored.

If utopianism in general is the way to renewal, it must nevertheless be said that *not all* utopianism is good. Actually, Bloch's work contains two kinds of utopianism: abstract and concrete. Only the latter is considered genuinely utopian and at the same time compatible with a Marxist *Weltanschauung*.

"Abstract utopia" is usually thought of as the *only* kind of utopia. It is synonymous with the land of milk and honey, fairy-talk kingdoms, and mythical heavenly cities. All these are seen as imaginative projections and therefore as *merely* utopian, in the pejorative sense. The allegedly "real" and the strictly "utopian" are separated into opposing realms (and even the revolutionary possibilities *within the real* are disparaged as "utopian"). The abstract utopia is transposed to a far-off, impossible age. The Christian "Kingdom," More's "Utopia," Campanella's "Sun State," and Voltaire's "El Dorado" are ideal solutions, but they are also abstract in that they discuss *no way to get there.* There are no maps, no instructions, no *Fahrplanen* (as Bloch says) to help the traveller get from the "now" to the "not-yet." Abstract utopias, then, are hypostatized fragments of human longing, or speculative reifications of man's hope for a better life. As such, they only project an ahistorical "leap" from the concrete to the ideal, from the present closed epoch to a future "new aeon." The responsibility for world renovation usually lies with saviours, mythical heroes, or miracle-workers who somehow transform the imperfect present into a perfect "not-yet." Much can be learned about a society that indulges in utopian fantasies, but very little can be gleaned from abstract utopias about how to *actually achieve* what is merely imagined. [33]

However, with concrete utopias, this is not true. The ideal is not postulated outside or beyond history but is "immanently joined with its epoch" and made realizable through the extension of existing tendencies. Similarly, it is not a miracle that brings the "new day" but men acting historically in a definite direction. "Utopia must be created in time." It is an ideal which must *and can be* actualized within the dialectical process of history. [34] For Bloch, Marxism properly understood is the most complete expression of concrete utopianism. In fact, the two terms are nearly interchangeable in Bloch's vocabulary, provided that by "Marxism," the essential, rather than the vulgar variant is understood. Both Marxism and concrete utopianism begin from man-in-process: the man of continuous and expanding wants, needs and aspirations. Marxism, however, emphasizes the dissatisfaction that drives man—his "lacks" and alienation—whereas concrete utopianism

---

33. Abstract utopias do, however, have some redeeming qualities. They may not giv specific guidelines for social change, but generally they do (1) express a rejection of existence as presently constituted, (2) declare themselves against accommodation or adjustment to the status quo, (3) offer a standard for measuring the shortcomings of the powers that be, (4) develop the rudiments of a critical consciousness, and (5) provide a sustaining hope for those who are certain that a better world is possible. See *Das Prinzip Hoffnung*, pp. 556-558; and *Tübinger Einleitung*, Vol. I, pp. 124-131.

34. *Tübinger Einleitung*, Vol. II, p. 178; *Man on His Own*, p. 184.

stresses the positive element of hope that draws man toward the future. [35] Alienation pushes one to become *other than* what one is, whereas hope pushes one to become more of what one is not yet.

Marxism and concrete utopianism relate to existing ideals in the same way. The notion of an ultimate fulfillment, an identity between subject and object, or a final *utopia* is not new to Marx or Bloch. What is new, however, is the obligation to make these abstract concepts real and concrete—to actually execute what was previously only represented. Just as Marx talked about throwing away the chain of religion but plucking the living flower, so too Bloch (in his concrete utopianism) wants to realize, rather than to abolish or reject ideals so far only sketched. He wants to actualize still other possibilities not yet adequately thought through or even visualized. With both concrete utopianism and with Marxism, it is assumed that the only way to accomplish these ends is through the historical process. Utopia—the realm of freedom—can be achieved by men working consciously and "hopefully" within the material dialectic, according to existing tendencies. Similarly, Marxism and concrete utopianism emphasize the same intimate relationship between immediate and distant goals. Both believe that distant goals can only be achieved through intermediate ones: there is always only the next step, and the step after that. No short-range goal can be successfully dealt with unless the ultimate end is present *immanently within it.* "If the goals of a man fighting for higher wages do not include the disappearance of a society that compels him to fight for higher wages at all, he will not get far in his fight for wages either." [36] Thus, there must be a constant dialectical interplay between what one wants in the final analysis and what one needs to accomplish in the short run to get there. The immediate goal is the *condition sine qua non* of the distant goal (which merely develops what has already been prepared for it). Likewise, the distant goal inspires and infuses hope and direction into the limited goals of the present so that they do not become blind or opportunistic, living only for the day. This mutual interpenetration is extremely important for Marx and Bloch. If one works only for immediate ends without the *ultimum* implicit in them, one becomes an abstract utopian—at best a Don Quixote, at worst a tyrant who uses any means available to realize fantastic or illusory ends. Only by striving for the "not-yet" *in and through the novum* can a society without alienation eventually be built. Neither can "leap over the route to the ideal"; instead, each must "follow its stages without abandoning the ideal." [37]

Finally, both Marxism and concrete utopianism offer a road map to the future, not leaving it as Hegel did in the "chaff and wind, mist and haze." For Marx, the map is specific and unequivocal. The misery at hand on which abstract utopias usually thrive must be transformed into revolutionary class power. Moreover, the economy must be closely scrutinized to grasp the various radical possibilities offered in its fissures,

---

35. *Subjekt-Objekt*, p. 515.
36. *Das Prinzip Hoffnung*, Vol. III, p. 1510; *Man on His Own*, p. 203.
37. *Tübinger Einleitung*, Vol. II, p. 172; *Man on His Own*, p. 86. See also Bloch's *Widerstand und Friede*, pp. 93 ff.

rifts and contradictions.[38] For Marx, it is important to find in the husks of the old society what is immanent and converging toward the future; this means focusing on *subjective factors* (the proletariat becoming conscious of itself within the matrix of existing relations) as well as *objective factors* (the accumulation of surplus-value, monopolistic tendencies, the conflict between social production and private ownership). Once these relationships are perceived, one can begin to comprehend the process of history and to hasten and direct it by concentrated human praxis. Thus, Marx was interested not in detailing the features of a "future state" (as all utopian thinkers before Marx did), but in describing existing tendencies and making understandable the dialectics of history.[39] In other words, he sketches a timetable; he tells how to make a revolution; how to operate through and transform upheavals in production and exchange; and how eventually to set up the conditions for communism as an identity between man and man, and man and nature.

Concrete utopianism attempts precisely the same thing: to open an "effective sphere" within the present and to unite with real-objective possibilities to bring about the "not-yet" still pending in the world process. This means combining concrete utopianism with historical materialism. What is needed, Bloch says, is "the establishment of the utopian in the concrete openness of history and even of nature itself," which "involves concrete utopia in dialectical materialism." Utopia must become the *novum* within Marxism, and one-dimensional materialism must be converted into "dialectical *utopian* materialism."[40]

In sum, what was wrong with all utopias before Marx was that they provided no specific directions, no concrete method of realizing what they sketched abstractly. What has been wrong with Marxism up to the present (Marxism *after* Marx) is that it has lost its utopian fire. Bloch wants to bring the two together by reactivating the latent utopian tendencies in Marxism, that is, by making it *"utopian* Marxism." This does not mean that Marxism should become less critical or less analytical. On the contrary, utopianism makes it possible to see how much is lacking in the present (in comparison with what could be), and how much still needs to be criticized in capitalism and socialism. In Bloch's view, the "spirit of utopia" actually brings greater realism to Marxism because it points out how much more there is to reality than ordinarily meets the eye. To be "realistic" is to be more conscious of both the "not-yet" which surrounds the edges of the present and the *novae* already hidden in the darkness of the lived moment. Utopianism not only makes it possible to achieve a more comprehensive grasp of the totality, but it also opens the way towards changing the world —and changing it in the *right* direction.

What does Bloch contribute to the solution of the question of consciousness and the problems of revolution? In regard to revolution, it must be said that he contributes very little. It does not appear that a social revolution is appreciably closer anywhere in the world simply because Bloch

---

38. *Das Prinzip Hoffnung*, Vol. II, pp. 723-724.
39. *Ibid.*, pp. 723-729.
40. *Ueber Karl Marx*, p. 176.

has written a dozen volumes of philosophy.

But in regard to consciousness, it can be said that Bloch has offered a great deal. He has made it clear *how much* revolution entails and what scope and depth it must have to be a genuine transformation. To seize the Winter Palace is not to "make a revolution" but only to begin it. The ultimate end is to establish what has not yet appeared: a true "homeland" for man.

Bloch also makes it clear that the way to revolution can never be simply political but must also be social, cultural, personal and interpersonal. In the past, Marxism has not made this point as strongly as it should have. Too often, it has de-emphasized the importance of consciousness, will, intentionality (the "active engagement of hope") and culture. Thus, Bloch sees the need to complete and enrich Marx's critique of pure reason with a more thoroughgoing critique of practical reason.[41] The dialectic must be followed into every corner of life, even into the recesses of consciousness, and into what now appears as only the shadow of possibility.

Here philosophy has a role. It can help expand man's awareness of his world and draw him into greater understanding of what has not yet become. As a medium, philosophy is open-ended and accessible to the future and therefore remains a crucible of utopian vision. However, this is not enough. Philosophy must also merge with dialectical materialism so that its projections will be rooted in concrete reality. For Bloch, the *elements of vision and concreteness must become inseparable*, just as the twin poles of theory and practice must be fused into a working synthesis. In an age of upheaval like the twentieth century, Marxist philosophy cannot be merely a revolution in consciousness; it must also prepare the way for a conscious revolution. As Bloch put it, the transformation of philosophy must be replaced by a "philosophy of world transformation." "Philosophy is nothing if it is not dialectical and material ... and dialectical materialism is nothing if it is not philosophical, that is, a penetra[tion] into the great open horizons [of the future]. This penetration means theoretical-practical work against alienation ... the expression of the coming homeland where the kernel of man's essential unity with the world may finally begin to manifest itself."[42]

---

41. *Widerstand und Friede,* p. 73.
42. *Subjekt-Objekt,* p. 519.

Existentialism and Marxism

Dick Howard

Men make their own history; but history makes its own makers. Without men and women, history cannot exist; but conversely, humankind would not exist without history. This is not a vicious circle which can only be escaped by a genetic account of its origins (either a zoological evolution from ape to human being, or a socio-historical evolution from primitive society). Rather, it is the condition of the intelligibility of its terms: without the one, the other cannot be understood, and vice versa. More precisely, the intelligibility here is *dialectical*. It is not a circle whose locus is the concepts used by the mind to understand the world: there is no "neutral" investigator contemplating a process, but only situated subjects whose understanding of their world is an understanding of themselves, and whose self-understanding implies that of the world. Like the absolute observer situated outside space and time, the isolated subject (or object) is a myth of analytic or positivist reason: the illusion of atomism or bourgeois individualism.

Dialectical materialism is that mode of comprehension by which the two poles, the individual and the collective (society, history), can be grasped without losing the variegated quality of either. Collective phenomena—such as surplus-value, accumulation of capital, imperialism—are not taken as things-in-themselves to be studied empirically and quantitatively; they are understood in terms of the human, individual relations which are the condition of their possibility. By the same token, individuals with their successes, failures, joys and fears, are seen not as isolated atoms determining themselves for themselves but are understood within their historical milieu and the possibilities it presents. Neither the individual nor the collective can be given logical (or historical) priority; they are reciprocally product and producer, in continual interaction and modification. Dialectical materialism is a method, an hermeneutic by means of which this richness can be retained and understood.

Although the give-and-take of the individual and the collective is a fundament of dialectical thought, under certain historical conditions what was a critical and self-critical method is fixed as a one-sided manifestation, becoming an ideology. The "theory" of the determination of the superstructure by the infrastructure is a classic example of non-dialectical thought parading under the banner of dialectical materialism; and those who accepted this mechanistic model paid dearly, for example, for their belief that Nazism was only a superstructural modification of the rotting capitalist infrastructure. This is only one illustration of the petrification of the dialectic in our time. There are many others, for example, in literary criticism. "There is no doubt," writes Sartre, "that Valéry was a petit-bourgeois intellectual. But not every petit-bourgeois intellectual is Valéry" (44).[1] The dialectic is not reductive; it has to be able to take account of the

---

1. All quotations, unless otherwise noted, are from Jean-Paul Sartre, *Critique de la raison dialectique* (Paris, 1960). This volume includes a preliminary essay, "Questions de méthode,"

individual as well as the general relations, and do justice to both. The dialectic must be critical and self-critical, continually putting itself and its results into question and justifying its own methodological claims. Otherwise, it becomes an ideology which is opaque and therefore alienating to its users who, no matter how skillfully they manipulate it, are in fact manipulated by it: a thing which they do not understand but blindly use.

Sartre's *Critique de la raison dialectique* is a monumental and multi-faceted attempt to establish the grounds of the intelligibility of dialectical materialism. As the parallel with Kant's *Critique of Pure Reason* suggests, Sartre's goal is not merely external criticism but a critique which would demand and permit dialectical reason to reveal its *a priori* necessity and ground. Thus: "If something like a dialectical reason exists, it reveals and founds itself in and by human *praxis* to men who are situated in a given society at a certain moment of its development. Starting from that discovery it is necessary to establish the limits and the validity of dialectical evidence: the dialectic will be an efficacious method as long as it remains *necessary* as the law of the intelligibility and the rational structure of being. A materialist dialectic only has a sense if it establishes from the interior of human history the priority of material conditions as they are discovered and undergone by human *praxis*. In a word, if something like a dialectical materialism exists it must be an *historical* materialism, that is, a materialism from within [*du dedans*]: it is the same thing to make it and to undergo it, to live it and to know it. For this reason, if it exists this materialism can only be *true* within the limits of our social universe..." (129). What is striking first of all is the stress on the limits and validity of admissible evidence, on the necessity of the dialectic as a law of the intelligibility and rational structure of being, and on the limits of the method itself. Sartre's concern that "dialectical reason, if it is to be rationality, must furnish the reason of its own reasons" (127) and his rejection of any type of empirical proof in favor of the self-justification of the dialectic point to an *ontological* goal whose parallel with Kant's is expressed when, playing on the title of Kant's "Prolegomena to Any Future Metaphysics," Sartre speaks of his own task as a "Prolegomena to Any Future Anthropology" (153). Sartre's effort is theoretical, in the strictest and most fundamental sense. He never tires of stressing that despite his use of abundant historical examples, the goal of the *Critique* is to analyze the *formal* preconditions for an understanding of human history as intelligible and rational.

The best way to begin the analysis of Sartre's *Critique* is to look first at his understanding of the conditions of dialectical intelligibility and his criticism of some common errors of "Marxist" and bourgeois thought. In this context, it will be useful to recall some of the fundamental insights and problems of *Being and Nothingness* in order to make the transition to the specific theoretical structure of the *Critique*. Second, it will be necessary to sketch the fundamental categories of Sartre's social ontology as it moves

---

which is translated into English as *Search for a Method*. An English translation of the entire book is due to appear, published by New Left Books and translated by Stanley Pullberg. In this essay, all translations are my own.

from individual *praxis*[2] through the different social pluralities, finally reaching the level of concrete history, with which this first (and so far only)[3] volume of the *Critique* concludes. Finally, a consideration of some of the theoretical problems raised by this social ontology will permit an evaluation of the import of the book and the directions in which it points.

I.

Imagine that we are an armed guerilla band, pursued by the army and pursuing it. They know of our existence and, more or less, our numbers and equipment; and we know theirs, the structure of their supply-lines, the nature of the terrain, and so on. In deciding our immediate tactics (vis-à-vis the army, and omitting here our strategic goal which takes precedence: winning the people to our side, demonstrating that resistance is not only necessary but possible) we must think not only of the enemy's present deployment; we must also consider what the enemy thinks, what his plans are, how he may be trying to lure us into ambush, and the like. We will consider too what the enemy thinks we think he thinks, for he may have deployed his reserves in such a way as to make us think (or to think that he has made us think) that we can surprise him if we attack from a certain position; and so on. From the point of view of the enemy, the same reflection is taking place. Each of the "factual" moves made by either side is subject to interpretation: the "facts" alone are meaningless, and are significant only in terms of the project or goal for which we are striving.

What does it mean here to "know" what the enemy is doing? On what kind of rationality will our plans be based? Surely not on the deliverances of analytic or positivist reasoning, for which the "facts" have one and only one existence and meaning which is fixed and unchanging. Certainly not on a schematic "dialectic" which predicts changes from quantity to quality, negations of negations and the interpenetration of opposites, and which imposes these blindly and formally on any and all circumstances. To "know" here is what Sartre calls comprehension or dialectical intelligibility. The key is the homogeneous circularity between the actor and the acted-upon mutually affecting one another and comprehending one another in terms of their mutual goals in a way which cannot be given to the outside neutral observer. This interpenetration and mutual determination of both poles is what Hegel was talking about when he said that the notion that "substance is subject" is the key to his system.

The dialectic is not a listless march from one lifeless concept to another, nor is it the limitless enumeration of positive facticity where each temporal moment is said to put into question, to relativize—to *aufheben*—the preceding one: in both cases the dualism which the dialectic overcomes is preserved, for while there may be a process on the side of the world, on that

---

2. I italicize *praxis* throughout this text because Sartre does so, to set it off from the notion of practice, thus showing its ontological usage in the *Critique*.

3. In a recent interview with M. Contat and M. Rybalka (*Le Monde*, May 14, 1971), Sartre indicates that the promised second volume will not appear. This is not, he insists, for theoretical reasons, but simply because he "will not have time ... before [his] death."

of the subject there is only the *reception* and sorting out of the images received (as, for example, in the naive materialism of Lenin's *Materialism and Empirio-Criticism*). The active engagement of comprehension is replaced here by the contemplative attitude typical of traditional philosophy and reinforced today by the "society of the spectacle."[4] What the analytical and positivist modes of understanding have in common, and what separates them once and for all from the dialectic, is their conflation of the totality and the totalization which results from contemplative reason's inability to grasp movement and change and to understand itself as both part of and conditioned by the movement it seeks to know.

Two common "Marxist" misunderstandings illustrate this point: the theory of the "dialectics of nature" and the analytical and reductionist model of "economism" (i.e., the idea that the economic structure of society determines all the other structures, right down to that of the individual). In both these modes of analysis, the human project and human responsibility are sacrificed on the altar of structural scientificity. As opposed to this, Sartre insists that if, for example, the structure of exploitation is to have a dialectical rationality, it must be understood not simply as a result but as a result of a specific *praxis* of specific individuals. In the case of colonialism, for example, it is not just a question of identifying and labeling a certain sociological process; the labeling process not only reveals but conceals the specificity of the experience. "The lifeless movement of appearances that economic Reason can study is intelligible only in relation to the anti-dialectical system of over-exploitation. But this latter in its turn is not intelligible if one doesn't begin by seeing in it the product of human labor which forged it and which does not cease to control it" (683). In other words, the type of knowledge derived from this economistic model is vitiated by the "objectivist" fallacy: the subject is separated from the observed object, which itself is radically purged of any trace of human subjectivity (humanity). Human *praxis* and freedom have no role, and the analysis devolves into the world of a Manichean materialism.

The condition of dialectical intelligibility is the homogeneity, the reflexion, the self-recognition or interpenetration of the interacting poles. With everything human eliminated from the world, it is *a fortiori* impossible for that world to be intelligible; at best, it remains an object for the quantitative sciences, which deal with the exterior presentation of a totalization frozen into a totality. Sartre opposes such a reduction. "But if one had to reduce the relations of practical multiplicities to simple contradictory determinations which are produced, simultaneously or not, by the development of a process; if one had, for example, to consider that the proletariat is the future destroyer of the bourgeoisie by virtue of the simple fact that the progressive decrease of variable capital and the increase of fixed capital, by increasing the productivity of the worker and reducing the buying power of the working class as a whole, will produce, passing from crisis to crisis, the economic catastrophe from which the bourgeoisie will not

---

4. See Lukács, "Reification and the Consciousness of the Proletariat," in *Geschichte und Klassenbewusstsein* (Berlin, 1923), on the former point, and on the latter, Guy Debord, *The Society of the Spectacle* (Detroit, 1970).

escape, then one ultimately reduces man to the pure antidialectical moment of the practico-inert" (731). The danger is that the notion of intelligibility will be sacrificed before the quantitative altar of positive science; that the human will be lost and that the world will lose its significance. Positive science takes the anti-dialectic or practico-inert (i.e., the material and cultural world) as solely inert facticity with no depth and with only one meaning. In fact, however, "that antidialectic is intelligible only because we produce it ourselves.... In a word, if in human history the mode of production is the infrastructure of every society, it is because work is the infrastructure of the practico-inert (and of the mode of production)" (671).

The problem can be seen in the works of Marx and Engels. When, in *The German Ideology*, they explain the origins of alienation genetically, in terms of the evolution of the division of labor and the formation of social classes whose interrelations are determined by the growth of productive technology, they fall into a non-dialectical mode of thought whose conclusions are not self-intelligible. The genetic account given in *The German Ideology* was the result of what seemed to be the failure of the *1844 Manuscripts*, namely, the circular deduction of private property from alienated labor and of alienated labor from private property. In Sartre's eyes, the earlier analysis was in fact the correct one, based on a dialectical understanding of the interpenetration of the individual and the social. What does the genetic account really tell us? Does it give a satisfactory account of the interaction between human needs and the growth of production explaining how, for example, at a certain level of production needs are no longer pre-formed by the mode of production but, inversely, create new types of machines? Doesn't it instead make technology, the thing, into a kind of demiurge whose mechanical machinery determines mankind's fate? More importantly, if the division of labor is natural, as Marx and Engels claim, and if its extension will ultimately extend its negative effects to the point at which the negation will be negated, then we are faced with the problem of the *origin of negativity*.[5] The dialectic needs negativity, without which there is no movement, no project, no present stage to surpass—indeed, without which there is not even a human world. The genetic account, as opposed to the dialectical one, cannot explain the origins of social negativity. The genetic account becomes a mechanistic determinism or a Bernsteinian evolutionary socialism; the human actor is left out and socialism is reduced to an inert reorganization of thingly relations.

The theory of the "dialectics of nature" makes an analogous mistake. Here too the source of the negativity in terms of which the dialectical movement occurs is occluded. Moreover, the theory of the dialectics of nature (at least in Engels' formulation) falls back into the dualism of subject and object. The scientific investigator is presented as if he or she were the neutral observer contemplating the activity of a world of objects to which the observer does not belong. These supposedly neutral observations are then tested in experiments whose chief epistemological characteristic is that by isolating the elements they want to study they end up reproducing the atomistic world which the subject-object dichotomy presupposes. All

---

5. On this, see *Critique*, pp. 214-224.

subjectivity is stripped from the supposedly dialectical nature, which is then fitted into a pre-formed mold, the trinity of "dialectical" laws. "But," Sartre objects, "in the historical and social world, as we shall see, there is *truly* a dialectical reason; in transporting this law into the 'natural' world, in engraving it there by force, Engels takes its rationality from it; it is no longer a question of a dialectic which man makes in making himself, and which, reciprocally, makes man, but of a contingent law of which one can only say: *this is how it is*, and not otherwise" (126). Because it cannot justify itself in its own terms but only through a schema borrowed from another domain, the "dialectics of nature" is irrational.

These modes of thought which have been criticized as irrational are not, for that reason, to be abandoned. They themselves must be understood dialectically, as products of a certain kind of human activity, and as human activity confronted with specific limits and problems. The reasoning of the quantitative historian, the economistic Marxist, or the academic sociologist with his ready-made categories is not simply wrongheadedness on the part of some individuals; it is a partial (in both senses of the term) approach to the truth which must be understood and used, not ignored or refuted with *ad hominem* argument. As noted above, these incomplete modes of thought conflate totality and totalization. When a totalization, a process, is treated as a totality, the human element is invariably lost: what is human in a completed process artificially isolated from other processes? In a totality all is fixed and finished; men and women are dead objects isolated from one another and from the observer contemplating them. They become things, objects without will and feeling, incapable of projects or *praxis*; and they are certainly not the dialectical subject-object which knows itself in its objects and its objects in itself. The observer is only a passive other contemplating the world.

Sartre's critique of the dialectics of nature (and, by extension, of the other deviations) was already present in his 1946 polemic "Materialism and Revolution," which attacked the mechanistic, objectivist bias of a schematic and sclerotic "diamat" as it flourished under Stalin. There, Sartre applied the basic insights of *Being and Nothingness* to a problem area which that book had barely touched. The confrontation of Sartre's early ontological insight with the Marxian *Weltanschauung* and, more importantly, with the concrete politics of his time, led to the reevaluation which is the *Critique de la raison dialectique*. Three problems were central to this development. (1) The problem of the "we-subject." In *Being and Nothingness*, Sartre can account for the "we-object"—social pluralities functioning as objects—but cannot explain how there can exist a "we-subject"—a plurality of social subjects harmoniously conjoined—because each *pour-soi* (subject) can only objectify (that is, negate) the being of every other *pour-soi* and therefore remains caught up in a world of its own reifications. (2) The problem of matter. The unforgettable descriptions of *Nausea* as well as the analysis of *Being and Nothingness* point to matter as something "opaque" or "massive" which interferes with the transparency of the *pour-soi*. Matter is sheer positivity to be manipulated and used by the negating activity of the *pour-soi*. Matter plays no positive role as mediating between the subjectivities which inhabit the social world, and Sartre risks falling back to a kind of Cartesian dualism of "thinking substance" and "extended substance." (3) The problem of history. The problem of history which is central to the Marxist problematic, plays no thematic role in *Being and Nothingness.*

II.

Dialectical rationality is *reflexive*, not reflective or contemplative. It depends on the homogeneity and reciprocity of self and other, subject and object, though in fact even these polarized terms are no longer strictly applicable since the dualism they are based on is the premise and condition of analytical thought. Sartre describes his project this way: "In a certain sense...man undergoes the dialectic as though it were a foreign power; in a another sense, he *makes it.* And if dialectical Reason is to be the Reason of History, then that contradiction must itself be lived dialectically. This means that man undergoes the dialectic in as much as he makes it, and that he makes it in as much as he undergoes it. Moreover, it is necessary to understand that Man does not exist: there are only persons, who define themselves entirely by the society which carries them. If we do not want the dialectic to again become a divine law, a metaphysical fate, then the dialectic must come *from individuals* and not from who-knows-which super-individual ensembles. In other words, we encounter this new contradiction: the dialectic is a law of totalization which makes for the existence of collectives, societies, history—that is, realities which impose themselves on individuals; but at the same time the dialectic must be the product of millions of individual acts. Thus, we will have to show how it can be at once a *result* (without being a passive means) and a *totalizing force* (without being a transcendent fate); how it can at each instant realize the unity of the dispersive pulsing movement and that of integration" (131). The dialectic makes sense only insofar as the individuals who constitute it are themselves dialectically constituted; and vice versa, the individuals in their social and historical milieu are dialectically constituted only insofar as this milieu is itself dialectical. Neither pole can be taken alone, for each is the condition of the other's intelligibility. This is the structure of reflexivity.

If we look at society in its historical context, we find that we cannot understand the collective structures society gives itself without the constitutive actions of the many individuals; but at the same time, we cannot understand the individual constitutive actions unless we understand their social context. If this dialectical circularity is not to imply relativism, it will be necessary to discover the formal, *a priori* structures which govern the relationship between the individual constitutive acts and the plural social structures they constitute, and which in turn reconstitute them. Sartre writes, "if it exists, the dialectic can only be the totalization of the concrete totalizations produced by a multiplicity of totalizing singularities. This is what I call the dialectical *nominalism*" (132). The task of the first volume of the *Critique de la raison dialectique* is to move from the most simple and abstract structures[6] through the stages of totalization and re-totalization,

---

6. "Abstract" in the sense that Hegel uses the term in the *Phenomenology of the Spirit,*

finally reaching the concrete, historically given society in all its complexity as the result of a continual ascent of intelligibility in which each later, more complex structure is comprehended as grounded by previously established principles. Once this formal, *a priori* task is completed, the second volume would have to show that these structures permit an intelligible understanding of History.

Sartre's project, in other words, is one of *transcendental social philosophy* and can be seen as an attempt to found and complete Marx's 1843 "Critique of Hegel's Philosophy of the State."[7] Marx's critique, it will be recalled, attacks the inversion of subject and object which permits Hegel to treat social categories as subjects of which the actual individuals are the determined predicates. For Marx, this view is a mystification which is unintelligible because the dialectical circularity is broken and the Spirit, not the people, determines the social categories. Sartre's task is to reconstruct, beginning from the individual, the increasingly concrete determinations of human society and its history.

Sartre's project is *transcendental* in the sense that it attempts to articulate a categorial structure based on a principle of which each successive development can be seen as a *principiata*; each moment must have its intelligibility in a ground of which it is the grounded. The dialectical circularity, with its comprehension of the interpenetration of the terms as totalization and not as fixed totalities, permits the ascent to ever more complex structures without falling back into an "atomism of the second degree" (152) insofar as the principle itself—as opposed to the Hegelian Spirit, which is present only in an incomplete form in each category and whose incompleteness motivates the ascent to higher concretions—is modified and enriched at each stage of development because of the reciprocal mediation of principle and *principiata*. In other words, from a methodological point of view Sartre's transcendental edifice is a philosophical departure. It represents the introduction of a *real ground* (the human being, as we shall see in a moment) which interacts with and is modified by experience but still remains what it was and avoids the static analysis of traditional philosophy. At the same time, as was noted above, Sartre modifies the (analytic) notion of a fixed and unchanging truth known by a contemplating neutral subject in favor of a dialectical philosophy of intelligibility.[8]

Sartre's transcendental-real ground is the immediate, "abstract" human individual and its *praxis*: "the critical experiment will begin from the immediate, that is, from the individual in his abstract *praxis*, in order to rediscover through more and more profound conditionings the totality of his practical relations with others, and by the same means, the structures of the diverse practical multiplicities, and, through the contradictions and

---

that is, least complex, most immediate moments which are therefore false in isolation but constitutive as moments of the totality. Abstract means the same thing as "immediate," as opposed to mediated structures which are, for Sartre and Hegel, the most concrete.

7. On Marx's critique of Hegel's view of the state, see my *The Development of the Marxian Dialectic* (Carbondale, 1972).

8. In fact, Sartre does not fully adhere to this method, and the reasons for his departure will be seen in Part III to give a ground for criticism and a suggestion for further work.

struggles of these multiplicities, to come to the absolutely concrete: historical man" (143). For the dialectical movement to begin, this individual and the as yet undifferentiated and inhuman world in which he finds himself must interact. Their interaction will define the initial negation, and the project of negating it, which will gradually enrich itself and assume greater concreteness as the dialectical interaction between man and the world develops and becomes more structures, more mediated.

The first totalizing relation between the individual and the environment is *need*: "Need is the negation of the negation in the measure that it reveals itself as a *lack* in the interior of the organism; it is positivity in the measure that by means of it the organic totality tends to conserve itself *as it is*..." (166). That is, the organic being, man, depends on the inorganic world which is external to it and which it must internalize in order to survive. In this process of internalization, the organic must externalize itself in order to appropriate inorganic nature. The organic thus gives unity to the brute factuality of the inorganic world, which becomes a thing-to-be-consumed. Simultaneously, the organic being opens itself up to the world and its risks: "the organism makes itself inert (man *weighs* on the lever, etc.) in order to transform the surrounding inertia" (174). The process is therefore a circular, dialectical one: "man is 'mediated' by things in exactly the same measure as things are 'mediated' by man" (165). Man externalizes his internal relation to the external world and in so doing negates its externality; man becomes a being-in-the-world and the world becomes a being-for-man.

There is, however, a "contingent and ineluctable" fact about the external world which is crucial for the development of the theory: *scarcity* (168). The internal relation to the world in terms of need, structures the world by externalizing itself and acting on it; but it cannot alter this brute fact (or, at least, has not yet done so; with the end of scarcity would come the end of what Marx called "pre-history" and at that stage the dialectical theory—Sartre's or Marx's—would no longer be applicable). Due to the dialectical reciprocity, the factual existence of scarcity is internalized (scarcity of food or raw materials; at a higher level, scarcity of time, clients, or even fresh air: scarcity is itself dialectical, modified by more complex developments). The internalization of scarcity introduces negativity (*le néant*) into the notion of the human subject in a dialectically intelligible manner, as opposed to the more phenomenological-descriptive approach of *Being and Nothingness*, and permits Sartre to develop the notion of *praxis*-as-project and to explain how the future acts as a negativity which affects the present as a facticity-to-be-totalized.

The dialectic of material scarcity permits Sartre to go beyond the negative understanding of matter as brute otherness (as portrayed in *Being and Nothingness*) to a positive appreciation of its role in the development of historical society. Indeed, matter becomes the condition or mediation which creates the possibility of social relations. "In effect, as the univocal relation of each and of all to matter, scarcity finally becomes the objective and social structure of the material environment and thus, in return, designates with its inert finger each individual as a factor and victim of scarcity" (207). The social relations thus established are antagonistic: "In pure reciprocity, the

Other than me *is also the same as me.* In reciprocity *modified by scarcity,* the same appears to us as the anti-man inasmuch as *this same man* appears as radically Other (that is, as carrying a threat of death for us)" (207-8). This threatening Other—which I may become at any time for any Other—is the "Excess Third." Negativity and conflict enter into human affairs because of scarcity-as-internalized, and not—as with Marx and Engels in *The German Ideology*—because of the division of labor, class-divisions, and the like. Sartre's account has ontological precedence over Marx's and Engels' descriptive analysis, which is caught up in an infinite (historical) regress and cannot explain its own intelligibility.

In the social world, each individual as an individual works upon matter and attempts to appropriate it (negate and form it) in terms of his own project. Though our projects may be different or similar, they are inscribed in one and the same material world, which accepts them as the wax does the seal: passively. Yet though it is the "inert memory of all" (200) and thus that in which our common history is inscribed, this matter also mediates our projects in precisely the measure that our projects mediate it. Consequently, it is not passive at all; it is actively passive. To give a simple example, the development of the material forces of production determines not only the kind of work done, but also the needs of the workers (by creating new and realizable possibilities: car, television, refrigerator, etc.; by demanding a rhythm of labor which dulls the senses and permits only certain kinds of leisure activities; by creating the civilization of massification with its attendant consumerism and passivity; by demanding new kinds of workers who must have a higher education or else face technological unemployment; etc.). Every material "advance" of civilization has its effect on the daily lives of men and women.

This active passivity of matter is interesting because its actions seem to be the result of the *praxis* of everyone and of no one. Each of our individual products is absorbed in its materiality and is reflected back at us as through a kaleidoscope. Matter becomes a "counter-finality," an "anti-*praxis*," a "praxis without an author" (235). Two of Sartre's illustrations are particularly clear. Chinese farmers eking out a bare living on a small plot of land each decide individually that they can grow more food if they cut down the trees on their plots in order to have a greater arable surface. The result of this *praxis*, however, turns against them *all* (though it was willed by *no one*) in the form of giant floods which occur on the treeless land. One could similarly analyze the introduction of massive quantities of gold into seventeenth century Spain. Each individual forms his own project for personal enrichment, but the results of the efforts of all as individuals, as they are inscribed in the material environment, is rather the opposite of their hopes: inflation, lowered domestic productivity, the flow of the imported gold to foreign middlemen, and finally the decline and impoverishment of the entire nation.

Because it does not have a univocal signification, Sartre speaks of matter as *practico-inert*. The etymology of the term indicates its dialectical origin: it is the product of plural individual *praxis*, but in the inertia of exteriority it has lost the translucidity of that *praxis*. This active passivity of the practico-inert is at the root of *alienation*. Insofar as our products escape from the project for which they were intended and dominate us, their makers, each of us can be said to be caught up in a machinery that we did not will but which we cannot escape. Each of us becomes Other; each is determined by the project of the Other; and each determines the project of the Other. "In a word," Sartre writes, "otherness comes to things from men and returns from things to men in the form of atomization..." (246). The practico-inert, then, is not simply any "thing": it is a frozen *praxis*-as-Other produced by each individual in his isolated project (as Other of each Other) which in turn reinforces the otherness of each as Other. It is not just a "thing" in the positivist sense; it also encompasses the domain of what Hegel calls "objective Spirit" and Marxists call "super-structures": art, language, history, the state—all of the structures formed by and forming social pluralities.

The practico-inert can be seen as a dialectical permutation of the onto-logical principle of man-as-*praxis*. Its intelligibility has its source in the interaction of men and matter in the world of scarcity. What is important here is that though the tool, the machine, and the other manifold products of collective individual *praxis* (including, it should be stressed, language and other cultural artifacts) can be understood as practico-inert—as products and producers, inhuman and human at once—*so can men*. Insofar as our human being is defined even partially by the non-human, we are no longer the free *praxis* on which the dialectical intelligibility is built. Yet this definition of the human by the inhuman Other can be understood dialec-tically as the product of an interaction that we ourselves produce. The definition of man as practico-inert does not violate the principles of intelli-gibility. On the contrary, it marks an important progress.[9] The analysis will become more complex as it becomes more concrete, but the fundamental schema of dialectical intelligibility—the interpenetration and reciprocal determination of individual and social *praxis*—remains the same. As Sartre wrote at the end of *Search for a Method*, "Anthropology will not merit its name unless it substitutes for the study of human objects the study of the different processes of becoming an object" (107).

In the world of the practico-inert, the social collectivity exists in a condition of *seriality*. Parallel to the active passivity of the practico-inert, the serial individual lives as a passive activity determined by the object (the Other) which totalizes the series. In an elevator, or waiting for a bus, for example, a plurality of persons are defined (passively) as a kind of unity by their object (riding-the-elevator, waiting-for-the-bus). Each is there as the

---

9. Sartre's *Critique* is important because it goes against the view which is too often held by "Leftists" or "New Leftists" today, that the working class is "alienated" and "sold out" to the point that, as Marcuse puts it in his *Essay on Liberation*, this has become a "biological charac-teristic." The crux of Sartre's argument is that the structures of alienation can only be under-stood as based upon free human *praxis*. As a result, many philosophical and practical prob-lems are avoided. It would be interesting, though this is obviously not the place to do so, to compare the Sartrean and Marcusian views of humankind: Marcuse's view errs by making consciousness too "thick" or "absorbent" of influences in the material-social-historical world, while Sartre's errs by making it too "thin." Sartre's position is superior to that of Marcuse in that, by accounting for the structures of unfreedom in terms of free action it permits the possibility of self-liberation as opposed to liberation from the outside.

result of a certain project (going to work, seeing a client, or visiting a friend); yet their unity comes not from their individual projects but from an external object. From the point of view of each, each Other is interchangeable; no internal, interpersonal community is established. Moreover, each recognizes itself as defined by Otherness (the coming-of-the-bus, the riding-in-the-elevator) which totalizes. This is a situation of *powerlessness*: the object which defines us is absolutely Other; the persons with whom we form a serial unity are interchangeable, faceless Others. We ourselves feel depersonalized and dehumanized by the knowledge that for each of the Others we are another Other, replaceable by any other of them: "...each is identical to the Other inasmuch as he is made, by the Others, an Other acting on the Others. The formal and universal structure of otherness is the *rationality of the series*" (314).

In the serial relation, I can affect the Other only insofar as I treat myself as Other (just as, in order to affect the material world, individual *praxis* must externalize itself and expose itself). Since we are replaceable one by the Other, I act as I would want the Other to act, I do what I think the ideal Other would do. Sartre illustrates serial rationality with such examples as the market place (328 ff), public opinion (338 ff), and racism (345 ff). What is important here is that there is a rationality involved which is intelligible to the dialectical analysis; human *praxis* remains at the root and remains free, though its results may be other than what it intended and even its goals may be travestied. In the serial situation, I act as I think the Other would act. I size up the "objective situation" (that is, the practico-inert which determines the unity of the serial collective), and I gauge my actions in terms of its demands. My projects become its projects; they become projects of the Other, of the Thing, and therewith of all of us who are determined by the Otherness of the Thing (the "system"). Our mutual Otherness determines us as belonging to the serial unity determined by an external Thing; but the totality which we form as a collective is always Other, a dead totality and not a living totalization. Though I may recognize this, I also recognize my powerlessness. I may choose to revolt, but the Other has a family and children, and cannot take the risk of sacrificing the material security guaranteed by the Thing. I finally internalize his fears and his desire for security and myself acquiesce to the passive determination by the practico-inert: "You can't fight city hall."

Take, for example, the classroom. We enter at the appointed time and sit in identical seats firmly riveted to the floor to prevent any but a linear arrangement with all heads facing the teacher. We take this class because "one" should take it (it is either interesting, useful, or required). We pay attention, take detailed notes (alongside our doodles), and look alert. To the teacher we are all Other, mutually interchangeable. We compete for scarce goods controlled by the teacher: grades. When one of us is questioned in class, or when we have to produce written work, we don't come together to aid one another, but compete: each is afraid of becoming an Excess Third (receiving a low grade), and we know that this is how students are supposed to behave. We ask few questions and hazard few original ideas, since "one" is supposed to fit in, to receive and not give ideas, to acquire an education like everyone else. What interpersonal and group relations we have spring from sources other than the classroom, since there we are a seriality defined by the Thing whose bidding we have internalized. The serial unity is a *lateral* relation of Other to Other. Inasmuch as its totalization comes from the external Thing, it may appear that the individual is acting freely when, for example, the exteriority is internalized in the (successful) attempt to make good grades—Sartre's point is that this is precisely the case! It is not a question of being duped or of selling out to the system, or even of an ingrained "false consciousness." What the dialectical analysis must show is the *intelligibility* of actions which seem to go against the possibility of human liberation. Its task is not to compare what is with what ought to be but is rather to explain in a consistent manner the structures of what is. If a person who obeyed the dictates of the Thing were irrevocably alienated, the possibilities of human liberation would indeed be slim. By showing the dialectical rationality of such alienated serial behavior, Sartre at the same time shows the possibility of social liberation.

The transition from the all-pervasive serial plurality to the *group*—the next stage in Sartre's categorial development—has the same dialectical intelligibility as the previous moments. "The group is defined by its enterprise and by the constant movement of integration which attempts to purify its *praxis* by attempting to suppress in it all the forms of inertia; the [serial] collective is defined *by its being*, that is, inasmuch as it makes all *praxis* into a simple *hexis*" (307). The group differs from the series in that the basic structure of the latter is the lateral relation of Otherness, whereas the group is founded on Sameness. The group is the active attempt to escape from determination by the Other (thing or person) and to create a self-determining social plurality—a *we-subject*. Because it is an active self-foundation, Sartre speaks of the group-in-fusion or a totalization-in-progress in order to clearly demarcate the active group from the passive seriality, the we-subject from the we-object. The theory of social groups and their relation to the practico-inert and to social pluralities is thus the solution to a problem already posed in *Being and Nothingness*.

The events of the French Revolution, to which Sartre often returns, can be used here as an illustration of the transition from the seriality to the group. The population of the quarters surrounding the Bastille in the days before July 14, 1789 was a mixed bunch, in effect united only by its geographical location, the fact of poverty, and discontent with the established order. It was, in a word, a seriality. As the situation worsened, as rumors flew (transmitted from Other to Other, reflecting a fear of the Other: the state-power), as demonstrations took place and as the people armed themselves (still in a serial context: each reacted to the menace of the Other, each saw his neighbor's actions as determining what "one" should do in this situation), a situation was created in which the seriality, by the very inertial force of its actions, created the possibility of its own reorganization as a self-determining, active group. What was needed for the fusion of the series into a group was a menace from the outside (the possibility of negation—death—for the collectivity and each individual as being potentially an Excess Third), and a "totalizing Third."[10] The external menace was the Bastille, that giant fortress in whose shadow they lived day in and day out. The Bastille was not only a prison but a fortress from which the government could bombard the quarter, menacing each Other in the populace. In the days of protest demonstrations, and as the population began to arm itself, the level of discontent rose, feeding upon itself; the temperature of the crowd, as Sartre puts it metaphorically, rose. Then, suddenly, someone (anyone!) galvanized the crowd: *"A la Bastille!"* Everyone ran, suddenly totalized by the voice of someone, anyone, one who was of the crowd and understood the danger that menaced. The hetero-geneous crowd fused into a group acting together for a common cause. Its organization was still determined by an external force (the-Bastille-as-a-menace-to-us-all). But at the same time, within the group-as-means, otherness was overcome and the Bastille was taken. "It is not that I am myself in the Other; it is that *in praxis* there is no *Other*, there are only *me's*" (420). The structure of serial otherness is replaced by a fusion of the Same. Belonging to the active, fusing group makes each individual the Same (mediation by the group) and the action of each Third (for anyone can be or become the totalizing Third; each action is called forth by some, any catalyst) mediates between the group and myself as Third.[11] The action here is not the active passivity of the serial individual, for it is now belonging to the group which defines all as the Same and which determines their action as homogeneous, not determined from the outside.

In the case from the French Revolution the group, however, was defined as a means toward an external goal, the negation of the menace which weighed over the group-in-fusion. Once the menace was overcome, the Bastille taken, the activity consummated and the group fused, then what? The group's mode of existence changed when, on the Sunday following the seizure of the Bastille, with no action having intervened in the meantime, individuals returned to the half-destroyed fortress, showed it to their families and children, and pointed out what "we" did. The group was no longer a fusion but a passivity. The heat of the action had passed, there was no longer any unifying force, and the fall back to seriality threatened. The

---

10. The role of the Third has already been prepared in the earlier discussion of individual *praxis*. There, Sartre asserted that "It is not possible to conceive of a temporal process which would begin with the dyad and conclude with the triad. The binary formation as an immediate relation of man to man is the necessary foundation for any ternary relation; but inversely, the ternary relation as the mediation of man between men is the foundation on the basis of which reciprocity recognizes itself as reciprocal liaison. If the idealistic dialectic made an abusive usage of the triad, it is first of all because the *real* relation of men among themselves is necessarily ternary. But that trinity is not an ideal signification or characteristic of human relations: it is inscribed *in being*, that is, in the materiality of individuals. In this sense, reciprocity is not the thesis, nor is the trinity the synthesis (or inversely); it is a question of lived relations whose content is determined in an already existing society, and which are conditioned by the materiality, and which one can only modify by action" (p. 189). The parallel between the two levels of the categorial (transcendental) analysis is striking, and points, once again, to the schema of dialectical intelligibility on the basis of a structure of reflexion.

11. Whereas, for the individual *praxis*, the Third menaced me, threatening to make me an "Excess Third," in the group-in-fusion each of us is made Other (hence, by analogy, excess) by the menace of an Other outside the group, and hence each of us is the Same.

Bastille became a monument, the symbol of a group that was, where *spectators* come to gape (yesterday's activists among them). I was one with my neighbor for the first time in a common action. Now our relations threaten to return to the polite formality and anonymity of seriality.

To hold the group together a new fear, a new threat from outside, and a new totalizing Third are needed. This may occur if, for example, the rumor [12] spreads that the royalists are coming from Versailles and the group decides that the threat to all is a threat to each, to the Same, and maintains its organization and awareness. However, the mobilization will only last so long; then fear becomes a habit, the pain is dulled, and seriality again threatens to reassert itself. If the group is to maintain itself, it needs a "practical invention," the Oath (439-40). Each individual as the Same swears on his life and person that the group and the we-subject it constitutes is to take precedence over all else. The Oath represents a form of negation or "alienation" of freedom, but a negation which is freely and consciously willed insofar as the individual makes itself into a *group-object*. I define my being as the being of the Same; I limit my freedom to the freedom of the group so that, in that we all act this way, we can count each upon the Other and can be certain that this "practical invention" has (artificially) created the fear-reaction needed for the group's preservation. The group now takes itself not simply as a means toward the negation (destruction) of an external menace to each Other-as-the-Same, but rather as an end in itself worthy of preservation. Written in the blood of each, the Oath permits the preservation of the group and the differentiation of functions within it (bound by the discipline of the oath, the group can send spies and infiltrators, form a fifth column, or deploy its reserves in such a way that the enemy will not realize its strength).

With the Oath is instituted what Sartre calls the Fraternity-Terror. Again, he illustrates this category with examples from the French Revolution. The tension and temperature of the group-in-fusion cannot be maintained indefinitely. The Oath, the bond of fraternity that each swears to himself and to his brothers and sisters, is only a spiritual force and will not be sufficient to maintain the coherence and unity of the group. "The oath is a free attempt to substitute the fear of all for the fear of oneself and of the Other in and by each inasmuch as it suddenly reactualizes violence as an intelligible move beyond the individual alienation by the common liberty" (450). That is, if after taking the Oath, you let the Other (the Enemy) appeal to you as Other-than-us, the group to whom you swore to remain the Same—and for whatever reasons you do so: fear for the ultimate victory of our group, desire to gain material wealth and comfort, fear for your family, etc.—then it is our duty, to you and to ourselves as a group, to eliminate you. And this violence that we do to you is "a practical relation of *love* among the lynchers" (455). It affirms to you, to the very last, that we still consider you one of us and at the same time it proves to us that we still exist as a coherent group. In a word, purges are necessary to maintain the

---

12. The rumor need not be true. This is the technique used by states, for example, which maintain their ideological cohesion by installing a permanent fear of the "red" or "capitalist" menace.

group and are justified in a manner not unsimilar to the theory of retributive justice.

The notion of the Fraternity-Terror and the measures which the group must take to preserve itself may make one stop and wonder in what direction the "existentialist" Sartre is pushing. Much of this sounds terribly like a philo-sophistical justification of Leninist-Stalinist practice. To clarify this, we should look for a moment at the structure of an athletic team, a more neutral example.

When we join a team in a sporting event, we voluntarily sacrifice our "freedom." We accept a certain clearly pre-defined goal which constitutes victory or defeat; we accept a set of rules inherited from generations of players—a set of rules on whose aptness to govern the game we were never consulted. We delegate the choice of who will play what position and who will be on the first or second team to a coach or manager. If we are serious about it, we accept the coach's or manager's orders about the foods we will eat, the hours we will keep, and even our dress styles. Of course, when the game actually begins, our action is determined not only by the neat game plan we have laid out in advance, but also by the "free" action of another team composed of individuals like ourselves, with the same goals and the same limitations. As a member of the team, I sacrifice my individuality to the common good; only in terms of our common goal can my individual actions (I am a decoy, I run certain patterns which to an observer who does not understand the game would seem silly, I pass the ball rather than score a point myself, etc.) be understood, not only by the spectator but by myself who has internalized that goal. In the course of the game each of my teammates and I find ourselves in the role of leader, of totalizing Third. At every moment of the game each of us gauges his action in terms of the action of an Other who, as teammate sworn to the same goal, is the Same. Thus, when I see you make a certain move or feint I know exactly what you will do next, why you are doing it, and what actions on my part your move calls for. You and I are the Same. Our team is a group of singular individuals each of whom is the Same as the next, united not by an external Thing but by an internal *praxis* in which, at any given moment of the match, each can be understood as regulating the action of all, and the All as regulating that of each.

The parallel of the athletic team and the political group can be pushed still further. Every coach knows that it is important that his team develop a kind of *esprit de corps*, that it be together both on and off the field, that it be conscious of itself as holding up a certain tradition (Homecoming game, "Win one for the Gipper," the winning tradition of the old Black and Red, etc.)—in a word, that the individuals who constitute the team internalize the Team-as-Sacred. Hence, there arise the traditions of pep rallies, letter sweaters, group get-togethers in the off-season, and the countless other psychological tricks employed by the successful coach.[13] In a word, there is a feeling that the group composed by the free unification of individual

---

13. In this latter function, the business world has of course gone even further than the sporting world, employing psychologists and sociologists in the attempt to "integrate" the worker into the firm, to make him or her into a "team-man."

praxis is in continual danger of breaking up precisely because of this free individual *praxis*. Thus, the tendency towards the *institutionalization* of the group appears.

Before looking at the forms in which the group may institutionalize itself, we must explain why this institutionalization is ontologically necessary. Sartre argues that "the group is *constructed* on the model of free individual action, and...produces an organic action without itself being an organism; it is a machine for producing non-mechanical reactions, and as with all human products, inertia constitutes its being and its reason for being" (544). The action of the group is the action of a *constituted dialectic* whose foundation is the *constitutive dialectic* of individual *praxis*. The constituted dialectic is not, Sartre insists again and again, some kind of hyper-organism or collective unconscious which would function like the *praxis* of a super-individual.[14] This is the crucial point, for the group thus becomes a functional but inherently unstable unity: "...born to dissolve the series in the living synthesis of a community, it is blocked in its spatio-temporal development by the insurpassable status of the organic individual, and finds its being outside itself in the passive determinations of the inorganic exteriority that it tried to suppress in itself. It formed against alienation, which substitutes the field of the practico-inert for the free practical field of the individual. But no more than does the individual, it does not escape from the practico-inert, and through it, falls back into serial passivity" (635-36). This is the ontological foundation of institutionalization. The group, "the practical organism is the unifying unity of the unification" operated by the constitutive individuals (431). The constitutive individuals are the rock-bottom foundation of Sartre's "dialectical nominalism" and their existential freedom can never be totalized from without. The institution is an attempt by the group to preserve its paradoxical unity.

The group does not have the existence of an object. It *is* not, but is—a perpetual *becoming* or fusion constituted by the multiplicity of individual totalizations, each of which seeks a goal common to each and freely chosen by all. As a constituted dialectic, however, the group is efficacious, produces an action, and tends to internalize that external effect as its definition. The inhabitants of the area around the Bastille did not originally exist and act as a group; but the product of their action, the destruction of the Bastille, presents itself to each individual as the product of a common *praxis*, and conversely as the definition of that same common or group *praxis*. Internalizing this result and definition, each member of the group recognizes himself as a group-individual. However: "...the group does not and cannot have the ontological status that it claims in its *praxis*; and it is, inversely, the fact that each and everyone produces himself and defines himself in terms of that non-existent totality. There is a kind of interior void, an impassable and indetermined distance, a malaise in each community, large and small. This malaise incites a reinforcement of integrative practices, and grows in the measure that the group is more integrated" (568). The group that destroyed the Bastille was a fusion in the historical heat of the

---

14. See *Critique*, pp. 417, 431, 507, 667, etc.

moment; it defined itself in its action. When the moment is past, only the result of the group-*praxis* remains; each individual as individual identifies with the result; and only through the mediation of the result, a thing, can the members of the group think of themselves as the Same. The group thus rests on a dead totality, losing its character as a living totalization. This is the foundation of the Fraternity-Terror which is, in a sense, the archetype of the general process of group socialization and internalization of norms. Because the fusion cannot be maintained naturally over a long historical time, the group must either institutionalize itself or disappear.

The institutionalized group represents "a beginning of circular massification whose origin is the *non-substantial existence* of the community. The *being of the institution*...is the *non-being* of the group producing itself as the relation between its members" (583). After the seizure of the Bastille the group tends to disperse, returning to daily life. Yet, there is a new danger: the revenge of the royalists, which may come today, tomorrow, or next week. The group must prepare to defend itself. It sends out small patrols to stand watch, it begins to think about organizing the defense of the quarter, it assigns responsibilities: in short, it begins to differentiate itself into subgroups each of which is determined by its belonging to the larger group. Each of these differentiated subgroups is defined by a task which the group assigns and as long as each individual has internalized the demands of the group in its historical situation, there is no danger of betrayal. Indeed, with the institution of the Oath and the Fraternity-Terror a first defensive means has been defined by the group to prevent such a betrayal—a betrayal which is always possible because once the fusing group cools down and the institution begins to emerge, the relation of each individual to the group again becomes serial and, thus, determined by Otherness. If the individual is determined by belonging and not by doing, this is a passive determination by the Other (even though the Other here is the group) and not an active self-definition. The function of the institution thus becomes, in increasingly more complex and subtle forms, the paradoxical task of preserving the being of a non-being (the group).

It is in this situation that the possibility of bureaucracy arises. With the increasing differentiation of subgroups within the group, it is necessary for the group to "consume a part of its strength...in order to maintain itself in a state of relative fluidity" (539). "That which constitutes the specificity of organized *praxis* is the pyramid of inertias which constitutes that organized *praxis*...and the fact that for any apparatus its object (its subgroups which must be united) appears as an internal-external inertia which as such must be manoeuvred, whereas the same apparatus, in its relations with other organs of the group, is itself manipulated as an inertia by the apparatus above it" (537). When the group, which originally constituted itself as a fusion which was a means to an end, takes itself as an end-in-itself and devotes its energies to its own self-preservation, each member takes on a dual status for each other member. Each is the Same, since each has internalized the same end-goal; yet each is an Other whose loyalty and efforts must be coordinated and structured. When the group becomes an end, its members become means. As the immediate goal for which the group was formed recedes in time it becomes necessary either to rule by bureaucratic means or to continually invent new external dangers (the threat of world imperialism, traitors in our midst, etc.) or both. In a word, the group-subject takes itself as a group-object, and treats itself as a thing. Its *praxis* becomes a *"praxis*-process" (549). Yet, even highly bureaucratized, the group retains a totalizing function which comes to it through the constitutive actions of individual *praxis*, and it would be wrong to study it *only* as an object. "Thus, the group constitutes itself in order to act, and de-constitutes itself in constituting itself" (573). The notion of the group as a *praxis*-process points to the necessity of keeping both functions and their interaction continually present in the analysis, since even in the form of a bureaucratized institution the group is constituted by the constitutive dialectic and retains the possibility of totalizing action.

At this point, the question of leadership arises. The notion of the regulative Third showed that the series needed *some* kind of catalyst to fuse. The fusion required a force which would create the subjective preconditions through which each could become the Same. The role of the regulative Third was the role of any one of us and rotated among us, depending not on any personal characteristics or charisma but precisely on our Sameness. Obedience to the call of the Third was in effect nothing but my obedience to myself. For the call of the Third to be effective, it was necessary that I recognize it as Mine. At this level of the analysis, the question of the relation between leaders and masses was not posed; the focus was on the abstract, formal structures which differentiate the group from the series.

Once the further evolution of the group has been studied in the abstract and the *praxis* of the group has become the *praxis*-process of the institutionalized group, we have reached the stage of concrete history. We have developed the formal avatars of the evolution of the constitutive dialectic as it becomes the constituted dialectic and we are prepared to deal with the interplay among the different formal structures as they actually exist in juxtaposition and conflict in the real world, what Sartre calls the *"champ commun"* (643). This transition is important for understanding Sartre's project. The suggestive concreteness of the examples which have been used to illustrate the different *praxical* structures must not be misunderstood. Often, Sartre introduces examples which can be understood only on the basis of principles not yet developed.[15] Up to this point, we have examined only formal categories; in concrete lived history none of these categories exists alone, in isolation, or in purity. The purpose of treating them in this formal manner was to demonstrate the principles of their dialectical intelligibility. Once that has been done, the analysis (in the remainder of this first volume of the *Critique*) can turn to concrete problems—the interaction of groups and series, the problem of leaders and masses, the nature of the

---

15. For example, the Spanish gold was used to illustrate the counter-finality of the practico-inert. Yet it brought into consideration social structures which were more complex, those of series, groups, institutions, etc. For a critique of Sartre on this point, see Klaus Hartmann, *Sartres Sozialwissenschaft* (Berlin, 1966). Hartmann finds the same problem in Marx's *Capital*, which is significant; Hartmann, *Die Marxsche Theorie* (Berlin, 1970).

state, etc.—and then (in the projected second volume) study the actual course of history as "a totalizing temporalization of our practical multiplicity [which is] intelligible even though that totalization carries with it no Great Totalizer" (152). In both cases, the point is to sort out the formal structures in their dialectical interaction so that the intelligibility of the whole can be demonstrated.

If we look at the working class as it exists at a given point in history, we see first of all that its being (as inert) is defined by the Other—by the state of technology, by the *praxis*-process of the economy (willed by all and by none, the result of factors that the dialectical categories we have studied thus far can clarify) which results in inflation and recession and accounts for the structure of the cities, the sorry state of public transportation, the nature of available leisure activities, etc., and by the *praxis*-process of trade-union activity. In short, the working class exists as a collective, powerless to control its destiny, the victim of forces it cannot control but can only accept inertly. Moreover, this collective is not homogeneous. The working class is composed of a series of series, each of whose interests may differ in one way or another from those of other series: the interest of the skilled worker differs from that of the unskilled, that of one sector of the economy from another; and, as the AFL-CIO's lobbying for a supersonic transport plane pointed out, peoples' interest as workers may differ from their interest as humans. The notion of seriality helps us understand such phenomena as racism and sexism which often appear within the class despite an "objective" long-run interest in fighting these divisive forces. It helps explain the reformism of the workers' unions, the structure of the prevalent upward-mobility-mindedness which workers may express in their value judgments and the "patriotism" of the "hard-hat." The point is not to make abstract value-judgments about these phenomena or to assimilate this behavior to some fictive model of "the" working class, but rather to understand the rationality of this kind of behavior.

The serialized working class does not exist in a vacuum. On the one hand, it has its institutionalized group(s), and on the other, it is determined by the action of other social groups and series. The encounter of series among themselves within the field of the practico-inert results in a more or less mechanical modification of the Other's determination of each which can be studied easily. The relation between a group and a series is more interesting, whether it be between the organized force of the bourgeoisie and the working class or between the mass media and the mass, or whatever. The series' determination by the Other is easily appropriated by the constituted group, which plays on the powerlessness of the serial individual and his desire to become like all the Others. Like belonging to a group, seriality is the result of a *praxis*; as such, the serial individual ("mass man") is—and this is the strict sense of the term—Other-directed. It is this Other-direction which accounts for phenomena like public opinion, bestsellers, and consumer society. Each serial individual strives practically to become what everyone and no one is, the ideal Other, which is that which gives meaning to his impotent existence. The choice of making oneself Other is a dialectically intelligible one. It is the choice to accept one's destiny, inscribed in and prescribed by the practico-inert. However, Other-direction accounts for such phenomena only at the concrete level where there exist not only the manipulated but the manipulators as well. This is the sense of Sartre's attack on economism, to which we have already referred. The theory of the "aristocracy of labor," which purports to explain the reformism of the working class in imperialist nations in terms of the surplus profits with which the bourgeoisie can placate the workers, is dialectically unintelligible because it makes the *praxis* of the individual dependent upon the brute facticity of the practico-inert without attempting to show not only the practical origins of this facticity but also the effect on this structure of the individual practice (of the class, of its institutionalized groups, and also of the bourgeoisie, the media, etc.). Moreover, this theory reduces the individual to the passive receptacle of stimuli to which it reacts in a predictable, machine-like manner. It is typical of the Leninist tendency to treat consciousness as a thing determined by other things external to it. The real situation is more complex and mediated.

Within the class itself, groups form and dissolve, unite serialities from without, and compete with one another. Clearly, these groups and series are formed on the basis of the existent social structure; and Sartre admits that "to become a bourgeois, one must already be one" (289). On the other hand, as the discussion of the practico-inert illustrates, the effect of the material conditions on the practice of the individual is not the direct relation of cause-effect. On the basis of an analysis of the social structure, I may decide that the correct course toward ending the war in Vietnam is to plant a bomb in a government building. Yet that very action and the end it has in view will have repercussions that may go contrary to those I intend: it may be the excuse for government repression or it may accidentally kill someone and turn public opinion against my cause. The *New York Times* may publish the "Pentagon Papers" because its analysis of the current social situation shows that the war is hurting the national interest. Yet the gross deception those Papers reveal may have a political effect going far beyond the *Times'* intentions. Sartre's analysis does not tell us how to predict these effects. It does, however, show that they are dialectically intelligible and it prevents us from falling into all too common errors. Moreover, it shows how free human *praxis* can be manipulated in a manifold of possible directions and, even more importantly, it warns against the error of identifying manipulated and manipulable *praxis* with pure externality. At the same time that it shows the intelligibility of alienated *praxis*, it also indicates other possibilities open to that *praxis* because, even in its alienation, its freedom remains.

What of the working class and its organizations? For Sartre, there is "no doubt that the entire class is present in the organized group which has constituted itself within it" (644). At the same time, however, he asserts that "the transformation of the class into an actualized group has never occurred anywhere, even in revolutionary periods" (644). This position rings paradoxical—and Leninist-Stalinist. Indeed, Sartre "explains" the need for Stalin to incarnate the will of the party as the will of all the people, since Stalin "is" the constituted dialectic which must direct the constitutive dialectic of the masses in order to unify it around a common goal (630).

Sartre bases his analysis of the party (and of the bourgeois state) on the previously elaborated formal structures. The class is a seriality of serialities. Periodically and under given conditions, the temperature rises and a fusion occurs. In this fusion, leaders arise, first as regulative Thirds. "Thus, the *leader* is produced at the same time as the group itself, and he produces the group which produces him—with this distinction, that in this elementary moment of the experience, the leader is *anyone*" (586). As the group begins to disintegrate back into seriality, the leader becomes the "authority" whose function is to integrate "the multiplicity of institutional relations and to give them the synthetic unity of a real *praxis*" (587). But due to the nominalism which indicates that this "synthetic unity" as institutionalized is in fact no longer a group but a fixed structure which takes itself as its own end, the position of the leader shifts. Where the leader was simply the expression of the group-as-all-of-us, now we become an expression of the leader, and he or she is no longer leader but sovereign. Of course, the leader may, like Lenin, devote himself to the structuring of the group as an end which is a means to another end. He may attempt to preserve the relation whereby we members of the group who agree with that final end remain related to one another and to the sovereign not as obedient subjects of the Other's will but as our own free choice of the Same. This would be the revolutionary party, formed either on a local level after action in a reduced arena or, with more difficulty, on a national level.

Inasmuch as the party exists within the class which is serially structured, its role is comparable to that of any group in relation to the series. The series is Other-directed, and the party is one of the Others competing for its attention.[16] Under these circumstances, the party may win votes, elections, and a share of the public opinion. It may recruit new members who choose to recognize themselves in it and its goals, subordinating themselves to it in order to become no longer Others-in-sympathy-with-the-cause but the Same as the other militants. Each militant identifies himself or herself with the party; and in discussions with non-party people (Others) will tend to identify the party as the truth and goal of the class. The problem with this (Leninist) view of the party is that it is based on seriality. If the party wins my vote, or if I follow its directions in a strike or a coup, I am still obeying the Other. It doesn't matter that the Other claims to be my representative, since I am nonetheless obeying. It may be for this reason that Sartre finds himself admitting that from this perspective the idea of the dictatorship of the proletariat "is itself absurd" (630).

To be sure, Sartre continually criticizes the party dictatorships in the so-called Socialist Bloc. His criticism is based on the same principles that he develops in the *Critique*. For example, in his brilliant Preface to the writings of Patrice Lumumba, he writes that "The government atomizes the colonialized people and unifies them *from the exterior*, as subjects of the King. Independence will be only a word if for that *cohesion from outside* a

---

16. It is significant that Sartre moves, in mid-paragraph, from this discussion to one of the role of the Hearst press as a manipulator of public opinion (pp. 605-606).

totalization from the interior is not substituted."[17] Indeed, Sartre's famous Preface to Fanon's *Wretched of the Earth* is based on the argument that revolt is necessary precisely in order to substitute an interior cohesion for the old colonial yoke. In the *Critique* itself, Sartre presents a discussion of the role of the cadre which clearly indicates that when the group does fuse, the old structure incarnated in the cadre disintegrates and new links replace it. Sartre recognizes that in any fusion, the party's directives are followed *only* if they are in fact the expression of the activity of the group. Yet, the necessity that Sartre's ontological analysis reveals—that the group is not a hyper-organism and that it must institutionalize itself or disappear—forces him to a position which gives the central role to the party.

III.

The scope of the philosophical project worked out in the *Critique de la raison dialectique* has few equals in the history of philosophy. The "experiment," as Sartre calls it, which leads from the most immediate level of the abstract individual and its *praxical* relation to nature through a series of more and more complex mediated structures to the level of concrete society and history can be appreciated on many levels. It is rich in insightful examples which would be of benefit to the specialized disciplines of anthropology, sociology, history, and so on. Sartre's experiment takes up and shows the dialectical rationality of, for example, Lévi-Strauss' work in kinship theory, contemporary historiography—particularly the work of the *Annales* school—sociology, demography, and even mathematics. What we are confronted with in the *Critique* is a project whose breadth and ambition are rivaled only by the work of Hegel, particularly the *Philosophy of Right*.[18] Rather than look at isolated insights or aspects of the *Critique*, it is better here to consider it as a whole, as a philosophical project. It is only in this way that the work can be appreciated and the lines between academic disciplines broken down, as the dialectical analysis indicates.

If we compare Hegel's *Philosophy of Right* with Sartre's *Critique*, the most apparent difference is that the former has a "happy ending." The *Critique*, on the other hand, is unable to account for any sort of stable totality because the group-in-fusion is always threatened by disappearance or by institutionalization. Its being is a non-being and it needs a state or party to hold it together. As the Hegelian analysis strides forward towards concrete history, it does encounter a moment—civil society—which is characterized by the "war of all against all," by economic exploitation and social injustice. Yet the social atomism of civil society is portrayed as only one categorial moment through which the Spirit must pass, but at which it does not remain. Civil society is transcended, *aufgehoben*, by the development of the state, in which its oppositions are at once preserved and

---

17. Sartre, *Situations V* (Paris, 1964), p. 213.
18. A systematic criticism of Sartre from the Hegelian point of view can be found in Hartmann, *Sartres Sozialwissenschaft*.

reconciled. The state is seen as the incorporation of Spirit in the world, the particular and the universal in a concrete social unity.

Like Sartre, Hegel uses concrete examples to illustrate his theoretical categories. Yet he is much more sparing in his use of examples, a point not without significance. Moreover, Hegel's theory of the state is *followed* by an outlined theory of history (expanded later into the lectures on the *Philosophy of History*). This is because Hegel's theory is a-temporal. It is the construction of an ordered hierarchy of categories arranged systematically (in terms of relative concretion or, what is the same thing, relative rational completeness). In this hierarchy each category is derived from the preceding moment, and the final stage is nothing but the full development and concrete instantiation of the beginning. The famous assertion that "The real is the rational and the rational is the real" was meant literally. Hegel's goal is to discover the categorial structure which justifies or grounds the existing society. The present moment is taken as positivity, as true. Hence, the theory must have a "happy end," demonstrating the stability of what is. Since there does not exist a state which is the unification of the multiplicity of particular individuals (for better or for worse), Hegel must show how this category fits into the hierarchy. The categorial levels that precede the state and the present are interpreted as "moments," categories whose logical existence is necessary and intelligible only in terms of the fully developed theory. Past historical stages, less-than-stately social forms, may in fact have existed; Hegel's concern, however, is not with them as existents but with them as grist for the categorial mill in which they are *aufgehoben*. The past has significance only when seen teleologically as a necessary (logical) stage in the move to the present.

The problem with the Hegelian theory, as Marx (and Feuerbach) saw, is that it has no room for the actually existing individual. It is a theory of categories, not of humanly constructed social pluralities. Marx points out that for Hegel it is the state (as the incarnation of the spirit) which gives reason to and defines the individuals which compose it, rather than vice versa. This is the famous inversion of subject and object which Marx points to and criticizes in detail through his "Critique of Hegel's Philosophy of the State." It should be noted, however, that Hegel can reply to this critique that he has already considered the individual at the very beginning of the *Philosophy of Right* where the individual is seen as incarnating itself and its individuality in private property, which in its turn moves forward in the categorial dialectic to higher and more complex categories. In each of these higher categories, Hegel could insist, the particular individual is still and always present-as-*aufgehoben*.

The Hegelian position is hardly satisfactory for the realist or existentialist who wants to keep continually in view the concrete human subject. Nor are the strictly logical transitions pleasing to the philosopher concerned to understand the actual, human genesis of the new categorial stages. It is precisely here that the Sartrean theory provides a counterpoint to the Hegelian. Rather than a theory of the successive stages of Spirit's incarnation, Sartre is concerned with the increasingly complex social structures created by and incarnating the human subject. In place of Hegel's abstract transitions (which, as Marx correctly observed, are accepted because they are already justified in the abstract principles of Hegel's *Logic*), Sartre proposes intuitively intelligible, temporal totalizations by the human subject; totalizations which cannot be understood by contemplative observation (another difference between the two theories) but only by the situated observer who participates in the intersubjective experience of the dialectic.

Thus, although their goals are analogous, the Sartrean and Hegelian theories prove to be nearly mirror-opposites. The virtue of Sartre's position is its ability to deal with the real, living individual; the advantage of Hegel's is its rejection of the transcendental nominalism which makes stable totalities impossible and necessitates the consequent "happy ending." Leaving aside any attempt at a mutual confrontation between the systems, the question remains: why does Sartre's theory have an "unhappy ending"?

Like Marx and unlike Hegel, Sartre proposes a *theory which is also* a critique. We have already discussed some of the different senses of this term in Part I. One which we haven't considered—because Sartre himself doesn't discuss it—is the meaning of "critique" for Marx, whose major writings, nearly without exception, were titled or subtitled "A Critique..."[19] As opposed to social *criticism*—which, implicitly or explicitly, examines and judges the present order in terms of an ideal or a paradigm of what society *should be* and which, therefore, can be called "utopian" because it cannot show the *mediations* which will lead from the "is" to the "should be"— Marx's critical theory is based on the *self-denunciation of the present order*; its task is to dis-cover, to reveal the underlying rationality of that order, letting it speak its own langauge and unfold its own logic. Marx's critical theory *is* theory. It is the attempt to articulate the dialectical intelligibility of what presents itself in its immediacy as sheer facticity. It is a theory which makes a truth claim; but it is the *truth of a false, self-contradictory society* which must negate itself (not *which must be negated*, which would imply a return to a kind of utopian *criticism*; it must, rather, contain within itself its own negation). This is why Marx wrote a book called *Capital* and not one called *Socialism*. This is why he always refused to predict the future, and this is the reason that—despite the practice of the so-called socialist countries—the categories of *Capital* are not valid under socialism. Moreover, the nature of this critical theory accounts for the difference between the Marxian and Hegelian systems: if the present is positive, then an Hegelian "happy ending" is necessary; if it is not, then the conclusion of the story remains in doubt, the circle is not closed, and the buckle remains unbuckled.

Sartre's theory is critical in this Marxian sense. More, it is an attempt to provide the ontological foundation for the social negativity which Marx's *Capital* takes for granted. That Marx was conscious of this theoretical need can be seen at the end of the first volume of *Capital* when—almost as an afterthought—he added the chapter on "Primitive Accumulation." That analysis, however convincing it may be to the intuitive understanding, is

---

19. On this notion of "critique," see my article "On Marx's Critical Theory," *Telos* No. 6 (Fall, 1970), and my *The Development of the Marxian Dialectic*.

merely a genetic account of the actual movement of history not unlike that given in *The German Ideology*, and it is open to the same reproach Sartre made against economistic explanations. It is not intelligible, for it does not account for the *origin* of the negativity but only illustrates its effects. In this context, Sartre's "unhappy ending" becomes clearer, especially if it is recalled that he continually asserts that scarcity, the foundation for the notion of the "Excess Third" which in turn serves to explain violence, strife, and exploitation among humankind, is a *contingent* principle which, though it has been present throughout past history, need not always exist. It is true that stable social pluralities in the sense that Hegel can account for them do not now exist, nor have they ever existed. This does not mean, however, that they cannot exist. Sartre is trying to understand history, as past and as presently lived; he is not trying to predict what will come in the future. Thus, Sartre's theory cannot have a "happy ending" for the simple reason that history (what Marx called human pre-history) has not ended.

The parallel between the Sartrean and Marxian theories can be extended still further. When he undertook his "revision" of Marx, Eduard Bernstein attacked what he saw as a "utopian" prejudice which, he thought, prevented Marx from seeing the impending evolution of capitalist social forms into their (structural) socialist resolution. Bernstein argued that Marx presupposed the necessity of socialism and was therefore led to see only contradictions, only crises, only increasing misery and exploitation, which could therefore only be remedied by an ultra-left Blanquist revolutionary position. Theoretically, continued Bernstein, this implied that Marx's analyses misunderstood the "facts," falling into a "dualism" which looked at the present only as a future-present and thus neglected the true facticity of the evolving economic structures. Replying to Bernstein in her brilliant pamphlet, "Social Reform or Revolution?" Rosa Luxemburg stressed that this "error" is nothing but the dialectical method itself, which makes sense only in terms of its final goal, socialism. "The secret of Marx's theory of value, of his analysis of money, his theory of capital, his theory of the rate of profit, and consequently of the whole existing economic system is—the transitory nature of the capitalist economy, its collapse, thus—and this is only another aspect of the same phenomenon—the final goal, socialism. And precisely because, *a priori*, Marx looked at capitalism from the socialist's viewpoint...he was enabled to decipher the hieroglyphics of the capitalist economy."[20] Bernstein's revisionism was based on analytic reason, on his inability to understand—as Lukács put it—"the present as history." Without an historical *telos*, a directed movement of history, the dialectical method cannot function; it remains caught up in the brute facticity of immediacy, the superficial contemplation of the surface of the phenomena. How is this *telos*, this final goal, socialism, to be understood? Is it merely an assumption, a City of God, portrayed in one way by Marxists and in another by Christians? Is it merely the arbitrary introduction into the theory of a surd or a lemma whose rationality can only be shown after the fact, on Judgment Day?

---

20. Howard, ed., *Selected Political Writings of Rosa Luxemburg* (New York, 1970), p. 101. See especially my "Introduction" to that volume.

Sartre's ontological principle of human *praxis* provides a foundation for the Marxian theory. In *Search for a Method*, Sartre defines *praxis*: "In effect, *praxis* is a passing from the objective to the objective by means of an interiorization. The project, as a subjective move from objectivity to objectivity, stretched between the objective conditions of the milieu and the objective structures of the field of possibilities, represents *in itself* the moving unity of subjectivity and objectivity... The subjective thus appears as a necessary moment of the objective process" (66). *Praxis* is nothing but the unity of theory and practice, of subject and object, of the ideal and the real. It is the result of a need in the organism, and represents the transcendence of that need in an active project. At another point, Sartre speaks of the difference between *praxis* and process (i.e., the movement inscribed n the things which determines the individual as Other), asserting that *praxis* is an "organizing project going beyond the material conditions towards an end, and inscribing itself by work in the organic matter as a restructuration of the practical field and a reunification of the means in order to attain the end" (687). But what is the "end" which *praxis* gives itself? There is a certain parallel here with the analyses of *Being and Nothingness*. Though still subjectively oriented, the individual (the *pour-soi*) was shown there to have a continual temptation and continual goal of becoming God, what Sartre defined as the *pour-soi-en-soi*, substance and subject at once. In the more historical presentation of the *Critique*, the individual is portrayed as a continual "totalization in progress" striving to become a totality (not *any* totality, but the totality possible on the basis of the historically given field of possibilities) and continually frustrated in that attempt. On the one hand, the individual is frustrated by the refracting action of the practico-inert and existence in serialities where each can only totalize the series by doing as the Other does, and on the other hand, he is frustrated by the very ontological irreducibility of the individual-as-principle.

Praxis is defined as resulting from a need whose transcendence is the result of an active project situated in a field of historically given materiality. Founded in scarcity, the need is continually present, modified by the interactions of groups, series, and matter as they exist in the field of historical possibility. For the series, the need itself (as incarnate in the practico-inert) totalizes each individual as Other, with the result that the individual's totalization is a false totalization of itself and the Other as Other. Yet the group in fusion does exist as an ontologically possible structure. It is a continual possibility both for the series and for the institutionalized group. The group in fusion is the true totalization, since in it I totalize myself and the Other not as an Other but as the Same. For the bourgeoisie, Sartre insists, [21] this true totalization is no longer a possibility; the bourgeoisie has already assumed its destiny as its own self-interest in

---

21. The parallel with Lukács here is interesting. Sartre nowhere refers explicitly to Lukács, though it is certain that he knew of *History and Class Consciousness*, which was not translated into French until after the writing of the *Critique*, but which is commented on in M. Merleau-Ponty, in *Les aventures de la dialectique* (Paris, 1955). Note also Sartre's use of the term "class-apocalypse," which brings to mind not only Lukács but also Ernst Bloch, though it is doubtful that Sartre knew of his work.

the atomistic society of competition. The proletariat, on the other hand, has assumed passively and as Other a materiality that it has not chosen but which, instead, has created it as proletariat. It is the revolutionary class; and its revolution is not defined by the changes it introduces into the structure of the practico-inert (nationalizations, etc.). Instead, the proletarian revolution is defined by what it does, not *to* but *with* humankind. "The worker," writes Sartre, "will not free himself from his destiny unless the entire human multiplicity changes itself forever into a group-*praxis*" (351).

The question now is, how can the working class actualize itself as a group? Sartre speaks of the "class-apocalypse" (660) and gives several possible phenomenological descriptions of this actualization. Toward the end of the book, he promises that "...we will see later the material conditions which make possible that *prise de conscience*," that changed consciousness which marks the revolution (742). But, as was seen, his discussion of proletarian politics implies consequences which seem to contradict the very goal of the self-determination of all as the Same which he posits as the *telos* of history. Here we must put forward some critical reserves about Sartre's theory.

At one point in his analysis, Sartre mentions the dispute between those who hold that the proletariat can only be organized as a class through the external action of the party and those who argue in favor of the necessary spontaneity of the masses (518). Sartre argues that the problem is a political one, since both solutions have the same ontological structure on the level of theory. If the group is truly a group, it is based on the Sameness of all, which implies that the party will succeed in effecting the fusion of the group only if it is the Same as the group, not external and Other to it. The fusion of a group is not the same thing, Sartre insists, as the agreement which might exist between a worker and his boss, or, for example, an agreement that the laws of physics are true. The agreement on a scientific principle is an accord about an Other, and as such does not affect the existence of either party, whose relation with the Other is unchanged. When a group forms and the necessity for tactical or strategic unity makes itself felt, the debate that is engaged is a life-or-death matter not only for the existence of the group but for each individual who composes it, because of the fact that here each is the Same. Within the group, no solution can be imposed on the Other, since that would imply the death of the group as such; and consequently the victory of the individual (or faction) imposing itself would be the pyrrhic success of the suicide. At this level of the theory, Sartre is certainly correct; but at the more concrete historical level, the political question becomes important. There, the neat theoretical structures developed in their formal isolation enter into conflict.

The ontological foundation of Sartre's system prohibits *a priori* the stabilization of the group in fusion, condemning it to dispersion or the petrification of an institution. In the concretion of history, the group, if it persists, enters into relations with other groups and series, relations which are themselves serial and which found the structures of domination whose archetype is the bourgeois state. The delicate relation thus established demands that the group-as-institutionalized take severe measures to preserve itself against the threat of inertia or dissolution. As a common member of the historical group, I must restrain myself, mold myself to the will of the institutionalized-group. Since the group is menaced by the outside world, in which it nonetheless exists, I must take care that despite my subjective goals my words and actions do not get deflected by the dialectic of seriality and turn back against the group. "The model of the institutional-group," says Sartre, "will be the *forged tool*" (585). In the same context, he speaks of the "systematic self-domestication of man by man" (585).

It appears, then, that even within the revolutionary organization the relations of reciprocity between myself and the Other-as-the-Same are degraded. Sartre may insist that formally, the structure of Sameness is preserved. He may argue that the institutionalized party-group is necessary as the incarnation of a permanent possibility of struggle for the class. He may assert the necessity (which he cannot explain) of a democratization and decentralization of the group and stress the importance of the workers' councils. He may talk of his dialectical understanding as a new kind of humanism different from and superior to the atomistic humanism of bourgeois individualism. However, ultimately he falls back to a position which I would call "structural idealism."

The motive force of Sartre's social theory is his attempt to formulate a consistent transcendental theory in which each stage can be understood in terms of a basic principle of which it is the concretion. It is this structure which guarantees the dialectical intelligibility. The principle of the system is the praxical individual, the constitutive ground of the constituted dialectic. On this basis, Sartre rejects analytic or positivist analyses which take the brute given as ultimate and inexplicable, and he tries to present a dialectical understanding of the origins of this givenness on the grounds of his constitutive principle. There is a danger here which Sartre recognizes explicitly: if the given "is *praxis* through and through, the entire human universe disappears in an idealism of the Hegelian type" (688). But although he sees this risk, Sartre nevertheless falls victim to it. This is why I spoke of a "structural idealism."

One of the major contributions of Sartre's *Critique* is the notion of the practico-inert. This category is clearly designed to answer the charge of "existential subjectivism" or "Cartesianism" raised against his early works, particularly by Maurice Merleau-Ponty. [22] Merleau-Ponty argued that Sartre's Cartesian bias led him to a subject-object dualism which was unbridgeable on the basis of its very formulation. The Sartrean dualism, he argued, is not an accurate description of the world in which we live, for in that world there exist not only pure subjects and objects but also what Merleau-Ponty calls an "*intermonde*," a world of bodies which are both

---

22. On Merleau-Ponty, see my essay, "Ambiguous Radicalism: Merleau-Ponty's Interrogation of Political Thought," in Garth Gillan, ed., *The Horizons of the Flesh: Critical Perspectives on the Thought of Merleau-Ponty* (Carbondale, 1973). Hubert L. Dreyfus is correct in seeing Merleau-Ponty's influence on Sartre, but incorrect in thinking that Sartre "accepts (without acknowledgement) all of Merleau-Ponty's specific suggestions." Dreyfus, "Introduction" to *Sense and Non-Sense* (Evanston, 1964), p. xx.

subjective and objective and which cannot be accounted for on the basis of the dualism. Because of his Cartesian premises, Sartre's theory must elevate *violence* into a constitutive principle. The same dualism is the basis of the Manichaeanism of Sartre's "Ultra-Bolshevism," most evidently expressed in *The Communists and the Peace* but still present, as we have seen, in the political theory of the *Critique*.

What is striking in the *Critique*, however, is that despite the revised notion of objects in the world as practico-inert and the notion of man-as-*praxis* which attempts to bridge the dualistic gap, the human individual never seems to have a *body*. In the early stages of the theory, the organism is seen as having to externalize itself in order to work on the environment. But the body is never explicitly analyzed as a constitutive variable of the social world. Parallel to this omission of the body—and this is not coincidental—is the lack of a theory of consciousness. As it has always been for Sartre, consciousness remains a void, nothingness. In the *Critique* its role is even smaller, decreasing with the increased emphasis on *praxis*. [23]

Because it is missing these two features, I spoke of Sartre's theory as a "structural idealism." The stress is laid on the ontological structures of the social world in a way which, paradoxically, recalls precisely the Engelsian dialectics of nature. The foundation of these social structures is seen to lie in the praxical dialectic acting in a world dominated by scarcity. However, the definition of *praxis* on which Sartre operates is vitiated by the principle of dialectical *nominalism* and by the inability to treat the human body and human consciousness as constitutive variables whose interaction, in the last analysis, is constitutive of that very *praxis*-as-principle. The absolutization of the individual *praxis* is not in fact necessary, and its result is "structural idealism" and the attendant problems for the analysis of successful group action and hence of revolutionary action.

Put another way, the difficulty of Sartre's nominalistic structural principle can be seen by comparing the two major divisions of the *Critique*: "From Individual *Praxis* to the Practico-Inert" and "From the Group to History." In presenting the broad lines of Sartre's analysis, two lines of thought sometimes seemed to emerge, only to fall back ultimately to the principle of dialectical nominalism. It appeared that Sartre's categorial principle—the abstract individual in his *praxis*—would raise itself to a first level of concreteness as the human individual living in the world of the practico-inert, and that this new, concrete human being would take on new depth at the same time that it became the principle for the second stage of development. That is, it seemed that Sartre's transcendental ground had a principle of movement, growth and change built into it. But this was only the appearance, and the abstract individual again became the determining force. The group was shown to be *a priori* doomed to institutionalization or

---

23. Merleau-Ponty makes the interesting point: "If a being is consciousness, it must be nothing but a tissue of intentions. If it stops defining itself by the act of signifying, it falls back to the condition of a thing—a thing being precisely that which does not know, which remains in an absolute ignorance of itself and the world, and which therefore is not truly a 'self,' that is, a 'for-itself,' and [therefore] has only a spatio-temporal individuation, an existence as an in itself." *La phénoménologie de la perception* (Paris, 1945).

dispersion. Sartre writes: "the concrete dialectic is that which reveals itself through the common *praxis* of a group. But we also know that the fundamental condition of historical rationality is the impossibility of going beyond...organic action as the strictly individual model; that is, the constituted dialectical Reason...must be related to its always present but always masked foundation, the constitutive rationality" (643). Sartre recognizes that this abstract individual has no real, concrete historical existence. At the same time, since he must reject the notion of the group as a hyperorganism, he has no choice but to found the existence of plural subjectivities (series, groups, or their combination and interaction) in this very same abstract individual. The ontological principle is thus taken one time as a real ground and at a second moment as a transcendental principle. The problem, ultimately, is Sartre's dualism, the inability to introduce the notions of the body and consciousness which would permit him to have an ontological principle which would itself develop dialectically. Here, the parallel between Sartre's and Hegel's systems works to Sartre's disadvantage, although one would have to ask whether Hegel's ground, the unchanging and pre-given Spirit, is not itself undialectical.

In summary, the political problems in the Sartrean social philosophy have their root in an ontological error or, perhaps, incompleteness. Sartre's contribution to the renewal of dialectical theory is immense, and the critic need not make an either/or judgment. There are problems with Sartre's theory. Some of them are fundamental, like the dualism; others could be more easily corrected, like the category mistakes that occur when Sartre concretizes his categorial levels too soon. But the direction in which Sartre's work points and the problems it poses cannot be lightly dismissed. He attempts to present the criteria of the validity of dialectical thought, and he has shown its utility—its indispensability—for understanding our present-as-history. When Sartre writes toward the end of the book that "at a certain level of abstraction, the class struggle is expressed as a *conflict of rationalities*" (742), he is also identifying one of the tasks incumbent upon us as radical intellectuals.

Phenomenological Marxism

Paul Piccone

Why "phenomenological" Marxism? Marxism needs no qualification and to so qualify it is an eclectic maneuver hiding a fundamentally anti-Marxist orientation. There is Marxism and anti-Marxism: no third way is possible. Any attempt to modify Marxism with some extraneous element is not only objectively anti-Marxist but also pro-imperialist, since it diverts attention from, and actually obfuscates, the really crucial issue of the day: the confrontation between communism and capitalism.

So runs the official line of Soviet Marxism, and its main objective is to apologize for a political strategy that has long ceased to be revolutionary. It is meant to reinforce the myth that the Soviet Union alone is the spearhead of true Marxism. Any questioning of this pretended theoretical hegemony is seen as counterrevolutionary because it allegedly threatens the unity of the working class movement. But this "unity" has long ceased to exist, along with the Soviet Union's revolutionary spirit. In fact, the history of the first "socialist" country is essentially a long series of failures: Kronstadt, the purge of the Left Opposition, the massacre of the Kulaks, the purge of the Right Opposition, the Stalin-Hitler pact, Yalta, the split with Yugoslavia, the Hungarian invasion, the split with China, the Czechoslovakian invasion, etc. It seems that the only predictable thing about the Soviet Union is that every five or six years it will produce some major counterrevolutionary disaster which can no longer shock any "orthodox" Marxist who, having put up with so much already, is conditioned to accept anything.

Within this frame of reference, it is not surprising that at the theoretical level—always a moment of the broader economic and political context—the bankruptcy is even more pronounced. "Orthodox" Marxism as a theory has become an empty shell held together by dogmatic slogans: only its supporters' cynicism can prevent it from being discarded as an intellectual aberration. The literature documenting this bankruptcy is too voluminous to quote. One need only recall Sartre's brilliant polemic against Lukács[1] to

---

1. Jean-Paul Sartre, *Search for a Method*, translated by H.E. Barnes (New York, 1963). Sartre's attack is directed at Lukács, *Existentialisme ou Marxisme?* (Paris, 1961). In the late 1940s during the most dogmatic period of his career, Lukács attacked not only existentialism but also any outlook other than "orthodox" Marxism as philosophies of imperialism. In a diabolical reversal typical of intellectuals who have attempted to collaborate with "official" Marxism, Sartre in 1953, during his ultra-Bolshevik period, charged Lefort with wasting his time in a useless "third way" independent of the French Communist party. Cf. J.-P. Sartre, "Réponse à Lefort," *Les Temps Modernes*, No. 89 (April, 1953). Three years later he praises Lukács, along with Tran Duc Thao, as the only authentic Marxists. Cf. J.-P. Sartre, "Réponse à Pierre Naville," *Les Temps Modernes*, No. 123 (March-April 1956). Simultaneously, Lukács was being criticized by the Hungarian Minister of Culture for developing a philosophy of the third way in aesthetics. Cf. Josef Revai, *La Littérature et la democratie populaire, à propos de G. Lukács* (Paris, 1950). Also, in 1956, after the Hungarian uprising, Lukács was briefly deported to Rumania and subsequently kept under house arrest (only because of his old age) for participating in the "counterrevolutionary activities" of the short-lived Nagy regime.

question why "orthodox" Marxism is even mentioned here. Yet "orthodox" Marxism typifies the crisis which has ensnarled Marxism for the past century; and to the extent that this anomalous situation persists, any attempt at a *critical* Marxism today must start out in contraposition to the "orthodoxy." This attempt must not only expose the bankruptcy of "orthodoxy," it must also explain it in terms of a critical Marxism whose fate hinges on its ability to penetrate and direct social realities wherein "orthodox" Marxism still plays an important—if negative—role. Unlike Sartre's approach, which prefers to go its independent way waiting for the day when "orthodox" Marxism finally comes of age and rejects the infantile nonsense that it now preaches and practices,[2] the task of radical theory today is to attempt to rescue Marxism from the dogmatic stranglehold—not by reforming its instrumentalized institutional cadavers, but by radically developing a new *critical* Marxism. Only a genuine *revolutionary* treatment—not a reformist substitute—will save Marxism from the ideological grave into which it has been forced.

Theoretically, the degeneration of "orthodox" Marxism is a function of its fixity. To the extent that historical content conditions theoretical form, the sanctification of "orthodox" Marxism to the level of an eternally valid metaphysics betrays it as an ideological fossil adequate, at best, for an historical phase long since gone.[3] Furthermore, in rejecting all qualifications and theoretical reconstitutions, "orthodox" Marxism becomes an abstract formalism which, without concrete social determinations, ends up as a set of slogans applying nowhere and thus everywhere at once. Not dialectically related to the social situations they are meant to conceptually articulate, these slogans manifest their arbitrariness in their ability to explain anything, anywhere, at any time (as well as the opposite). This ability is what makes this kind of Marxism so useful to the bureaucracy which sanctifies it. Lacking any foundation, it becomes a powerful tool of intellectual mystification based on a faith in the progressive teleology of its users.

---

2. Sartre, *Search for a Method*, pp. 30 and 181. He writes: "Marxism is still very young, almost in its infancy; it has scarcely begun to develop." As long as this state of affairs persists, "...existentialism will follow its own path of study...as a fragment of the system." Of course, given Sartre's long history of flirting with the French Communist party, it is hard to tell how much longer he will hold such a position. From his "Materialisme et revolution" to "Les Communistes et la paix," to the *Critique de la raison dialectique*, there have been so many changes that it is difficult to ascribe to him any definite position. In fact, Sartre cuts the tragic figure of a radical intellectual attempting to catch up with history. Yet, whenever he finally apprehends any event into his philosophy after much compromising and doubt, the event exhausts itself, leaving the philosopher in a state of chronic obsolescence. Thus, Sartre has had the dubious distinction of becoming a Stalinist precisely at a time when Stalinism was on the way out after thirty years of unchallenged hegemony in official Communist parties, and of denying the possibility of major revolutionary events in the West four months before the May uprising in France in 1968. Cf. his interview in *Le Point*, January 1968. For a history of Sartre's political engagement, see Franco Fé, *Sartre e il Comunismo* (Florence, 1970).

3. In his *Soviet Marxism* (New York, 1958), Marcuse has shown to what extent Soviet Marxism has actually changed. Yet, to the extent that no concrete or determinate negation is allowed any longer, all these changes are quantitative and cannot transcend certain well-fixed ideological limits. Thus, in its changes, it remains fundamentally the same.

All this is well known. The crudeness and barbarism of Stalin were exposed long ago, and Zhdanovism is allegedly a thing of the past.[4] Unfortunately, Krushchev's attempts to de-Stalinize "orthodox" Marxism have failed; and to the extent that they were Stalinist in their very anti-Stalinism[5] they have reinforced precisely what they were meant to eliminate, finally shipwrecking in Brezhnev's doctrine: computerized Stalinism. It is unnecessary here to deal with the apologetic gymnastics meant to show that this state of affairs is only a temporary aberration caused by the backwardness of Russia's "objective conditions." First, as Deutscher and others have repeatedly pointed out, all the suffering and repression, both physical and intellectual, were really unnecessary: the same ends could have been attained through other means. Secondly, the mechanistic doctrine according to which the quality of Soviet society and culture would radically change with the improvement of objective conditions was fundamentally misconstrued from the very beginning. It assumed a radical separation between subject and object, i.e., although the object (Soviet society) manipulated by the subject (the bureaucracy) would change, the subject would remain throughout this process essentially unchanged in its teleology and perseverance. But one of the basic tenets of Marx as well as Hegel is that the subject makes itself in and through making the object: a leadership *operating as* a manipulative bureaucracy can only make itself into a manipulative bureaucracy! And Marxism in the hands of a manipulative bureaucracy necessarily becomes the "orthodox" travesty which confronts us today.

Thus, the "phenomenological" qualification appended to Marxism, far from being a mere philosophical afterthought, is the conceptual otherness of a determinate socio-historical problem: the need to develop a critical approach to social reality able both to apprehend as well as direct the historical process according to a genuinely humanistic project. It is not surprising, therefore, that "orthodox" Marxism overcomes the ambiguities and doubts of the philosophies of the third way[6] by means of the mechanistic doctrine of "partyness" (*Parteilichkeit*) according to which the party is not to be questioned in its decisions after they are made, since it is the true representative of the interests of the working class—the agency of historical change. But since only the top echelons of the party ever participate in making these decisions, eventually everyone but the leaders ends up as a mere executor of the sacred mandates. To the extent that these executors

---

4. For an excellent analysis, even if occasionally exaggerated, see István Mészáros, *La Rivolta degli Intellettuali Ungheresi* (Turin, 1958).

5. As Birnbaum points out, Krushchevism "continues the 'cult of personality' by attributing much of [the failures] solely to Stalin's personal defects rather than to the structure of Soviet society." Cf. Norman Birnbaum, *Toward a Critical Sociology* (New York, 1971).

6. Calling attempts at a critical Marxism "philosophies of the third way" is tantamount to falling into a Stalinist trap since it assumes that "orthodox" Marxism *is* already a *second* way or an alternative to bourgeois ideology rather than one of its abstract negations. To the extent that "orthodox" Marxism is a positivistic metaphysics, it rates no better than any other dogmatic religion. Thus, it is no alternative. The confrontation today is between bureaucratism and *critical* Marxism: *tertium non datur.*

cannot question party positions taken by "orthodox" Marxists as party functionaries, all culture is immediately reduced to the level of a weapon committed to fighting battles in which the sides are predetermined by the objective requirements of Soviet policy—which means, purely and simply, its destruction as culture. Since the philosophy of "orthodox" Marxism is nothing more than a means for the attainment of ends safely guarded within the Kremlin walls, all intellectual activity reduces itself to apologetics and, as such, to an act of faith and mystification. Thus "orthodox" Marxism is really a theological Marxism: a contemplative ideology meant for popular consumption in a society which has been turned into a spectacle; a spectacle in which the working class spectators are constantly forced to applaud the ludicrous nineteenth century reruns dished out by *Pravda* as the road to the future.[7]

As a possible alternative to the sclerosis of "orthodox" Marxism, phenomenological Marxism is no novelty. In fact, the earliest documented efforts at a synthesis between Marxism and phenomenology go back some years to Herbert Marcuse who, immediately after the publication of Heidegger's *Sein und Zeit*, in 1928, wrote a long essay on the subject.[8] But the issue must have been in the air for at least a couple of decades prior to this. Thus, Goldmann argues that the crucial *rapprochement* between phenomenology and Marxism takes place much earlier and that even Lukács' early works such as *The Theory of the Novel* (written during World War I) can be seen as being situated "in the crossing-point of the three great currents of German academic thought of the period: the neo-Kantianism of Heidelberg, the elucidation of the concepts of meaning and understanding by Dilthey, and Husserlian phenomenology."[9] According to Goldmann, the very vitality of Lukács' Marxism in *History and Class Consciousness* consists in "the decisive progress that the work entails by substituting the

---

7. For an excellent analysis of the dialectic of contemplation, see Guy Debord, *Society of the Spectacle* (Detroit, 1970).

8. Herbert Marcuse, "Beiträge zu einer Phänomenologie der historischen Materialismus," *Philosophische Hefte*, No. 1 (July 1928), pp. 45-68. This essay has been translated into English in *Telos*, No. 4 (Fall 1969), pp. 3-34. The same issue of *Philosophische Hefte* also includes a note by the editor, Maximilian Beck, indicating the close connection between the Marxian notion of *class* with Heidegger's *Man* and *Mitsein*. According to Beck, both *Class* and *Mitsein* mediate between the individual and society in general. An earlier version of the following history of phenomenological Marxism has already appeared as part of the Translators' Introduction to Enzo Paci, *Functions of the Sciences and the Meaning of Man* (Evanston, 1972), translated by Paul Piccone and James E. Hansen.

9. Lucien Goldmann's "Introduzione" to the Italian translation of György Lukács, *Teoria del Romanzo* (Milan, 1962), p. 13. It would have been more correct if Goldmann had substituted Kierkegaard and Sorel for Husserlian phenomenology. As Lukács put it in the Preface to the new edition of 1967 (written after Goldmann's work): "...on the one hand, Kierkegaard had played a significant role in my early development and in the immediate pre-war years in Heidelberg I even planned an essay on his criticism of Hegel. On the other hand, the contradictions of my social and political views brought me intellectually into contact with syndicalism and above all with the philosophy of Georges Sorel." Georg Lukács, *History and Class Consciousness*, translated by Rodney Livingstone (London, 1971), pp. ix-x. For a broader analysis of this issue, see Andrew Arato, "Lukács' Path to Marxism (1910-1923)," *Telos*, No. 7 (Spring 1971), pp. 128-136.

phenomenological idea of *atemporal* meaningful structure...with the Marxist and dialectical concept of meaningful structure which is both dynamic and temporal, based on the idea of the Totality."[10] Furthermore, he sees the birth of German existentialism as an attempt to answer the early Lukács. "We hold that it is impossible to understand such a philosophical rebirth [existentialism], anxious and decadent, unless it is seen in relation to the fact that it is always elaborated in relation to a provisionally absent thinker [Lukács], forgotten and isolated in silence, who nonetheless has preceded this rebirth by outlining the area and the level of the discussion and the problems to be dealt with, but who has always asserted man's dignity, the value of clear consciousness, courage, and hope... It is not by chance that the two most important thinkers of such a philosophical rebirth, Heidegger and Jaspers, belong to the same generation as Lukács and come from the very same restricted university circle: that of the southwest German 'school'."[11] Hence, according to Goldmann, what Merleau-Ponty called "Western Marxism"[12] (as opposed to "orthodox" Marxism) has been inextricably connected with phenomenology from its very origin at the end of World War I—even if in an unacknowledged way. Even Heidegger's *Sein und Zeit* has been interpreted by Goldmann in his doctoral dissertation as mainly a confrontation with Lukács' work. Allegedly, Heidegger's book "cannot be understood without realizing that it constitutes largely, though perhaps implicitly, a debate...with Lukács' work *History and Class Consciousness*."[13]

Although a close reading of Lukács' later works such as *Die Zerstörung der Vernunft* indicates a limited knowledge of Husserlian phenomenology—in fact, whenever he attacks phenomenology he ends up confusion Scheler's and Heidegger's variety of phenomenology with Husserl's[14]—it is undeniable that the cultural climate of Middle Europe between the two world wars was saturated with these issues. Whether or not Heidegger consciously meant his work as an answer to Lukács, it was *in fact* taken as such in some quarters. This was not so much a result of the profundity of Heideggerian existentialism as it was a result of the inner contradictions of Lukács' position and the crisis of European working class movements—the repository of hope for all the Marxist thinking of the period. In reaction to the mechanistic Marxism of the Second International which had fizzled out in reformism and political irrelevance during the first part of the century, Lukács sought to dialectically articulate a dynamic Marxism free of the metaphysical shackles of scientism and positivism. He did so by vindicating

10. Goldmann, *op.cit.*, p. 43.

11. *Ibid.*, pp. 48-49.

12. See Maurice Merleau-Ponty, *Les Aventures de la dialectique* (Paris, 1955), chapter II, "Le Marxisme 'Occidental'," pp. 43-80. An English translation of this crucial chapter has appeared in *Telos*, No. 6 (Fall 1970), pp. 140-161.

13. Lucien Goldmann, *Immanuel Kant*, translated by Madeline Duclas and Theophile Spoerri (London, 1971), p. 25.

14. For an excellent analysis of Lukács' critique of phenomenology, cf. Guido Neri, *Prassi e Conoscienza* (Milan, 1966), pp. 128-135.

the Hegelian heritage of Marxism and uncompromisingly approaching every problem in terms of the Totality. His whole effort, however, was fundamentally vitiated by objective idealism, since it did not deal with the concrete realities of the time but substituted for them a set of highly articulate categories lifted out *tout court* from Marx's works. Although dynamic, these categories remained foreign to Lukács' historical situation and rendered his whole analysis hopelessly obsolete. This prevented Lukács from dealing with *real* historical forces and led him into political dead ends entailed by his uncritically accepted Marxist categories.

Thus, it is not surprising that *History and Class Consciousness*, a work spouting revolutionary fire from every page, appears as the most untimely book of the period, published precisely when it had already become evident that Marxist revolutions in Western Europe had been defeated and that there would be absolutely no opportunity to carry them out for the next few years. It can be argued that the main aim of this work was to counter the theoretical and political flattening of Marxism by the Soviet epigones. Yet, later developments in Lukács' thought seem to rule out such tactical considerations. The problem with Lukács' book was that despite all its rhetorical lip service to materialism, it operated entirely with an idealistic dialectic which brilliantly articulated Marxist categories transposed lock, stock and barrel from Marx without, however, retaining their grounding in socio-historical reality, i.e., their materiality. Despite its penetrating philosophical analyses of reification, social democracy, and bourgeois thought, in practice *History and Class Consciousness* was a beautiful dream altogether lacking any mediation to meaningfully relate it to the desperate realities of 1920 Middle Europe. Lukács himself must have been painfully aware of this, since in the last essay of the book, "Towards a Methodology of the Problem of Organization," and in another little booklet written immediately thereafter on *Lenin*, he directed his entire theoretical apparatus to justify the Leninist notion of the party and its mechanistic consequences.[15]

Whereas Lukács became a Stalinist and thus considerably dulled his theoretical edge, this was not true of a "whole host" of young radicals whom Lukács himself mentions as being greatly impressed by his Hegelian Marxism.[16] Unwilling to accept the "Leninist mediation"[17] (on Hegelian

_____

15. As Merleau-Ponty points out, Lukács tried to salvage his dialectical edifice within the limited field of aesthetics to which he dedicated the better part of his life: "Although [Lukács] has generally accepted the lessons of philosophical Leninism and like everyone else he speaks the language of reflective consciousness, thus leaving the door open for less comprehensible detours and giving a free hand to the history makers, in principle he still upholds the autonomy of truth, the possibility of reflection, and the life of subjectivity in the cultural realm where these cannot be subordinated to a tactic or it will mean their death. Everything happens as if, having accepted the unavoidable in action and in historical engagement, he now attempts to preserve for the future the conditions necessary for a healthy culture." Merleau-Ponty, *op.cit.*, pp. 91-92. An English translation of this chapter has appeared in *Telos*, No. 7 (Spring, 1971), pp. 112-121. The quoted passage appears on pp. 117-118. For a more elaborate analysis of Lukács' theoretical trajectory, see my "Dialectic and Materialism in Lukács," *Telos*, No. 11 (Spring 1972), which is wholly devoted to Lukács.

16. Lukács, *History and Class Consciousness, op.cit.*, p. xxii.

17. This, of course, was not genuine Leninism but a Stalinist aberration which traces back

grounds this turns out to be romantic *external* mediation and consequently undialectical pseudo-mediation), these young radicals remained confronted with the problem of how to mediate between their theory and the reality to which it was to apply. Not surprisingly, a few years later when Heidegger published *Sein und Zeit,* young radicals like Marcuse took it to be the kind of mediation needed to make Hegelian Marxism viable. With its stress on the things themselves, phenomenology seemed to remedy the scandal of Hegelian Marxism, i.e., its inability to relate to the existing state of affairs. "A fundamental distinction must be drawn between the immanent meaning of an ideology and its historical sense (location). One of the most fundamental theses of historical materialism is that the *definition* of an ideology (its immanent meaning) is not consistent with its *historical meaning.* Historical materialism is interested only in the latter, since only the latter can be dealt with by its dialectical method. The explication of immanent meaning requires precisely an approach completely opposed to the dialectic."[18]

This approach, of course, is Heideggerian phenomenology. Lukács had already separated "immanent meaning" from "historical meaning,"[19] but he assumed throughout that Marxism could easily deal with both, although he had severely curtailed its domain of application by altogether excluding dialectical methodology from nature.[20] Confronted with this contradiction

---

to Lenin's early turn of the century days when he was still essentially a Kautskian. For an elaboration of this point, see Mandel's contribution to Nicolas Krassó, ed., *Trotsky: The Great Debate Renewed* (St. Louis, 1971).

18. Marcuse, "Contribution to a Phenomenology of Historical Materialism," *Telos,* No. 4 (Fall 1969), pp. 27-28.

19. Thus, he writes, "On the one hand, all the categories in which human existence is constructed must appear as the determinants of that existence itself (and not merely of the description of that existence). On the other hand, their succession, their coherence and their connections must appear as aspects of the historical process itself, as the structural components of the present." Lukács, *op.cit.,* p. 159.

20. In fact, Lukács had reproached Engels for attempting a dialectics of nature: "It is of first importance to realize that the [dialectical] method is limited here to the realm of history and society. The misunderstandings that arise from Engels' account of dialectics can in the main be put down to the fact that Engels—following Hegel's mistaken lead—extended the method to apply also to nature. However, the crucial determinants of dialectics—the interaction of subject and object, the unity of theory and practice, the historical changes in the reality underlying the categories as the root cause of changes in thought, etc.—are absent from our knowledge of change." *Ibid.,* p. 24n. Lest this early Marcusean attempt be discarded as trivial, it is to be remembered that Sartre's *Critique* is also beset by the same problem. In fact, having rejected any dialectic of nature, Sartre puts forth existentialism as a means to deal with the particular or, in Marcusean language, with "immanent meaning" since he is forced to claim that Marxism can only give a valid historical interpretation ("historical meaning"). Any account of Marxism which denies the possibility of a dialectics of nature is necessarily condemned to finding mechanistic complements for an equally mechanistic Marxism. As Gramsci put it, "the masses 'feel' but do not always comprehend or know; the intellectual 'knows' but does not always comprehend or 'feel.' The two extremes are thus pedantry and philistinism on the one hand, and blind passion and sectarianism on the other." Antonio Gramsci, *Il Materialismo Storico e la Filosofia di Benedetto Croce* (Turin, 1966), p. 114. Very penetratingly, Gramsci identifies the two tendencies as typical of the masses on the one hand, and the intellectuals on the other. The fact that twentieth century Marxists have to look at phenomenology or at existentialism as a crutch to make Marxist intellectuals "feel" once again is a sign of the distance that has come between Marxism as an abstract ideology, and concrete reality.

and openly attacked in the political arena by social democrats as well as Bolsheviks, Lukács chose simply to discard the entire problematic, even though the political attacks of his opponents such as Zinoviev and Kautsky had nothing to do with the *real* shortcomings of his work. [21]

Marcuse's proposed synthesis, however, sought to remedy the real problems of Hegelian Marxism. As Habermas claims, [22] Marcuse's early effort anticipates a whole series of similar attempts, even though it is beset by insuperable intrinsic difficulties. The forced synthesis of the two mechanically juxtaposed frameworks is bound to fail from the very beginning: either phenomenology dissolves in the dialectic, in which case it ceases to be phenomenology, or the dialectic is frozen in the phenomenological foundation and loses its dynamism, thus ceasing to be dialectical. [23] Merleau-Ponty seems to have understood this, and his philosophy of ambiguity sought to handle both Marxism and phenomenology without ever really mixing them. To the extent that both Marxism and phenomenology are not separate but merely distinguishable moments of the same broad perspective, what resulted with Merleau-Ponty was neither an exclusively phenomenological nor an exclusively Marxist perspective, but a phenomenology that paved the way for structuralism and a tamed Marxism that gave way to social democracy.

Efforts to reconcile phenomenology and Marxism often take the form of a *synthesis*. And this is precisely what is wrong with them. Mechanically contraposed as self-contained entities, they are from the very start condemned to fail: the result is the shotgun marriage of two ideologies which cannot accommodate each other. Only by seeing Marxism as the outcome of phenomenology and phenomenology as an inextricable moment of Marxism, is it possible to attain any reconciliation which simultaneously produces a relevant phenomenology and an undogmatic Marxism. Marxism can only be a valid historical mediation as a function of its ability to concretely articulate and direct social reality. Phenomenology, critically understood, is the tracing back of all mediations to the human operations that constitute them. Thus, it is to be expected that the crisis of Marxism—its

---

21. The real shortcomings were clearly pointed out by Gramsci who wrote: "It seems that Lukács asserts that one can only speak of the dialectic for the history of man but not for nature... If his assertion presupposes a dualism between nature and man, he is wrong, because he falls into a view of nature proper to religion, Greco-Christian philosophy, and also idealism, which in reality does not manage to unite man and nature and relate them together other than verbally. But if human history should also be conceived as the history of nature (also through the history of science) how can the dialectic be separated from nature? Perhaps Lukács...has fallen...into a form of idealism." Gramsci, *op.cit.,* p. 145.

22. Thus Habermas writes: "After the war, the left existentialists of Paris and the philosophers of *Praxis* of Zagreb and Prague substituted the analysis of the life-world of the late Husserl for Heidegger's analysis of being, yet both 'schools' are based on a phenomenological foundation of a Marxism that Marcuse had himself anticipated." Jürgen Habermas, ed., *Antworten auf Herbert Marcuse* (Frankfurt, 1968).

23. A dialectical solution to this problem consists in seeing phenomenology as a *moment* of Marxism and Marxism as the logical outcome of phenomenology. For a detailed elaboration of this topic, see Enzo Paci, *Function of the Sciences and the Meaning of Man.*

becoming frozen in a set of abstract categories that no longer meaningfully articulate social reality but instead cover it with an impenetrable veil of ideas—necessitates a phenomenological reconstitution. New content can be expressed only in new forms (phenomenological Marxism) dialectically related to older forms (classical Marxism). Similarly, to the extent that the human operations to which phenomenology reduces all mediations are themselves historical, they take place within a context preconditioned by the sedimentations of the past which equally affect all the subjects caught in it—hence, the *intersubjective* character of every subjectivity.[24] Thus, phenomenological analysis unavoidably ends up in Marxism as the class-analysis that explains different kinds of consciousness in terms of class position (a result of social sedimentation) and labor (the teleological activity which allows the class engaged in it to reach the *true* consciousness[25] of its situation and the possibility of changing the world by means of the mediations that it itself creates).

After Marcuse, the most important figure engaged in developing a phenomenological Marxism and a Marxist phenomenology is Tran Duc Thao, who came from the same cultural milieu as Sartre and Merleau-Ponty. As early as 1946, Tran Duc Thao published a long article on "Marxisme et Phénoménologie"[26] in which he gave a phenomenological

---

24. Without belaboring this point, it should be noted that it is precisely here that Husserlian phenomenology differs radically from Sartrean existentialism. Whereas for Husserl subjectivity is always intersubjectivity, this is not the case with Sartre, for whom the ego is uncaused and unmotivated, and all attempts at its self-constitution are necessarily mediated by objectifications. Unlike the Husserlian *Ur-Ich* which is essentially an I-can, an operating subject in flesh and blood, the Sartrean ego is a nothing which becomes a something only through the project it freely undertakes. Thus, this constituted something is monadic in character and is constantly caught in the need to assert itself through free acts at every turn. This leads to sado-masochism in interpersonal relations, and prevents the persistence of stable groups (or intersubjectivity). The series—monadized individuals—constitutes itself into a group by overcoming otherness through the objectification that is collectively bestowed upon it by the other. The group remains a group (intersubjectively constituted) only as long as the other remains to carry out the objectification. But this artificial unity contains the seeds of its own destruction since it defines itself through a project whose realization entails the very dissolution of the unifying agency. Consequently, the dialectic of group formation necessarily entails its dissolution and, as such, the group rapidly degenerates back into its natural state of seriality: a bunch of monadic egos floating around in meaninglessness. For concise articulation of this dialectic, see Jean-Paul Sartre, "The Risk of Spontaneity and the Logic of the Institution," *Telos*, No. 4 (Fall 1969), pp. 191-205. There, Sartre applies his analysis to explain what happened in the U.S.S.R. and why the October Revolution, having attained its goal, necessarily degenerated into bureaucratism and recreated the serialization it was meant to eliminate.

25. True consciousness here does not refer to any kind of absolute reflection of reality, but simply to a consciousness that expresses the objective interests of the subjects possessing it. It is *true* because it is constituted by the subjects that have it.

26. Tran Duc Thao, "Marxisme et Phénoménologie," in *Revue Internationale*, No. 2 (1946). In the very same issue, there is another article by Jean Domarchi, "Les Théories de la valeur et la phénoménologie," which operates very much within the same frame of references. Domarchi writes: "In the first chapter of *Capital*, Marx carries on in the same way as the phenomenologists. Through a discursive process very close to Husserl's reduction, he has determined the essence (or the *eidos*) expressing the economic meaning of a thing, and he has subsequently described how, on the level of the *world* (especially the capitalist world) the thing *appears* as a commodity, i.e., it takes on a form that *masks its authentic economic existence.*" *Ibid.*, p. 159.

interpretation of the Marxist notions of "structure" and "superstructure." Unlike Marcuse, Tran Duc Thao's approach was not an arbitrary synthesis of Marxism and phenomenology, but a genuine articulation of the two within their own framework: a dialectical interpenetration of both. This work, however, met much opposition in "orthodox" Marxist circles [27] and, as Tran Duc Thao became increasingly involved in Communist politics, [28] he eventually came to reject the whole attempt in his *Phénoménologie et Materialisme Dialectique* (1951). Put forth as an attempt to show that phenomenology cannot resolve its inner contradictions except by becoming dialectical materialism, the presentation in this book is utterly inconclusive. The work is two separate books: the first a commentary on Husserlian phenomenology and the second a mediocre reiteration of the theses of "orthodox" Marxism in roughly the form espoused by Lukács in *Existentialisme ou Marxism?* published a couple of years earlier. [29] Despite this suspicious turnabout, it is not altogether obvious that Tran Duc Thao actually rejected *in toto* the phenomenological approach, and his latest work on language indicates a strong reliance upon tacitly accepted phenomenological techniques. [30]

The most important figure who has attempted to articulate the phenomenological basis of Marxism is Karel Kosik, whose work, *Die Dialektik des Konkreten*, [31] marks the high point of critical Marxism in Eastern

---

27. Cf. Pierre Naville's reply, "Marx ou Husserl," in the next issue of the same journal, where not only Tran Duc Thao but also Sartre and Merleau-Ponty, are directly or indirectly rebuffed.

28. For an account of Tran Duc Thao's intellectual trajectory in the late 1940s, see Roberta Tomassini, "Fenomenologia e Materialismo Dialettico in Tran Duc Thao," *Critica Letteraria*, No. 9 (July 1971), and Pier Aldo Rovatti, "Introduzione" to the Italian translation of Tran Duc Thao, *Fenomenologia e Materialismo Dialettico* (Milan, 1970).

29. It is to be remembered that the late 1940s and early 1950s are the most dogmatic and Stalinist years of Lukács' entire career. The other main work of this period, in addition to *Existentialisme ou Marxisme?* is *Die Zerstörung der Vernunft*, where all of Western philosophy from 1848 to the present is reduced to an increasingly irrationalistic apologetic. In this dogmatic rejection, Lukács' account was typical of the "orthodox" Marxist treatment of the subject. For a later work on the same level, see Jean T. Desanti, *Phénoménologie et Praxis* (Paris, 1963), devoted exclusively to Husserl's *Cartesian Meditations* which are found to be caught in a vicious circle. A major exception to the "official" treatment of Husserlian phenomenology can be found in the work of Antonio Banfi who, as a leader and Senator of the Italian Communist party, always paid very close attention to Husserlian phenomenology and other "decadent" philosophical trends. Although highly critical, he never summarily dismissed either Husserl or existentialism. For a good example of his account, see his posthumously published work, *La Ricerca della Realtà* (Florence, 1959), two volumes.

30. Tran Duc Thao's latest works consist in a series of four articles published in *La Pensée* under the titles: "Le Mouvement de l'Indication comme Forme Originaire de la Conscience," No. 128 (August 1966); "Du Geste de l'Index a l'Image Typique (I)," No. 147 (October 1969); "Du Geste de l'Index a l'Image Typique (II)," No. 148 (December 1969); and "L'Avéole de la Dialectique de la Connaissance," No. 149 (February 1970). For an analysis of these works see Silvia Federici, "Viet Cong Philosophy: Tran Duc Thao," *Telos*, No. 6 (Fall 1970). The same issue of this journal also includes the English translation of one of Tran Duc Thao's articles, "The Rational Kernel in the Hegelian Dialectic and its Real Content" (originally published in *Les Temps Modernes*, No. 36, 1948).

31. Karel Kosik, *Die Dialektik des Konkreten* (Frankfurt, 1967). The original Czech edition, however, dates back to 1961. An English translation of the first part of this work has

Europe after World War II. Through a devastating criticism of Heideggerian philosophy, Kosik reexamines key Marxist notions such as praxis, labor, consciousness, and economy, free of the empty and mechanical "orthodox" Marxist slogans. The result is a Marxism sounder than anything produced since Lukács and Gramsci. Indirectly exploding established myths such as knowledge as reflection, class structure as reducible to ready-made categories, and the economy as a limited sphere of human activity, Kosik's Marxism was a covert threat to the official ideology. Inextricably connected with the Czech "New Course" of which it was the best theoretical articulation, Kosik's work was one of the victims of Soviet tanks. Forgotten in Eastern Europe and ignored in the West, it seems bound for the same fate as Lukács' *History and Class Consciousness*, although it is theoretically much more sound.

The most pressing problem facing any serious Marxist today is the crisis of Marxism, seen not solely on a *practical* but also on the theoretical level. It would be abstract and idealistic to suppose that a fundamentally sound Marxism could have resulted in the unsound consequences that it has had; something must have been wanting in Marxism from the beginning. And it is precisely the locating of this original flaw which must allow an analysis of Stalinism and its consequences. Phenomenological Marxism can be preliminarily described as that approach which constantly reduces all theoretical constructs—including Marxism—to their living context in order to guarantee the adequacy of the concept not only to the object it claims to apprehend but also to the goals it seeks to attain. In fact, its point of departure is the rejection of the theory of reflection, so dear to "orthodox" Marxists, but actually an untenable remnant of positivism. Merleau-Ponty was right: "Marxism needs a theory of consciousness."[32] This is the task of phenomenology.

What does it mean to claim that a concept "reflects" the reality to which it refers? Concept and object are qualitatively different; there is not and cannot be any *necessary* connection between the two. If there were, then not only would absolute knowledge be possible, but it would have long ago been attained. The problem of knowledge is much more complicated. The attempt to determine reality metaphysically ends up in Kantianism and Hegelianism as soon as it is realized that the apprehended object can never be apprehended in its very being—which is fundamentally pre-conceptual—and that what is eventually apprehended is a set of projected categories which claim to describe the object. Kantianism is the realization that our intellectual relationship to reality is always mediated by these categories which, as such, constitute an impregnable shield protecting it from our grasp. Thus, according to Kantianism, the "materialist" theory of reflection is a crude form of objective idealism unaware that the very materiality of its object is constituted by projected categories which are subsequently seen as

---

appeared in *Telos*, No. 2 (Fall 1968), and in No. 4 (Fall 1969). No further reference will be made to this work in what follows since it would be too cumbersome. The debt to this work is too great to be documentable.

32. Merleau-Ponty, "Western Marxism," *op.cit.*, p. 148.

independent of the subject doing the projecting. Hegelianism is the further realization that the projective process is both *necessary* and *partial* such that the metaphysical "thing in itself" becomes superfluous, and absolute knowledge—in terms of which the partial conception appears as partial and whose very partiality presupposes a totality of which it is a part—turns out to be an unavoidable consequence. As Husserl has forcefully shown in his later writings,[33] far from being irreconciliably opposed, idealism and materialism are intimately related and are both the logical results of the same metaphysical matrix: objectivism. The difference between Marxist and bourgeois philosophy does not concern the metaphysical quandary whether consciousness precedes matter or vice versa. The difference is between a dynamic, creative philosophy which explains man's making of himself by making the object, on the one hand, and on the other, contemplative philosophies which counterpose an abstract subject to an abstract object, both equally inert.

As the self-consciousness of bourgeois society,[34] Marxism is a creative and not a contemplative philosophy, based on *labor* as man's teleologically directed activity. Bourgeois philosophy is contemplative precisely to the extent that it is the world outlook of a class that does not produce but passively consumes what other classes produce for it. Thus, the philosophy of bourgeois consciousness is neither idealism nor irrationalism, but *objectivism*, according to which both subject and object passively confront each other as full-fledged, ready-made, metaphysical entities. Objectivism takes the form of mechanical materialism, idealism, or irrationalism at different times in its futile effort to reconcile the two poles: subject and object. Ignoring labor, which is not a part of its social reality, bourgeois thought moves from system to system in the desperate search for a solution to its intrinsic contradictions. Thus, in mechanical materialism it lays its hopes on a preconstituted material world and in idealism it relies on a system of ideas. Marxist philosophy, not concerned merely with reflecting the world but with changing it, reconstitutes the world not only physically but also conceptually.

The relation between concept and object is not one of reflection or symmetry, but one of *adequacy*. To the extent that the concept is qualitatively different from the reality it apprehends and to the extent that it is necessarily partial in its depiction, the criterion of truth cannot be correspondence between concept and object; rather, it must be the correspondence between the concept and the fulfillment of the goal for which the concept was originally devised. Since the concept cannot reflect reality and, as Marx put it, is not attached to it,[35] the concept must be created. Furthermore,

---

33. See Edmund Husserl, *The Crisis of European Sciences and Transcendental Phenomenology*, translated by David Carr (Evanston, 1970). Robert Havamann, in *Dialektik ohne Dogma? Naturwissenschaft und Weltanschauung* (Hamburg, 1964), comes to roughly the same conclusions, although starting from a fundamentally different viewpoint—at least concerning crude materialism being identical with objective idealism. See the section on "Objektiver Idealismus und mechanischer Materialismus," pp. 27-32.

34. Lukács, *History and Class Consciousness*, p. 229.

35. Marx, *Capital*, (Moscow, n.d.), Vol. I, p. 74.

since an infinite number of possible partial concepts can be created to describe the same object—at least to the extent that the object is determined by the totality of the relationships into which it enters—the criterion determining the character of the unavoidable partiality of the concept is always a function of a social situation with its own needs and problems. In other words, the process of concept production should not be seen as at all different from the process of commodity production.[36] Both processes are teleological and based on labor. Thus, it is possible to talk about *all* knowledge, including science, as class-determined. If the concept bears not a necessary but only an historically contingent relation to the object, and if that relation is determined by a certain teleology inextricably connected with a certain social situation (class), then *all* knowledge is the result of a certain mode of social production and, consequently, is subject to the same dialectic described by Marx in *Capital.*

The structural symmetry between commodity production and conceptual production can be roughly described as follows. The crisis of capitalist society consists in the fact that whereas man makes himself through labor, under capitalist conditions of production he destroys himself in the process. The subject making the object through labor makes himself as a *creative* subject; but under capitalism the object is taken away from the subject and, to the extent that the object embodies his subjectivity, capitalism deprives the subject of his subjectivity and his humanity. Further, since under capitalism all decisions are made by the owners of the means of production, the subject is reduced to the level of an object which, however, must remain minimally a subject so that he can continue producing. Simultaneously, his product becomes first a commodity in the capitalist market, and subsequently *capital*, once it becomes universalized through the process of exchange. Thus, alienation results: the original producing subject is reduced to the level of an object to be bought and sold in the labor market just like any other commodity, while the object he originally produced, in becoming capital, has become the abstract subject. It requires no elaboration to see how capital in a capitalist society functions like a subject in the process alienating not only the worker but the capitalist as well. Essentially, the crisis of capitalism can be described as follows. The capitalist productive system originally developed to satisfy human needs (even if, from the beginning, these needs were not really universal but only particular, i.e., those of the rising bourgeoisie). However, with the reversal of subject and object, the productive system became counterproductive to its original goal. No longer connected with the producing subject, collapsed into the object-become-subject, the original goal of satisfying human needs is completely forgotten. Horkheimer and Adorno have described this process in *Dialectic of the Enlightenment* as one of rationality embodying both means and ends: when technological rationality becomes its own criterion, atomic destruction and Nazi barbarism face no significant opposition. Far from being a departure from bourgeois rationality, such atrocities are its logical outcome.

---

36. This insight, along with many others, can be found, *undeveloped*, in Sartre's *Search for a Method*, p. 179.

What is crucial here is that the framework of the capitalist crisis is wholly objectivistic. The subject-reduced-to-object faces a seemingly self-determined and independently-given rationality within which he can fit only as a mere object determined by that very same Frankensteinian rationality.

Precisely the same process takes place in the case of knowledge.[37] As a scientist, the scientist performs *specialized* labor: what he produces is as much a commodity in capitalist society as any other commodity. Originally developed to attain a certain universal goal, once the produced science is separated from the subject (the scientist) who produced it, science loses its *telos* and, instead of remaining a *means*, becomes its own criterion. Like capital, to the extent that it embodies the alienated subjectivity of the scientist, science functions as if it were a subject by redefining the original subjects as mere things in a universe of things. The crisis of the sciences consists in the alienation of the scientist into a robot characterized by what Husserl called the naturalistic outlook: the subject's failure to see anything but what the conceptual constructs he himself has created allow him to see. Thus, not only does he fail to see the pre-conceptual reality presupposed by his scientific constructs whose primacy is a necessary condition to it, but he also loses sight of the original *telos* which functioned as the criterion in constructing those categories. To the extent that means make sense only in relation to the end in terms of which they are means, once the end disappears these means lose their meaning; and, although the resulting scientific system exhibits a high degree of rationality, its foundation is precisely a thoroughgoing irrationality because there is no longer a *telos* to give it any meaning.

This process not only produces the atomic bomb and bacteriological warfare as allegedly "neutral" results, it also prevents science from making any progress, since science does not and cannot thematize the original abstractive process that produces the mathematizable forms which are alone susceptible to formal scientific treatment. To the extent that this abstractive level is not penetrated by science and remains its outer limit, a science that has lost sight of the subject can never explain the circularity of

---

37. A similar thesis seems to be put forth by Jürgen Habermas, "Knowledge and Interest," *Inquiry*, Vol. 3 (Winter, 1966), pp. 285-300. Strangely enough, Habermas' account is meant as a broadside attack on Husserl who is accused of reversing the order of primacy between the theoretical and the practical. For Habermas, "in the power of self-reflection knowledge and interest are one," such that both the crude and pretended value-free objectivism of positivist social science and the aloof "idealism" of Husserl are swept aside simultaneously. But in placing knowledge and interest on the same level, Habermas falls precisely into the one-dimensionality which Husserl characterizes as the crisis of the European sciences. The *telos* cannot collapse into the knowledge that it itself generates without being destroyed in the process. Need, as the precategorical basis of the *telos*, like the object that the concept seeks to capture, can never be exhausted in the latter and, if identified with it, loses its function and meaning. When the end itself is demoted to the level of a means, the means themselves no longer make sense as means. The fetishization of the *telos* by collapsing it to the level of knowledge leads to the occlusion of precategorical needs and their replacement by categorical ones. In this sense Habermas, rather than having gone beyond Husserl and Marx, is still pre-Marxian and pre-Husserlian. For an excellent critique of Habermas along these lines, see Pier Aldo Rovatti, "Critical Theory and Phenomenology," *Telos*, No. 15 (Spring 1973), pp. 25-40.

its own professed objective methodology.[38] At this point, it becomes possible to talk about class science since the original *telos* which has long been forgotten but which nonetheless permeates all of science was, and had to be, grounded in a social situation which gave it relevance—its pretended universality notwithstanding. Since the universal can concretely present itself only in the form of a particular, concrete universality is not the denial of particularity but its affirmation. Thus, science was from the very beginning *bourgeois* science. Yet, to the extent that the bourgeoisie claimed to be the *universal* class, its science sought to be universal and the crisis of science is inextricably connected with the crisis of bourgeois society. When the bourgeoisie revealed itself as a *particular* class with material interests radically different from those of a nascent *universal* class, the *universality* of its science became an ideological tool of social manipulation. The fact that there is no other science only shows that presently there is still no alternative, fully-constituted, social class which, caught in a radically different social context, can produce a different science in the same way that the bourgeoisie, in the Renaissance, succeeded in producing an alternative to replace feudal science.[39]

The same process applies to Marxism, which originally put itself forth not as a dogmatic metaphysics but as a specific type of consciousness developed in a specific historical stage to perform an equally specific social goal: the overcoming of class societies and the installation of a new social order with classless—and therefore universal—aims. Like labor, or science as specialized labor, Marxism comes about as the objectification of a certain class which—to use Sartre's term—is in fusion. Marxism is not the *empirical* consciousness of the proletariat since, as a result of alienation, such a consciousness necessarily reflects the ideology of the ruling class. Rather, Marxism is the objective consciousness that the proletariat *ought* to have once it becomes fully constituted as a class *for itself* as well as *in itself.* This process was to have taken place through the development of the subject-object identical. An understanding of why this failed to occur is the key to an understanding of the crisis of Marxism.

What is this subject-object identical? Lukács himself, who articulated this notion in *History and Class Consciousness*, eventually rejected it as an idealist construct.[40] In a nutshell, the subject-object identical is both the historical outcome of the alienation resulting from the capitalist mode of production and, at the same time, the necessary condition for its overcoming. According to Marx, under capitalism the worker becomes increasingly alienated. Thus, at first sight, it would seem that revolution is impossible since one of the manifestations of alienation is precisely the inability to realize one's objective interests and to fight for them. This

---

38. This, of course, is roughly Husserl's analysis in the *Crisis*. For an account of what consequences this is having on some sciences, see Gianni Trogú, "Vasco Ronchi's Revolution in Optics," *Telos*, No. 8 (Summer 1971).

39. General indications of this type can be found in the last chapter of André Gorz, *Le Socialisme Difficile* (Paris, 1967).

40. Lukács, *History and Class Consciousness*, p. xxiii.

conclusion, however, is undialectical; it fails to take into consideration the qualitative change that takes place *in* the process of alienation. What is destructive about the process of alienation is not that men objectify themselves through their labor, but that their objectifications are taken away from them. Since these objectifications are his *embodied subjectivity*, the subject is reduced to the level of a passive object, but with one crucial qualification. To the extent that the worker must continue to produce, he must remain minimally a subject. Total objectification is death, and dead workers cannot produce. Thus, although the worker is reduced to the level of a mere object, he remains throughout a subject. His alienation, manifested through his acceptance of the ruling class ideology, is the result of the separation of the subject from his produced object whereby the object becomes subject and vice-versa. However, this reversal sets the stage for the overcoming of alienation, since the very process that separated subject and object also ends up by reuniting them. As a commodity on the labor market, the worker finds himself as the product of bourgeois society and, as such, is reunited with his objectified subjectivity. This is how the subject-object identical comes into being and, with its creation, the worker is in an objective position to realize what his own objective interests are.[41]

Of course, given the state of emiseration and exploitation of nineteenth century industrial workers, the first and most immediate manifestation of this *prise de conscience* is the putting forth of trade union demands. But this, by itself, is only a *reformist* consciousness which does not yet question the whole productive system and, as such, does not pose a *revolutionary* threat. It is, however, a *moment* in the development of revolutionary consciousness. According to Marx, the competitive and closed character of capitalism does not allow the owners of the means of production to meet even these minimal demands. If the system were, in fact, competitive and closed, it would be impossible to grant trade union demands without simultaneously raising costs, and therefore prices, thus becoming noncompetitive. To the extent that the system cannot meet these demands, the trade unions

---

41. Much more concrete than Lukács, Gramsci shows not only that this subject-object identical is possible, but that it is the necessary product of modern capitalist modes of production: total enslavement becomes equivalent to total freedom. He writes: "The medieval scribe who took interest in the text that he copied, changed the grammar, the morphology and the syntax of the copied text: he left out entire paragraphs that he did not understand because of his low level of culture and the train of thoughts generated in him by his interest in the text led him to interpolate clarifications and notes; if his dialect or his language was different from that of the text, he introduced clarificatory details; he was a bad scribe because he actually 'rewrote' the text. The slowness of medieval copying techniques explains many of these deficiencies: there was too much time to reflect and, therefore, 'mechanization' was more difficult. The typographer must be much faster, he must continually keep his eyes and hands in movement and this facilitates his mechanization. But, to think about it, the effort that these workers must make in order to isolate the graphic symbolization from the intellectual content of the text—occasionally very engaging (in which case the work is slow and bad)—and concentrate on it, is maybe the greatest effort required of any job. Yet, it is done, and it does not spiritually kill man. When the process of adaptation has taken place, what results is that the worker's brain, *rather than becoming mummified, has attained a state of complete freedom.*" Antonio Gramsci, *Note sul Machiavelli, sulla Politica e sullo Stato Moderno* (Turin, 1966), pp. 336-337. Emphasis added.

change from reformist to revolutionary organizations seeking to overthrow the entire oppressive, historically obsolete system.

This explains why Marx did not bother much with elaborating a theory of the party. The party is itself the product of the spontaneous activity of the working class *under specific socio-historical conditions.*[42] Lenin's insistence in *What Is to Be Done?* on the need to bring revolutionary consciousness through the party to the working class from outside that class stems from what has earlier been indicated as that "something wanting" in Marxist philosophy from the very beginning: a premature totalization of the capitalist mode of production. Lenin took the voluntarist road in the face of social democratic reformism *à la* Bernstein because the trade unions and their political organs did not make the qualitative turn and become *revolutionary* organizations. Ironically, this political failure is precisely the result of their success. To the extent that the demands of trade unions were at least partially met, they became stable organizations effectively mediating the class struggle and freezing working class consciousness at the level of reformism.

With the onset of imperialist expansion toward the end of the nineteenth century, the full burden of exploitation was passed on to the new working classes of underdeveloped countries while the proletariat in the imperialist countries was gradually elevated to a relatively privileged economic position. Lenin's theory of the working class aristocracy, developed to account for the degeneracy of the social democratic leaders of the Second International, actually applied to the majority of the members of the working classes in advanced industrial societies. Prophetically, the first volume of Marx's *Capital*, the only one published during his lifetime and, therefore, the only one that can be regarded as a *finished* work, concludes with a chapter on colonialization. However, his purpose there was only to better show the inner mechanism of advanced capitalism in the mother country.[43] Marx's discussion of colonialism was focused almost exclusively on the then

---

42. Thus Marx and Engels wrote: "...the workers begin to form combinations (Trade's Unions) against the bourgeoisie; they club together in order to keep up the rate of wages; they found permanent associations in order to make provisions beforehand for these occasional revolts. Here and there the contest breaks out into riots. Now and then workers are victorious, but only for a time. The real fruit of their battles lies, not in the immediate result, but in the ever-expanding union of the workers. This union is helped on by the improved means of communications that are created by modern industry and that places the workers of different localities in contact with one another. It was just this contact that was needed to centralize the numerous local struggles, all of the same character, into one national struggle between classes. But every class struggle is a political struggle... *This organization of the proletarians into a class and consequently into a political party* is continually being upset again by the competition between the workers themselves. But it ever rises up again, stronger, firmer, mightier." Marx and Engels, "Manifesto of the Communist Party," in Marx and Engels, *Selected Works* (Moscow, 1968), Vol. I, pp. 42-43. Emphasis added.

43. One need only recall the last paragraph of the volume: "However, we are not concerned here with the condition of the colonies. The only thing that interests us is the secret discovered in the new world by the Political Economy of the old world, and proclaimed on the house-tops: that the capitalist mode of production and accumulation, and therefore capitalist private property, have for their fundamental condition the annihilation of self-earned private property: in other words, the expropriation of the laborer." Marx, *Capital*, Vol. I, p. 774.

sparsely populated North America and Australia. He overlooked the densely populated areas in Asia, Africa and Latin America which were rapidly being drawn into the economic orbit of capitalism. It was the colonial peoples in these areas who became the major revolutionary forces in the twentieth century and thus redefined the battle lines of class struggle.

Thus, at the close of the nineteenth century it became evident that Marxism as it had been developed by Marx and Engels was not entirely adequate. Because of the new lease on life given to capitalism by imperialist expansion, Marxism ceased to be the self-consciousness of the proletariat and became, at best, a *separate* ideology for manipulating workers and mediating the thawed class struggle. The same process at work in commodity production obtains here: the subject is separated from his object (Marxism) which, precisely because of this separation, becomes an independent entity. Because of the human subjectivity embodied in it, and the capitalist structure within which it operated, Marxism lost its *universal* character and was presented as the ideology of the proletariat as a particular social class with *particular* interests. Alienated Marxism took many forms. For Bernstein it was an "objective" science. For Lenin, it was merely what was positive in bourgeois ideology—what the bourgeoisie could not realize because it was a decadent class. And with Stalin it finally turned into a fixed metaphysics. Separated from its class foundations and redefined as an externally valid, objectively given structure,[44] Marxism has even, in certain cases, become another tool of oppression.

To the extent that Marxism was a premature totalization, it took a prerevolutionary situation as a revolutionary one. As a result, the revolutionary model it presented—capturing in theory the social forces of mid-nineteenth century Europe—has long been historically obsolete. A new critical Marxism adequate to today's realities must start out by reconstituting first and foremost the notion of class, particularly the working class. This is not a *new* problem; it has been around at least since the turn of the century. In fact, social democratic economism and Bolshevik voluntarism are opposite solutions to the same problem. Recognizing that the objective interests of the European proletariat had become inextricably connected with those of the national bourgeoisie, social democracy embarked on reformism as the political expression of those objective interests. Aware of this state of affairs, Lenin invested the revolutionary intelligentsia with the task of radicalizing the otherwise reformist working class. In both cases, Marxism degenerated from the level of revolutionary theory to that of mere *ideology*.

---

44. Gramsci was very much aware of this and, in a review of Bukharin's exposition of Marxism, he wrote: "If Marxism theoretically claims that any 'truth' believed to be eternal and absolute, has had practical origins and has been a 'temporary' value (the historicity of every world-view), it is very difficult to 'practically' explain that such an interpretation is also valid for Marxism, without at the same time shaking those convictions necessary for action." Thus, he explains Bukharin's theoretical aberrations in terms of tactical requirements: "Thus, it happens that Marxism itself tends to become an ideology in the bad sense, i.e., a dogmatic system of absolute and eternal truths." Cf. Gramsci, *Il Materialismo Storico*, p. 95. What Gramsci does not deal with, and which is a major problem today, is how it is possible to return to a genuine Marxism after these theoretical aberrations have compromised it. The failure of Krushchevism shows the problem to be extremely complex.

In the first case it ceased to be *universal* since it came to represent the *particular* objective interests of a privileged social class—the proletariat of advanced industrial societies—while in the second, it remained *universal* at the cost of no longer spontaneously arising from social praxis—thus becoming the *abstract* philosophical construct of alienated intellectuals.

The Russian Revolution took place in a backward country with highly industrialized centers (Petrograd, Moscow) where the proletariat was still a mere island within a sea of peasants. Thus, the revolution was essentially a result of World War I destruction, the organizational readiness of the Bolsheviks, the open collaboration of the peasantry, and the revolutionary ferment of a proletariat not yet integrated by the privileges of imperialism. However, the backward objective conditions immediately checkmated revolutionary hopes by necessitating the New Economic Policy (NEP), concessions to the peasantry, etc. By the time of Lenin's death, it had become obvious that the European revolutions, on whose success the Bolsheviks had staked their own survival, were not going to take place. If the Russians were to have socialism, they would have to do it alone. Thus "Socialism in One Country" was not just a Stalinist disaster, but the objective result of imperialist stabilization and the impossibility of revolution in the rest of Europe. By literally destroying both the Left Opposition and the Right Opposition, Stalin succeeded in industrializing Russia at the price of (among other things) debunking Marxism in the process. The result was state capitalism operated by a ruthless bureaucracy and controlled by the military. Thus, during the late twenties and early thirties, Marxism became the theoretical justification of Stalinist practice, and the attainment of the classless society became identified with the national interests of the U.S.S.R. It is precisely at this time that phenomenological Marxism began to develop as an attempt to return to a genuinely living and dialectical Marxism.

Thus, phenomenological Marxism is a response to the crisis of Marxism. Yet the task of a critical Marxism is, as has been indicated, nothing less than the radical reconstitution of Marxism itself. How can phenomenology be of any help here? Without entering into a discussion of the merits and shortcomings of phenomenology as a bourgeois philosophy, it can be shown that certain notions developed by Husserl in his later writings can be extremely useful in the reconstitution of Marxism, i.e., in the development of fundamental categories of analysis which can deal adequately with present socio-historical realities. Husserl's critique of science centers on the failure of science to change reality; instead, according to Husserl, it has occluded reality with its categories checkmating man as the historical agent and reducing him to the level of a passive object operating among similar objects. In fact, Husserl's analysis of science is a paradigm analysis of any knowledge whatsoever, including Marxism. As has already been shown, the dialectics of commodity production apply equally well to modern science and to Marxism. Whereas Marx "materialized" Hegel, critical or phenomenological Marxism must "materialize" Husserl by interpreting the base as the *Lebenswelt* and the worker as *transcendental subjectivity*. Only by doing so is it possible to vindicate the need for revolution and the quest for a qualitatively different way of life.

The *Lebenswelt* is that domain of experience which is both precategorical and categorical. It includes our relation to reality as such—free from any conceptual mediation, the array of concepts we use to conceptually articulate reality, and the conceptualized reality resulting from apprehending reality through concepts. Far from being a passive process, perception is itself a form of labor—the very process of perception exhibits the structure of labor. It involves the preconceptual apprehension of reality, the sorting out of concepts needed to abstract certain crucial features of that reality, and the conceptualizing of those features of reality deemed relevant, i.e., determined as essential in relation to some *telos* itself given to us as need in the *Lebenswelt*. It is inappropriate to identify the *Lebenswelt*, like Marcuse [45] and Schutz, [46] with the "empirical" or with the "common sense" world, since doing so ends up occluding precisely the crucial dialectic that makes the notion fruitful and relevant. The *Lebenswelt* does include the empirical and the commonsense world, but it also encompasses much more. In fact, its usefulness here lies precisely in this "much more." Although it is true that *ordinary* perception involves the mere identification of preconceptual entities through conceptual structures, this is not all that takes place or can take place. The *Lebenswelt* is also the domain in which concepts are invented and historical projects are formulated. Although *most* experience is of the *mundane* type whereby precategorical content is mechanically matched with pre-given conceptual forms (in fact, as recent developments in optics indicate, the identification is between the concept and its projection which is substituted for the precategorical reality it seems to be grasping), [47] this mundane experience is parasitic on the original constitutive experience that generated the conceptual repertory. It is only a moment of the whole but it ends up being considered as the whole itself. Husserl tried to uncover the transcendental subjectivity which generated these concepts and which is constantly repressed in *mundane* experience, i.e., the alienated experience of everyday life under certain socio-historical conditions. However, he was unable to draw the revolutionary conclusions implicit in his own analysis and he thus ended up identifying the crisis as first and foremost a *philosophical* crisis resolvable through a philosophical solution: the new phenomenology. [48]

This philosophical *cul de sac*—itself an epiphenomenon rather than a solution of the crisis—should not detract from the revolutionary character of Husserl's analysis. According to Marx, revolution is necessitated not just by material or even by cultural deprivation but, more importantly, by dehumanization; under capitalism men and women (both capitalist and proletarian) are limited to *mundane* experience, i.e., to a non-human level

---

45. Herbert Marcuse, "On Science and Phenomenology," in Robert S. Cohen and Marx Wartofsky, eds., *Boston Studies in the Philosophy of Science* (New York, 1965), pp. 279-290. Cf. also Herbert Marcuse, *One Dimensional Man* (Boston, 1964), pp. 162-169.
46. Alfred Schutz, *Collected Papers*, Vol. I, Maurice Natanson, ed. (The Hague, 1967).
47. In optics, of course, it is more appropriate to talk about "images." For a concise analysis of this, see Gianni Trogú, *op.cit.*
48. For a detailed criticism of Husserl along these general lines, see Antonio Banfi, "L'Humanisme et la culture contemporaine," *Comprendre*, No. 5 (1956).

of existence. The proletariat ends up as the revolutionary agency not because of any inner superiority or higher moral character but because having to work continually forces the worker into the role of a *transcendental* subject who not only *mundanely* transposes pre-given categories into a pre-given reality but also transforms that pre-given reality and, in laboring, is constantly faced with the limitations of the given categories. Thus, he must constantly function as a *transcendental* subject without even admitting this to himself. Anyone who has ever worked in a modern factory knows that the most difficult part of learning a job is not mastering the techniques designated by the existing division of labor, but establishing a *lebensweltliche* relation to the subject matter so as to relate creatively to it and, subsequently, to learn how to do this while pretending to adhere to the categorical procedures laid down by management. In a nutshell, the worker, as a worker, must function as a *transcendental* subject while at the same time presenting himself at all times as a passive, manipulatable, object-like thing. [49] Revolution is necessitated by the need to be an openly transcendental subject, i.e., really *human*. In fact, communist society can be defined as a society in which *transcendental* subjects can function as such. Communist society is not—as "orthodox" Marxism assumes—a streamlined and more efficient version of present society, projecting into every worker the life style of the capitalist. (This explains why workers in Eastern Europe and in the U.S.S.R., constantly bombarded with such an ideology, see an idealized American way of life as the wave of the future.) Instead, communist society must be a qualitatively different society in which every subject can be a real subject in a genuinely intersubjective society.

An immediate consequence of this analysis is a reinterpretation of the key Marxist notion of the economy. The economy cannot be seen as a separate sphere among other spheres such as leisure, education, rest, play, etc. The economy is fundamental precisely because it deals with the production and reproduction of everyday life. In fact, as Vajda and Heller have stressed, [50] revolution cannot mean simply a change from private to collective

---

49. Of course, this is not possible under capitalist or bureaucratic modes of production for, if a worker were to reveal his *transcendentality*, i.e., his better acquaintance with reality, this would only open the door for intensified exploitation. In fact, the discrepancy between the *categorical* technique and the transcendental relation of the worker to his job, acts as a shield of protection for the workers—even though management, especially in small and nonunionized enterprises, very often compensates for this in an immediate empirical manner: the worker can always do better than is expected. Gramsci, as usual, was very much aware of this contradiction. He wrote: "The active man of the masses operates practically, but does not have a clear theoretical consciousness of his own functioning which is nonetheless a way of knowing the world to the extent that he transforms it. Rather his theoretical consciousness can be historically in contrast with his functioning. It can almost be said that he has two theoretical consciousnesses (or one contradictory consciousness), one implicit in his functioning and which really unites him to all of his collaborators in the practical transformation of reality, and one superficially explicit or verbal which he has inherited from the past and has uncritically accepted." Gramsci, *Il Materialismo Storico*, p. 11.

50. Mihaly Vajda and Agnes Heller, "Family Structure and Communism," *Telos*, No. 7 (Spring 1971), pp. 99-111. Cf. also Agnes Heller, "The Marxian Theory of Revolution," *Telos*, No. 6 (Fall 1970), pp. 212-223.

management; that would leave everyday life unchanged and, as such, would be utterly irrelevant. Revolution must be interpreted, first and foremost, as a qualitative change in this everyday life through which today's fragmented and robotized workers will become subjects consciously (politically) engaged in determining their destiny (concretely, not through bureaucratic party representatives).

The most glaring failure of Soviet society is not in economics understood in the bourgeois sense (growth in production, GNP, etc.). In quantitative terms Soviet society might be judged a moderate success. It is in terms of economics as the production and reproduction of everyday life that Soviet society must be judged a failure. The Soviet worker is probably the most atomized, depoliticized and alienated worker in the world. "Orthodox" Marxism, relating to Marxism not as a living philosophy of human self-becoming but as a fixed metaphysics, can only conceive of it in the abstract. Thus, it can regard socialism as practically attained once collective owner-ship of the means of production has been attained. However, collective ownership is only a means to the attainment of a qualitatively superior humanity. If the means no longer attains the end, the means must be changed. Unfortunately, reified Marxism has been reduced to an abstract formalism in which the dialectical tension between means and ends has been collapsed in the facticity of a bourgeois rationality purely concerned with technological efficiency. It cannot penetrate the living reality it hides and thus it perpetuates a form of the very bourgeois alienation it claims to have eliminated.

This is why phenomenological Marxism interprets the base-superstruc-ture distinction as what Husserl calls the categorical and the precategorical. Tran Duc Thao did this preliminarily in "Marxisme et Phénoménologie." Thus, the base is not simply the domain of production—which can be easily understood in a mechanistic way as the physical means of production—but the sphere of teleological human activity: what was earlier defined as the economy. The superstructure is not the ideological reflection of the base but rather the domain of cultural and spiritual objectifications. A qualitative change of the base and superstructure (revolution) cannot, therefore, be identified with either industrialization or collectivization of the means of production, but must be seen as a radical change in the *quality* of life. In our historical context, this means that what must change is not only the mode of production (the abolishment of the private ownership of the means of production), but also the way we relate to ourselves and others. In fact, for Marx, the change in the mode of production makes sense only to the extent that it is a *precondition* of a qualitative change in the life style which is both categorical and precategorical: we live not only as biological and physical beings but also as thinking entities. Revolution, therefore, can only mean a qualitatively different life. The technological and productive para-phernalia come in only to the extent that it is necessary to this end. An alienated Marxism is one that forgets this means-ends dialectic and considers socialism realized once private property has been abolished and industrialization carried out, without perceiving that it might be possible to realize what were thought to be the means without at the same time necessarily guaranteeing the attainment of the ends. The experience of Soviet Marxism is precisely of this nature.

Theoretically, this dialectical and phenomenological articulation of the base and superstructure prevents the occurrence of reactionary mystifications such as Stalin's "infrastructure." Stalin interpolated the infrastructure between base and superstructure understood—not as the domain of subjective operation conditioned by earlier objectifications and the domain of objective results produced according to a determinate teleology—but instead as material forces and ideological reflections thereof. Stalin invented this altogether new fundamentally non-Marxist and non-dialectical category as a sort of epistemological limbo in which to place things such as science and linguistics.[51] These and other troublesome entities could be located neither in the base nor in the superstructure without generating all kinds of difficulties. For, if science is part of the base, then it ought to change radically with a shift from bourgeois to socialist society. This however, did not happen in the U.S.S.R. In Stalinist Marxism, the very notion of base gradually gives way to the "infrastructure." This is understandable. If the Soviet Union wants to present itself as the society of the future or as a step beyond bourgeois society, it must show a base different from the bourgeois base. Since it cannot do this—its base is not technologically superior to that of the U.S. nor has it succeeded in abolishing the division of labor and individual remuneration—both science and the means of production must be evaporated from the base into the neutral mid-air of the infrastructure. It should also be evident why science cannot be placed in the superstructure. If science is part of the superstructure then science would have to be different in the Soviet Union from bourgeois science— which it is not. Thus, the infrastructure as the domain of reified and unchanging bourgeois reality camouflaged as neutral existence, becomes a very handy category in a society which, although it claims to be socialist, is still very far from reaching that goal. It becomes a means for hiding the blatant contradictions of Soviet society.

This interpretation of economy, base, superstructure and revolution also leads to a reinterpretation of the very notion of class, with all its organizational and political consequences. If revolution is first and foremost a qualitative change of everyday life for the entire society, and revolutionary consciousness—as well as bourgeois consciousness—is a function of a

---

51. See Giuseppe Stalin, *Il Marxismo e la Linguistica*, Italian translation by Bruno Meriggi (Rome, 1968). Interestingly enough, in this work Stalin puts forth a theory of linguistics very close to Wittgenstein for whom "*the limits of my language* are the limits of my world." Cf. Ludwig Wittgenstein, *Tractatus Logico-Philosophicus* (New York, 1961), 5.6, pp. 114-115. Stalin argues that language is not distinguishable from thought and that it belongs in the infrastructure as a neutral domain. It is to be remembered that the identification of language and thought has been one of the major tenets of Italian Idealism (Croce) and that, although in the *Grundrisse* Marx wrote that "ideas do not exist separate from language" (cf. Karl Marx, *Grundrisse des Kritik der politischen Oekonomie* [Berlin, 1953], p. 80), he also makes it very clear that language has its class character. Cf. Marx, *Selected Writings in Sociology and Social Psychology*, translated by T.B. Bottomore (New York, 1964), p. 71. In the *German Ideology* Marx writes: "the very language is a product of the bourgeoisie and therefore, even in language as in reality, commercial relations are placed at the base of all others." Marx and Engels, *L'Ideologia Tedesca*, Italian translation by Fausto Codino (Rome, 1967), p. 213.

certain socio-economic situation that determines one's life style, then the criterion for class-belonging is a function not of the relationship to the means of production but of the quality of life that results from that relationship. Furthermore, to the extent that in advanced capitalist societies life style is no longer exhaustively determined by the relationship to the means of production, the bourgeoisie proletariat dichotomy must be reexamined. The very fact that modern society produces different life styles which, accordingly, find parallel political expressions, i.e., women's liberation, Black liberation, student movements, etc., indicates that class lines are much more complicated than classical Marxism assumed and "orthodox" Marxism has since uncritically parroted. If oppression is first and foremost a function of sex, race, etc., and only after considerable Marxist theoretical mediation becomes a function of the proletarianization process produced by the bourgeois mode of production, then it does not make much sense to retain the old class analysis. In fact, the old proletariat has been so fragmented and disintegrated in the development of advanced capitalism, that all the king's horses and all the king's men (or even the Leninist party), could never succeed in putting this Humpty Dumpty back together again.

The structure of revolutionary political organizations also needs to be radically reexamined. The classical Leninist concept of the party as outlined in *What Is to Be Done?* has become *official* Stalinist dogma—although Lenin himself abandoned this position as early as 1906.[52] This position now appears utterly obsolete. As Gorz put it, the kind of revolutionary organization adequate to contemporary objective conditions "...can no longer follow the Leninist model. It is no longer confronted by a despotic and repressive State, but by a State which is essentially political and which bases the legitimacy of its repressive actions on its ability to mediate politically between contradictory interests that are continually reduced to forms of ideological expression which makes this mediation possible. And it is no longer confronted by a homogeneous upsurge of popular forces against repression, but by a number of upsurges, all relatively distinct in their anti-capitalist aspirations, all pursuing at differentiated and specific levels a sovereign self-determination by social individuals of the conditions, ends, and framework of their social activity."[53] Unfortunately, Gorz's account, which reflects the needs exemplified by the failure of the May 1968 revolt in France, fails to deal with the theoretical problems the account itself generates. It is not at all clear why the general totalizing element which Gorz posits as being able to unite all these classes according to the new

---

52. See Marcel Liebman, "Lénine en 1905," in *Les Temps Modernes*, No. 285 (April 1970). Liebman distinguishes between Lenin and Leninism and succeeds in showing how Leninism was always at least two steps beyind Lenin's living dialectic. In fact, interestingly enough, in 1905, when Lenin changed his position and came out favoring the Soviets that had spontaneously arisen, the Petrograd Bolsheviks *refused* to publish Lenin's views on the subject. The monolithic and authoritarian character of Leninism is ascribed by Liebman to the reactionary lull that ensued in Russia after 1906. Although Lenin fought these tendencies, after his death they became "official." For a very similar analysis of Lenin's notion of the party, see Antonio Carlo, *Lenin sul Partito* (Bari, 1970).

53. André Gorz, "The Way Forward," in Arthur Lothstein, ed., *"All \ Are Saying..."* (New York, 1971), pp. 336-337.

definition—i.e., socialist society—will be accepted by these very groups. The *particularity* of their demands easily falls prey to bourgeois mediation: to the extent that demands remain particular they do not constitute a threat to bourgeois society. Thus, the abolishing of racism or the granting of full equality to women is not something altogether impossible for modern capitalism. These things could be attained without at the same time qualitatively changing the character of capitalist society. On the other hand, if the source of the problem is traced back to property relations and capitalism, this already presupposes the *universalization* of the criticism and, therefore, the transcendence of the organization of these groups as *autonomous* groups. Thus, the paradox seems to be that either the demands of these new classes are particular, in which case no political glue will ever succeed in joining them into anything but a mechanical political coalition ready to fall apart at every juncture; or their demands are universal, in which case the original analysis of these groups as autonomous entities is questioned and their coalescing into a larger federation is really unnecessary since they are all parts of the same class to begin with.

This criticism, however, is abstract insofar as it freezes the fluid reality of these groups into fixed stereotypes. In reality, all these groups are in fusion and include both particularized and universalized self-understanding within them. Thus, to the extent that the present situation is characterized by overwhelming bourgeois cultural hegemony, it is easy to see how, lacking any counter-cultural interpretation which would reinforce the universalized tendency within these groups, they are eventually condemned to bourgeois integration and, therefore, easily defused of their revolutionary content. This is precisely what makes the existence of a revolutionary organization able to challenge bourgeois cultural hegemony all the more necessary: its very existence can prevent the shipwreck of revolutionary potentialities into integrated standardization. The reformist trends within women's liberation, Black liberation, etc., i.e., the framing of the issues purely in terms of race and sex, is, to a great extent, due to Marxists' inability to provide a Marxist analysis of these problems free of the trivialities and irrelevancies of "orthodox" Marxism. This is where phenomenological Marxism can become very useful.

Given the present state of bourgeois hegemony whereby *all* constituted opposition is trapped into sharing the fundamental assumptions of precisely that order that has to be qualitatively altered, a concrete analysis of society and culture is a *sine qua non conditio* of any meaningful political project. Marxism, through its two main theoretical tenets—the dialectic and the theory of alienation—can provide such an analysis if, and only if, it is itself cleansed of the naturalism and objectivism that has reduced it to a third-rate duplication of standard bourgeois theory. Thus, in its naturalized form, alienation becomes a direct result of economic relations such that, once private ownership of the means of production is replaced by state ownership, it becomes a logical impossibility. But alienation is first and foremost the result of *domination*, and capitalist exploitation is only one of many possible forms of alienation. Thus, removing capitalist exploitation is no guarantee that domination is abolished. Only a *subjectivist* analysis of domination can plot out its actual overcoming since to be a subject is not the result of a logical deduction from reified categories, but something which must be experienced in the first person in the process of freely creating and recreating the environment and oneself. Alienation will be overcome only when everyone becomes a subject in the Husserlian sense, independently of juridical relations such as the ownership of the means of production.

The same goes for the dialectic. Unless it is understood as primarily a precategorical creative process, the dialectic itself becomes naturalized and deteriorates to a rhetorical dance of abstract categories. This denaturalization of both the theory of alienation and of the dialectic can only be carried out through a rigorous phenomenological cleansing with the reintroduction of the subject as the crucial element throughout. Otherwise, Marxism may very well remain the nineteenth century ideological remnant that it has become, peacefully rusting in the junkyard of abstract negations.

Hegelian Leninism

Raya Dunayevskaya

"The group of editors and contributors of the magazine *Under the Banner of Marxism* should, in my opinion, be a kind of 'Society of Materialist Friends of Hegelian Dialectics'."

—*Lenin, 1922*

During the disintegration of the entire world and of established Marxism in the holocaust of World War I, Lenin encountered Hegel's thought. The revolutionary materialist activist theoretician, Lenin, confronted the bourgeois idealist philosopher Hegel who, working through two thousand years of Western thought, revealed the revolutionary dialectic. In the shock of recognition Lenin experienced when he found the revolutionary dialectic *in Hegel*, we witness the transfusion of the lifeblood of the dialectic, the transformation of reality as well as thought: "Who would believe that this— the movement and 'self-movement' . . . spontaneous, *internally-necessary* movement . . . 'movement and life' is the core of 'Hegelianism,' of abstract and abstruse (difficult, absurd) Hegelianism??"[1]

"The Dialectic Proper"

Lenin the activist, Party man and materialist underwent "absolute negativity." While reading "The Law of Confrontation," he concluded his new appreciation of the dialectic by saying: "the principle of all self-movement: The idea of universal movement and change (1813 *Logic*) was conjectured before its application to life and society. In regard to society it was proclaimed earlier (1847) than it was demonstrated in application to man (1859)."[2] The illumination cast here on the relationship of philosophy to revolution in Lenin's day is so strong that today's challenges become transparent and reveal the ossification of philosophy and the stifling of the dialectics of liberation. Russian philosophers refuse to forgive Lenin for this. Their underhanded criticism of his *Philosophic Notebooks* continues unabated even on the hundredth anniversary of his birth. They have blurred the distinction between the vulgar materialist photocopy theory of *Materi-*

---

1. The first English translation of Lenin's *Abstract of Hegel's Science of Logic* appeared as Appendix A of my *Marxism and Freedom* (New York, 1958). This translation will hereafter be referred to as *M&F*. I will also cite parallel passages in the Moscow translation (Lenin, *Collected Works*, Vol. 38, 1961) and will refer to it as Vol. 38. Here, see *M&F*, p. 331; Vol. 38, p. 141.

2. *Ibid.* In this quotation, the date 1847 refers to the writing of *The Communist Manifesto* which, however, was published only in 1848. The date 1859 is the date of publication of Darwin's *Origin of the Species*.

alism and Empirio-Criticism (1908) and Lenin's totally new philosophical departure in 1914 toward the self-development of thought.

In the *Notebooks*, Lenin wrote: "Alias: Man's cognition not only reflects the objective world, but creates it."[3] B.M. Kedrov, director of the Institute of History of Science and Technology, reduces Lenin's new appreciation of "idealism" to philistine semantics: "What is fundamental here is the word 'alias,' meaning otherwise or in other words, followed by a colon. This can only mean one thing, a paraphrase of the preceding note on Hegel's views.... If the meaning of the word 'alias' and the colon following it are considered, it will doubtless become clear that in that phrase Lenin merely set forth, briefly, the view of another, not his own."[4] Professor Kedrov's zeal to deny that Lenin's 1914 *Notebooks* "are in fundamental contravention of *Materialism and Empirio-Criticism*" has led him to such cheap reductionism that "in defense" of Lenin, Kedrov can only attribute to Lenin his own philistinism: "Lenin categorically rejects and acidly ridicules the slightest slip by Hegel in the direction of ascribing to an idea, to a thought, to consciousness the ability to create the world."[5] With this single stroke, Kedrov deludes himself into believing he has closed the philosophic frontiers Lenin opened.

The West's deafness to Lenin's break with his philosophic past (in which cognition had only the role of "reflecting" the objective or the material) has produced an intellectual incapacity to cope with Communist emasculation of Lenin's philosophy.[6] However, anyone who invokes Lenin's name "favorably" should at least remember either "the objective world connection" to which Lenin incessantly referred or men's "subjective" aspirations, the phrase by which Lenin "translated" his concept of consciousness "creating the world": "the world does not satisfy man and man decides to change it by his activity."[7] Even independent Marxists have been sucked into the theoretical void following Lenin's death and have lazily avoided the rich, profound, concrete *Notebooks*. They bemoan the "jottings" which make the *Notebooks* seem so "scanty" that any attempt to understand them could only be "idle speculation." Sticking to "provable" politics as if that were sufficient, they call for "application" of the dialectic. No doubt, the proof of the pudding is always in the eating, and Lenin's "application" of the *Notebooks* was in politics. But were we to begin there

---

3. *M&F*, p. 347; Vol. 38, p. 212.

4. B.M. Kedrov, "On the Distinctive Characteristics of Lenin's *Philosophic Notebooks*," *Soviet Studies in Philosophy* (Summer, 1970).

5. *Ibid.*

6. Professor David Joravsky senses that Lenin's comments on Hegel's *Science of Logic* are "tantalizingly suggestive of a new turn in his thought" in *Soviet Marxism and Natural Science, 1917-1932* (New York, 1961), p. 20. He exposes Stalin's transformation of Lenin's alleged "partyness" in the field of philosophy into pure Stalinist monolithism. Nevertheless, by excluding from his own work a serious analysis of Lenin's *Philosophic Notebooks*, Joravsky leaves the door wide open for lesser scholars to write as if there were a straight line from Lenin to Stalin instead of a transformation into opposite. As for Lenin's *Materialism and Empirio-Criticism*, Lenin himself was the one who stressed its political motivations. He wrote in his letter to Gorky, "The Mensheviks will be reduced to politics and that is the death of them." See the chapter "Lenin and the Partyness of Philosophy" in Joravsky's work.

7. Vol. 38, p. 213.

and dwell on politics apart from Lenin's new comprehension of the dialectic, we would understand neither his philosophy nor his politics. It is the interaction of the two which is relevant for today.

During the critical decade of war and revolution between 1914 and 1924, Lenin did not prepare the *Notebooks* for publication. However, his heirs had no legitimate reason to delay their publication until six years after his death. When they were published in 1929-1930, neither Trotsky, Stalin, Bukharin, nor "mere academicians" (whether mechanists or "dialecticians") took them seriously.[8] A new epoch of world crises and revolutions and the birth of the Black dimension in Africa and the U.S. finally compelled an English publication in 1961.

Lenin began reading Hegel's *Science of Logic* in September, 1914, and finished on December 17. Even from his comments on the Prefaces and the Introduction, it is clear that Lenin's concrete concerns (to which he referred in his "asides" as he copied and commented on quotations from Hegel) were "the objective world connections," the Marxists and the Machists, and above all Marx's *Capital*. Reading Hegel's Introduction, in which he speaks of logic as "not a mere abstract Universal, but as a Universal which comprises in itself the full wealth of Particulars,"[9] Lenin wrote: "cf. *Capital.* A beautiful formula: 'not a mere abstract universal, but a universal which comprises in itself the wealth of particulars, individual separate (all the wealth of the particular and separate)!! *Trés Bien!*"[10] No matter how often Lenin reminded himself that he was reading Hegel "materialistically," no matter how he lashed out against the "dark waters" of such abstractions as "Being-for-Self," and despite the fact that in his first encounter with the categories of the Doctrine of Notion (Universal, Particular, Individual) he called them "a best means of getting a headache," Lenin grasped from the outset not only the deep historical roots of Hegel's philosophic abstractions but also their historical meaning for "today." Therefore, Lenin sided with Hegel's idealism against what he called the "vulgar materialism" of his day: "The idea of the transformation of the ideal into the real is *profound.* Very important for history—Against vulgar materialism. NB. The difference of the ideal from the material is also not unconditional, not excessive (*überschwenglich*)."[11]

The significance of Lenin's commentary is that he made it while he was still reading the Doctrine of Being. To all Marxists after Marx, including Engels,[12] the Doctrine of Being had meant only immediate perception, or the commodity, or the market, i.e., the phenomenal, apparent reality as against the essential exploitative relations of production. Even here, Lenin

---

8. The first publication of the *Philosophic Notebooks* was edited by Bukharin who, however, had nothing to say about it. The introduction of 1929 by Deborin and that of 1930 by Adoratsky apeared only in the Russian edition. See *Leninski Sbornik* (Moscow), Vol. XII. It is also worthwhile to consult Joravsky, *op.cit.,* pp. 97 ff., regarding Bukharin and Trotsky on the *Philosophic Notebooks.*

9. Hegel, *Science of Logic* (New York, 1929), Vol. I, p. 69.

10. *M&F,* p. 328; Vol. 38, p. 99.

11. *M&F,* p. 329; Vol. 38, p. 114.

12. The two letters of Engels to Conrad Schmidt dated November 1, 1891 and February 4, 1892 are most applicable: Engels cites "a good parallel" between the development of Being into Essence in Hegel and the development of commodity into capital in Marx.

escaped "vulgar materialism," which sought to erect impassable barriers between the ideal and the real. In Lenin's new evaluation of idealism, however, there was neither "sheer Hegelianism" nor "pure" Maoist voluntarism.[13] Instead, Lenin's mind was constantly active, seeing new aspects of the dialectic at every level, whether in Being or in Essence. Indeed, in the latter sphere Lenin emphasized not the contrast between Essence and Appearance, but instead *self*-movement, *self*-activity, and *self*-development. For him it was not so much a question of essence *versus* appearance as it was of the two being *"moments"* (Lenin's emphasis) of a *totality* from which even cause should not be singled out: "It is absurd to single out causality from this. It is impossible to reject the *objectivity* of notions, the objectivity of the *universal* in the particular and in the individual."[14] Reading the Doctrine of Notion, Lenin broke with his philosophic past. The break began in the Doctrine of Essence, at the end of Causality, when he began to see new aspects of causality and of scientism, which could not possibly fully explain the relationship of mind to matter. Therefore, he followed Hegel's transition to the Doctrine of Notion, "the realm of Subjectivity, or Freedom" which Lenin immediately translated as "NB Freedom = Subjectivity ('or') End, consciousness, Endeavor, NB."[15]

Lenin was liberated in his battles with the categories of the Doctrine of Notion, the very categories he had called "a best way of getting a headache." First, he noted that Hegel's analysis of these categories is "reminiscent of Marx's imitation of Hegel in Chapter I."[16] Second, Lenin no longer limited objectivity to the material world but extended it to the *objectivity of concepts:* freedom, subjectivity, notion. These are the categories through which we gain knowledge of the objectively real. They constitute the beginning of the transformation of objective idealism into materialism. By the time he reached Hegel's analysis of the relationship of means to ends, he so exalted in Hegel's genius in the dialectic, "the germs of historical materialism,"[17] that he capitalized, boldfaced, and surrounded with three heavy lines Hegel's statement that "in his tools man possesses power over external Nature even though, according to his ends, he frequently is subjected to it."[18] In reaching that conclusion, Lenin had projected his new understanding of objectivity by writing: "Just as the simple value form, the individual act of exchange of a given commodity with another, already includes, in undeveloped form, *all* major contradictions of capitalism,—so the simplest *generalization*, the first and simplest forming of *notions* (judgments, syllogisms, etc.) signifies the ever-deeper knowledge of the *objective* world connections. It is necessary here to seek the real sense, significance, and role of the Hegelian Logic.

---

13. The pretentious French Communist Party philosopher Louis Althusser is working hard to kill the dialectic and at the same time to present himself as a "Leninist." But such absolute opposites cannot coexist, not even when one is inventive enough to add Mao and Freud to the hodgepodge. See especially his lecture to bourgeois French philosophers, since reproduced as a pamphlet, *Lénine et la Philosophie* (Paris, 1968).
14. *M&F*, p. 339; Vol. 38, p. 178.
15. *M&F*, *loc.cit.*; Vol. 38, p. 164.
16. *M&F*, *loc.cit.*; Vol. 38, p. 178.
17. *M&F*, p. 342; Vol. 38, p. 189.
18. Hegel, *op.cit.*, Vol. II, p. 338.

This NB."[19] Thirdly, Lenin began striking out not only against Hegel but against Plekhanov and all Marxists including himself. Although Moscow's English translator omitted the emphasis in "Marxists," there is no way to modify Lenin's conclusion that "none of the Marxists understood Marx. It is impossible fully to grasp Marx's *Capital*, especially the first chapter, if you have not studied through and understood the *whole* of Hegel's *Logic*."[20]

Naturally, like the aphorism on "cognition creating the world," this cannot be taken literally. Long before Lenin seriously studied the *Logic*, no one had written more profoundly on economics, especially on Volume II of *Capital*, both as theory and as the concrete analysis of *The Development of Capitalism in Russia*. Nevertheless, the world had changed so radically by the outbreak of World War I and the collapse of the Second International that Lenin became dissatisfied with everything Marxists had written before 1914 on economics, philosophy, and even revolutionary politics. These writings lacked the sharpness and the necessary absolutes of his dictum, "Turn the imperialist war into a civil war." Of course, Lenin did not bring a blank mind to the study of *Science of Logic*. Even as a philosophical follower of Plekhanov, who never understood "the dialectic proper,"[21] Lenin was a *practicing* dialectician. The actual contradictions in Tsarist Russia prepared him for these new conceptions of the dialectic, the "algebra of revolution," which he now began to spell out as "subject" (masses) reshaping history. As Lenin prepared himself theoretically for revolution, dialectics became pivotal and ever more concrete to him. He had begun the study of the *Logic* in September, 1914, at the same time he completed the essay "Karl Marx" for the *Encyclopedia Granat*. Lenin was not fully satisfied with what he had written when he *finished* the *Logic* on December 17, 1914. On January 5, 1915, with the world war raging, he asked Granat if he could make "certain corrections in the section on dialectics.... I have been studying this question of dialectics for the last month and a half, and I could add something to it if there was time...."[22] By pinpointing the time as a "month and a half," Lenin indicated the specific book, *Subjective Logic*, which had opened his mind to new philosophical frontiers. The *Notebooks* themselves, of course, make clear beyond doubt that it was while reading the Doctrine of Notion, directly after the section of the Syllogism, that Lenin exploded with criticism of turn-of-the-century Marxists for having made their philosophic analyses "more in a Feuerbachian and Buchnerian than in a Hegelian manner," and with the realization that it was "impossible fully to grasp Marx's *Capital*, especially the first chapter, if you have not studied through and understood the *whole* of Hegel's *Logic*."[23]

The Russians ignore that Lenin not only concentrated on *Subjective Logic* as a whole but also devoted fifteen pages to the final chapter, the Absolute Idea. But they have to acknowledge that "Lenin evidently assigned

19. *M&F*, p. 339; Vol. 38, p. 179.
20. *M&F*, p. 340; Vol. 38, p. 180.
21. *M&F*, p. 354; Vol. 38, p. 277. Cf. "On Dialectics," in Vol. 38.
22. *The Letters of Lenin* (New York, 1937), p. 336.
23. *M&F*, p. 340; Vol. 38, p. 180.

great significance to Hegel's *Subjective Logic*, since the greater part of his profound remarks and interesting aphorisms are expressed during the reading of this part of the *Logic*." [24] But in the three decades since the first publication of the *Notebooks*, Russian philosophers have not drawn any conclusions from this fact; much less, in their favorite phrase, have they "applied" it. Instead, they have taken advantage of Lenin's philosophic ambivalence and have refused to see his philosophic break in 1914 with his Plekhanovist past. Certain facts, however, are stubborn. One such fact is that whereas Plekhanov, *the* philosopher of the Second International, reverted to the materialist of the seventeenth and eighteenth centuries, Lenin eventually came to concentrate on Hegel. Lenin regarded Hegel as crucial to the task of the Russian theoreticians. Lenin saw the need to "arrange for the systematic study of Hegelian dialectics" which, though it was to be done from a materialist standpoint, was not to be reduced to mere interpretation. Also, it was necessary to "print excerpts from Hegel's principal works." [25] Another stubborn fact is that Lenin's advice to Russian youth to continue studying Plekhanov cannot alter the task he set for himself: "Work out: Plekhanov wrote probably nearly 1,000 pages (Beltov + against Bogdanov + against Kantians + basic questions, etc. etc. on philosophy (dialectic). There is in them *nil* about the Larger Logic, *its* thoughts (i.e., dialectic proper, as a philosophic science) nil!!" [26] The third stubborn fact which Communist philosophers disregard is the significance of Lenin's swipe (which included Engels) at "inadequate attention" to dialectics as the unity of opposites. "The unity of opposites is taken as the sum total of examples ('for example, a seed,' for example, primitive Communism)." [27] Lenin forgave Engels this defect because he wrote deliberately for popularization. However, this cannot touch the deeper truth that, although he always followed Marx's principle that "it is impossible, of course, to dispense with Hegel," Engels considered that "the theory of Essence is the main thing." [28] Lenin, on the other hand, held that the Doctrine of Notion was primary because, at the same time that it deals with thought, it is concrete. It is subjective, not merely as against objective but as a unity in cognition of theory and practice. Through the Doctrine of Notion, Lenin gained a new appreciation of Marx's *Capital*, not merely as economics but as logic. Lenin now called *Capital* "the history of capitalism and the analysis of the notions summing it up." [29] Lenin, and only Lenin, fully understood the unity of materialism and idealism present even in Marx's strictly economic categories.

Marx founded historical materialism and broke with idealism. But he credited idealism rather than materialism for developing the "active side" of "sensuous human activity, practice." [30] On the road to the greatest

24. *Leninski Sbornik, op.cit.,* Introduction by Deborin to Vol. IX.
25. Lenin, *Selected Works* (New York, 1943), Vol. IX, p. 77.
26. *M&F*, p. 354; Vol. 38, p. 277.
27. Lenin, *Selected Works, op.cit.,* Vol. XI, p. 81. "On Dialectics" also appears both in Vol. 38 of the *Collected Works* and in Vol. XIII (1927) as an addendum to *Materialism and Empirio-Criticism*! It is also wrongly attributed there to "sometime between 1912 and 1914."
28. Engels to Conrad Schmidt, November 1, 1891.
29. *M&F*, p. 353; Vol. 38, p. 320.
30. I have used the latest Moscow translation of the "Theses on Feuerbach" in *Marx and Engels—The German Ideology* (1964), pp. 645 and 647.

material (proletarian) revolution, Lenin likewise saw the indispensability of the Hegelian dialectic. He summarized in an article what he had just completed in the *Notebooks*: "Dialectics *is* the theory of knowledge of (Hegel and) Marxism. This is the 'aspect' of the matter (it is not 'an aspect' but the essence of the matter) to which Plekhanov, not to speak of other Marxists, paid no attention."[31] Having reestablished continuity with Marx and Hegel, Lenin fully grasped what was new in Marx's materialism: its human face. He was not, of course, familiar with the *Economic and Philosophic Manuscripts of 1844*, in which Marx defined his philosophy as "a thoroughgoing naturalism or humanism."[32]

At the opposite pole stand the official Russian philosophers. There is, of course, nothing accidental about this situation: it has deep, objective, material roots. It is outside the scope of this article to discuss the transformation of the first workers' state into its opposite, state-capitalism.[33] What must be stressed is the new quality which Lenin discerned in the dialectic. Because he lived in a historical period entirely unlike Engels', Lenin did not stop at essence versus appearance but proceeded to the Doctrine of Notion. Because the betrayal of socialism came *from within* the socialist movement, the dialectical principle of transformation into opposite, the discernment of *counter*revolution within the revolution, became pivotal. The uniqueness of dialectics as self-movement, self-activity, and self-development was that it *had* to be "applied" not only against betrayers and reformists but also in the criticism of revolutionaries who regarded the subjective and the objective as separate worlds. Because "absolute negativity" goes hand in hand with dialectical transformation into opposite, it is the greatest threat to *any existing* society. It is precisely this which accounts for the Russian theoreticians' attempt to mummify rather than develop Lenin's work on the dialectic. They cannot, however, bury Lenin's panegyric to the dialectic: "the living tree of living, fertile, genuine, powerful, omnipotent and absolute human knowledge."[34]

The contradictory jamming up of the opposites, "absolute" and "human," is *true*. Toward the end of *Science of Logic*, Lenin stopped shying away from "Absolute" and grasped that the true "Absolute" is "absolute negativity." Absolute lost its godlike fetishism and revealed itself as the unity of theory and practice. The dialectical development through contradiction, which is an "*endless* process, where *not* the first but the *second* negativity is the 'turning point,' transcends opposition between Notion and Reality." Since this process "rests upon subjectivity alone,"[35] Lenin adds, "This NB: The *richest* is the most *concrete* and *most subjective*."[36] These are the actual forces of revolution, and we will now turn to the dialectics of liberation just as Lenin turned then to the practice of dialectics.

---

31. Vol. 38, p. 362.

32. *M&F*, p. 313.

33. See chapter 13, "Russian State Capitalism vs. Workers' Revolt," *M&F*. For the development of the state capitalist theory from its birth in 1941 until the present, see the Labor Archives, Raya Dunayevskaya Collection, Wayne State University.

34. Vol. 38, p. 363.

35. Hegel, *op.cit.*, Vol. II, p. 447.

36. Vol. 38, p. 232.

Dialectics of Liberation

Until 1915, Lenin was satisfied with Marxist economic studies of the latest stage of development of capitalism, which had first been analyzed by the bourgeois liberal economist Hobson in his 1902 book, *Imperialism*. The first Marxist study of the new phenomenon was *Finance Capital* by Hilferding (1910). It was praised for singling out a new feature, bank capital, and for asserting that this highly developed stage of capitalism made it easier for the dictatorship of the proletariat "to take over" the organization of industry. Like the categories of Essence, the new economic categories all led to Absolute Substance. Hilferding's analysis disclosed *no new beginning, no self-developing Subject that would determine its own end.* No Marxist noted this deficiency, however. There seemed to be no need of any deeper awareness of the dialectic, of an awareness that the jamming up of opposites is far more complex and more concrete than the general counterposition of labor against capital.

In 1913, Rosa Luxemburg published *Accumulation of Capital*, concentrating on the relationship of capitalism to non-capitalism, that is, on colonialism. What began as a supplement to Marx's *Capital*, an updating of "primitive accumulation of capital" to comprehend the actual ongoing accumulation of capital, ended as a *revision* of Marx's greatest theoretical work.[37] Lenin opposed Luxemburg's underconsumptionism and wrong counterposition of theory to reality. However, what concerns us here is that despite claims by Paul Sweezy and youthful exponents of the "Third World" that colonial people are "the only revolutionaries," Rosa Luxemburg denied that she had unearthed a new subject either in theory or in fact. She insisted that "long before" capitalism could exhaust itself by running out of non-capitalist areas to exploit, the proletariat would overthrow it.

In 1915, Bukharin published *Imperialism and World Economy*. Lenin was very satisfied with this updated study, which lashed out against the betrayers and their apologetic Kautskyian theory of "ultra imperialism" as merely "bad policy" instead of as the actual stage of world economy. He wrote an introduction for Bukharin's book without realizing that it treated the proletariat like an "object" or, as Bukharin expressed it, a "substitute" for "finance capital." As with Hilferding, for Bukharin it was merely a question of "taking over" capitalist economy instead of totally uprooting it.

Suddenly, Lenin became dissatisfied with all other studies of imperialism. His uncompromising stand against betrayers and reformists extended even to his Bolshevik co-leaders. He decided to embark on his own dialectical study. Empiricists without method cannot recognize method in others. They still consider the economic analyses of imperialism so similar in all Marxist studies that to them the dispute during the same period on national self-determination seems "only political." In fact, the first thing disclosed in Lenin's *Notebooks on Imperialism* (begun immediately after completion of the *Philosophic Notebooks*) is that they are by no means limited to the

---

37. My 1941 study of Luxemburg's work has been republished as an appendix to the pamphlet *State Capitalism and Marxist Humanism* (Detroit, 1967).

economic study of the latest phase of capitalist development but also include outlines of articles on the war, on the National Question, and on "Marxism and the State" (which later became *State and Revolution*). Even an inspection of the "strictly economic" work alone, which was published by itself in 1916 as *Imperialism, A Popular Outline*, shows that the methodologies of Lenin and Bukharin are poles apart. As opposed to Bukharin's concept of capitalist growth in a straight line, or via a quantitative ratio, Lenin was fiercely loyal to the dialectical principle of transformation into opposite. Tracing the self-development of the *subject* (not an "objective" mathematical growth) makes it possible to see transformation into opposite both in the transformation of competitive capitalism into monopoly capitalism *and* of a part of the labor force into a labor aristocracy. *Also*, such a study makes clear that this transformation is only the "first negative." The development through *this* contradiction compels analysis toward the "second negative" or, as Marx expressed it, "lower and deeper" into the masses, to find the *new* revolutionary forces. Thus, Lenin held that *just when* capitalism had reached this high stage of "organization," i.e., monopoly (which extended itself into imperialism), the time had grown ripe for new national revolutionary forces to act as "bacilli" for proletarian revolutions. [38] Whereas Lenin saw in imperialism a new urgency for national self-determination, Bukharin vehemently opposed the latter as "impossible of achievement" and "reactionary." Nothing short of a *direct* road to socialism was acceptable to him. This plunge from concretely developing revolutionary forces to abstract revolutionism, which Hegel would have considered a jump into the "absolute like a shot out of a pistol" and which politicos called "ultra-leftism," was to Lenin *"nothing short of imperialist economism."* [39]

On the surface, it seems fantastic for Lenin to apply that designation to a Bolshevik co-leader. Yet Lenin continued to use it against revolutionaries including "the Dutch" (Pannekoek, Roland-Holst, Gorter), whom he characterized in the same breath as the "best revolutionary and most internationalist element of international Social Democracy." Long before the National Question emerged as his final battle with Stalin, whom Lenin accused of "Great Russian Chauvinism" and whose removal as General Secretary he demanded in his *Will*, [40] long before Lenin thought that a proletarian revolution would succeed in backward Russia and that national and world revolutions would become questions of the day, and at a time when the horrors of imperialist war were everywhere and no emergent proletarian revolution was in sight, Lenin became uncompromising in his struggles with Bolsheviks on self-determination. He saw it *not only* as a

---

38. Lenin, *Collected Works*, Vol. 19, p. 303.

39. *Ibid.*, pp. 213-263. See Gankin and Fisher, *The Bolsheviks and the World War* (Stanford, 1940), pp. 222-223.

40. Lenin's *Will* was first published by Trotsky as "The Suppressed Testament of Lenin" (New York, 1935). Khrushchev quoted it in his famous "De-Stalinization Speech" in 1956. When it finally appeared in English in Lenin's *Collected Works*, Vol. 36, in 1966, it was called "Letter to the Congress" (pp. 593-611) and included much more than the *Will*: there are the final battles between Lenin and Stalin on the Nationalities Question and on "Autonomisation," i.e., the structure of the state. There is also a difference in the translations. On this dispute see Moshe Lewin, *Lenin's Last Struggle* (New York, 1968).

"principle" (to which all Bolsheviks agreed) but as "the dialectic of history," the revolutionary force which would be the "bacillus" of socialism: "The dialectics of history is such that small nations, powerless as an *independent* factor in the struggle against imperialism, play a part as one of the ferments, one of the bacilli, which help the *real* power against imperialism to come on the scene, namely, the socialist proletariat."[41] The word *dialectic* kept springing up because Lenin recognized an old enemy, "Economism," which had never understood mass revolutionary struggle. All revolutionaries had fought Economism when it first appeared in Russia in 1902. It had been easy to recognize it as the enemy of revolution then because the Economists openly tried to limit the activities of the workers to economic battles on the ground that, since capitalism was "inevitable," "therefore" political struggles should be left to the liberal bourgeoisie. Yet in 1914, during an imperialist war, revolutionaries rejected the national struggles of colonial and oppressed peoples on the ground that self-determination was "impossible" and "therefore," as Bukharin put it, "utopian and reactionary." They would only "divert" the struggle for "world revolution." This super-internationalism proved to Lenin only that the world war had "suppressed reason" and blinded even revolutionaries to the fact that "all national oppression calls for the resistance of the broad masses of people ...."[42] Not even the great Irish Rebellion changed the abstract revolutionism of these internationalists, who were concerned with "imperialist economy" instead of the self-mobilization of the masses. Lenin fought them and branded their thinking "imperialist economism" *not* because they were against revolution but because they were so undialectical that they did not see in the throes of imperialist oppression the new revolutionary force which would act as a catalyst for proletarian revolution. Lenin extended his constant emphasis on the dialectical transformation into opposite to the transformation of imperialist war into civil war. The defeat of one's country became the "lesser evil." Whereas other revolutionaries including Luxemburg[43] and Trotsky[44] still thought of the struggle for "peace without annexations" as the "unifying force," Lenin was preparing for socialist revolution and for "the day after," when the population "to a man" would run society.

---

41. Lenin, *Collected Works,* Vol. 19, p. 303.

42. *Ibid.,* p. 248.

43. *Ibid.* See "The Pamphlet by Junius" and, of course, Luxemburg's own illegal pamphlet *The Crisis of Social-Democracy,* which she signed "Junius."

44. The full collection of Trotsky's articles on the war *before* the Russian Revolution appears only in the Russian edition *War and Revolution* (Moscow, 1923), Vol. I. The essays are concentrated against social patriotism, of course, but they are also hostile to Lenin's counterposing of "defeatism" ("Turn the imperialist war into a civil war") to the "struggle for peace": "Comrade Lenin adequately revealed, especially at the preliminary conference, as earlier in his essays and articles, that he personally has an entirely negative attitude to the slogan of the struggle for peace." English readers can see this to some extent in Gankin and Fisher, *op.cit.,* p. 17, which quotes Trotsky's reply to the Bolshevik call for a special conference of Russian revolutionaries: "Furthermore, under no condition can I agree with your opinion, which is emphasized by a Resolution that Russia's defeat would be a 'lesser evil.' This opinion represents a fundamental connivance with the political methodology of social patriotism... What is necessary is a rallying of all internationalists, regardless of their group affiliation or of the tinge of their internationalism."

When the Russian proletariat smashed Tsarism and created a still newer form of self-mobilization, the Soviets, Lenin further concretized his revolutionary perspective: "No police, no army, no officialdom. *Every* worker, *every* peasant, *every* toiler, *everyone* who is exploited, the whole population *to a man*" must run production and the state; otherwise, no new society could be created. With the new concrete universal "to a man," Lenin completed his theoretical preparation *to be there*. As he phrased it when he found himself without time to finish *State and Revolution*, "It is more pleasant and useful to go through the experience of the revolution than to write about it."

According to Lenin, the smashing of the old state between October, 1917 and February, 1918 was the easiest part of the job. The difficult, decisive task followed. The population "to a man" must run the state and manage the economy, and thus it was "necessary to abolish the distinction between town and country as well as the distinction between manual workers and brain workers." [45] That, Lenin said, is the goal of genuine communism. The formula of genuine communism differed from the pompous phrase mongering of Kautsky, the Mensheviks, and the Social Revolutionaries and their beloved "brethren," in that it reduced everything to the *conditions* of labor. [46] To further stress that the role of labor was *the* proof of a workers' state, Lenin maintained that even the smashing of the old state, which marked the proletarian revolution, did not distinguish it: "The petty bourgeoisie in a frenzy may also want as much." [47] What did distinguish the socialist revolution was its accomplishment from below. "We recognize only one road, changes from below, we want workers themselves to draw up, from below, the new principles of economic conditions." [48]

If the Communist party did not become bureaucratized and did not begin thinking it could do for the masses what only the masses could do for themselves, then, *and only then*, people could progress to socialism. "Every citizen to a man must act as a judge and participate in the government of the country, and what is most important to us is to enlist all the toilers to a man in the government of the state. That is a tremendously difficult task, but socialism cannot be introduced by a minority, a party." [49] There is not one critical question, from the National Question and the dominant role of workers in a workers' state to his own unique contribution on organization, the "Vanguard Party," [50] that is not tested by the dialectics of liberation.

The aspect that concerns us most is Lenin's development of the relationship of the National Question to internationalism, where he set forth new theoretical points which are relevant today and where he fought his final battle with Stalin. Indeed, his declaration of "war to the death on dominant

45. Lenin, *Selected Works*, Vol. IX, p. 433.
46. *Ibid.*, p. 439.
47. *Ibid.*, Vol. VII, p. 337.
48. *Ibid.*, p. 277.
49. *Ibid.*, Vol. VIII, p. 320.
50. I have stressed this point at length in chapters 11 and 12 of *Marxism and Freedom*, stressing the many changes Lenin introduced into the concept during 1902-1923. Here, I limit the discussion to the last two years of his life.

national chauvinism"[51] was based not only on the Russian situation but on the state of world revolution. When the first German revolution was beheaded in 1919, Lenin wondered if world revolution could become a reality through Peking. Later, he reminded the White world that "in the last analysis, the outcome of the struggle will be determined by the fact that Russia, India, China, etc., account for the overwhelming majority of the population of the globe."[52] Lenin projected a totally new departure in theory[53] when he developed the dialectic of world revolution and said that Russia, although it had experienced a successful revolution, must be ready to subordinate its interests *if* it were possible to overthrow world capitalism through colonial revolutions. "Petty bourgeois nationalism declares the recognition of the equality of nations, and nothing else, to be internationalism, while preserving intact national egoism... proletarian internationalism demands, firstly, the subordination of the interests of the proletarian struggles in one country to the interests of the struggle on a world scale..."[54]

Impatient academic Marxists like Marcuse notwithstanding, *the* theoretical departure for the dialectic of world revolution was laid down in 1920, nearly half a century before Marcuse. Trying to dispense with Marx's concept of proletarian revolution, such Marxists contend that Lenin saw national revolutions as only "auxiliary" whereas today, with the rise of the Third World, we can see matters "globally."[55] It is essential, dialectically and historically, in tracing Lenin's "Hegelianism" to grasp his philosophical and national heritage, part of which erupted spontaneously and part of which grew out of organization, and which he extended all the way to

51. It took over fifteen years to make public this letter of Lenin to Kamenev. See Moshe Lewin, *op.cit.*, p. 52. Trotsky reproduced some of these letters in *The Stalin School of Falsification* (New York, 1937). But the official texts and some fuller ones did not appear in English until 1966, in *Collected Works*, Vol. 36, p. 606. See especially the note on "The Question of Nationalities or 'Autonomisation' ": "the apparatus we call ours is, in fact, still quite alien to us; it is a bourgeois and tsarist hodgepodge and there has been no possibility of getting rid of it in the course of the past five years... unable to defend the non-Russians from the onslaughts of that really Russian man, the Great-Russian chauvinist, in substance a rascal and a tyrant, such as the typical Russian bureaucrat is."

52. "Better Fewer but Better," in Lenin, *Selected Works*, Vol. IX. I prefer the translation in Lewin, *op.cit.*, p. 172.

53. "Theses on National and Colonial Questions," in Lenin, *Selected Works*, Vol. X.

54. Lenin, *Selected Works*, Vol. X, p. 235. The Black dimension first appeared in Lenin's work in 1912 in "New Data on the Laws of Development of Capitalism in Agriculture." See Lenin, *Selected Works*, Vol. XII, pp. 190-282. This work was often cited in the disputes in the United States among Communists, Trotskyists, and others as to whether the "Negro Question" was a National Question and whether there was a relationship between U.S. slavery and serfdom in Russia. In 1915, in *Notebooks on Imperialism*, Lenin had referred to the fact that the I.W.W. had a more correct position on the Negro Question than did the Socialist Party which, Lenin stressed, "Built separate locals for Negroes and whites in Mississippi!!" The question arose a third time in Lenin's debates with Bukharin, whose reference to the Hottentots he criticized; finally, it was made into a new category which combined nationalism and internationalism in the "Theses on the National Question." See *Selected Works*, Vol. VIII, pp. 311-367; and Vol. X, pp. 231-244. See also Claude McKay's speech to the Fourth Congress of the Communist International.

55. Herbert Marcuse, "Re-examination of the Concept of Revolution," *New Left Review*, 56 (July-August, 1969).

leadership and organization.

It was not only the Asian majority that became a new dimension of world revolutionary development. The Black dimension and minority problems in general became *moving* forces. Thus, in the "Theses on the National and Colonial Questions," Lenin listed as revolutionary forces the Negro in the United States and the Jew in Poland.[56] The appearance of the Garvey movement gave new urgency to the Black dimension (which Lenin had long studied) just when the German revolution was failing. The central point in Lenin's new relationships of theory to practice had nothing to do with the old concept of practice as "the carrying out of a line" elaborated by the party leadership. Instead, the relationships involved the leadership listening to and *learning from mass practice:* theoretical advances must come *from* the one source of theory which is also its soul.

One thing the Lenin Institute did provide in their empty introductions to Lenin's *Philosophic Notebooks* is the list of Lenin's requests for books.[57] Clearly, he had not stopped studying the Hegelian dialectic once the revolution succeeded. Nor was this study "academic" or limited to his asking "the theoreticians" who edited the new theoretical organ *Under the Banner of Marxism* to act as "Materialist Friends of the Hegelian Dialectic" and to continue publishing Hegel's works. Lenin applied the dialectic in life, in theory, in battles with his co-leaders, and in his revolutionary perspectives.

Death of the Dialectic

There is no more tragic document in history than Lenin's *Will*. His criticism of his Bolshevik co-leaders was directed not only against Stalin, whom he asked to be "removed," and against Zinoviev-Kamenev, who by "no accident" published in the bourgeois press the date of the planned seizure of power, and against Trotsky's "administrative mentality"; also damning was Lenin's criticism of Bukharin. "Bukharin is not only the most valuable and biggest theoretician of the party; but also may legitimately be considered the favorite of the whole party; but his theoretical views can only with the very greatest doubt be regarded as fully Marxian, for there is something scholastic in him. (He has never learned, and I think never fully understood, the dialectic)."[58]

---

56. Lenin. *Selected Works,* Vol. X, p. 231.

57. The 1966 English publication of Vol. 38, although it claims to be more complete than the early Russian editions, does not repeat in its Introduction the listing of books Lenin requested. Therefore, see Adoratsky's Introduction to the first Russian edition (1930) of *Leninski Sbornik, op.cit.* "Despite the fact...[of] the extreme situation and the necessity to give all attention and all energy to practical questions, Lenin continued to interest himself in questions of philosophy. This is evident from his readings.... On June 24, 1921, he asked [for] ... a Russian translation of Hegel's *Logic* and *Phenomenology* [see *Notes of the Lenin Institute,* Vol. III, pp. 94-95].... Lenin not only read but wrote in that period on the questions of philosophy. Nine-tenths of the remarks on Bukharin's *Economics of the Transition Period* concern the question of method."

58. Compare this passage from the English edition of the *Will* published in 1935 by U.S. Trotskyists, to the corresponding passage from the Moscow translation (1966) in *Collected*

Writing the *Theses* and the *Will*, Lenin summed up a lifetime in revolution just as that movement was achieving the greatest proletarian revolution in history. In his last struggle, dialectics became the *pons asini* of Lenin's philosophical thought. It was no small, abstruse matter that the major theoretician of the party did "not fully understand" the dialectic, nor was it unimportant that *if* factional struggles reflected actual class divisions then nothing whatever could prevent the collapse of the proletarian state. [59] And nothing did. When the Russian revolution failed to extend even to Europe, world capitalism gained more than a breather. The isolation and bureaucratization of the workers' state led to its transformation into its opposite. The young workers' state based itself not on the creativity of the masses but on its authority over them; the determinant was not labor but the state plan. The state party and the monolithic state became isolated from the masses and the party was not checked by the "non-party masses," [60] but was impelled by world production. The state had achieved a new stage of world capitalism: state capitalism. Lenin feared this movement "backwards to capitalism," and in his last speech to the Russian Party Congress he warned that history had witnessed many retrogressions and that it would be "utopian to think we will not be thrown back."

Because of this awareness, Lenin did not limit his critique of his Bolshevik co-leaders to the "politicians" but extended it to the "major theoretician," Bukharin. Lenin lay writing not only in physical pain but in agony over the early bureaucratization of the workers' state and its tendency to move "backwards to capitalism." He felt that Bukharin's theoretical positions on the National Question, the trade unions, and the economics of the transition period would stifle rather than release the creative powers of the masses. Lenin sensed "a passion for bossing" in revolutionaries who wielded state power. Unfortunately, in this state capitalist age the New Left, when it does not support the Russian state power, supports the Chinese. But uprisings, especially those in Eastern Europe, have shown that people hunger for freedom *from* the state party, *from* the state plan, *from* the state; what they hunger *for* is decentralization of rule as in workers' councils, intellectual councils, and youth councils.

Works, Vol. 36, p. 595: "Bukharin is not only a most valuable and major theorist of the Party; he is also rightly considered the favorite of the whole Party, but his theoretical views can be classified as fully Marxist only with great reserve, for there is something scholastic about him (he has never made a study of dialectics and, I think, never fully understood it)."

59. Trotskyism makes it necessary to say that if the factional struggle between Trotsky and Stalin had been a *class* question, it would have meant nothing as simplistic as Stalin "representing" the peasantry and Trotsky the proletariat.

60. Lenin, *Collected Works*, Fourth Russian Edition, Vol. 26, p. 475. "We are badly executing the slogan: arouse the non-party people, check the work of the party by the non-party masses." In English, the concept of the importance of the non-party masses checking the party is found in *Selected Works*, Vol. IX, pp. 253-254. The same volume contains Lenin's final speech to the Eleventh Party Congress (pp. 324-371), in which he invents words to describe his disgust for the party leadership and its "passion for bossing" and "Communlies" (communist lies). See also "What Happens After," in *Marxism and Freedom*, p. 205, where I summarize Lenin's attitude on vanguardism. It was valid *only if* the party reflected "the actual spontaneous movement of the masses. *Outside of that relationship* the Party would become anything its worst enemies could think of. It did."

Mao Tse-tung has always been terrified of the *objectivity* of the "Hegelian" contradiction, the actuality of Left opposition to the communist state. Thus, in 1937 during the heroic Yenan period when he made his major contribution to dialectics (or, more accurately, to its revision), Mao invented a new distinction between *the* "principal" and *a* "principal aspect" *of* contradiction which neither Marx nor any Marxist had perceived. From this distinction he drew the conclusion that *class* conflict need not be the decisive contradiction. "When the superstructure—politics, culture, and so on—hinders the development of the economic foundation, political and cultural reforms become the principle and decisive factors." [61] The practical reason for the invention was to fight "dogmatism" in the anti-Japanese struggle and to foist upon the masses "the leadership of Chiang Kai-shek." In 1957, Mao gave another twist to this philosophical contribution. This time, he drained contradiction of its class content in order to advise Krushchev to crush the Hungarian revolution and to tell the Chinese masses that, since the contradictions in China were "non-antagonistic" and "among the people," they could be "handled." [62] Similarly, in 1966, though it was supposedly a "Second Revolution," [63] the resolution of contradictions depended entirely on the thought of one man, "The Great Helmsman, Chairman Mao." At the same time, although a "war to the end" is directed against "capitalist-roaders" like his co-founder Liu Shaochi, it is no accident that the "revolution" is not against the actual rulers but is confined to "culture."

A hundred and fifty years ago Hegel pinpointed the inverted relationship of thought to reality which is characteristic of "culture." "Inversion of reality and thought, their entire estrangement of one from the other; it is pure culture." [64] And, "This only led to voluntarism, [for which] 'the world' is absolutely its own will." [65] Mao, of course, has long known that culture is only "the superstructure" as distinct from the determining production relations; thus, he has surrounded his "revolution" with the adjectives "Great, Proletarian, Cultural." It is no coincidence that impatient modern Marxists, who talk glibly of revolution, leave out the proletariat. Though they project nothing short of world revolution, their perspective for intellectuals is only "Radical Enlightenment of others." [66]

What we need instead is "seriousness, labor, patience, and suffering of the negative" [67] on two levels. It must start where Lenin left off. That is the

---

61. Mao Tse-tung, "On Contradiction," in *The Political Thought of Mao Tse-tung*, Stuart Schram, trans. (New York, 1963), p. 133.

62. The whole question of "handling contradictions among people" produced the famous "One Hundred Flowers" struggle, for which see Roderick MacFarquar, *The Hundred Flowers Campaign and the Chinese Intellectuals* (New York, 1960). Every issue of *Peking Review* carried documents from the Cultural Revolution, and these in turn were published in separate pamphlets by the millions. Some of the major documents can also be found in A. Doak, *China After Mao* (Princeton, 1967).

63. The expression is from K.S. Karol, *New Statesman* (September, 1966). He has since become so apologetic for Mao that he has hit out against Castro. See *The Course of the Cuban Revolution* (New York, 1970).

64. Hegel, *Phenomenology of Mind* (New York, 1931), p. 549.

65. *Ibid.*, p. 601.

66. Marcuse, *op.cit.*

67. Hegel, *Phenomenology of Mind*, p. 81.

indispensable foundation, but not the whole. The new reality of our age cannot be considered a mere updating. Rather, the comprehension of what is new begins by *listening* to new impulses arising from below, from practice. This process, as opposed to the elitist practice of theoreticians "going to the peasants," involves theoreticians *learning from* the masses, at which point they begin to develop theory. For our era, the new reality first erupted in East Berlin on June 17, 1953, and has continued not only in Eastern Europe and throughout the Third World but also in the technologically advanced countries, in the May, 1968 revolt in France and in the new revolutionary forces in the United States.

These new forces of revolution, which begin from and always return to the Black revolution but also include the youth, women's liberation, Chicano, and Indian movements, are not a substitute for the proletariat but are in solidarity with it. The continuous, persistent, never-ending revolt of the Black revolution constantly emphasizes the vital struggle of labor and forms its most militant part. [68] At least verbally, Mao recognizes the role of labor. But what everyone notices is his voluntarism. As if one day could "equal twenty years"! Because so much of the New Left feeds, if not on Maoism, on the American bourgeois philosophy of pragmatism, it is necessary to contrast Mao's dialectics to Lenin's. "Mao's failure to grasp dialectic logic has nothing whatever to do with 'understanding philosophy.' Dialectic logic is the logic of freedom and can be grasped only by those engaged in the actual struggle for freedom. Therein lies the key to the fulfillment of human potentialities and therein lies that new relationship between theory and practice which could lessen the birthpangs of industrialization. Anything else is the type of subjectivism which hides Mao's compelling need to transform the struggle for the minds of men into a drive to brainwash them. . . . It is sad commentary on our times and exposes how totally lacking in any confidence in the self-activity of the masses are today's claimants to the title 'Marxist-Leninist.' Their militancy gains momentum only where there is a state power to back it up. . . . The challenge is for a new unity of Notion and Reality which will release the vast untapped energies of mankind to put an end, once and for all, to what Marx called the *pre*-history of humanity so that its true history can finally unfold." [69]

Lenin began from this standpoint in 1917 and worked from it until his death in 1924. Mao's *new* revolutionary opposition, Sheng-wu-lien, tried to begin in a similar way in its Hunan Manifesto of 1968. "Contemporary China is the focus of world contradictions. . . . For the past few months, the class struggle has entered a higher stage. . . . It is 'to overthrow the newborn bourgeoisie and establish the People's Commune of China'—a new society

---

68. See Charles Denby, "Workers Battle Automation," *News and Letters,* 1960. See also his "Black Caucuses in the Unions," which is appended to the *News and Letters* Editorial Board Statement "American Civilization on Trial: Black Masses as Vanguard," *News and Letters,* 1970. Along with these statements by a Black production worker, see those of Black, Chicano, and white women and theoreticians in "Notes on Women's Liberation: We Speak in Many Voices," *News and Letters,* 1970.

69. *Marxism and Freedom,* second edition (New York, 1964), pp. 329-330.

free from bureaucrats, like the Paris Commune."[70] As the Hunan Manifesto shows, it is impossible to bring about the death of the dialectic simply because the dialectic is not *merely* philosophy. Above all, it is *life*, the extremely contradictory life of *state as well as private* capitalism. The young Chinese and French revolutionaries, and in the United States the anti-Vietnam War movement, the Black revolution, and most recently women's liberation, all give the lie to rumors of the death of the dialectic. Neither Stalinism nor the "de-Stalinized" communists, much less the "vanguardists" who as yet have no state power but hunger for it, can stop the forward movement of the new generation of revolutionaries. It is imperative, therefore, to fill the theoretical void left by Lenin's death. Surely, future generations will marvel at the relentless resistance of today's so-called Marxists against "the dialectic proper" and the dialectics of liberation worked out by Lenin both while gaining power and after power (but not socialism) had been achieved. Lenin concluded that "socialism cannot be introduced by a minority, a party," but only by the population "to a man" taking control of their own lives. Only when this ideal ceases to be merely the underlying philosophy of revolution and becomes its *practice* as well will freedom no longer be "philosophy" but reality.

---

70. "The Hunan Manifesto" as well as three other documents of opposition within China, and the attacks upon the young group of revolutionaries by the official leaders of China's "Cultural Revolution," are reproduced in Klaus Mehnert, *Peking and the New Left: At Home and Abroad*, China Research Monographs (Berkeley, 1969).

The Theory of the Crash

Lucio Colletti

Marx's attitude towards capitalism is a function of two different perspectives. The first is the *revolutionary* perspective, which aims at the overthrow of bourgeois society in order to reestablish on a new basis the human relationships which have been reversed and turned "upside down" in this society. The second is the *scientific* perspective, which aims at reconstructing the way the system functions and develops. Although quite different, these two perspectives do not appear juxtaposed in Marx's work: rather, they are closely connected so that each is supported and reinforced by the fact that it follows as a consequence of scientific analysis; and the latter is pushed to its extreme conclusions by the orientation and impulse of revolutionary teleology. These dual requirements and the way they are interconnected can be grasped in general outline by briefly examining Marx's critique of utopian socialism and then integrating this critique with that developed against the major classical political economists.

On the first point, Marx primarily stresses the fact that utopian socialism opposes to modern bourgeois society a "moralistic" viewpoint, i.e., an abstract, subjective viewpoint. It denounces the system's "injustices" without, however, penetrating its real mechanisms from within. Its condemnation proceeds from ideals and criteria lacking foundation in the reality being criticized. Under these conditions, writes Engels, "the solution of social problems...the Utopians attempted to evolve out of the human brain. Society presented nothing but wrongs: to remove these was the task of reason. It was necessary, then, to discover a new and more perfect system of social order and to impose this upon society from without by propaganda, and, wherever it was possible, by the example of model experiments. These new social systems were foredoomed as utopian; the more completely they were worked out in details, the more they could not avoid drifting off into pure fantasies."[1]

Naturally, the immaturity of this early type of socialism must itself be considered a product of the objective situation. "The utopians...were utopians because they could be nothing else at a time when capitalist production was as yet so little developed. They necessarily had to construct the elements of a new society out of their own heads, because within the old society the elements of the new were not as yet generally apparent."[2] Yet, these "qualifications" do not prevent Engels from seeing the profound innovation made in this field by historical materialism: it changed radically the critique of bourgeois society. It became no longer a matter of opposing abstract ideals to existing reality; rather, "the means of getting rid of the incongruities that have been brought to light must also be present, in a

---

1. Frederick Engels, "Socialism: Utopian and Scientific," in Karl Marx and Frederick Engels, *Selected Works* (Moscow, 1962), Vol. II, p. 121.
2. Engels, *Anti-Dühring* (Moscow, 1962), p. 121.

more or less developed condition, within the changed modes of production themselves. These means are not to be *invented*, spun out of the head, but *discovered* with the aid of the head in the existing material facts of production."3

This new program is executed in Marx's *Capital*, compared to which utopian socialism's limitations stand out all the more clearly. In fact, writes Lenin, in criticizing capitalist society, the old socialism "condemned and damned it, it dreamed of its destruction, it had visions of a better order and endeavored to convince the rich of the immorality of exploitation. But...[it] could not indicate the real solution. It could not explain the real nature of wage-slavery under capitalism, it could not reveal the laws of capitalist development or show what *social force* is capable of becoming the creator of a new society."4 In Marx, on the other hand, all these shortcomings seem to be eliminated. The system's laws are investigated and discovered in their objective consistency as if they were processes of natural history. And when they remain, the moral indignation, invective and condemnation are framed and imprisoned in the network of scientific discourse and its rigorous demonstrations. "And even when a society has got upon the right track for the discovery of the natural laws of its movement," writes Marx in the "Preface" to *Capital*, "—and it is the ultimate aim of this work, to lay bare the economic law of motion of modern society—it can neither clear by bold leaps, nor remove by legal enactments, the obstacles offered by the successive phases of its normal development... My standpoint, from which the economic formation of society is viewed as a process of natural history, can less than any other make the individual responsible for relations whose creature he socially remains, however much he may subjectively raise himself above them."5

The most obvious sign of the transformation the subject matter of utopian socialism undergoes in Marx is the way *Capital* treats the problem of exploitation. This theme, traditionally an object of "moral" considerations, becomes the argument of the theory of surplus value. There is no longer any appeal, as in Proudhon, to the idea of *justice éternelle*. Exploitation is no longer denounced as a theft, an "injustice," or a violation of legality. Rather, *Capital* attempts to demonstrate how the production of surplus value is perfectly compatible with the law of exchange of commodities based on equivalence. As Marx put it, "The circumstance, that on the one hand the daily sustenance of labor-power costs only half a day's labor, while on the other hand the very same labor-power can work during a whole day, that is consequently the value which its use during one day creates, is double what he pays for that use, this circumstance is, without doubt, a piece of good luck for the buyer, but by no means an injury to the seller."6 The same notion is reiterated some years later in the so-called *Randglossen zu Wagner* where, after denying that the profit made by the capitalist can be called a "theft" from the worker, Marx writes: "I

3. *Ibid.*. pp. 365-366.
4. V.I. Lenin, *Collected Works* (Moscow, 1960), Vol. XIX, p. 27.
5. Karl Marx, *Capital* (Moscow, n.d.), Vol. I, p. 10.
6. *Ibid.*, p. 194.

depict the capitalist as a necessary functionary of capitalist production and show very extensively that he not only 'detracts' or 'steals,' but forces the *production of surplus-value* and therefore helps to create what is subsequently detracted. In addition, I simply show that in the very exchange of commodities *only equivalents* are exchanged, and that the capitalist—as soon as he has paid the worker the actual value of his labor-power—expropriates the *surplus-value* with full right, i.e., with the right corresponding to this mode of production."[7]

For Marx, this is the explanation of the genesis of surplus value, which in the old socialism was the object of moral considerations concerning "justice" and "equality." Throughout his work, Marx follows it in its activity as the propulsive element of capitalist accumulation. And from surplus value, always seen as the antithesis of wage labor, he derives other categories such as profit, rent, and interest in a way which, in broad outline, reconstructs the entire social mechanism.

Thus, Marx frees himself from utopian socialism by becoming an economist and a scientist, i.e., by undertaking the investigation where Smith and Ricardo left off. The antithesis of bourgeois society is no longer depicted as a subjective ideal *external* to it; instead, it is discovered within this very society: it is the contradiction between capital and wage labor. Since from the strictly economic viewpoint wage labor itself is part of capital (i.e., variable capital), and, as Mill put it, "the term capital in this sense includes both capital and labor," the contradiction between the two ultimately results in a contradiction embodied in capital itself, i.e., an *internal* contradiction in the mechanism of capitalist accumulation.

So far we have dealt only with the first point: Marx's attitude towards utopian socialism. Concerning the second, Marx's attitude towards classical political economy, the argument must in a sense be reversed. Whereas Marx answers the utopians as an *economist*, he answers Smith and Ricardo as a *critic of political economy*. In both cases, his critique hinges on history. There is a difference, however, that must be pointed out. Marx contraposes history to the utopians in the sense that history is synonymous with adherence to real processes, i.e., the actual and not the imaginary penetration of existing conditions, and therefore, the scientific comprehension of the mechanism of accumulation. On the other hand, the same argument is opposed to the economists in the sense that history, with the relativism it entails, disposes us to recognize types of society other than the existing one—both those existing in the past and those *possible in the future*—and can prevent economists from "becoming immersed in bourgeois production as production in itself." Thus, in the first case Marx points out that Sismondi "convincingly criticizes the contradictions of bourgeois production without *understanding* them, thus also failing to understand the process of their dissolution."[8] In the second case, he observes that "bourgeois economists consider capital as an external and *natural* (not historical) form of production," that is, "bourgeois limitations

---

7. Marx, "Randglossen zur Adolph Wagners *Lehrbuch der politischen Oekonomie,*" *in* Marx and Engels, *Werke*, Vol. XIX.

8. Marx, *Storia delle Teorie Economiche*, (Turin, 1958), Vol. III, p. 59.

consider capitalist forms of production as its absolute forms, i.e., as the eternal natural forms of production."[9]

In other words, although the first fundamental point of dissension with the utopian socialists dealt with the inability of their analysis to penetrate *within* the mechanisms of capitalist production, the crux of the critique of political economy is the opposite. It is that Smith and Ricardo failed to see the historical relativity of the capitalist system, and, mistaking it for the absolute form of production, remained its prisoners, unable to stand outside it enough to grasp it as a whole and criticize it in its totality. This critique is quite evident in the analysis of commodities at the beginning of *Capital* and permeates the theory of value. In fact, in considering the production of commodities as the universal, inevitable form of production in every possible society, Smith and Ricardo end up regarding the "commodity-form" taken by all the products of labor under capitalist conditions as a constant and a datum of their investigation, i.e., as a non-problematic fact. Marx writes: "If Ricardo believes that the *commodity form* is neutral, this follows from his hypothesis that the bourgeois mode of production is absolute and therefore a mode of production without more precise specific determinations."[10]

It follows from this perspective that, first of all, since Smith and Ricardo assume that the product of labor *always* assumes the commodity form, economics as a science simply reduces to the "science of commodity-production." Unable to imagine other modes of production, political economy makes the particular historical mode of production what the motion of bodies is for mechanics, a datum which cannot be gone beyond and which cannot be left out of consideration. Secondly, since political economy regards commodity production as the universal, inevitable form of every possible social production, economic problems assume a purely quantitative character: political economy never poses the problem of why the product of human labor in determinate historical conditions takes on the "commodity form" and why, therefore, social human labor appears as the "value of things." Instead, having assumed commodities as the irreducible datum, it restricts itself to investigating the basic quantitative relations whereby commodities are exchanged among themselves, i.e., it investigates "exchange value" rather than value proper and the social relations hidden in it.

With Marx all of these problems undergo a profound transformation. Commodity-production, far from being the universal, inevitable form of economic life, becomes only *one* of its possible forms. Obviously, this form has been customary for centuries and still dominates the modern era; yet it is nonetheless an historically conditioned form which cannot in any way claim to be a direct manifestation of "human" nature. At the same time, as Paul Sweezy points out, the economist "cannot limit his attention to the quantitative relations arising from the production of commodities," but "must also pay attention to the character of the social relations underlying

9. Marx, *Grundrisse der politischen Oekonomie* (Berlin, 1953), p. 364.
10. Marx, *Storia delle Teorie Economiche*, Vol. II, p. 582.

the form of 'commodities'." And, "More concretely, in the case of exchange value there is, as Adam Smith saw, the quantitative relation between products; hidden beyond this, as Marx was the first to see, there is a specific, historically conditioned, relation between producers." [11]

This broadening of the domain of political economy, which follows from the need to go beyond that commodity-production which was the last element for Smith and Ricardo, corresponds in Marx to the fact that his theory of value is *also* a *theory of fetishism* of commodities and of capital. It is a theory through which he not only limits the confines of the whole system from the outside but also uncovers the character of the "upside-down" reality in which human relations appear as relations among things and things appear to have social qualities.

In other words, the knowing or scientific perspective, pushed to its extreme consequences, becomes for Marx a revolutionary project. The need for the *socialist* transformation reappears from within the economic analysis. Thus, it is not sufficient to understand and *explain* the production of commodities: it must be *abolished*, i.e., the material and social conditions within which the fetishistic inversion takes place must be reversed. Even when explained and understood, the mechanism whereby social human labor appears in the objective form of ownership of things and the world of products dominates the producer does not thereby cease to exist and function. "The recent scientific discovery, that the products of labor, so far as they are values, are but material expressions of the human labor spent in their production, marks, indeed, an epoch in the history of the development of the human race." But, Marx continues, it "by no means dissipates the mist through which the social character of labor appears to us." "The fact that in the particular form of production with which we are dealing, *viz.*, the production-of commodities, the specific social character of private labor carried on independently, consists in the equality of every kind of that labor, by virtue of its being human labor, which character, therefore, assumes in the product of the form of value—this fact appears to the producers, notwithstanding the discovery above referred to, to be just as real and final, as the fact, that, after the discovery by science of the component gases of air, the atmosphere itself remained unaltered." [12]

Thus, science is not enough, since it is not just a matter of correcting Smith's and Ricardo's *interpretation* of reality but of correcting this very *reality*. The mystification is continually generated by the objective processes of capitalist production, even before it reaches the economists' level of reflection. The basic inversion, according to which wage labor—the source of capital—becomes dependent on it while capital—only its product—comes to dominate the producer, is not brought about by Smith and Ricardo. This *quid pro quo* is written in the very mechanism of capitalism, in which "it is not the worker that uses the working conditions, but, on the contrary, the working conditions that use the worker." [13]

---

11. Paul M. Sweezy, *The Theory of Capitalist Development* (New York and London, 1968), p. 25.
12. Marx, *Capital*, Vol. I, p. 74.
13. Marx, *Il Capitale* (Rome, 1951), Vol. I, Book II, p. 129.

In a nutshell, science is not enough if "in this mode of production everything is represented upside-down." The very social process must be inverted. In fact, political economy is not a true science. Only the revolution is the true science. Since labor must dispose of capital instead of the reverse, the only treatise that can enunciate this scientific axiom is the socialization of the means of production.

In this total *negation* of the capitalist system, all the themes enunciated by utopian socialism reappear in an even more pronounced and audacious form. In fact, the socialization of the means of production means only this: the abolition of commodity production and, therefore, the abolition of money as well; the abolition of the market, i.e., of buyer-seller relations and, therefore, of all the contractual and juridical forms that have come about with exchange; the abolition of the state and, therefore, the transformation of politics into the "administration of things." All the "utopianism" reappears from within science itself.

Yet, the true remaining difference with respect to utopian socialism is the nature of the *negation* of the system. It is no longer merely an ideal or an external subjective criterion but a real factor inherent in capitalism itself. In this case, the negation is wage labor or the working class. It produces its own means of subsistence and, at the same time, surplus-value, i.e., profit, rent and interests. By its labor, it supplies the revenues of all fundamental classes of society. In fact, as long as it is subordinated to capital, the working class is only a gear in the capitalist mechanism. It appears only as "variable capital," i.e., as part of that capital which is actually its own product. This is the inverted or "upside-down" society mentioned earlier. However, reinforced as it is by capitalist development, the working class organizes itself and its consciousness matures in opposition to the whole system. It becomes the lever that can overthrow the whole society: the *negation* that can become real.

To summarize: all of Marx's work appears as both a revolutionary project and a scientific analysis. It is the reconstruction of the system's functioning and development while at the same time it is the consciousness of the fact that under this mode of production everything appears "upside-down." In the first case, Marx the *economist* continues Smith's and Ricardo's work. In the second, Marx is the *critic of political economy*, precisely in the sense that political economy is *bourgeois* political economy. Two different interpretations of the theory of value, which must be indicated, correspond to these two different perspectives.

The first is the interpretation whereby the theory of value appears to be a "regulative principle" which allows the explanation of the system's internal functioning. Hilferding writes that "If we consider the complexity of proportional relations which are indispensable in a system of production, no matter how anarchic it may be, we immediately face the problem of who cares to uphold these relations. Clearly, only the law of prices can perform this function since capitalist production is regulated by prices, and their variations determine the expansion or the limitation of production, the starting of new production, etc. Here, too, we find the indispensability of an objective law of value as the only possible regulative element of capitalist economics."[14] Sweezy also considers this interpretation when, after noticing that "the law of value is essentially a theory of general equilibrium," he points out that "this implies that one of the primary functions of the law of value is to make clear that in a commodity-producing society, in spite of the absence of centralized and coordinated decision-making, there is order and not simply chaos." And he goes on: "No one decides how productive effort is to be allocated or how much of the various kinds of commodities are to be produced, yet the problem does get solved, and not in a purely arbitrary and unintelligible manner. It is the function of the law of value to explain how this happens and what the outcome is."[15]

Along this same line, and with the advantage of being able to indicate its birthplace in Smith and Ricardo, he also adheres to Dobb's interpretation of the law of value. "Only with the work of Adam Smith, and its more rigorous systematization by Ricardo, did political economy create that unifying quantitative principle which enabled it to make postulates in terms of the general equilibrium of the economic system—to make deterministic statements about the general relationships which held between the major elements of the system. In political economy this unifying principle, or system of general statements cast in quantitative form, consisted of a theory of value."[16]

As can readily be seen here, the theory of value is the "live-wire" that allows us to understand how everything which appears at first sight irrational and fortuitous in the system is actually regulated and dominated by an internal rationality. From value to prices of production and even up to market prices; from surplus-value to profit and up to equalization of profits themselves through competition; the entire capitalist system, which appears at first sight to be totally chaotic, turns out to be a fundamentally balanced organism in which every party is in harmonious correspondence with the others. From this viewpoint, political economy appears to Marx himself as a science whose structure is not at all different from that of all other sciences. In the same way physics studies falling bodies, economics as a science analyzes and describes the "natural laws" of capitalist production, the same laws discussed in the "Preface" to *Capital.* These laws are objective material processes—"actual operating *tendencies* functioning according to their own iron law." Moreover, like the natural sciences, political economy also turns out to be in a *positive* relation to its object. Here, in fact, the object, i.e., "the development of the economic formation of society" understood "as a process of natural history," is not qualified as an "upside-down" reality to be "negated" (from the scientific viewpoint, these qualifications are meaningless since science's task is to explain "facts" or "sure phenomena" and nothing else). Rather, it is treated as a self-sufficient reality whose functioning must be understood. This aspect of the theory of value is clearly indicated in the expressions of the authors just quoted. The law is a law of "general equilibrium." It explains how, notwithstanding all

14. Rudolf Hilferding, *Il Capitale Finanziario* (Milan, 1961), p. 335.
15. Sweezy, *op.cit.,* p. 53.
16. Maurice Dobb, *Political Economy and Capitalism* (New York, 1945), p. 5.

friction and contradictions, the system functions, and how a new order constantly reappears from chaos.

In the other interpretation, the law of value is the theory of *fetishism*. In this case, too, it is claimed that "the production of commodities...has its peculiar, inherent laws" which obtain "despite anarchy" and which "affect the individual producers and in antagonism to them, as inexorable natural laws of their particular form of production."[17] But in this case, the "natural" and "objective" character of these laws is only the *fetishistic* projection of the very social relations operating when, instead of being dominated by man, they have escaped human control. In this sense, the laws of the market obtain for men with a "natural necessity" and the movements of the market are as unpredictable as earthquakes, not because the market is a "natural" phenomenon like the fall of bodies but because what has taken the objective form of *things* and of *processes among things* are the social relations among men themselves.

The difference is evident: in the first case the law of value is a theory of "general equilibrium" which *explains* the functioning of the system; in the second it is a theory which enunciates the reasons why men must *overthrow* the system (eliminate commodity production and proceed to full socialization) if they want to free themselves from the determinism of the market and to dominate their own relations. It is in this context that Engels correctly talks about "a leap of humanity from the reign of necessity to the reign of freedom." Furthermore, this second interpretation of the law of value not only expresses the fundamental contradiction through which labor, the source of capital, becomes its product; it also clearly implies that the only force which can overthrow the system is not a mechanical factor but the proletariat's ability to transform itself from a subordinate internal element of capitalism into a *subjective, political*, external agent antithetical to the whole system.

In the opposing pull of these two different perspectives, all of Marx's work seems to break in an unbridgeable rupture which gives rise once again to old antinomies.

But before surrendering to philosophical skepticism, it is worthwhile to extract from the mind everything it can yield. It is true that the law of value is both the principle that regulates the *equilibrium* of the system and the principle that expresses its fundamental *contradiction*. It is true that it is both the principle that *explains the existence* of the system and that of its *negation*. But the point is that although capitalism is a mode of production mined with radical contradictions, it is still an existing, functioning system and theory must deal with it simultaneously in two ways. It must be able to demonstrate both how lack of harmony and radical contradiction constantly interact in an "equilibrium" marked by "proportions" and "measure" (for, otherwise, the system would not exist), and how this order constantly breaks down in a disordered movement. Marx is very clear on this point from the very beginning of his investigations. "The economists say that the *average price* of commodities is equal to the cost of production; that this is a *law*.

---

17. Engels, *Anti-Dühring, op.cit.*, p. 372.

The anarchical movement, in which rise is compensated by fall and fall by rise, is regarded by them as chance. With just as much right one could argue the fluctuations as the law and the determinations by the costs of production as chance, as has actually been done by other economists." Marx concludes: "The total movement of this disorder is its order. In the course of this industrial anarchy, in this movement in a circle, competition compensates, so to speak, for one excess by means of another." [18]

This is not empty sophism, as it might appear at first sight. The hidden problem here is real. In fact, if Marx's work were not both a *critique* of capitalism, i.e., an analysis of the *internal* contradictions undermining it, and at the same time an exposition and reconstruction of the way in which, despite everything, the contradictions are overcome and the system *exists and functions*, it would be stuck with the empty simplicity of one of the following two errors. It would either "demonstrate too much": overemphasize the internal contradictions of the system and thus demonstrate not just the contradictory nature of the existing system but also the *impossibility* of its existence and functioning (e.g., Sismondi or even Rosa Luxemburg). Or else, it would be forced to repeat the opposite error of those who, caught and impressed by the *existence* of the mechanism under investigation, play down and minimize its internal disequilibrium to the point of rendering its existence *absolute and eternal* and, therefore, fail to see why the system cannot function and last forever (e.g., Tugan-Baranovskij and, in a certain sense, even Hilferding and Otto Bauer).

Similarly, it seems that even the antinomy discussed earlier can somehow be resolved, i.e., the antinomy whereby Marx's work is seen sometimes as the discovery and the *noticing* of objective material processes, and at other times as the unmasking of that false *fetishistic* "objectivity" in which human social relations are transformed when they escape social control. Although it is impossible here to analyze this fully, the solution could probably be found by reconsidering the unity of economic-material-objective factors and socio-historical or subjective factors upon which the unity of economics and sociology is built in Marx. In fact, as Schumpeter put it: "in the Marxian argument sociology and economics pervade each other. In intent, and to some degree also in actual practice, they are one. All the major concepts and propositions are hence both economic and sociological and carry the same meaning on both planes—if, from our standpoint, we may still speak of two planes of argument. Thus, the economic *category* "labor," and the social *class* "proletariat," are, in principle at least, made congruent, in fact identical. Or the economists' functional distribution—that is to say, the explanation of the way in which incomes emerge as returns to productive services irrespective of what social class any recipient of such a return may belong to—enters the Marxian system only in the form of distribution between social classes and thus acquires a different connotation." [19] Yet, after having evaluated everything, one difficulty remains.

---

18. Marx, "Wage, Labour and Capital," *Selected Works*, Vol. I, p. 87.
19. Joseph A. Schumpeter, *Capitalism, Socialism and Democracy* (New York and Evanston, 1962), p. 45.

Let us face the problem squarely. Granted that a "theory of the crash" aims at demonstrating *scientifically* the certain, well-determined reasons why the system has had it, the question here is whether or not there is a theory of the crash in Marx. If we examine the debate on this point between Marx's followers and interpreters, we notice that all divergences eventually boil down to this. For some, denying that Marx's work contains a theory of the crash amounts to betraying his thought, emasculating it, and depriving it of meaning. For others, it is a betrayal to attribute one to him, even in good faith. In the uncertainty of these alternatives, it would be very useful, at least in terms of a preliminary orientation, if it were possible to associate either of these positions with a political tendency. But another complication surrounds the theory of the crash: it has been upheld both by interpreters on the "right" and on the "left." In fact, both the father of "revisionism," Bernstein, and his most ferocious and intransigent adversary, Rosa Luxemburg, attributed a theory of the crash to Marx. On the other hand, both Kautsky and Lenin, along with the social democrat Hilferding and the then left-wing Bolshevik Bukharin, claimed the opposite.

My own opinion is that there is a theory of the crash in Marx's work but that it also contains reasons to deny, in principle, the validity of any such theory. Let us leave aside the question of the periodic recurrence of crises and their progressive worsening which is elaborated less conclusively in Marx's work. "The law of the tendential fall of the rate of profit" is a genuine theory of the crash. The term "tendential" should not mislead us. In fact, it indicates that the law as such is restrained by the action of antagonistic causes which "counteract and neutralize the action of the general law, thus giving it the character of a simple tendency." But this does not mean that the law is annihilated or overcome but rather that its "complete" realization is obstructed and slowed down," i.e., the law operates, but over a longer time span and through a more complicated process. In fact, were it not this way it would be difficult to understand how we can talk about it as a *law*.

Because of its very structure, this law allows us to understand what Marx means when in the "Preface" to *Capital* he talks about "laws of nature, i.e., of objective material processes of the capitalist mode of production." In fact, since the law outlines a process in which the increase of the "organic composition" of capital cannot in the long run be compensated by the increase in the rate of exploitation or the rate of surplus-value, the relationship which counts is that between "constant capital" and "variable capital" (elements internal to capital itself) rather than the relationship between classes. Because subjective-historical agents, the capitalist class and the working class, are not central to its functioning, the law operates mechanically.

The mechanism is this: to increase surplus-value and therefore profit, the capitalist must increase the productivity of labor, i.e., introduce technological innovations. The introduction of these new techniques (better machinery, etc.) increases the "organic composition" of capital (the percentage of constant capital with respect to all the invested capital); in other words, it increases a factor which decreases the rate of profit more than it can be increased by raising the rate of exploitation. The process is that of a motor which runs into trouble because of the very mechanisms that make it function, without the process itself being influenced in any way by the class struggle or by the participants' consciousness. So much so, in fact, that in interpreting this law an author who has accepted it, Maurice Dobb, feels the need to submit it to such severe limitations that its very consistency is threatened. He writes: "This law of motion could not be given a purely technological interpretation: could not be made a simple corollary of a generalization concerning the nature of changes in productive technique. The actual outcome of this interaction of conflicting elements might be different in one concrete situation from what it was in another and different situation. There is often a tendency...to give Marx's view of this matter a too mechanistic twist, depicting it as though it relied on the forecast of profit falling in a continuous downward curve until it reached a point at which the system would come to a abrupt stop, like an engine with insufficient pressure of steam behind the piston. The true interpretation would seem to be that Marx saw tendency and counter-tendency as elements of conflict out of which the general movement of the system emerged."[20]

Dobb's concern is legitimate. Unfortunately, he ends up defending the law in the very same way that critics reject it. Tendency and counter-tendency balance each other; the result of this interaction varies with different situations; there is no way of predicting which of the two tendencies will eventually prevail. These are the same arguments adduced by Sweezy to attack the law. "If both the organic composition of capital and the rate of surplus-value are assumed variable, as we think they should be, then the direction in which the rate of profit will change becomes indeterminate."[21] More specifically, "Whether their [the capitalists'] actions will succeed in restoring the rate of profit, or whether they will only act to hasten its fall, is an issue which cannot be settled on general theoretical grounds."[22] Certainly, the "subjective" elements reassert themselves here; but the validity of the law is completely destroyed. The system is not destined to an inevitable "crash" through a mechanical impasse. The only factor that *can* destroy it is the clash of classes, a clash in which, besides objective material conditions, all the subjective factors like "class consciousness," the degree of class unity and organization, and the efficacy of each class' "political instrument" participate.

It can be objected that this last formulation is closest to the spirit of Marx's doctrine. In fact, Marx was never a determinist. The statement which best summarized all his thought is that it is men who make history, even though they do it in conditions not of their choice. But to the extent that the subject of *Capital* is capital itself and not the human wage labor that produces it (which appears instead as a simple moment in the self-evaluation of capital, i.e., as "live" labor *incorporated* in its "dead" objectivity), it is understandable that the end of capitalism could at times be seen in this

20. Dobb, *op.cit.*, pp. 109-110.
21. Sweezy, *op.cit.*, p. 102.
22. *Ibid.*, pp. 105-106.

work precisely in terms of a "brisk stop" in the functioning of the motor of accumulation.

Let us leave aside all the hypotheses that come to mind: the "young" and the "old" Marx and Korsch's arguments in *Marxism and Philosophy* about the different historical characters of the two periods Marx dealt with (the first dominated by the revolutionary climate of 1848 and the second by the stabilization of capital and the absence of working class initiative). Let us also leave aside the question raised by Carr in *1917* about the possibility of defining Leninism as "a return to the young Marx." What must now be stressed is how, even in terms of a sure interpretation, the consciousness of what has been said occasionally seems to flash through Marx's own pages. In Chapter 15, Volume III of *Capital* (precisely in the section dealing with the "tendential fall of the rate of profit"), recalling Ricardo's uneasiness on this point, Marx writes: "What worries Ricardo is the fact that the rate of profit, the stimulating principle of capitalist production, the fundamental premise and driving force of accumulation, should be endangered by the development of production itself. And here the quantitative proportion means everything. There is, indeed, something deeper behind it, of which he is only vaguely aware. It comes to the surface here in a purely economic way —i.e., from the bourgeois point of view, within the limitations of capitalist understanding, from the standpoint of capitalist production itself—that it has its barrier, that it is relative, that it is not an absolute, but only a historical mode of production corresponding to a definite limited epoch in the development of the material requirements of production."[23]

If our interpretation is correct, the falling rate of profit and the *quantitative* relation it expresses are considered as the way the historical and therefore transitory character of capitalism appears. Yet that way, and the "purely economic way" in which it is expressed, are considered correlative to the "bourgeois viewpoint," i.e., the viewpoint which remains "within the limitations of capitalist understanding," "the very viewpoint of capitalist production." Unless we are completely wrong, the fallibility of capitalism should not appear to those who see the system from another perspective in the form of the "theory of the crash" and, therefore, not in "purely economic" terms.

In other words, objective tendencies such as the falling rate of profit make sense only to the extent that they appear as the conditions and real premises of the class struggle, i.e., of the clash at a political and subjective level. Alone, they have no decisive value. The illusion that they have such value generates the various theories of the crash. On the other hand, although the true conditions of capitalism are always class contradictions, it is also true that the outcome of the clash cannot be predicted in advance. It can be objected that subjective factors are always themselves moments of reality. But then the problem becomes the following: either the subjective datum is itself as calculable as an objective datum, in which case we are back in the theory of the crash, or it is not, in which case social science can never come up with the predetermination of the outcome of the process. In the latter case, however, the problem remains as to whether social science

---

23. Marx, *Capital*, Vol. III, p. 254.

can remain this open and still be called "science," e.g., Sweezy's argument in opposing the law of the falling rate of profit, when he assumes that "both the organic composition of capital and the rate of surplus value are assumed variables" and concludes that "the direction in which the rate of profit will change becomes indeterminate." Here, the course of the historical process turns out to be "open," not predetermined; but the proposition asserting the possible equivalence between the increase in organic composition and the increase in the rate of surplus value seems more like a simple restatement of the problem than its solution.

Here, the opposition between Bernstein and Luxemburg seems to contain something typical. If the end of capitalism cannot be scientifically demonstrated, then the foundation of the socialist program falls back on subjective ideals. In other words, it becomes an idealistic foundation and there is no longer any objective necessity, i.e., the foundation based on the material-social process. On the other hand, if that end is scientifically demonstrated as the unavoidable outcome of objective laws, then we somehow end up in the theory of the crash; and the subjective intervention, the consciousness of the participants, while it "can shorten and lessen the birth-pangs" of the new society, as Marx put it in the "Preface" to *Capital*, can "neither clear by bold leaps, nor remove by legal enactments, the obstacles offered by the successive phases of its normal development."

Marxism in the United States

Paul Buhle

American socialism, communism, and "New Left" radicalism have been non-Marxian to a degree unique among Left social movements in the West. The sources of this historic peculiarity are complex, rooted both in the unequalled success of American capitalism and in the particularities of the intellectual climate that have affected all American critical thought.

The most fundamental obstacle discerned by American Marxist historians to the development of Marxist theory and practice has been tenacity of an attitude DuBois called the "American Assumption." The apparently boundless free land which lay in front of seventeenth, eighteenth and early nineteenth century immigrants, the lack of class constrictions in the specific old world sense, and the relative insulation of Americans from the mass bloodshed of war and social revolution all operated as real forces to create for Americans a sense of exceptionality from the fate of Mankind.[1] To be sure, some critics, especially literary figures, comprehended and sought to explicate the "blackness," the other side of the American success story.[2] Since colonial times, class and social movements have protested against special privileges and demanded the extension of democracy to ever wider groups. Yet the practice of criticism and the criticism of practice have remained for the most part discontinuous and episodic; palliated by the recurrent upsurge of the economy and/or successfully isolated from the mass of the population.

The slow and uneven development of a coherent class consciousness among workers has been central to the fate of American Marxism. As the history of early class-reform movements indicates, American workers organized politically to demand not only amelioration of their working and living conditions but also access to cheap land in the West, in the hope that it would provide a chance to escape the pauperization-through-proletarianization which faced the European poor.[3] The Civil War cleared the path for a modern proletariat by eradicating the principle political competitors to industrial capital. However, it also left in its wake four separate and badly divided sectors of the working class: Southern laborers both black and white, generally lacking in non-agricultural skills and with few exceptions unable to perceive even the possibility of a common fate as proletarians; unskilled Northern workers (divided among themselves by ethnic and

---

1. David Noble, *Eternal Adam and the New World Garden* (New York, 1968), pp. 3-8; W.E.B. DuBois, *Black Reconstruction* (New York, 1938), pp. 29-30; and William Appleman Williams and Harvey Goldbert, "Thoughts about American Radicalism," in Goldberg, ed., *American Radicals, Some Problems and Personalities* (New York, 1956), especially pp. 4-5.

2. A brilliant discussion of Melville, Poe, and Hawthorne is contained in Harry Levin, *The Power of Blackness* (New York, 1963).

3. Note Williams' suggestive remarks on forms of "surrogate socialism" such as Bryanesque people's capitalism and corporation socialism, in *The Great Evasion* (Chicago, 1964), especially pp. 129-165.

language differences) and Northern skilled laborers, who led the organization of the first successful trades unions, but usually to the exclusion of the other three sectors.[4] Marx and Engels, along with many American Marxists, thought that America's extraordinary industrial development would be accompanied by the growth of a strong political working class movement. However, in spite of militant flares of industrial struggle in 1877, 1885-86 and the 1890s, by the turn of the century there were still no significant, stable working class institutions in America.[5]

In the twentieth century, American imperialist institutions have operated so as to continue to frustrate opportunities for continuity of working class development. Although the ethnic divisions, which had obfuscated working class unity in the late nineteenth and early twentieth centuries, had been substantially alleviated by the 1930s, conflicts between white and Third World workers and between male and female workers contined to erode the path to unification. Although great industrial unions were built after a half-century of strenuous effort, under the impetus of imperialist expansion and government manipulation these same unions became devices for disciplining the working class. Thus, the continuing viability of the capitalist order challenged the Marxian notion that the development of the system's inner contradictions would lead to a widely perceived sense of common proletarianization, and thus through class solidarity to revolution. Following Lukács, one might suggest that through rapid industrialization with a widely heterogeneous work force, American capitalism bypassed the critical moment of European proletarian socialism's birth; and that the delayed comprehension of labor-power as a *commodity* sold by the worker was succeeded in America not by a reassertion of the producer as subject of the machine-process but rather by an alienation of the worker from all social institutions and a redoubled sense of isolation from the steady development of class forces.[6]

Concurrently, American critical thought has lacked the vitality of its European counterparts. As T.B. Bottomore has noted, there was only one "great issue" in the century following the American Revolution, and that issue resolved itself in the Civil War which absorbed all the energies of the reformers and helped create an industrial society which confounded the old framework of expanding agrarian social democracy. While European intellectuals sought a systematic theory for the construction of a future society, Americans continued to be lured by the vision of the old, small property-owning "Golden Age" society whose possibility had passed.

In the final decades of the nineteenth century, American social analysis followed Herbert Spencer, not Karl Marx. "Reform Darwinists" like E.A. Ross looked to the state for a modulation of social tensions, and utopian writers like Edward Bellamy envisioned a future order run like an army.

---

4. DuBois, *op.cit.*, p. 216; also David Montgomery, *Beyond Equality* (New York, 1967).

5. A recent insightful summary and analysis of European Marxist thought on the United States is R. Laurence Moore, *European Socialists and the American Promised Land* (New York, 1970). See Chapters 1-3 on the Europeans' attitude in the late nineteenth century.

6. Lukács, "Reification and the Consciousness of the Proletariat," *History and Class Consciousness* (London, 1970), pp. 168-172.

During the first two decades of the new century, a critical social science was promulgated by such outstanding thinkers as John Dewey, Thorstein Veblen, Charles Beard, and James Harvey Robinson. These writers shared a desire to lend scientific rigor and historical depth to American intellectual thought and were often in outspoken opposition to the mainstream academic apologetic for then existing institutions. At times, they flayed the corrupt, inefficient bourgeoisie which benefited from the exploitation in American industry and politics. But with few exceptions, they felt uncomfortable with Marxism, an intellectual system which they considered hopelessly narrow for American society. Methodologically, they felt the need to shun transcendental or dialectical systems of thought for the sake of drawing conclusions from life *as it was* and as it might be scientifically reorganized. [7]

The elaboration of the American Empire abroad and the concomitant institutions at home increased the intellectuals' involvement with and control over the details of American life but effectively limited their understanding of fundamental social and philosophical questions. The search for a kind of truth—however confused and eclectic that search may have been—was increasingly supplanted by a search for prediction and calculability. The humanist view of intellectuals serving society was vitiated by the increasing bureaucratization of the public sector; and what radical tendencies permeated intellectualism were severely disrupted by the disillusionment following the World Wars. [8] Indeed, even self-avowed radical intellectuals were not freed from the mainstream pragmatist conceptions of "social engineering." The groupings which founded social reform clubs in the 1880s and 1890s popularized the Socialist party among the middle class reform groups during the Progressive era, and supported the Soviet Union inside the liberal milieu in the 1930s; all shared a collectivist but non-Marxist view of the future in which the dominant feature of progress was man's increasing *control* of himself and his world. [9] As Max Horkheimer noted, it has been precisely this "disease of reason," the faith in Americans' own domination of nature, which has precluded a dialectical solution to the individual alienation created by increasingly powerful technology. [10]

Understandably, then, American Marxism could not draw its intellectuals either from the working class or from sympathetic bourgeois circles. Most of the Socialist party's populists came directly from reform movements with little background in Marxism and fled from the movement at the outbreak of World War I. The Marxists in the 1930s were mainly

---

7. The best brief discussion is contained in T.B. Bottomore, *Critics of Society, Social Criticism in North America* (New York, 1969), pp. 22-23.

8. Max Horkheimer's little known work, *The Eclipse of Reason* (New York, 1949), contains a wealth of dialectical analysis of American twentieth century thought. See also Charles Forcey, *Turning Point in American Liberalism* (New York, 1961).

9. James Gilbert is preparing a manuscript on several "collectivist" thinkers (including W.E. Walling and Charles Steinmetz), which has been a great source of insight for me. The best analysis of left-liberals in the 1930s is Frank A. Warren, *Liberals and Communism, the Red Decade Revisited* (Bloomington, 1966). As Warren shows, it was not the liberals who were deluded, but the Communists who believed in their own power of manipulation.

10. Horkheimer, *op.cit.,* pp. 176-177.

literary figures with a poor understanding of history and economics. These writers were, in Bottomore's words, "living off borrowed Marxism" until another war brought the payments due. For the few intellectuals actually drawn to Marxism, there has been little substantive encouragement. Universities in the United States have been unwilling to tolerate "Marxists of the Chair" until quite recently; and neither a trade union nor a party bureaucracy of any size or strength has ever existed to offer a friendly base for theoretical analysis.[11]

Through most of its history, American Marxist thought has been confined to a relatively small, self-educated scattering of intellectuals. On one level, this has meant an interpretation of doctrine imported from Europe—primarily from Germany before 1920 and from the Soviet Union afterward. On another level, American Marxism has concentrated on interpreting the whole of life for the faithful in and around party ranks, in the simplest form possible. At both levels, the analysis has been so thin and often so self-serving that "orthodox Marxism" has necessarily remained an abstraction to be fitted alongside the political problems of daily life, an abstraction which became increasingly unintelligible for theory or practice as America changed. By the late 1940s, at least, the momentum of the initial conceptions of inevitable economic collapse and class struggle (with a brawny proletariat emerging under the guidance of a Marxist organization) had been lost; and Marxism as an ill-digested set of ideas used for social prediction had been all but destroyed.

Only with the emergence of the mature American empire at approximately the same time was there the beginning of a distinctively *native* Marxist thought. The question of imperialism, which had been treated as secondary in the Socialists' and Communists' relationship with the masses of workers, could no longer be ignored. Further, America's role in the world could no longer be obscured by hopes of alliances with liberalism. At the same time, the question of racism emerged as never before, creating the basis for a rethinking of America's role in the world economic and cultural systems. Finally, by the end of the 1960s, there were definite indications that Left political movements in the United States were in some ways more advanced than their counterparts in Europe. The birth of the free speech movement, youth culture, and the women's movement have conclusively proven that American Marxism can no longer be artificially constructed from foreign examples. The growing crisis in the empire has forced widespread public reexamination of American society as it fell increasingly into disrepair. And the crisis in the political New Left which resulted in the collapse of SDS has almost as forcibly restimulated *class* analysis. Although after a full century of development there is still no mature Marxism, the conditions for its emergence have never been so good.

The origins of American Marxism lie in the small bands of German-Americans, mostly skilled workers, who during the late nineteenth century formed organizations to gain ideological understanding, to obtain some

---

11. Paul Sweezy, "The Influence of Marxian Economics on American Thought and Practice," in D.D. Egbert and Stow Persons, eds., *Socialism and American Life* (Princeton, 1952), p. 485 and note 58.

political and economic leverage, and to help share a common exile within American culture. The doctrines of Marxism were little understood by these men, and their contact with American workers was obstructed by language barriers and the physical superiority of their own situation as skilled, often organized, workers.[12] From the end of the Civil War to the 1890s, these groups sought intermittently to indoctrinate the small organized labor movement and to strike an arrangement with the populist movements in the West. With few exceptions their efforts failed, and the ideological eclecticism that marked their literature reflected their difficulties. In it the doctrines of Ferdinand Lassalle, the non-Marxian writings of socialist economists, the single-tax theories of Henry George, and an amalgam of other sources were mixed eclectically with writings by Marx, Engels, Bebel, and Lafargue.[13] As Marx and Engels noted in their letters to American correspondents, there was no immediate need to make deeper theoretical literature available in the U.S. because native Americans were not ready to understand it, and the German refugees only used Marxism to monopolize the socialist movement and prevent the linkage of socialism to the "impure" workers' movement.[14]

During the 1890s the United States endured one of its first true social crises. In the midst of the longest depression in the country's history, millions of farmers were set in motion around political populism while workers staged frequent and bloody battles to maintain subsistence living conditions. The life of the "official" Marxist movement, the Socialist Labor party, only indirectly reflected these struggles. After decades of relative isolation eased only by some trade union work and periodic local political labor insurgences (most notably the Henry George United Labor party campaign for the Manhattan mayorality in 1886), the SLP turned toward inward concern for its thin ranks as the future leaders of the proletariat. While the rise and fall of Populism passed by, the Socialists sought to build their bases for power in the American Federation of Labor and the Knights of Labor. Due to the widespread economic distress and the SLP's political agitation, various middle-class reform tendencies gravitated toward it. And on a local level, working class communities in Cleveland, St. Louis, and Milwaukee, as well as elsewhere, began to support socialist and left labor papers. Portentiously for American socialism, the growing Russian-Jewish community in Manhattan also began to turn in considerable numbers toward several varieties of socialism.

Yet for all this activity, English-language Marxism remained rare. Far more than in Europe, American Marxism was seen as *one* socialist view of

---

12. There is no adequate discussion of American Marxism's earliest period. For analysis of certain individuals, see David Herreshoff, *American Disciples of Marx* (Detroit, 1968). See also Howard Quint, *The Forging of American Socialism* (Columbia, S.C., 1952).

13. The New York Labor News Co. was founded in the mid-1880s as a publication outlet for the Socialist Labor party but offered only a sparse group of "Marxian" publications in English until the 1890s when, with the party's growth and DeLeon's leadership, the Labor News Company began a publication program which ultimately included Bebel's *Women Under Socialism*, Marx's *The Eighteenth Brumaire of Louis Napoleon*, and many other classics, frequently translated by DeLeon himself.

14. Marx and Engels, *Letters to Americans* (New York, 1938), pp. 178, 220, 257-58.

life, stronger than any other single view because of its all-encompassing logic but hardly a total conception for American conditions. At best, it provided an economistic sense of prediction which, however, frequently caused socialists to wait for the masses to follow their "correct" political position instead of attempting to infuse socialism within existing movements. The leading Marxist paper in America remained the *New Yorker Volkzeitung*, edited by Marx's aging correspondent, Hermann Schleuter. In English, only the SLP's organ *The People*, a fiercely sectarian sheet, could be called avowedly Marxist.

With the emergence of the Socialist party in 1901, American socialism approached maturity. The success of the party was due substantially to its ability to promote the amalgamation of the various, sometimes contradictory, forces of American radicalism. Several major groupings managed to live side by side within the party framework, retaining considerable autonomy and thereby preserving the unique perspective they had brought into the socialist movement. However, virtually none of these segments were drawn to Marxism as a methodological tool for analyzing social change. Nearly all utilized Marxian catch-phrases when convenient, drew an almost instinctive sense of class background and perspectives, and shunned the would-be theorists of American Marxism.

Skilled socialist workers, disproportionately but by no means entirely German-American, brought a reformist but ardently proletarian vision of social transformation. In Milwaukee, where a unique ethnic and political situation existed, the socialist movement used a base of skilled workers to win the city over to municipal socialism. While in other areas like St. Louis, Cleveland, and Manhattan, socialists were unable to attain power, they did manage to build powerful socialist blocks within the labor movement. The Marxism of these movements was viable in the short-run but inevitably archaic. Socialism was seen as the inevitable outcome of gradual emiseration and steady socialist education for the "real American proletariat" (i.e., excluding blacks, often recent immigrant groups, and for the most part, women). These movements projected a vision of a post-capitalist society run entirely by the state in which the family and other social institutions under pressure from capitalism would be firmly reestablished. The self-sufficient world view of these groupings revolved around belief in a "material determinism," and a common-sense socialism which drew its lessons from daily life and which projected the future as visible to any working man who would open his eyes to socialism.[15]

The politically moderate, industrially conservative views of the skilled workers' groups were linked logically to those of the "parlor socialists," recruits from the middle class who streamed into the socialist movement, especially between 1906 and 1914. For the most part, these socialists were close in spirit to the Progressive movement for the scientific adjustment of modern society through the instrumentality of the state. Because of their relatively high level of education, socialists of this kind became the outstanding popular writers, and sometimes actual leaders of the Socialist

---

15. See Paul Buhle, "Introduction" to the *Social Democratic Herald* (reprint, Greenwood Publishing Company, 1970), for some suggestive comments on Milwaukee socialism.

party. A few of the "parlor socialists" became ardent revolutionists, stirred by the efforts of the IWW to reach the unorganized workers. Others became dedicated Socialist party workers, providing much of the infrastructure for propaganda and agitational efforts. As a group, however, the middle class socialists remained distant from Marxism proper. Even when they read Marxian texts, the current reading matter of the time (especially Veblen and Nietzsche) often seemed equally important. Generally, Marx and Engels were perceived as pioneer social scientists like the more modern scientific minds of America (e.g., John Dewey).[16] In fact, all texts were considered by important middle class socialists as secondary to the ethical values that had been passed from the heritage of early Christianity to the modern socialist movement. The "parlor socialists" had little internal unity, but they shared at least a predisposition for intellectual fashions in which Marxism was only one important element.

Perhaps the most uniquely American segment of socialism was the conglomerate group of tenant farmers, small property owners, and small town residents in the middlewest and southwest. American socialism's remarkable agrarian successes flowed from an adaptation of class analysis to the plight of the rural poor. Rural socialism inherited considerable energies from populist movements, but it added a sharpened class perspective by insisting that, true to Marx's prediction, land was becoming more concentrated and that a rural proletariat was being created. The future society was not seen as a workers' republic but rather as a cooperative commonwealth in which the land would belong to those who used it. The rural socialists were often avowedly revolutionary and commonly opposed to the "possibilist" reformism of other socialist segments; but they saw little connection between the fine points of Marxian doctrine and the job of organizing the farmers. Rather, socialist analysis was conducted with the most indigenous common sense attitudes, uninformed about or indifferent to possible sophistications.

American socialism had, from its earliest years, a disproportionately weak relationship with the class segment most ideal (in abstract terms) for a Marxist movement: the unskilled worker. Blacks were only rarely seen as a force toward which special efforts should be spent, and therefore they played no significant role in socialist struggles. Similarly, poor southern whites were often seen as beyond the ken of a political socialist movement. White laborers in the mines, lumberyards, ships and elsewhere, however, often turned toward revolutionary socialism. In the West especially, the IWW made headway among native American workers in some of the most brutalizing occupations. Yet the peculiar experiences of these workers failed to promote any ideologically sophisticated radicalism. Migrant work patterns and long hours left little time for study and tended to weaken

---

16. There has been no good treatment of Debsian Socialist writers as a group. However, James Weinstein, *The Decline of Socialism in America, 1912-1925* (New York, 1967), and James Gilbert (unpublished manuscript mentioned above) offer general characteristics and helpful insights. See also Paul Buhle, "Debsian Socialist Intellectuals," *Radical America*, Vol. IV (April, 1970).

17. My analysis is drawn from James Green, "Socialism in the Southwest," (unpublished dissertation, Yale University, 1971).

interest in anything beyond obvious and immediate questions of organization. There were scarcely any radicals less inclined to intellectual discussion than the hard-bitten "Wobbly" rank-and-filers. The influx of recent immigrants from eastern and southern Europe could scarcely speak each other's languages, let alone listen to socialist theoretical discussions in English. While several of the new immigrant nationalities, like the Italians and the Finns, brought a tradition of radicalism, none save the Russian Jews developed an immediate, close relationship between intellectuals (usually socialist, sometimes anarchists) and workers. Of all the rank-and-file socialists in America, perhaps only Jewish proletarians *as a group* corresponded to the Marxian conception of an exploited but proud working class on the lowest rung of white labor who were increasingly influenced by Marxism. [18]

Thus, with few exceptions, American socialism provided little space for the Marxian theorist. The Socialist party united for the national presidential campaign and the distribution of literature, but in general it remained a kind of confederation of regional movements. The national office never published a theoretical organ. Of all the nationally-circulated magazines and newspapers, only the post-1908 *International Socialist Review* could be considered both popular and Marxist, and its Marxism was agitational, not exegetical or exploratory. On the whole, intellectuals were primarily used as popularists for the socialist press, as public speakers on agitational campaigns, and as authors of "socialist lessons" for internal dissemination through the party. Radical theory which did not have a direct and immediate application to day to day party activity was thoroughly mistrusted.

Yet, in the first phase of American socialism (roughly corresponding to the first decade of the century), several intellectuals with a real knowledge of Marxism appeared in Socialist party ranks. The most venerable was Schleuter, an editor of the *Volkzeitung* until his death in 1919. Schleuter wrote a German-language history of American workers in the nineteenth century, and a *History of the Brewery Workers*. He also published a collection of documents with his own commentary on *Lincoln, Labor, and the Civil War*. Unlike most socialist history, Schleuter's work was unpretentious and craftsmanlike. The study of the brewery workers was in fact a history of the brewing industry in the United States, with the rise of a socialist-influenced industrial union as a final, almost triumphant chapter. The commentary on the Civil War sought to place the event in international perspective and to provide a balanced account which viewed racism as a significant obstacle to progress. Schleuter's studies, however, provoked little interest. His German language work was never even translated into English, and his other two works received scant circulation in party circles. Schleuter himself was venerated, but only as the main spokesman of a dying culture within American socialism.

---

18. Little is actually known about the internal life of the Socialist party Language Federations. However, Charles Leinenweber has provided a helpful discussion of the party's generally negative attitude toward them in "Socialism and the New Immigrants," *Science & Society*, 32 (Winter, 1968).

The efforts of two self-educated Marxian economists to achieve recognition for their work in party circles was even less successful. Ernest Untermann was well versed in Marx's writings but was consistently discouraged from any work deeper than popularizations of Marxian texts and occasional translations (including several volumes of *Capital*) of the work of European theorists. As a result Untermann came to lead a strange but characteristic double life. While he did various forms of local agitation for American socialism, he completed a seven-hundred page text on Joseph Dietzgen's theories of cognition for publication in Germany. At best, Untermann provided study classes for individuals (including Jack London) willing to take the time and effort to read philosophy and economics. At worst, Untermann was an impatient parent of American Marxism who criticized false starts in economic theory but was unable or unwilling to produce his own *magnum opus*. Untermann's barbs were often aimed at the best known American Marxist economist, Louis Boudin, whose *Theoretical System of Karl Marx* was widely praised even in Germany. Though Boudin's work suffered from a lack of philosophic grounding, American socialists ignored it not because it was too simple but because it was too difficult. Boudin regarded himself as a personal Permanent Opposition to the party's political leadership in New York. He was considered a carping intellectual complainer by moderates and a lawyer (his profession) by revolutionary proletarians. Thus, like Untermann, he produced simple historical lessons for the New York *Call's* Sunday magazine section; and sent his best theoretical studies to Germany.[19]

During the same period, a scattering of "Americanizers" of Marx sought to introduce a Marxist logic (usually via Kautsky or Engels) to a larger American reading public. The most prolific of these was A. M. Simons, an author and the editor of the *International Socialist Review* during its years as a theoretical journal (1900-08). Simons was a figure of some importance in the Socialist party, particularly as editor of the short-lived *Chicago Daily Socialist*. Yet his theoretical labors on the *ISR* were little appreciated, and his most important historical work appeared just as he was drifting to the right, away from socialism. Simons' "theoretical" work was most popular when it provided an easy explanation for the conspiratorial control of American institutions by the bourgeoisie. Yet his efforts never achieved the popularity—either within the party or among its sympathizers—of writers like Robert Hunter and Charles Russell, whose muckraking efforts were only incidentally connected with socialism.[20]

Schleuter, Untermann, Boudin and Simons shared with the rest of the early socialist movement a nineteenth-century mode of class analysis which was ill-equiped to comprehend a rapidly changing American society. By 1910, the socialist movement was faced with a crisis. The mass of skilled

---

19. Some further discussion is offered on the contributions by Schleuter, Untermann, and Boudin in Paul Buhle, "American Marxist Historiography, 1900-1940," *Radical America*, Vol. IV (November-December, 1970), and on Untermann and Boudin in Buhle, "Debsian Socialist Intellectuals," *op.cit.*

20. One of the few published biographies of a Socialist party intellectual is Kent and Gretchen Kreuter, *An American Dissenter: The Life of Algie Martin Simons* (Lexington, 1969).

workers in most cities had remained aloof from the socialists, while farmers, middle class radicals, and others had actually diluted the proletarian content of the organization. To represent the working class in formation, the socialists would necessarily have to reach the mass of unskilled workers, predominately recent immigrants who showed little interest in voting or in educational activities generally. Temporarily, the socialist movement rode in the crest of municipal electoral victories and the large presidential vote for Debs in 1912; a few years later, socialists of all factions would turn from socialist agitation to anti-war work, thus further suspending questions about the future of the movement. But a few socialists probed the crucial problem of the new workers, and these few provided the outstanding expressions of the creative Marxism in Debsian socialism.[21]

Ironically the precursor of these theorists was Daniel DeLeon, sectarian chieftan of the Socialist Labor party. Because of the domination of American socialists at that time by the politics of the German-American skilled-workers' groups and because the movement seemed further threatened with inundation from middle class reformers, DeLeon and his coterie had sought to purify the SLP for a proletarian leadership role the moment for which, however, never arrived. DeLeon's opposition to modern unionism and the SLP's intervention in the IWW after 1905 caused the old editor to formulate a conception of a reorganized socialist movement in which, through revolutionary unions, the working class would dominate and control movement activities and goals. In DeLeon's mind, Socialist party leaders' conceptions of electoral victories and/or struggles at the barricades were utopian and archaic for an advanced proletariat. By 1911-12, DeLeon had long since been expelled from the IWW and his SLP was reduced to a sect. But radicals who sought an alternative to Socialist party strategy, or a way to reconcile their hopes for the revived IWW with their Socialist party activities, discussed their problems within a framework which DeLeon had done the most to establish.

Particularly in the *New Review* and in the transformed and popularized *International Socialist Review*, writers such as Louis Fraina, Austin Lewis, and S. J. Rutgers explicated the "New Socialism" or "Industrial Socialism" in the light of the wave of strikes by unskilled workers which struck the continent and America. For a brief period, a concomitant theoretical flourishing seemed to promise the development of a richer and more profound Marxism. In the *New Review* criticism of cultural events like the Armory Show was mixed with discussions of the need for an aggressive socialist policy toward special Black problems, the philosophic problems of pragmatism, and a variety of other subjects. However, this growth of Marxism hardly affected socialism outside the New York area; and it symbolized in the writers' minds, instead of actually representing, the fusion of proletarian interests and Marxist analysis. The commentaries like that of DuBois, who declared in the *New Review* that the "Negro problem"

---

21. Perhaps the most suggestive single essay on the dilemma of the Socialist party after 1910 is by Gabriel Kolko, "The Decline of American Radicalism in the Twentieth Century," in James Weinstein and David Eakins, eds., *For a New America, Essays in History and Politics from Studies on the Left, 1959-1967* (New York, 1970).

was the "great test" of American socialism, remained theoretically unelaborated and were never practically taken up by American socialism.[22] The effect of the World War wiped out the *New Review's* financial base, resulted in the postal suppression of the *ISR*, and drastically reduced the capability of the Socialist party to seek a way out of its dilemmas.

Certain real possibilities remained for American Marxism in the socialist movement. During the war years, Louis Fraina and a scattering of other writers continued to elaborate their analyses of American society. Fraina correctly foresaw that after World War I the spread of imperialism would strengthen capitalism and that the middle classes would turn sharply to the Right. Meanwhile, nearly fifty thousand new immigrants were brought into the socialist movement by successful agitation and the hopes raised by revolutionary movements in eastern and southern Europe. However, when the great potential thrust represented by the steel strike of 1919 failed to provide a mode for organizing the unorganized, and when the world revolution failed to take place, the potentialities for American Marxism disappeared. In the wake of the Socialist party's failure to encompass its new working class membership and the fragmentation of the party by the formation of two Communist factions, the promising theorists disappeared or became mere factional ideologues.

For nearly a decade, Marxist analysis fell to a point approximating that of the first years of the century. The Communists founded *The Communist* as a theoretical organ in 1928, but most of their magazines and newspapers were dominated with agitational writings, factional demagogy, reportage from Russia and Europe, and efforts to explicate the ever-changing Comintern "line." As in the first years of Debsianism, much effort was spent translating the "classics," only now the writings of Lenin were added to those of Marx and Engels. Despite the confidence Communist publications expressed about the bright future for socialism, the Communists' own movement in America was essentially defensive.

For the socialists and the Communists the 1920s was a period of enclaves. Both movements found their remaining trade union strength primarily within the largely Jewish garment industries. The Communists failed to make significant interventions except in under-capitalized, "sick" industries like the garments trade (as in the Gastonia and Passaic strikes) or occasionally the coalfields. The socialists maintained influence only by their adaptation to the unions as integrative agents within capitalism. In such a period of isolation, European intellectuals might allow Marxism to become abstract, a product for the academy and for the remaining party faithfuls. In America, even such a role was not possible.

The long-term prospects for American Marxism were, however, fundamentally affected by changes in the work-force and the productive process. These changes were largely outside the ideological purview of socialists and Communists. Black workers had streamed north during the World War I, increasing the number of Blacks in manufacturing to around

---

22. DuBois, "Socialism and the Negro Problem," *New Review*, Vol. I (February 1, 1913), pp. 138-141. DuBois' critique of the Left unfortunately remains unexplored.

nine million. This number increased in 1920s despite the far higher unemployment rates for non-white laborers. Thus, in the North a distinct Black proletariat evolved in the face of the hostility of white workers. This resulted in rioting and in general a repetition of the black-white labor competition in the South. While Marxists continued to speak in the name of a raceless, undifferentiated proletariat, the birth of Black Nationalist struggles such as the Garvey movement demanded a more sophisticated theoretical treatment. Also in the 1920s, the remaining bases of craft unionism were undercut by the transformation of production and the introduction of time and motion studies and other Taylorist methods on the production-line. [23] Finally, the continuing process of Americanization, especially amidst a developing consumer market for automobiles and other relative luxuries, bore down upon the ethnic communities, foreshadowing both the eclipse of ethnic radicalism and the possibility of working class cultural homogenization. [24] In all, the passing of one radical period had opened the way for a period of relative reaction which, however, concealed the formation of a demographically and culturally transformed working class.

The second wave of Marxist thought began shortly after the onset of the depression. Ironically, the Communists had by then embarked on a policy which limited the number of sympathetic intellectuals their activity could attract. Whereas during the 1920s the young Communist movement had maintained a relatively easy-going attitude toward literary allies who were not direct factional opponents of the Party, in 1929-31 the party functionaries' position hardened. V. F. Calverton, the adamantly independent but unquestionably friendly editor of the *Modern Quarterly*, was blasted for "social fascism" over slight theoretical differences. Similarly, the collection of intellectuals attracted to the League of Professional Groups for Foster and Ford (including such notables as John Dos Passos, Edmund Wilson, and Clifton Fadiman) was driven away from the party milieu by sectarian Communist tactics and personal demands. [25]

At least in part, the American Communist party's shift in attitude toward intellectuals was a response to the political line of the Comintern's "Third Period" (roughly 1929-35). Following the explusion of the Left Opposition (Trotskyists) in 1927 and the "Right Opposition" (Lovestoneites, including the editor of the *Communist*, Bertram Wolfe, and several key theoretical

---

23. Hal Baran has written an extremely suggestive major essay, "The Demand for Black Labor: Historical Notes on the Political Economy of Racism," *Radical America*, Vol. V (March-April, 1971), especially pp. 20-25, delineating major shifts in the Black work force. The relation of the Communists to the Black community is sketched in Mark Naison, "Marxism and Black Radicalism in America: Notes on a Long (and Continuing) Journey," *Radical America*, Vol. V (May-June, 1971).

24. An important contribution to the comprehension of the 1920s as a transitional period of American capitalist social develoment is by Martin J. Sklar, "On the Proletarian Revolution and the End of Political-Economic Society," *Radical America*, Vol. III (May-June, 1969).

25. There is still no published work on the life and activities of Calverton, a key figure among non-Communist party Marxists. The only extensive treatment remains Haim Gnizi, "V.F. Calverton, Independent Radical" (unpublished dissertation, City University of New York, 1968).

contributors), the party attempted generally to put itself into fighting shape for a seizure of power in the foreseeable future. Thus, intellectuals who showed hesitancy toward accepting complete discipline, and especially intellectuals who seemed to show sympathy toward the Opposition groups, were publicly attacked and separated from party functions. The *Communist* and the *New Masses* were "politicized": genuine discussion of Marxism and the participation of non-Communist intellectuals was reduced to a minimum and replaced by self-serving polemical bursts and tactical reports of Communist successes. [26]

During this period there were certain other attempts to reformulate Marxian theory to fit American society. Calverton had since the twenties sought in his *Modern Quarterly* and through a stream of books of his own on sexuality, American literature, and history, to penetrate areas not discussed in radical analysis. Calverton was a shallow thinker, "up to date" in keeping up with the non-Marxist intellectual trends of the day toward psychoanalysis, sociology and literary commentary, rather than a Marxist absorbing and describing new areas of interest. Inadvertently, his magazine became a journal of thought for radical, non-Communist intellectuals including Max Eastman, Robert Briffault, Sidney Hook and Bertram Wolfe. The *Modern Quarterly* reached its height in 1933-34, becoming a monthly with considerable influence among the Left-leaning intelligentsia.

At various points, independent radicals sought to cooperate with non-Communist organizations to create a new party and a basis for Marxian discussion free of Communist polemics. Around 1934, several of the *Modern Monthly* intellectuals including Hook and Calverton joined with other intellectuals (most notably James Burnham and the trade unionist writer J.B.S. Hardman) to promote the American Workers' party. Using the Committee for Progressive Labor Action headed by A.J. Muste as its basis, the American Workers party was an attempt to create a specifically "American" revolutionary movement. A small but energetic movement searching for a theoretical and political position, the AWP linked itself to the equally small Trotskyist organization. Over the next several years, this slight organizational tendency provided a meeting-point for anti-Stalinist intellectuals. Especially while a theoretical journal was being published (1934-35 and 1937-40), the Trotskyists offered a lively analysis with a range of views and an open-endedness scarcely present in the regular Communist press. Trotsky's own sweeping commentary, George Novack's historical and philosophical discussions, cultural commentaries by Dwight MacDonald, and debates involving such figures as John Dewey, Sidney Hook and Max Eastman all provided vigor to Marxist discussions. Around the same period, the revived *Partisan Review*, edited by William Phillips and Philip Rahv, was under heavy influence from Trotskyists seeking to draw together

---

26. In 1935, Earl Browder bragged that the Communists would "burn out any tendency to irresponsible gossip with a red-hot iron," quoted by M.V. Venkataramani, "United Front Tactics of the Communist Party (USA) and Their Impact on the Socialist Party of America, 1932-1936," in *International Studies* (New Delhi), Vol. I, p. 180n. For one treatment of the Communist attitude toward intellectuals, note Paul Buhle, "Louis Fraina-Lewis Corey, 1892-1953," (unpublished M.A. thesis, University of Connecticut, 1968).

Left-Oppositional politics with their own developing literary and cultural critique. [27]

Independent Marxist intellectual activity reached a sort of peak in 1935 with the founding of the *Marxist Quarterly*. Its editorial board included such notables as Louis Hacker, Lewis Corey, James Burnham, George Novack, Felix Morrow, Bertram Wolfe and Sterling Spero. However, the short life of this journal (three issues) was typical of independent Left developments. With the intelligentsia moving either toward the New Deal, the Communist Popular Front, or both, the ground was cut away from any other real possibility. Indeed, even as the journal was founded its "Marxian" editors were moving away from Marxism toward the higher ground of "Collective Democracy" nearly all would adopt during World War II. With the beginning, the *Partisan Review* writers along with most of the intellectuals in the Left Opposition abandoned Marxism. Trotskyist Marxism could not survive the slightness of its organizational importance and the decay of the promise of world revolution into the new crisis of a world war. Too little ground had been taken or defended even in terms of fundamental Marxian theory, let alone new analysis of the social situation in the United States and elsewhere, to constitute another stage of Marxian theoretical development. Like Luxemburg and her allies at the time of Bernstein's revisionism, the Trotskyists pleaded primarily that Stalinism was a perversion of Marxism, but themselves had little beyond the framework of the previous period (in this case, classic Leninism) to offer in explanation of the new world situation and especially of the new conditions of the American proletariat. [28]

Meanwhile, the Communists had gained hegemony over the political Left and seemed, more than any movement since the socialists in their heyday of 1912, to have gained real links with working class movements. Fortuitously, the Comintern's turn rightward toward anti-fascism and participation of Communists in progressive social movements coincided with the formation of the CIO in 1935-41. While new unionism, even with its militant tactics, did not pose a clear revolutionary alternative, the sweep of working class struggles indicated, as the Communist trade union leaders analyzed, a new maturity. While the working-class offensive continued and the New Deal attempts at economic retrenchment faltered, a revolutionary perspective was widely held within the Left. Communists gained leadership in several of the most important industrial unions and formed a temporary working alliance with center-Left union leaders such as John L. Lewis. [29]

Concurrently, the Communist Popular Front broadened its political base through alliances over anti-fascism, the Spanish Civil War, and to a certain

---

27. See James Gilbert, *Writers and Partisans* (New York, 1969), for a valuable commentary on the *Partisan Review* milieu and that of the literary Left generally.

28. For one account of the *Marxist Quarterly* and the Trotskyists' relationship with intellectuals, see George Novack, "Radical Intellectuals in the 30s," *International Socialist Review*, Vol. XXIX (March-April, 1968). Perhaps the fullest analysis of the *Marxist Quarterly*, its significance and its disintegration, is contained in Paul Buhle, "Louis Fraina-Lewis Corey."

29. The best treatment of the subtle relationship between the new unionism and the Left is in Len DeCaux' autobiography, *Labor Radical* (Boston, 1971).

extent anti-racism. These alliances transformed the party from a nationwide movement with an almost totally working-class membership into a movement geographically concentrated in New York State with nearly half of its members outside the working class. [30] Despite massive efforts throughout the 1930s, the party never gained a mass base among industrial workers. Thus, like the Socialist party in an earlier period, while the Communist movement had contacts and influence within the workers' movement, the fundamental support for its position was among other sectors.

Communist political and theoretical attitudes reflected a dichotomy. On one level, all-out support was lent to New Deal policies and Franklin Roosevelt's liberal leadership. On another level, Roosevelt's failure to give full support to struggling workers and, more fundamentally, his avowed intent to save capitalism, was denounced in traditional class terms. Party leaders and theoreticians sought formulae by which to justify these conflicting political positions, but though the "line" changed several times between 1934 and 1941, the formulizations became increasingly makeshift and unreal. [31]

Little theoretical effort was made before 1935 to broaden the horizons of Marxian thought within Communist circles. Like the socialists, Communists whether rank and filers or leaders disdained intellectual work which lacked immediate practical application. Anthony Bimba contributed a notable *History of the American Working Class* based on secondary sources and an admirable small volume on *The Molly Maguires*; Granville Hicks wrote the *Grand Tradition*, an interpretation of literary history in the United States; and Herbert Morais wrote a history of deism as political thought in the eighteenth century. But there was little or nothing of substance produced on philosophy, international history, capitalist economics, or other key subjects of traditional Marxian investigation.

During the period of the Popular Front, there were at least some stirrings among the Communist intelligentsia for wider discussion of theoretical matters. Their central vehicle for theoretical discussion was *Science and Society*, created in 1935 as an alternative to the more independent *Marxist Quarterly*. At its formation, *Science and Society* boasted an impressive list of editors and contributors including Franklin Frazier, Fulmer Mood, Granville Hicks, Broadus Mitchell, Matthew Josephson, Kurt Lewin and Robert Lynd. In its first several years, the journal promised to provide wider currency for Marxism among the academic community than had been seen in America, certainly wider than that since the demise of the *New Review* in 1917. However, pressure from the Communists for politicization, the reduction of academic freedom within the universities from 1939 onward, and the generalized rightward move of the academic Left, all combined to decisively narrow *Science and Society's* milieu. Though a handful of

---

30. Nathan Glazer, *The Social Basis of American Communism* (New York, 1963), p. 92.

31. See George Charney, *A Long Journey* (Chicago, 1969), on the internal mechanisms of the United Front and Popular Front. Also, for a valuable survey of literature on the Communist party and the working class during this period, see Brian Peterson, "Working Class Communism," *Radical America*, Vol. V (January-February, 1971).

Communist scholars including Herbert Aptheker and Philip Foner emerged during these years, the impetus for a broader and deeper Marxism was essentially lost and their contributions remained individual and limited in scope.

There were a few notable efforts to expand American Marxism, but these were virtually all written outside Left political movements. In 1932, Louis Boudin completed a two-volume history of American constitutional law, *Government by Judiciary*, which argued in a Beardian fashion that the rights of the people had been eroded step by step since Revolutionary days and that Americans possessed fewer rights than they imagined. Lewis Corey (earlier known as Louis Fraina, a proto-Communist intellectual of Debsian era) wrote the limited but incisive study of the Gilded Age ruling class, the *House of Morgan* (1931), and several years later completed the major economic work by an American Marxist, *The Decline of American Capitalism*. Its nearly seven hundred pages of conceptually poor, repetitive, and sometimes self-contradictory analysis provided at least a tremendous *effort* to update Marx. Most important, W.E.B. DuBois wrote his monumental *Black Reconstruction*, whose significance may be measured by C.L.R. James' comment that it is "one of the finest history books ever written." DuBois was a profound scholar who moved toward Marxism in an effort to conceptualize the saga of Blacks in America. Through them, the whole of American civilization at the most critical period of their history. DuBois surpassed not only the efforts by other Marxists, but also those of American bourgeois historians. He placed the Civil War and its aftermath in the context of world history and in the context of the West's failure in the twentieth century to achieve the progress its bourgeois revolution had promised. *Black Reconstruction* laid bare the failure of the working class to reach in reality the universal class-consciousness that Marxists had abstractly predicted as its destiny. For DuBois, the dilemma of Blacks was also the dilemma of Marxism.[32]

Characteristically, none of these singular efforts became building blocks for American Marxism. The close of the 1930s was marked by the Left's confusion over the diplomatic actions of the Soviet Union and its despair over the possibility of world conflagration. This confusion and despair which gripped the Left for nearly twenty-five years. Despite its actual size, its influence within sectors of the working class, and its considerable intellectual following, American Marxism had not been strong enough to resolve the fundamental questions of race, class, and international position which made American society unique. And if there remained unanswered problems in 1939, the problems were to grow far more complex with the rapid changes over the next decade. With few exceptions American Marxism established basic patterns of theory and practice which were far from adequate for the new tasks ahead.

Ironically, the immediate effect of World War II prosperity was to buoy the Left. While anti-Communist efforts intensified in some sectors of the

---

32. See Paul Richards, "W.E.B. DuBois and American Social History: the Evolution of a Marxist," *Radical America*, Vol. IV (November-December, 1970), for an outstanding analysis of DuBois' *Black Reconstruction*.

CIO, the organization of workers continued to spread. Despite the Communist party's acceptance of the "No Strike" pledge, working-class militancy continued during the war and in 1945-47 reached a new level. Communist membership continued to rise through 1943 to a level near that of the Socialist party in 1912 and in 1919. Despite Smith Act attacks Communists felt a new respectability during the war.

Beneath the hopefulness, however, the Left was undergoing agonizing internal decay. With the Molotov-Ribbentrop Pact, the Communists lost support and defense in liberal circles which they were never to fully regain. Communist recruiting efforts within the middle class were dashed by a post-war conservative turn similar to that which cut middle-class support for the Socialist party after World War I. Most important, the Left strength within the unions proved to be more apparent than real. Increasing government intervention in union affairs, postwar economic affluence, the union's bureaucratization posed challenges to existing Left strategy for which radicals were unprepared. The internal conflict on the Left, including most notably the expulsion of Earl Browder and the wide Communist swing toward sectarianism, reinforced a widespread sense of confusion. Trotsky had predicted that World War II would lead to world revolution; radicals of all varieties had held that war's end would bring another depression, the expectation of capitalist recovery in Europe and America was scarcely believed, and the shock of the Left at its failure to comprehend the shape of reality at first historical glance should not be surprising.

Only in one specific sense was the American Marxist vision substantially vindicated. Since the 1920s, initially at the behest of the Comintern leadership, the Communists had pointed to the unique position of Blacks in American society. The Communists' sense of the Blacks' future role in working-class, intellectual, and cultural circles in American society, the Marxist understanding of the CIO as a tremendeous potential force in the Black Community, and the Communist scholars' efforts to uncover and trace the tradition of Black resistance all showed a special insight. Yet there was little indication through the 1940s that white Marxists could view the problem of racism as central to American civilization. Rather, and with important exceptions both within the Communist movement (Harry Haywood) and among its competitors (C.L.R. James), Marxism continued to gloss over the pervasive racism throughout American society and to seek an abstract conception of a unified working class. [33] Throughout the 1940s, Blacks were viewed as *supporting actors* when, as was shown a decade later in the South, they were actually moving toward the center-stage.

For many Marxists, the problems of post-1940 reality were so tremendous that they defied Marxist analysis. A few continued to explain them away through repetition of the old formulae. Some, however, attempted to create an open-ended Marxist analysis capable of growth and development. One

---

33. The most exceptional works include C.L.R. James' conversations with Trotsky and the resolutions of the Trotskyist movement which James authored, published in *Leon Trotsky on Black Nationalism and Self-Determination* (pamphlet, New York, 1967), and in the "C.L.R. James Anthology," published as *Radical America*, Vol. IV (June, 1970); and Harry Haywood, *Negro Liberation* (New York, 1948).

small group with an historical background in Trotskyism undertook to translate essays from Marx's 1844 *Economic-Philosophic Manuscripts*. Led theoretically by C.L.R. James and Raya Dunayevskaya, they articulated an analysis of the Soviet Union as "State Capitalist," and as a bureaucratic reversion from its socialist origins: more important, they derived from Marx a notion of working-class self-activity through which they sought to show the bureaucratization of American unions as they had developed and the means for workers to recapture self-identity as the subjects of the production process through the creation of workers' councils. In at least one important sense, James, Dunayevskaya, and their followers made a conceptual advance from the current state of American Marxism: they recognized the critical link between the philosophy of the "Young Marx" and the class struggle of modern times. [34]

Dwight MacDonald's magazine *Politics* reflected the realization that the world view of the Left needed complete reconstruction. *Politics'* contributors drew on the cultural critiques of the "Frankfurt School" of Marcuse, Adorno and Horkheimer and it succeeded in indicating the problems of mass society that orthodox Marxists had not foreseen. In *Politics*, the reality of successful mass manipulation of public opinion, the threat to humanity posed by atomic weapons, and the cultural degeneration which mass advertising produced were all viewed with a pessimism which made Marxism itself seem irrelevant and the Left hopeless. [35]

In less than a decade the circles of American Marxism had narrowed to a few intellectuals and the various sects (a category in which, by 1950, the Communist party could be included). The Marxism of the parties had become, except for the historical writings of Communist scholars like Herbert Aptheker and Philip Foner, little more than a defense of the faith for an ever-decreasing group of believers.

Paradoxically, the overwhelming fact of an American empire, a major factor in the dissolution of the "Old Marxism" and the Old Left, proved a source of insight for a New Marxism and a New Left less ridden with illusions of working class solidarity and more realistic about popular acceptance of Cold War economic dividends. The first major sign of this new Marxism was the appearance of the *Monthly Review*, founded by economist Paul Sweezy and popularist Leo Huberman. Sweezy's *Theory of Capitalist Development* (1942) had been one of the significant individual works of American Marxist thought, the first treatment of Marxist economics by a professional economist. The outstanding feature of *Monthly Review* was the "Review of the Month," which described with considerable adeptness the changes in the American economy toward war production and waste consumption. *Monthly Review* provided encouragement for Paul Baran, whose *Political Economy of Growth* was later recognized as the outstanding Marxist work on the effects of imperialism on the Third World. In the late 1950s, Sweezy and Huberman comprehended far more clearly

---

34. The most easily available document from the James-Dunayevskaya group is *State Capitalism and World Revolution*, 2nd ed. (Detroit, 1970).

35. There has been no adequate critique of *Politics* magazine. See, however, Hannah Arendt, "Introduction" to *Politics* (reprint, Greenwood Publishing Co., New York, 1969), and various essays in MacDonald, *Memoirs of a Revolutionist* (New York, 1956).

than other American Marxists the significance of the Cuban Revolution. By the mid-1960s, the editors' focus had widened to encompass the nature of the Sino-Soviet division and the significance of Chinese support for Third World struggles. Over the last decade, *Monthly Review* has delineated most clearly the monumental implications of the Indochina conflict for American and Western society as a whole. In addition to their work with *Monthly Review,* Baran and Sweezy coauthored *Monopoly Capital,* a masterful analysis of the changes American capitalism has undergone in the twentieth century.

A second major sign of the emergence of a New Marxism was the historical writing of William Appleman Williams, the leading radical historian of foreign policy at the University of Wisconsin. Williams' analysis, unlike that of the *Monthly Review* editors, concentrated on the implications of the American empire for American social relations. In a series of seminal works (most notably *Contours of American History* and *The Origins of the Modern American Empire*), Williams depicted the *corporate* character of life in America. In the formative period of the United States, Americans had attempted to define the good life and derived a vision of empire as a hedge against the metropolitan, class-ridden society that seemed to defile Europe. By the end of the nineteenth century, farmers, workers, and others who saw their dream collapsing sought new frontiers, specifically, foreign markets, and lent mass popular support to the imperial thrust. In the twentieth century these elements along with big business helped shape a corporate order not unlike Mussolini's Italy. All components (business, labor, farmers, etc.) had a determined place fixed against both complete impoverishment and the possibility of revolutionary change. Thus, Americans avoided Marxism and its hard truths with a "great evasion" of social reality throughout the world, America's contribution to continuing misery. Thus, Williams sought in his work to pinpoint America's unique role, the particularity of its historical development, an effort that previous Marxists had always shunned. [36]

Williams' influence at Wisconsin in the late 1950s, particularly his intellectual leadership of graduate students, was one important sign of the changes in American society that created the new basis for the social movements and the Marxism of the next decade. Growing at an accelerated pace after the Second World War, by the mid-1950s the "multiversity" was inhabited by a stratum of relatively leisured students no longer confined by the scarcity of the 1930s and 1940s, but faced instead with the tremendous cynicism and callous manipulation of America's institutions of higher learning. Through the 1930s and 1940s, there had been relatively small Left movements within American universities but they had been no more than "youth groups" for the adult Left. In the 1950s, the predominant attitude of American college students was one of sullenness. Most students refused the patriotic-idealistic conceptions of "student activism" expressed by university presidents but few were willing to demonstrate open opposition. The dissolution of the Left, however, freed some notable young intellectuals

---

36. One of the most valuable summaries of Williams' labors is by Michael Meeropol, "W.A. Williams' Historiography," *Radical America,* Vol. IV (August, 1970).

to return to school at places such as Wisconsin and made possible the self-recognition of students as an authentic self-constituted base of radical change, one wing of a variegated proletariat with its own desires and demands.[37]

Throughout the 1940s and 1950s, changes in the black community had simultaneously opened up new outlets for social struggle. The mass transfer of black communities from South to North had brought millions of black people into factory labor, multiplying the size of the black proletariat and transforming the demographic structure of metropolitan areas. While in the long run the new bases of black strength would make their position more threatening to the bourgeoisie, in the short run the small size of the black population remaining in the South made possible concessions which were renegotiated through the civil rights movement and the integration struggles of the late fifties and early sixties.[38]

A significant shift in the position of women in American society made possible and necessary the development of the modern women's liberation movement. Women had been an important force in American industry from its beginning (there were a million female laborers as far back as 1890). However, women have constituted, by and large, an *impermanent* labor force, largely because of the turnover created by marriages and the birth of children. By 1956, there were twenty-one million women workers, most of them permanently employed. However, in opposition to the new opportunities in industry, a social lag in mores existed and constituted in part an actual counterrevolution. Since the death of social feminism in the 1920s, neither the Left nor any other American institution had offered an outlet for class or personal political awareness. Sexual changes in that decade had remained in effect, providing relative liberty from nineteenth century patterns but bondage compared with the position of men. The momentary encouragement given women for new status during World War II, when their labor was so much in demand, had been reversed by the decreasing need for their work and the suburban social patterns which prescribed the family on the young woman in the 1950s even more strongly than it had been prescribed for her mother.[39]

Social developments of the 1960s, above all the widening Asian war, "liberated the dialectic" of struggle inherent in the situation of students, Blacks, and women. As Goran Therborn has commented, the Vietnamese resistance "shattered the cemented unity of American society" and provided the impetus for movements which, once begun, carried their own sources of energy.[40] The reopened struggle in the center of the world empire was in one sense an unprecedented event in twentieth century revolutionary history, for it situated the conflict where class struggle in the orthodox forms was *least* likely to dominate the multifaceted struggle.

37. See James O'Brien, "History of the New Left, 1960-65," (unpublished dissertation, University of Wisconsin, 1971), Chapter 1.

38. H. Baran, *op.cit.*

39. See Robert W. Smuts, *Women and Work in America*, 2nd ed. (New York, 1971), Chapter 4, pp. 110-156; see also Betty Friedan, *Feminine Mystique* (New York, 1963).

40. Goran Therborn, "From Petrograd to Saigon," in Arthur Lothstein, ed., *All We Are Saying: the Philosophy of the New Left* (New York, 1970).

Moreover, since Second International and Third International Marxism had been unable to explain the nature of social forces and class developments in the United States, the new shape of things vanquished the Old Marxism more quickly and totally in the U.S. than in any other nation. America as the most advanced capitalist civilization became the center for the display of the most advanced contradictions in capitalist world society. As Marx had predicted, social struggles in the United States were *uniquely* modern, involving whole blocs of young, an increasingly conscious black internal nation, and women. In the U.S., more than anywhere else, the revolutionary thrust would necessarily be total, unlimited by the sectoral constraint of Europe and the Third World. The Marxism which could comprehend this totality would also have to be uniquely modern.

Judged by the limitations of its background and the tasks which faced it, American Marxism of the 1960s could scarcely have been expected to build a comprehensive critique of the society around it or to portray the path to revolutionary victory. Still, Marxists in America took substantial steps foward in comprehending orthodox theory and in providing some original contributions to practical understanding. There was above all a growing sense of the American past and the nightmarish weight it placed on current prospects. Significant numbers of young scholars began to use Marxism as a methodological tool, rather than as an ideology expressing faith in the progress of the "socialist countries." There was widespread interest in the effects of American imperialism. Also, there was a significant interest in the questions posed by European Marxism: the concept of the "new working class," the culture critique of the Frankfurt School, and the discussions of the "Young Marx."

The development of the journal *Studies on the Left* during its history (1959-1967) indicates some of the problems and strengths of the New Marxism in America. Significantly, several of its editors came from an Old Left background and had been liberated for theoretical activity precisely by the collapse of the Communist party in the mid-1950s. Of equal significance, the editors as a whole were deeply influenced by William A. Williams' theories of American society and foreign policy. During the first years, writers were concerned less with the exposition and modernization of Marxist doctrine proper than with specific historical studies designed to elucidate the formation of the "corporate society." Although the editors specifically sought the recreation of a socialist politics, as isolated intellectuals practically they were able to do little more than propose a "Radicalism of Disclosure" (the title of *Studies'* first editorial), a scholarly commitment to radical interpretation. With the broadening of Left opportunities in the early and mid-1960s, *Studies* sought to continue probing social theory while relating itself to the New Left initiatives of community organizers, anti-war activists, and others. Yet the dualities of *Studies* were never successfully overcome. The editors found little in the "movement" which led to an overtly socialist struggle; and activists were never attracted to Marxism (or any coherent theory) in great numbers. The Marxism of *Studies* remained an uncompleted project: it was neither deepened to encompass the philosophic framework of classic Marxism in any consistent way, nor was it able to link its own analyses with a vibrant social movement. Yet, like *Monthly Review, Studies* did provide a vehicle for young intellectuals who sought a form of Marxism which actually explained the functioning of American capitalism and offered suggestions on prospects for change. [41]

Studies on the Left helped New Left activists to break with the Old Left conceptions of political activity. Most New Left activists instinctively realized that the ideology expressed by politicians, business leaders, and labor bureaucrats represented the New Deal's success and not a repudiation of it by reactionary forces. Similarly, observation of Soviet diplomatic intrigues taught the New Left to discard the dichotomy posed by the Communists of the "progressive nations" and the "capitalist countries." But there was nothing specifically Marxian in these insights, and indeed many of the New Left analyses seemed merely to reverse the Old Left attitudes. If, for instance, the Popular Front had attempted to aid blacks in successful integration, New Leftists became sycophantic around the most violent Black groups. If all Old Leftists united in their fidelity to the working class, New Leftists conceived a series of explanations for indifference toward the industrial worker.

At first, young radicals sought to become activators of the poor and dispossessed through community organizing. By the mid-1960s, the most ideologically concerned sectors of SDS took up the "new working class" theory, which in several forms sought to explain the peculiarly radical nature of students in terms of their status as future workers. Within several years, the growth of "underground culture" caused young radicals to embrace youth culture, a purposefully classless analysis of "Amerikan society" and its cultural opposition. The frustration the New Left experienced in their search for a successful strategy is reflected in the ideology of the Weathermen: anti-imperialism increasingly entangled with a youth-culture critique which sought to evaluate the reactionary nature of the white population in "Amerika" and saw only a miniscule fragment even of youth culturists as potential revolutionaries.

In the late sixties, the political New Left moved toward premature postures and internal crisis, while its various sectors commonly adopted a Marxist-Leninist vocabulary. At the 1966 National Convention of SDS, for instance, only "Old Left" factions openly styled themselves Marxists. The political position of the mass of activists and their leaders was a kind of vague liberalism mixed with an existentialism which spurned ideological fineries. By the time of the disastrous 1969 convention, when the organization had swelled to several times its earlier size and many times its importance, all major factions (which embraced practically all attending members) were overtly "Marxist-Leninist." This change represented no great doctrinal transformation or change in the class basis of SDS membership. Rather, "Marxism-Leninism" represented an almost exclusively *political* designation of support for Third World revolutions abroad (especially those under the leadership of People's China) and Third World peoples within America. The expression of a dying organization, such Marxism proved incapable of creating a comprehensive analysis or even of

41. See Weinstein and Eakins, "Introduction" to *For a New America, op.cit.*

maintaining itself for any period of time. Thus, the brief but widespread overt identification of a new group of Americans with Marxism ended with the movement's own negation. By 1970, the overriding realities of the step by step collapse of the empire, the brutalizing cultural conditions at home, and the fervent desire for personal liberation by millions of youths had clouded over any clear perception of a Marxist analysis and had rendered impossible the recreation of a Marxist political movement.

In a specific sense, the early stages of an autonomous women's movement added to the doubts about Marxism and the problematic aspects of its application. Unlike the problems posed by the Black movement, which past Marxists had belatedly recognized and sought to handle, those raised by women's oppression were fundamentally outside the boundaries of orthodox Marxist theoretical practice. Except for the basically agitational efforts by feminists in the Socialist party and the translation of a scant few "classics" on women (such as Bebel's *Women under Socialism*), Marxists had glossed over women's special oppression with simple explanations, e.g., its expressing economistic demands for equal opportunities. By 1970, militant feminists could see that the problems of women were philosophical as well as practical, relating indeed to Marx's and Hegel's very concept of labor.[42]

Throughout the brief history of the political "New Left," the struggles of industrial labor had been considered at best secondary, sometimes irrelevant, and often as tainted with the "white-skin privilege" of most workers. Thus, whatever its other virtues, the Marxism which arose in the late 1960s bore a peculiar and finally unresolvable relationship to the older Marxist orthodoxy. Even when Marx's methodology could be accepted, his means to revolution and perhaps even the kind of revolution he had envisioned remained questionable for many in the New Left. Yet, as the new variants of Marxism were thrown into crisis by the collapse of the movement, the rekindling of the industrial struggle appeared on the stage of history and provided the context for a newer theoretical approach which showed possibilities for reconciling the *sectoral* insurgencies of the 1960s (Blacks, youth, women) with the fundamental philosophical-historical heritage of Marxism.

In reality, the class struggle between industrial labor and capital had never disappeared in America, although imperial elaboration had provided boundaries on its levels and social implications, especially since World War II. The great strike wave after World War II prevented the return of 1930s wages but failed to deflect the increasing bureaucratization of the unions. The failure of the CIO to play a significant social role within American politics and the success of government-directed "Red Purges" had transformed the context of labor efforts by the 1950s. Increasingly, protests could be made against employers, government, and bureaucratized unions only through wildcat strikes, which contained no means of coordination and which had no potential for returning industrial workers to the offensive. Stalemated by overwhelming opposition, working class forces continued to bear the contradictions of production within capitalism, contradictions

---

42. This problem is touched upon in a very useful survey of women's history in America by Mari Jo Buhle, Ann Gordon, and Nancy Schrom, "Women in America," *Radical America*, Vol. V (July-August, 1971).

which could surface under changed conditions.

Even while the New Left ruminated about the need for a "constituency," conditions within the industrial work force moved toward a new phase of struggle. As Paul Booth has noted, labor in the early 1960s defeated the attempt to scale wage gains to productivity, and by 1967 embarked upon a "kind of spontaneous wage offensive," stirred by the "vague sense of declining working class living standards (for the first time since Korea)." This offensive has not been coordinated from the top of the labor movement, and in the meantime stronger forces within the government have pushed for a wages policy directed at further limiting labor's share. Yet, although fundamentally defensive, class initiatives have resulted in a massive strike wave nearly equal to that of 1946, including several remarkable new developments (e.g., the postal workers' strike).[43]

In a deeper sense, the basis for a new labor movement had been laid earlier by the changes in the nature of the work force. During the 1950s and 1960s, black labor had become a central force in key industries such as the auto industry. This black worker was, as Harold Baron eloquently noted, a "veritable devil in the flesh" for the capitalists, who seek black labor but cannot dismantle the racial sources of social explosion without dismantling the very institutional bases of legitimate authority in the society. During the same years, women became more than ever before a permanent labor group comprising nearly half of the work force and the dominant factor in many sectors. Here, too, the very demands for equality were by their nature radical, for they posed a restructuring of fundamental roles in society. Over the last decade, there has been yet another significant minority of workers with their own peculiar demands: the youth, unstable in their positions, unwilling to tolerate the old discipline, eager for openings toward militancy.[44]

There has been almost no apparent comprehension within the Left of a new, variegated proletariat emerging as a class force. Within the Old Left and traditionalist sectors of the New Left, intra-class divisions were frequently ignored or their implications in active protests against union policies were considered disruptions to labor unity. Among the bulk of New Leftists, the oppression of blacks, women, or youths within the working class has been seen as merely another sign of the irrelevance of class lines and as an encouragement to choose the side of the most oppressed workers against the less oppressed.

Only through a theortical comprehension of such intra-class dynamics could Marxism as a *system of thought* become relevant for American society. Yet only with a thorough analysis of social mechanisms within the empire as a whole could such a class analysis be made real, i.e., concrete and operable for revolutionary strategy. The task of Marxism has become nothing less than the understanding of the social relations of capitalism at the system's most advanced point, when the advancement of contradictions has thrown the role of all social classes and groups into profound crisis.[45]

---

43. Paul Booth, "Theses on Contemporary Trades Unionism," *Radical America*, Vol.V (January-February, 1971).

44. See the special issue on young workers in *New Generation*, 52 (Fall, 1970).

45. There have been considerable accomplishments by "New Left" Marxists which were

The problems posed for Marxists by American society have always been unique to a degree Marxists themselves could rarely perceive. The overwhelming fact of a New World with an expanse of nature which seemed to require only conquering and civilizing to create a human paradise, unique divisions promoted by slavery, external and internal migration, and the astonishing speed and pervasiveness of American industrial development in its various phases all posed insurmountable problems for men who read Marx abstractly and economistically. Yet, as American society faces its last frontier, the erosion of imperialism, the problems are fundamentally universal and their resolution will deeply affect the social patterns of all humanity. Never before have the antinomies of eros/repression, white/black, male/female, and humanity/nature so nearly approached a practical and simultaneous transformation. Never before has it been so clearly possible to see, within the womb of the old society, the forms of the new order groping for life and readjustment. Never before, therefore, has the task of American Marxism been so fundamental. There is no certainty that Marxists over the next several decades will successfully probe these contradictions and derive answers which help clarify the revolutionary forces. But certainly, a Marxism which fails to accomplish these basic tasks will perish and in perishing will contribute to the victory of barbarism.

---

not analyzed here, however, Particularly notable are Eugene Genovese's *Political Economy of Slavery* (New York, 1966), and David Montgomery's *Beyond Equality* (New York, 1967), both in American social history. In the 1960s, furthermore, the Marxist economic critique by Paul Mattick, Sr., has finally been made available in *Marx and Keynes* (Boston, 1970). Mattick, a council communist theorist, has lived and worked in the United States since the late 1920s, almost totally obscured from an American audience.

The Marxist-Christian Dialogue

Howard Parsons

What is, or can be, the good of Marxist-Christian dialogue?

To answer this, we must look at the conditions which have produced the dialogue and the concrete revolutionary demands of Marxists and Christians as they have arisen out of these conditions and have been shaped by them. We must also look at the conditions that prevail today and consider what good the dialogue could possibly do. And we must consider the *human* value of dialogue.

With the formation of the first Marxist state, Lenin repeatedly emphasized the necessity of peaceful coexistence between states of differing social systems. His reasons were two: first, the belief in the uneven development of capitalism and hence the necessity for Marxist states to cope and compete with capitalist states; and second, the belief that war as an instrument for settling disputes between nations is destructive and inimical to socialism. The policy of peaceful coexistence included the renunciation of war as a national policy, negotiation in international disputes, mutual understanding, non-interference, respect for the rights of national self-determination, and economic and cultural cooperation and exchange. It opens the way, I believe, for the policy of dialogue, i.e., discussion between Marxists and non-Marxists on basic principles and, where possible, cooperation in cultural and political matters for securing the survival, welfare and fulfillment of all people.

The rise of fascism in Germany and Italy in the 1930s put this policy of peaceful coexistence to a test and called for a policy of unity among states (not all Marxist) desiring to maintain peace against the war-making policies of the fascist nations. Thus, Dimitrov's *Report to the VII Congress of the Communist International* (1935) called for a united front of all persons and nations against fascism and war. As a corollary action, the French communist, Maurice Thorez, offered "the outstretched hand" in April, 1936, to Catholics and others, as an effort to achieve dialogue and unity of anti-fascist political action. But, as we know, the communist policy of collective security did not succeed. The war that the fascists and their supporters desired fell like a devastating pestilence on much of mankind. In the Soviet Union alone, twenty million people were killed, millions more were invalided, and twenty-five million were left homeless; industrial production was cut in half; and virtually all agricultural machinery was destroyed. The war was socialism's greatest enemy. Is it any wonder that Soviet and other Marxists then as now are committed to a policy of peaceful coexistence among nations? Now, a third and pre-eminent reason has been added to Lenin's reasons for peaceful coexistence—the danger of the annihilation of all life in the next war between nuclear powers.

Since World War II a number of events have stimulated the development of a spirit of peaceful coexistence, dialogue and collective security against war. These are as follows:

(1) The creation and exponential growth of the means of atomic, chemical and biological warfare and hence the threat of genocide. The American bombs dropped on Hiroshima and Nagasaki were opening blows in the cold war, but they also ushered in a unique period in human history. During this period governments and men would either control their weapons or be destroyed. Some realistic people have understood this; and some of the governments that have worked the hardest to effect the control of atomic and other genocidal weapons have been socialist.

(2) The establishment of a number of Marxist states in Eastern Europe and Asia and the emergence of revolutionary Marxist movements for national liberation in various parts of the world. These revolutionary facts have meant a considerable change in the distribution of power in the world. In addition to its effect in containing and checking imperialism's operations, these movements have generated a new atmosphere of revolutionary hope among peoples in the Third World and in the world of capitalism, including the colored peoples. The Black movement in the United States and the socialist successes in Latin America, for example, owe a good deal to this atmosphere. The revolutionary movements have forced the United States government to recognize the power and growth of socialist as a world wide fact and have indirectly contributed to that government's gradual accommodation to the Soviet Union.

(3) The presence of a sizeable number of Christians in the new communist nations. Many millions of Roman Catholics, Protestants and Orthodox believers live in the Soviet Union, Poland, the German Democratic Republic, Czechoslovakia, Hungary, Romania, Bulgaria and Yugoslavia. They represent a fact of life in these socialist countries. As a consequence, socialist leaders have increasingly sought to secure their cooperation in building socialism and world peace. This effort is a result of the recognition that the vinegar of over-militant atheism may not diminish religion as much as the honey of a more persuasive approach.

(4) The post-Stalin criticism and democratization in the socialist countries of Eastern Europe. These changes have had both domestic and foreign consequences. At home institutions and policies have been subjected to new examination. In Poland, about a decade ago, after much strife between the strong Catholic Church and the Communist party, Gomulka acknowledged that this strife had harmed the state and that religion would survive for a long time to come. Polish Marxists began to differentiate between reactionary, moderate and progressive Catholics, and shaped their policies accordingly.[1] While during Krushchev's regime the number of Russian Orthodox Churches was reduced by more than half,[2] Krushchev himself supported the policy of peaceful coexistence and on April 20, 1963, had this to say about Pope John's *Pacem in Terris* encyclical: "We welcome the Pope's statement for peace...in favor of ending the arms race, the prohi-

---

1.   Howard L. Parsons, *Humanistic Philosophy in Contemporary Poland and Yugoslavia,* Occasional Paper No. 3, American Institute for Marxist Studies (New York, 1967).

2.   *New York Times,* March 7, 1966. See also Richard H. Marshall, Jr., ed., *Aspects of Religion in the Soviet Union 1917-1967* (Chicago, 1970).

bition of nuclear weapons and the stopping of nuclear tests, in favor of disarmament under effective international control, the peaceful coexistence of countries, equal relations among countries and peoples, and elimination of war hysteria... I am no theologian, but if I remember rightly, according to the Gospel, Christ preached peace and not war."

The Krushchev general shake-up of bureaucratic and other attitudes produced new attitudes toward religion as well. For example, the leading organ for atheism in the Soviet Union, *Nauka i Religiya*, has left behind the old policy of a frontal and altogether negative attack on religion. While it puts forward a scientific outlook and tries to persuade believers to leave religious doctrine, it acknowledges that religion provides values and orientation for believers. The policy of the journal is to treat believers with respect, engage them in discussion, and strive to help them solve their problems.[3]

Under Krushchev, Lenin's principle of different roads to socialism was revived, as was the principle of peaceful transition to socialism under certan conditions. In 1956 the Twentieth Congress of the CPSU rejected the principle of the inevitability of war. This rejection opened the way for the search for methods to minimize the dangers of wars between states of differing social systems—wars that might escalate into thermonuclear annihilation. This has been taken as a position of weakness by some self-styled "revolutionaries" who hold that an armed clash between capitalist and socialist nations is inescapable and even desirable. But virtually all analysts are agreed that such a clash between nations employing nuclear weapons would be suicidal for both sides and probably genocidal for humanity. Is that strength? Is it not strength to strive to reduce the possibilities of human genocide? Such "revolutionaries" sometimes appeal to the example of Lenin. But Lenin consistently sought peaceful relations and friendship with other nations, including capitalist ones. He was constantly ready to make compromises when principles and long-range goals of communism were not affected or were advanced.

(5) The initiative of the Vatican in opening the doors for dialogue. Three encyclicals—*Mater et Magistra* (1961), *Pacem in Terris* (1963), and *Populorum Progressio* (1967)—affirmed the urgency of dialogue and cooperation between Christians and others in working for peace and friendship among states. Such initiative was received with approval and reciprocated by communists in socialist countries. In this atmosphere the dialogues arranged by the Paulus Gesellschaft at Munich, Cologne, Salzburg, Herrenchiemsee and Marienbad between Christians and communists were successful, according to the testimony of many participants.[4] This initiative from Pope John XXIII and Pope Paul VI was the consequence of the aforementioned events—the genocidal threat of new weapons; the strength and influence of the socialist nations and the revolutionary national liberation movements in the world; the existence of millions of Roman Catholics in socialist countries and in countries where revolution was brewing (especially

---

3. Such are the aims as indicated by the editors to the author in an interview August, 1970.

4. Some of these dialogues have been published. See Erich Kellner, ed., *Christentum und Marxismus—Heute* (Vienna, 1966).

in Latin America, where twenty-five percent of all professing Catholics live); and the policy of peaceful coexistence pursued by the socialist states. The Vatican, like all national states, wishes to maintain and extend its influence. As a capitalistic institution and the largest stockholder in the world, the Vatican confronts a formidable competitor in the form of Marxist states. Within the past fifty years, Marxism has conquered the loyalties of one billion people, or one third of the world's population. After two thousand years of effort, The Roman Catholic Church now commands the loyalties of more than half a billion people. Moreover, Marxism is expanding, in word and deed, while Catholicism is in relative decline: in the last thirty years, while the world's population increased by some seven hundred million people, the Catholics increased by one hundred million. To maintain and extend its influence the more realistic leaders of the Church understand that they must appeal to the insurgent groups of the world who are shaping twentieth century history. These are the peasants, the industrial workers, the urban poor, the colored races and the women (*Pacem in Terris* discussed and implicitly supported the legitimate demands of such groups.) The upshot has been that there is a tendency among many Catholics to forsake the century-old anti-communism of the Church and to support dialogue and progressive causes. In turn, the communists for the most part have abandoned their harsh anti-religious campaigns and have shown themselves ready for dialogue. In doing so such Christians have reactivated their humanistic heritage, while the communists have reexamined their historical and philosophical relations to Christianity.

(6) The radicalization in Western European, North American, and South American nations. This radicalization is the result of the factors mentioned above as well as the crises and failures of capitalism in these parts of the world. The extent of this radicalization is shown in the postwar growth of the Communist parties in Italy (two million members) and France (one fourth of the vote for the Communist party); in the rise of the radical movement among the Blacks, the poor, the youth, the intellectuals, and the women; the massive demonstrations in the United States against the Vietnam War, the first of their kind since the Civil War; in socialist Cuba; in the recent expropriation of foreign capitalistic holdings in Peru and Bolivia; in the spread of radical political activity throughout all countries of Latin America; and in the recent election of socialist Salvador Allende Gossens to the presidency of Chile.

The developing economic crises and consequent developing radicalism in Western European, North American, and South American nations during the last twenty-five years have opened the way for Marxists and progressive Christians to come together in dialogue and cooperation on common goals. The literature on the subject of dialogue is now extensive.[5] Beginning in

5. A summary of the recent work on dialogue is Douglas C. Stange, *The Nascent Marxist-Christian Dialogue: 1961-1967—A Bibliography* (New York, 1968). Additional bibliographical materials may be found in Leslie Dewart's Introduction to Roger Garaudy, *From Anathema to Dialogue*, trans. by Luke O'Neill (New York, 1966), pp. 6-7. Recent important books pertaining to dialogue are Giulio Girardi, *Marxism and Christianity* (New Y rk, 1968); Roger Garaudy and Quentin Lauer, *A Christian-Communist Dialogue* (Garden ity, New York,

France and Italy, where both the Catholic Church and the Communist party were strong and many individuals were struggling with dual commitments within themselves, the dialogue spread both eastward and westward. Eventually it was taken up by official organs on both sides. In the United States, the center of world anti-communism, the dialogue and the spirit of *Pacem in Terris* with respect to Communists were at first resented by Catholic leaders. Hence, the dialogue in the United States is in fact less than a decade old, and is proceeding slowly.

Scholars from Eastern European socialist countries have entered into the dialogue with their Western counterparts not out of a sense of internal economic crisis but out of a sense of urgency for a united front against the forces of war and fascism in the world. Within the Soviet Union and other socialist countries, both Marxists and believers normally agree on the socialist goals of the society.

By contrast, the problems of the societies of Western Europe and the Americas have multiplied during this recent quarter of a century—war, racism, hunger, repression, ill health, unemployment, inadequate housing, poor education, pollution, crime, etc. A pervasive deterioration of the material standard of living and of the quality of human life has set in. Dehumanization is a common fact of life and a common theme discussed by scholars. How is such a situation to be corrected? A limited number of general answers has appeared: the fascist, the conservative, the liberal, the anarchist, and the socialist. More broadly, there are two alternatives: the humanistic and the anti-humanistic. The humanistic answer would preserve human life and nurture the conditions of its fulfillment. The anti-humanistic alternative would undermine and destroy such conditions.

The anti-humanistic alternative is most fully illustrated in the genocidal policies of the Nazis and of the present American military-industrial-political complex in Indochina. In south Vietnam nearly half the population has been killed, wounded, maimed, displaced, or rendered wards of the state since the start of the war; one third are refugees;[6] and the millions of tons of bombs dropped by American planes have made completely useless an area the size of Connecticut.[7] In the face of public opposition, the genocidal war has been expanded to Cambodia and Laos. The American aerial bombing of Laos has led to the deaths of more than two hundred thousand civilians, making one out of three Laotians a refugee.[8] The bombing of Laos in early 1971—three to four thousand tons of bombs per day—is the most massive bombing in world history.[9] The domestic counterpart of this

1968); Paul Oestreicher, ed., *The Christian-Marxist Dialogue* (New York, 1969); Thomas W. Ogletree, ed., *Openings for Marxist-Christian Dialogue* (Nashville, 1969), Helmut Gollwitzer, *The Christian Faith and the Marxist Criticism of Religion*, trans. by David Cairns (New York, 1970). A survey of the dialogue in Latin American is given by Alberto Moreau, "Catholics and Marxists in Latin America," *Political Affairs*, Vol. XLV, No. 7 (July, 1966), pp. 64-73.

6. Dale S. de Haan and Jerry Tinker, *Refugee and Civilian War Casualty Problems in Indochina*, Staff Report of the U.S. Senate Subcommittee on Refugees (Washington, 1970).

7. Barry Weisberg, *Ecocide in Indochina* (New York, 1970), p. 66.

8. *Refugee and Civilian War Casualty Problems in Laos and Cambodia* (Washington, 1970).

9. *American Report*, February 26, 1971.

genocidal imperialism is the economic and political oppression of ill-fed, ill-clothed, ill-housed millions, particularly Blacks, and all their political allies, who are struggling to affirm their human rights.

The most radical, thoroughgoing and powerful humanistic alternative to this imperialist oppression—which appears in all those regimes around the world supported by the U.S. imperialist apparatus—is socialism. (Liberals and anarchists are only partially and ineffectively humanistic, for their theories of social change—gradual parliamentary reform for the liberal, terrorism or withdrawal for the anarchist—cannot produce long-range humanistic improvement; and in crises conservatives either flop over to the fascist side or become liberals.) Immediately someone will call for "socialism with a human face" and cite the crimes that have been committed in the name of socialism. But while such crimes have been and will continue to be committed (though not on the scale depicted in the capitalist press), they violate the basic theory or principles of socialism, which are totally humanistic. Fascism and imperialist capitalism as theories have never claimed to be humanistic but are openly anti-humanistic, elitist and brutalizing—Hitler, Mussolini, Herman Kahn, Henry Kissinger, et al. In judging any economic, political and social system, we must ask what are the *practical* alternatives, and the record shows that on the humanistic criteria of the fulfillment of the basic needs of people—employment, food, shelter, clothing, medical care, old-age security, literacy, education, mental health, equality of opportunity without discrimination, peace-keeping, etc.—more people are better situated under socialism than under fascism or capitalism. And this is true even though all or nearly all socialist countries have developed out of relatively undeveloped economies.

The response of the genuine Marxist to the problems of the modern world is therefore based on a deep-seated humanism. This humanism dates from Marx himself. It was formulated by the young Marx in his early writings and provided the foundational convictions impelling and guiding Marx's mature work in economic studies.[10] Marx's humanism in turn was derived, step by step, from the philosophical idealism of German thought (especially that of Hegel), the French Enlightenment (by way of Feuerbach's humanism), British and French political economy, the ideals of the French Revolution, French socialism, and proletarian movements. The humanism had two major roots—the scientific-Renaissance-Greco-Roman tradition, and Judaic-Christian sources.

Thus, Christianity shares with Marxism a common humanistic origin, and that is a primary reason why Christians respond to the dehumanization of the modern world in a way similar to that of the Marxists, and why they are destined by their traditions for dialogue and cooperation.

Norman Cohen in his richly documented work, *The Pursuit of the Millennium*,[11] shows how from the time of the Jews and through Christian history to the Middle Ages one continuous apocalyptic dream recurred: a dream of the coming of a millennium in which all persons equally possessed of the

10. Howard L. Parsons, *Humanism and Marx's Thought* (Springfield, Mass., 1971).
11. Norman Cohen, *The Pursuit of the Millennium* (New York, 1957).

divine spirit would be perfected and happy. Such a dream was eschatological and revolutionary: it foretold, as Isaiah had foretold, that "Every valley shall be exalted, and every mountain and hill shall be made low: and the crooked shall be made straight, and the rough places plain."[12] It foretold what Jesus foretold: "Blessed are you poor, for yours is the kingdom of God. Blessed are you that hunger now, for you shall be satisfied. Blessed are you that weep now, for you shall laugh... But woe to you that are rich, for you have received your consolation. Woe to you that are full now, for you shall hunger. Woe to you that laugh now, for you shall mourn and weep."[13]

This dream of a community of equals enjoying the fruits of their labors appeared in the Jewish prophets and sometimes, as in Amos in the eighth century B.C., climaxed in denunciations of the exploitative ruling class: "They sold the righteous for silver, and the poor for a pair of shoes."[14] In the same century Isaiah cried out: "What mean ye that ye beat my people to pieces, and grind the faces of the poor?"[15] At times this challenge to ruling class exploitation became an open prophecy of the overthrow of the ruling class, as in the song of Jesus' mother as she anticipated the birth of her son: "My spirit hath rejoiced in God my Saviour. For he hath regarded the low estate of his handmaiden... He hath put down the mighty from their seats, and exalted them of low degree. He hath filled the hungry with good things; and the rich he hath sent empty away."[16]

Engels compared early Christianity to the modern working-class movement: both were movements of oppressed people, both preached forthcoming salvation from bondage, both were persecuted and baited, both forged ahead toward triumph.[17] We should add that both were humanistic movements, bent on bettering the vast mass of humanity—though early Christianity was limited in its concept of humanism by its belief in a supernature and an afterworld.

Much evidence points to the conclusion that Jesus and the early Christians comprised a revolutionary movement that challenged the foundations of the Roman Empire: the repeated harsh judgments against the rich ruling class passed by Jesus, James, Saint Clement, Saint Ambrose, Saint John Chrysostom and many other Church Fathers; the basis of the movement in the proletarian poor; the primitive communism of consumption among the Christians; the words of Jesus that emphasize struggle and violent conflict ("I came not to send peace, but a sword"); and the fierce and unrelenting state persecution of Jesus and his followers.[18]

Whether or not the early Christians were an armed insurrectionary band, the ruling groups of Jews and Romans in Jesus' day and for three centuries

---

12. Isaiah 61: 1.
13. Luke 6: 20-21, 24-25 (Revised Standard Version).
14. Amos 2: 6.
15. Isaiah 3: 15.
16. Luke 1: 47-48, 52-53.
17. Engels, "On the History of Early Christianity," in Marx and Engels, *On Religion* (Moscow, n.d.), p. 316.
18. See Karl Kautsky, *Foundations of Christianity*, trans. by Henry F. Mins (New York, 1953). Archibald Robertson, *The Origins of Christianity* (New York, 1954).

thereafter viewed Jesus and Christians as a threat to the establishment. People loyal to the establishment were not normally crucified or thrown to the lions. In fact, Jesus at his trial was accused of subverting the nation, opposing the payment of taxes to Caesar, and claiming to be Messiah, a king.[19] The evidence strongly suggests that the beliefs and actions of Jesus and his followers gave the authorities of the Roman Empire ground for regarding them as dangerous to the Empire in word if not also in deed. Certainly a great number of Christians throughout two thousand years of Christian history have taken his teachings and his example as ground for revolutionary action of one kind or another: the Donatists, the Cathari, Arnold of Brescia, the Waldenses, Francis of Assisi and the radical Franciscans, Joachim of Fiore, the Brethren of the Free Spirit, John Wycliffe, the Lollards, John Ball, the German mystics, the Gottesfreunde, the Brethren of the Common Life, Jan Huss, Thomas Münzer, the Anabaptists, and others in the left wing of the Reformation, Levellers and Diggers, the Christian socialists of the nineteenth century, and those "troublesome priests" like the Berrigan brothers today.

The ideas of radical humanism in Judaism and Christianity are available for discovery by those who have eyes to see when they look at the Scriptures of those traditions. But people have often not seen them because the ideas are mixed with a great mass of legend, history, law, homilies, poetry, and the like; because the institutional leaders of religion, law and education screened out the radical parts; and because people themselves were not prepared psychologically to see. But today, as in previous periods of intense class-conflict and crisis, religious people have been forced under the pressures of the problems of postwar capitalism to take another look at their sources. The result: a resurrection of the radical humanism of early Christianity. Born out of a crisis situation which pitted a ruling class against the ruled, these radical ideas of Jewish prophets and Christians speak to a similar situation today. Christians who struggle against the dehumanizing conditions of feudalism and capitalism—against war, racism, poverty, political oppression, inequality, alienation—become radicalized and humanized. And their feelings and the actions get articulation, support and guidance from the recovery of their ideological sources in the past.

To the extent that this radicalization and humanization has occurred and is occurring among religious people—and here we are speaking of Christians, though the same principle applies to Jews, Muslims, Buddhists, Hindus, etc.—to that extent they are ready for dialogue and common action with Marxists. For Marxists hold to a similar humanism—a humanism which Marx himself learned as a youth through the commanding ideals of the Greek and Judaic-Christian traditions and the humanized Christianity of Hegel, and which he transformed into his own materialistic, dialectical humanism.

But the radical humanism of Christianity is not obvious to many non-Christians. What is obvious are the anti-humanists among the Christians: the Hitlers, Mussolinis, Francos, Salazars, Greek juntas, Nixons, Carl

---

19. Luke 23: 2.

McIntires, Cardinal Cushings, and all the slaughterous popes, parasitic priests, and rich, racist Christians who have strewn the earth with the blood and guts of the poor from Rome to Rio and from Dixie to the Mekong Delta. It is not likely that a Marxist or even a persuasive, pacific Christian can have useful dialogue with such oppressors. It is not thought initially but only changes in material conditions of life accompanied by reeducation that will alter the feelings and thoughts of such "ravenous wolves" in sheep's clothing, as Jesus called them. [20]

But it would be a grave and even fatal mistake for nonreligious people committed to humanistic goals to damn all Christians in consequence of the deviltry of a few (or even many), or to write off Christians as insignificant. The Church, its leaders and its laymen are in change. Under the impact of technological, economic and social forces, its people are increasingly split and are rapidly polarizing into humanistic and anti-humanistic camps. Large numbers of Christians are still blindly tied to the dictates of their anti-humanistic leaders. But large groups are breaking away, under the leadership of humanistic popes like John XXIII and courageous bishops and priests in Europe, North America and especially Latin America. Particularly striking is the revolt of nuns and priests against the authoritarianism of a feudal Church and the barbarities of feudal and capitalistic governments (in the United States, Latin America, Spain, etc.). Protected in the sanctuaries of their educational and monastic institutions, these nuns and priests have suddenly been forced out of their pure, feudal isolation into the conflicts, competition, exploitation and sufferings of the modern capitalistic world. Having been nurtured in the purity of feudal devotion and the principles of early Christianity, they find themselves unable to accept the greed and money-grubbing of capitalist society. But once having broken loose from the cloistered walls of their religion, they realize they cannot go backward to a feudal order, nor can they accept capitalism. So the more clear-sighted and courageous go straight forward toward some form of socialism. And this decision is supported by their search of the Scriptures and their discovery of primitive communism there as an ideal and as living practice.

The old Marxist attitude that assailed religion as an enemy of the people was appropriate and effective in certain times and places—as in old Russia, where the Orthodox Church was identified with Tsarism's degradation of the masses. Two out of three believers in old Russia (in the European part) were illiterate and almost completely imprisoned in the ideological grip of the Church. In Latin America today the same proportion of people are illiterate. But the difference is this: the masses of peasants, attracted to the cities, can see with their own eyes the splendors of wealth; the priests and educated laymen can read and have access to the news from abroad which tells of challenges within the Church to arbitrary authority, feudalism and capitalism, of national liberation movements, and of the scientific and socialistic changes in places like the Soviet Union, China, Cuba and Chile— in a word, of humanistic advance in various parts of the world. The result is a ferment of revolutionary ideas and hopes among religious people.

---

20. Matthew 7: 15.

For example, the Archbishop of La Paz, Bolivia, Jorge Manrique Hurtado, recently declared in a pastoral letter that "neo-socialism presents no conflict of faith for Christians." He said that many Christians have indicated to him "the necessity for a social revolution that would radically transform the system of private property, eliminate marked distinctions between classes and families, and increase state control of the nation's economics." Such people, he said, do not want violence but "would not exclude it as a possibility if they felt it were justified." They are "anti-imperialist in international politics and ideologically they're socialists, not Marxists. An increasing number of Christians are finding in this neo-socialism an authentic expression of their desire for justice and solidarity." (The Archbishop went on to reject the materialism, atheism, alienation from God, hate, and class struggle of Marxism.)   Though the Archbishop disowned Marxism, what is significant is that he acknowledged the demand on the part of many Christians for a "social revolution that would radically transform the system of private property," eliminate marked class distinctions, and increase state economic control. In Italy eighty priests and seventy-five laymen of the synod diocese of Bolzano-Bressanone went farther. They said, "The society in which we live commits a grave sin against the plan of God by placing capital at the center of everything and subjecting man to the law of profit." Marxist philosophy, they continued, has built a model of a society "in which exploitation of man by man is impossible or at least very difficult." That model "appears more attuned to God's plan than capitalist society." [22]

The conditions of living in North America, Latin America and elsewhere which are producing these changes toward revolutionary ideology are unprecedented in world history. "Marxists" who are blind, indifferent, or even opposed to such conditions represent counter-revolutionary tendencies. In the words of Fidel Castro, Marxism must "come out of a certain stagnation, to interpret objectively and scientifically today's realities." It is a paradox of history, he added, that certain sectors of Marxism should become "ecclesiastical forces" at a time when some members of the Roman Catholic clergy are becoming revolutionaries. [23]

We cannot afford to be fastidious about metaphysical matters in this time of crisis. The basic choices in our part of the world—and in most other parts—are between humanism and anti-humanism. The basic changes required cannot be effected by any one group of humanists—Marxists, Christians, liberals, or others. A united, common front is needed. This principle has been illustrated again and again in our struggles in the United States for civil rights and for peace. One's view of the world is important, and differences in world views should not be overlooked, since world views influence action. But where men with different world views can unite on important action, those differences should not be allowed to obstruct the united action.

---

21. *Catholic Transcript*, October 23, 1970.
22. *New York Times*, March 10, 1971.
23. In a speech before the International Cultural Congress, January 12, 1968.

We can of course dwell on the vast and untold crimes and sins of the Church. But there are many crimes and sins on the other side. As Leslie Dewart has pointed out, Christians have two thousand years to repent of and the Communists have fifty, so the Christians, being forty times as sinful as the Communists, should take that much longer to repent.[24] But we can't spend a lot of time in accusation and repentance. We may have only a very short time in which to work together to save one another, our world and our children. We must go on with that collective task.

A great deal has been said about the human values that Marxism and Christianity share: man, man's fulfillment and progress, truth, justice, love, brotherhood, peace, cooperation. This convergence on human values can be most succinctly summarized in the words of Jesus in the twenty-fifth chapter of Matthew: "For when I was hungry, you gave me food; when thirsty, you gave me drink; when I was a stranger you took me into your home, when naked you clothed me; when I was ill you came to my help, when in prison you visited me."[25]

The Marxist equivalent (in *Theses on Feuerbach*) is social, "revolutionizing practice." The goal is the mutual fulfillment by people of human needs; the procedure is practice. The revolutionary element in Christianity is not stated in the above. But the revolutionary implications were pursued by John Ball in the fourteenth century, the Taborites in the fifteenth century, Thomas Münzer in the sixteenth century, the Diggers and Radical Levellers in the seventeenth century, the American Revolutionists in the eighteenth century, the partisans of the Social Gospel in the nineteenth century, and A.J. Muste, Martin Luther King, Jr., the Catonsville Nine and many other members of the noble army of martyrs in the twentieth century.

I do not have time here to develop the common theoretical values shared by the radical humanism of Marxism and Christianity. The simple truth is that people in capitalist countries like our own who feel the urgency of solving the vital human problems—war, poverty, racism, fascism—need all the help and all the cooperation they can muster. In the Soviet Union and other Eastern European countries, believers are not admitted to membership in the Communist party. In Western countries, it is quite the reverse: in Italy, France, England, the United States, and Latin America, membership is open to believers. The significance of this is that in old Russia religious people and institutions played an almost totally reactionary role, whereas in the West, partly because the church's association with the bourgeois revolution, they have played and are now playing a progressive and even revolutionary role. Moreover, in Eastern European countries the power of capitalism has been broken and people are building socialism, whereas in the Western countries people need all the help they can get in destroying capitalism.

The urgency of our situation requires the practical, united front approach. The basic philosophical issues between Marxists and Christians should be discussed and argued in a cooperative search for the truth, so as

24. Leslie Dewart, *Initiative in History: A Christian-Marxist Exchange*, occasional paper published by The Church Society for College Work (Cambridge, 1967), p. 27.
25. Matthew 25: 35-36.

to make more effective their work and more secure their comradeship. But as John Lewis has said: "when the house is blazing I do not want to drag the fireman away from his hose to discuss the Laws of Thermo-dynamics, or the nature of the Trinity or the essential doctrines of Dialectical Materialism." [26]

Marx and Engels of course fought religious supernaturalism as an illusion that diverts man from the task of radical social action. But they recognized the *human* struggle against oppression in religion, and Engels in particular was appreciative of the revolutionary roots of Christianity. Both opposed intolerance and anarchistic terrorism toward religion. Lenin at one point accepted conscientiously working priests within the party. [27] His approach was a flexible, practical one, without falling into opportunism or compromise on basic principles.

More than half of the people in the United States belong to some Christian church. If radical, revolutionary, humanistic changes are germinated in a society by the increasing incapacity of the ruling classes to rule, the deepening suffering of the oppressed classes, and the increasing activity of the masses—as Lenin said [28]—then it is important for Marxists to seek their allies wherever they may be found. I submit that there are many potential allies among the religious groups of the population. The activities of many Catholics and Protestants in opposing the Vietnam War, racial oppression and poverty, and other forms of oppression are evidence of this. For example, the Catonsville Nine—priests and laymen who in May, 1968, burned the draft records of Catonsville, Maryland with Napalm—acted with a kind of courage which is widespread amongst their brothers and sisters in the Church. Such courage should be wholeheartedly supported by Marxists through dialogue and common political activity. In the United States, an increasing number of Catholic scholars—Father Frederick Adelmann, Father Louis Barth, Professor Fred Carrier, Professor George Hampsch, Father Quentin Lauer, Justus George Lawler, Father George McLean, and others—have for some years shown openness and friendliness toward Marxism. In Canada, leading Christians like Breweter Kneen, Reverend James G. Endicott, Father Arthur Gibson, and Professor Leslie Dewart have responded positively to the openings of dialogue. It is assumed that in honest dialogue each side will try to influence, persuade, or convert the other. But at this stage of the dialogue what is important is the development of common ground of conviction and action. The fact is that the views of Christians are undergoing transformation primarily as a result of the material, political and ideological struggles shaking the foundations of our whole society and the world, including the foundations of Christianity. The point of Marxists' dialogue with them at this time should be not so much to convert them ideologically as to develop a mutual understanding and fellow-feeling that will lead to cooperation at the practical, political level. Actions speak louder than words and ultimately actions

---

26. In *Dialogue of Christianity and Marxism*, James Klugman, ed. (London, 1968), p. 105.
27. "The Attitude of the Workers' Party Towards Religion," in V.I. Lenin, *Religion* (New York, 1933).
28. *The War and the Second International* (New York, 1932), p. 13.

change minds more effectively than words.

The conditions in Latin America, where more than ninety percent of the people are nominally Roman Catholic, graphically illustrate the need and opportunity for an alliance between Marxists and Christians. There three-fourths of the people are constantly hungry and two-thirds are illiterate. While the mean income in Latin America is $253, most people earn much less. In Peru, for example, more than half the people have no money whatsoever, one hundred families own ninety percent of the native wealth, and "naked children, some too young to know how to walk, [compete] with pigs for a few bits of food scraps accidentally discarded by the garbage men."[29]

What is the Church doing here? For the most part it is holding onto its land (it is the biggest landowner in some countries) and blocking progressive social change. But an increasing number of bishops, priests and laymen are taking seriously the radical and revolutionary message of the Gospel. In 1967 three hundred Brazilian priests noted that the infant mortality rate among the poor sometimes reached fifty percent: they called for the Church "to face courageously the rules that govern capitalist production, but to help the church attain complete freedom from economic powers." In Colombia Father Camilo Torres shed his cassock, joined the guerrillas, and died as a revolutionary. "I am a revolutionary," he declared, "because I am a priest and because I am a Catholic." Others, such as Father Santiago MacGuire in Argentina, have cast their lot with the poor, living and struggling with them. There have been hundreds of such conversions,[30] and there are growing numbers of red priests like Comrade Torres. The Bolivian government recently expelled four Roman Catholic priests and a Protestant minister for cooperation with revolutionaries.[31]

In Chile where the Church has been more progressive than elsewhere in Latin America, Salvador Allende Gossens, the Marxist president, has described the situation as follows: "Before, for centuries, the Catholic Church defended the interests of the powerful. Today the church, after John XXIII, has become oriented toward making the Gospels of Christ a reality, at least in some places. I have read the declaration of the Bishops at Medellin, and the language they use now is the same that we have used since we were born into political life thirty years ago... I believe that the church will not be a factor against the Popular Unity government. On the contrary, they are going to be a factor in our favor, because we are going to try to make a reality out of Christian thought. Furthermore, there will be the widest religious pluralism...all [religious groups] will be absolutely respected."[32]

Who would quarrel with that, except the political and religious reactionaries who wish to see socialism destroyed in Chile?

The point is that there are two major sources of revolutionary thought in Latin America—and indeed in North America and in the western hemi-

29. John Gerassi, *The Great Fear in Latin America* (New York, 1965), p. 20.
30. *New York Times*, March 16, 1966.
31. *New York Times*, October 7, 1970.
32. *New York Times*, October 4, 1970.

sphere. They are Marxism and Christianity—or more accurately, Marxism and the Judaeo-Christian tradition. For we find Jesus in his first appearance in the synagogue after his temptations in the wilderness reading the radical passage from Isaiah: "The spirit of the lord is upon me because he has annointed me; He has sent me to announce good news to the poor, to proclaim release for prisoners and recovery of sight for the blind; to let the broken victims go free; to proclaim the year of the Lord's favour."[33]

And he then announced that it was he—the pious son of Joseph, the Camilo Torres of Galilee—who had come to fulfill such a mission. Jesus preached the power of the poor, the corruption of ruling classes, the hypocrisy of religious hierarchs, the idolatry of riches, the evil of exploitation, the primacy of love, the virtue of brotherhood, and the glory of living (and, if necessary, of dying) for mankind. He led an insurrectionary movement against the Roman state, and he was crucified as a blasphemer and a subversive. It is such a faith, both as creed and deed, that has sustained millions of oppressed people through two thousand years of history. In relation to such a faith, Marxism historically is, as Herbert Aptheker remarked, "a latecomer." It is an effort to constitute what Marx in "The Jewish Question" called "the human ground of Christianity."

Thus it should not surprise us that in a time when the crises of Western societies require revolutionary answers, Christians and Marxists arise to respond. Nor should it surprise us that Christians and Marxists desire to cooperate in dialogue and action.

But dialogue is important not only as a tactic but also as a value vital to man's nature and health. What marks us as distinctively human is that we are dialectical (speaking together), dialogic (reasoning together), sympathetic (feeling together), and cooperative (acting together). So far as these activities are impaired, we cease by so much to be human; and if they are seriously impaired we lose our sanity. To be engaged in this kind of creative mutuality with others, to be in this way creating the conditions of social life and nature so as to develop ever wider bonds of mutuality, is to escape the extremes of conformist conservatism, compromising liberalism, sectarian adventurism, and anarchist violence and despair. Without faith and hope in himself, others, and the processes of history created by people together, man will not only fall away from effective and humanistic political action, but will also fail in the basic biological, social and ecological functions of human life itself. The ground of faith and hope is a creative interaction between person and person and between persons and the non-human world —an interaction working toward the welfare of all persons. In such interaction we are transformed in the direction of fulfilling our distinctive human potentialities, and the world around is progressively humanized. This is the most important principle to be found in both Marxism and Christianity. This is why we call them forms of radical humanism. They serve themselves and others best when they lead men to this fulfillment instead of turning them to their own specific doctrines and institutions. Most of the sins and crimes of Christianity and Marxism have been the

33. Luke 4: 18.

result of the confusion of means with ends, of creation with the creative process itself. The economy and ideas, the church and the state, according to the founders of Marxism and Christianity, should be made for man. But what is man? He is a creative, social, interactive, growing being. Hence, dialogue should be both the means toward and end of his humanization.

One "Marxist" argument against dialogue and cooperation is that Marxists have nothing to gain and everything to lose by it. We have nothing to gain, the argument runs, because the Christians are naive and sentimental; we have everything to lose because mingling their idealistic holy water with our materialistic red wine can only weaken the vividness of our truth and the militancy of our action. But this is a pretentious and proud isolationism, when Marxists and all progressives need all the friends and allies they can find. This was certainly not the tactic of Marx, Lenin or Mao. We should recall words of that peasant-priest, Pope John, who in speaking for Christians also spoke for all of us: "The person who errs is always and above all a human being, and he retains in every case his dignity as a human person. . . . Besides, in every human being, there is a need that is congenital to his nature and never becomes extinguished, compelling him to break through the web of error and open his mind to the knowledge of truth. . . . [W]ho can deny that those movements [working on historical situations], in so far as they conform to the dictates of right reason and are interpreters of the lawful aspirations of the human person, contain elements that are positive and deserving of approval?" [34]

I say that John speaks for us; what he says is neither a Catholic nor a Marxist truth but a *human* truth that belongs to all. The truth is that dialogue, and the cooperative search for truth and a better world are precious and important human values—more important, may I add, than the fixed doctrines and practices of Marxism and Christianity. And this, indeed, is what both Christianity and Marxism at their best affirm.

So we need friends not only for numbers and their strength but also for our own humanization in thought and feeling. We cannot assume—unless we are operating on some new doctrine of infallibility that no Marx, Engels, or Lenin pronounced—that we already possess all the wisdom and courage possible. We can learn from those who in good will are concerned to eradicate the same evils as we. We need to have our blind spots corrected and our errors purged. And in a genuine give-and-take and a relation of trust, our friends might help us do that. We need to learn to live with a variety of persons in the party of mankind and convictions in the camp of humanism. We are lost in our struggle if we draw the line too strictly now. The world we are aiming for in the future must be a world of variety of truly human values and persons or it will not be a world worth having and enjoying and fighting for. The kind of human relations we build now will be promissory of the human relations we will have in the future. Let our criterion be: we will have dialogue with those who are ready to have genuine dialogue, to speak honestly, to listen sensitively, and to respond with integrity; and we shall hold up the same standard for ourselves; and we will

---

34. *Pacem in Terris.*

engage in common action with those who are committed to the same vital human ends as we—peace, equality, freedom, brotherhood.

The cooperation of Marxists with Christians should not in the slightest diminish the commitment of the Marxists to their own distinctive theory and practice; it is this, indeed, which is the Marxist contribution to the dialogue and to common practice. Cooperation should not diminish the Marxist's ideological struggle against what he considers to be false ideas and theory, inhuman values, and misleading ways of getting and testing knowledge. Certainly Christians will struggle in the defense and propagation of their own ideas, values, and knowledge. The sharp differences between Christianity and Marxism should not be overlooked or obscured. For example, institutionalized Christianity is supernaturalistic in its theology, while Marxism is dialectical and materialistic; institutionalized Christianity supports capitalism, while Marxism holds it to be the root of evils of the modern world. Dialogue and cooperation do not require that one relinquish one's own distinctive position on such matters. On the contrary, one's position can be enriched if each participant holds to what is distinctive, learns from the other, and strives to widen his understanding and appreciation. The frank and open dialogue of a Marxist with a Christian who believes in capitalism must expose the Christian to the evils of capitalism while enlarging the Marxist's understanding of what it is he opposes. It is by no means necessary to agree with or to approve of what the other believes, in order for dialogue to be fruitful. In his dialectical relation with the Christian, the Marxist must maintain both the unity of cooperation and the opposition of ideological struggle. The most effective relative balance between these will vary with circumstances. But two errors must be avoided: the dialogue and cooperation that tend toward absorption in the other position (opportunism), and the ideological struggle that becomes so intense that dialogue and cooperation tend to be destroyed (sectarianism).

At this stage of history we are engaged in a struggle with vital practical problems whose solutions are so urgent and determinative of the future of mankind that theoretical problems and conflicts must not be allowed to retard them. Such is the problem of ending wars like those in Indochina and the Mid-East, the problem of the control of nuclear, chemical and biological weapons, the problem of reducing armaments, the problem of correcting poverty and overpopulation. If these problems increase, then the solutions of other problems become progressively improbable. Moreover, in both Christianity and Marxism, practice is always the final and best way of assessing a person's theory and character. Judge a man, said Jesus, by his fruits. "Every step of the actual movement," said Marx, "is more important than a dozen programs." Marx never slighted theory. On the contrary, for him it was an indispensable guide to action. But an important feature of such theory is that it shall not impede necessary and effective action and that we must go ahead with social action in order to test, correct and extend our theory. Marx's theory was a scientific, exploratory practice and hence open to new problems and facts the discovery of which would continuously modify the basic theory.

Our enemies in the United States and the world are evident. They are driving our people toward disaster. Is it not clear that the hard hats, the hard heads, and the hard hearts are destroying us? Let us seek out the human-hearted and sensible people, the ones ready to be humanized in dialogue and common struggle. Let us bind ourselves together in order to eradicate from the earth those Molochs of imperialism and racism. The first way to do this is to extend the outstretched hand toward our friends. Let the closed hand, the uptight personality, the tight fist, the stiff neck, and the stuffed shirt stay unmoved, if so it must be. We must be the loose ones, flexible and free, resolute and creative. And if we and many other can be so, in dialogue and in deed, we will conquer the land for ourselves and for future mankind. We will—if we become united with our friends and with the people; and if we can keep the faith, the hope, and the vision; and if we embody and work toward all that is truly human.

Index